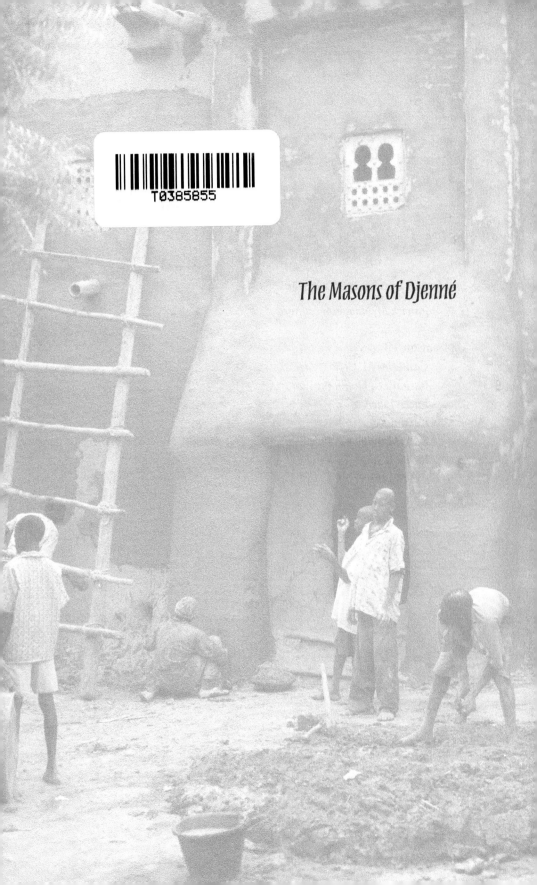

The Masons of Djenné

African Expressive Cultures

Patrick McNaughton, editor

Associate editors
Catherine M. Cole
Barbara G. Hoffman
Eileen Julien
Kassim Koné
D. A. Masolo
Elisha Renne
Zoë Strother

The Masons of Djenné

Trevor H. J. Marchand

Indiana University Press · Bloomington & Indianapolis

This book is a publication of

Indiana University Press
601 North Morton Street
Bloomington, IN 47404-3797 USA

http://iupress.indiana.edu

Telephone orders   800-842-6796
Fax orders   812-855-7931
Orders by e-mail   iuporder@indiana.edu

♾The paper used in this publication
meets the minimum requirements
of American National Standard for
Information Sciences—Permanence
of Paper for Printed Library
Materials, ANSI Z39.48-1992.

Manufactured in the United
States of America

**Library of Congress Cataloging-
in-Publication Data**

Marchand, Trevor Hugh James.
  The masons of Djenné /
Trevor H. J. Marchand.
    p. cm.
  Includes bibliographical
references and index.
  ISBN 978-0-253-31368-3 (cloth : alk.
paper) — ISBN 978-0-253-22072-1
(pbk. : alk. paper)
  1. Construction industry—
Mali—Djenné. 2. Architects and
builders—Mali—Djenné. 3. Marchand,
Trevor Hugh James. I. Title.
  HD9715.M423D546 2009
  331.7'6931096623—dc22

                    2008042660

1 2 3 4 5 14 13 12 11 10 09

To John

All art worthy the name is the energy—neither of human body alone, nor of the human soul alone, but of both united, one guiding the other: good craftsmanship and work of the fingers, joined with good emotion and work of the heart.

John Ruskin, 1859

Contents

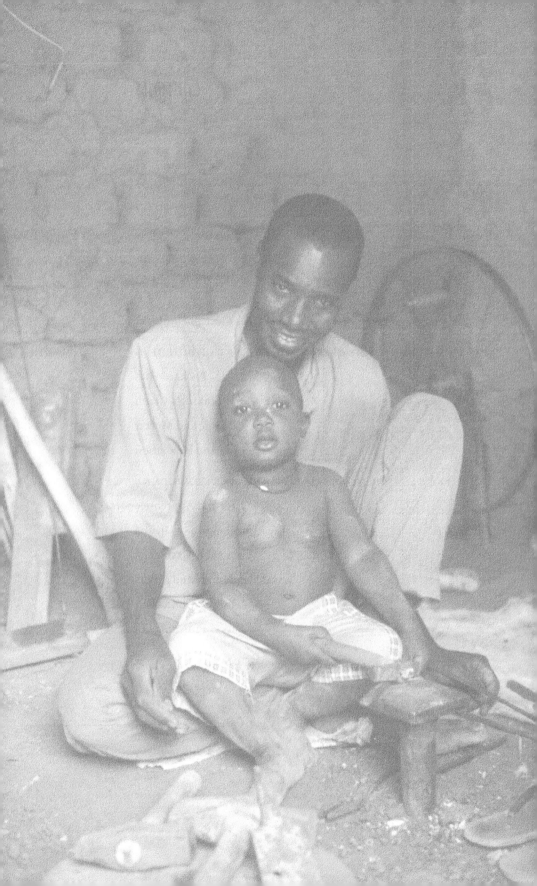

Acknowledgments

My first thanks go to the masons of Djenné who welcomed me onto their building sites and allowed me to participate in their daily work. All that I learned during my fieldwork I owe to them. Bayeré Kouroumansé generously introduced me to my sites and masons, and remained a springhead of knowledge throughout my study. Of the numerous masons I came to know, I am particularly indebted to the Kouroumansé brothers, including al-Hajji, Baba, Bamoy, and Hasey, as well as to Bamoy and Ibrahim Sao, to Konmusa and his father, Konbaba Tennepo, and to my dear friend Konamadou Djennepo. I gratefully acknowledge all the laborers and apprentices I worked with during the two building seasons and who I continue to visit on my excursions to Djenné. Their names are too many to mention, but their stories fill the pages of this book.

I also extend a special thanks to Rogier Bedaux, former curator of the Africa department at Leiden's Volkenkunde Museum. His scholarly studies of the region and his tireless devotion to Djenné's architecture were a guiding inspiration to my work. I am grateful to Pierre Maas and Geert Mommersteeg for charitably sharing their tremendous wealth of knowledge about the town and to the knowledgeable Amadou Camara at the Cultural Mission who entertained my endless questions about daily life and local culture. Members of the Djenné Patrimoine association, including Joseph Brunet-Jailly and Amadou Tahirou Bah, also kindly furnished important information. I am very grateful to Patrick McNaughton, Mary Jo Arnoldi, and especially Geert

Mommersteeg for their generous comments and advice on earlier drafts of the manuscript. Thanks to Hady Ballo who shared his knowledge of Bozo legends; to Mody Sounfountera who reliably responded to e-mail queries about vocabulary and spellings of Djenné-Chiini terms; to Anna Portisch who assisted me with digitizing the photos and figures; to Linda Feinstone for getting me back and forth to Mali on several occasions; to John Peel for his wisdom and steady support; and to my brother, Keith, and to Barbara Heywood who kindly edited early versions of my text. I also owe a debt of gratitude to Dee Mortensen at Indiana University Press for her consistent guidance, and to copyeditor Rita Bernhard. Above all, I am indebted to John Heywood whose care and encouragement throughout this work helped to make the task a pleasure.

During fieldwork my stay was graciously hosted by the director of Djenné's Cultural Mission, Boubacar Diaby. Official support for my research was sponsored by the director of the Musée National in Bamako, Samuel Sidibé, and permission was granted locally by the traditional chief of the town (*Djenné wéré*), Ba Hasey Maïga. The fieldwork for this book was generously supported by the British Academy and the School of Oriental and African Studies (SOAS), and the final stages of writing and editing were funded by a Fellowship from the Economic and Social Research Council (ESRC) of Britain (Award Reference RES-000-27-0159) in support of my ongoing studies of building-craft knowledge.

A Note on Language

Throughout the book I introduce the masons' local vocabulary to describe tools, building materials, architectural features, and other salient objects and concepts. Djenné represents a complex multilingual context where several languages are regularly employed in daily communication. Most prominent is the town's lingua franca, Djenné-Chiini, which is a dialect of the Songhay languages spoken in Timbuktu and Gao. Bamanankan and French, Mali's two official languages, are also widely spoken; and a host of other languages including Fulfuldé, various Dogon dialects, and Mossi are used on building sites between laborers who come from outlying regions and Burkina Faso. Arabic words and expressions pepper everyday speech, and point to the strong historic trade links between the Sahel and North Africa, and to the dominant Islamic identity of the town and the pervasiveness of Qur'anic education. Notably, although the majority of masons are Bozo, few speak their ethnic language and, like most urbanized citizens of the town, Djenné-Chiini is their mother tongue.

For the benefit of non-linguist and non-specialist readers, I have employed a simple form of transliteration whereby the spelling of non-English terms is restricted to roman letters and diacriticals to stress pronunciation. For example, Mandé scholars sometimes use the symbol η in spelling such words as *nyama,* but, like many other authors, I have chosen to use the close phonetic equivalent "ny." Readers familiar with literature on the region will find that spellings for words from this West African region vary depending on the author and date of the text. Most local languages were not written and still lack standard transliteration into the roman alphabet. I have tried to maintain the most conventional spellings taken from popular sources whenever possible in order to facilitate the reader's recognition of terms, and I use Heath's *Dictionnaire Songhay-Anglais-Français,* volume 2, for the spelling of Djenné-Chiini terms. In the case of Arabic, which has its own alphabet, I have included the Arabic spelling for words in parentheses. This will be useful to those familiar with the language and those interested in the root source of many popular expressions and salutations used throughout West Africa.

Definitions for non-English terms are provided in the text at first mention, and a glossary is included at the end of the book.

The Masons of Djenné

View of Djenné's eastern perimeter

Introduction: The Field and the Work

Locating the Field

As a brand new architecture graduate, I set off to discover the faraway towns and cities that had fired my imagination during my studies. Mali was an essential destination. I yearned to see the dazzling mud architecture of Djenné, the cliff-side houses and granaries of Dogon country, and the ancient Djinguéré Ber Mosque in Timbuktu. It seemed so very other-worldly to me who had been weaned on a combination of classical proportion and modernism, and I needed to experience these extraordinary spaces and touch their surfaces to know they were real.

I arrived in Mali in January 1989 during the troubled years of President Moussa Traoré's regime and the heavy-handed control of his security forces. Travel around the country with a backpack, no vehicle, and little money was challenging at best, and every route was strewn with checkpoints extorting hefty tolls for onward passage. Good fortune soon landed me in the hospitable company of two better-heeled travelers—an archaeologist and a tour operator—who together were scouting the country's sites by jeep. One Monday I accompanied them to Djenné to visit its famous weekly market that features in every guidebook published since Michelin's earliest editions to the French Sudan.

After a long journey we crossed the calm jade waters of the Bani with two turbaned men, tall and sleek, who silently poled the ferry to the other side. We

Map of Mali

continued driving for several kilometers along a graded road raised above the parched and scrubby floodplain. A lone arch with a crowning comb of miters sat sentinel on the flat expanse, framing our first view of the island town silhouetted against a cloudless sky. The jeep crossed a tiny bridge into Djenné, and we steered vigilantly over the bumps and ruts of a long snaking road squeezed between foreboding mud walls of two-storey houses before finally emerging at the edge of the bright and open marketplace.

The perimeter of this vast irregular space was lined by handsome merchant houses fortified with slender buttresses that framed carved wooden doorways and tiny screened windows, and that terminated in orderly rows of pointed crenulations along the rooftops. On its western side, the marketplace was dominated by Djenné's majestic mosque. A scattering of vendors, mainly women loosely draped in colorful wax-print cottons, were seated on the ground in full sunshine amid their groupings of tattered baskets. Pungent balls of *soumbala;*[1]

Map of Mali's Inland Niger Delta region

a small variety of shriveled smoked fish; spare quantities of papayas, tomatoes, squashes, and limes neatly stacked in tiny pyramids; and dried chili peppers and okra—little else comprised the market offerings. A series of droughts across the Sahel over the past two decades had been severe and the economy was in ruins. People and animals were underfed, disease was rife, and crops were meager. Compared to what I would witness twelve years later, the market was bare.

Following our tour of the stalls and an exploration of the narrow streets in a neighborhood quarter, we entered the mosque. At that time the prayer hall was open to non-Muslim visitors, and we climbed the minaret staircase that ascended from the dark cavernous interior to the roof that looked out over the

View over Djenné's roof terraces and towering *sarafar* miters

The Djenné Mosque

market.[2] The immense surface of this fantastical roofscape was embossed with tiny mounds, evenly spaced and arranged in neat columns. Each mound was capped by a crudely made ceramic dish that, when removed, let a constellation of tiny daylight apertures pierce the darkness of the prayer hall below and permitted rising heat to escape. A high parapet wall enclosed the rectangular terrace, and smooth mud pinnacles soared loftily at the corners, balancing gleaming white ostrich eggs on their pointed tips. The three colossal towers that projected outward from the facade rose like ziggurats, and their staggered tops also bore giant eggs gracefully poised at the apex. The mosque towers loomed high above all other buildings, orienting Djenné eastward toward Holy Mecca. We stayed among the softly sculpted formations for a long while, peering over the thick rounded parapet in all directions to drink in the market activity and contemplate the angular compositions of rooftop terraces encircling us. Unknown to us at the time, the old town and nearby archaeological site of Djenné-Djeno had recently secured a prestigious place on UNESCO's growing roster of World Heritage sites.

I did not return to Djenné until many years later. After my second diploma in architecture I went to Nigeria supported by an award from the Canadian International Development Agency (CIDA). There I researched Hausa masons and their baroquely decorated mud architecture in the northern Emirate of

Zaria.[3] This was my first taste of fieldwork and, as the project progressed, I found myself turning increasingly to anthropology to frame emerging questions about the daily lives and skilled expertise of these men who both design and build their works. The study led me to pursue a Ph.D. in anthropology, and I selected a new field site, this time working with masons in the south Arabian city of Sanʿa. For more than a year I labored alongside a team specialized in erecting towering mosque minarets of kiln-baked brick. The subject of inquiry that intrigued me above all others—including structural and aesthetic concerns, site politics, cultural and religious practices, and social organization—was the nature of training and the progression of young men who entered the trade. With so little offered by mentors in way of explanation, how do apprentices come to perform their tasks and eventually master their trade? And what personal characteristics and other types of knowledge, in addition to laying bricks and making solid structures, constitute a qualified and recognized mason?

The hierarchy on the Sanʿani building site was stark, and the training regime was regimented and at times severe. What I witnessed and experienced firsthand fueled my thesis that formal craft apprenticeship involves a great deal more than the transmission of trade skills and the conditioning of bodies. Central to the Yemeni mason's development was a formation of person firmly grounded in proper Islamic comportment, professional demeanor, and social responsibility.[4] Morals, muscles, and mind were tightly integrated with one another in this context, and the competent craftsperson was conceived within the trade and by their public as an embodiment of all three.

With much anticipation I returned to Mali in late 2000 to conduct postdoctoral fieldwork. My aim was to write an ethnography on the masons of Djenné by comparing building-craft knowledge and apprenticeship in West Africa to what I had learned from Arabia. Before taking up residence in the town, I traveled for several weeks to reacquaint myself with the country and to observe the momentous changes wrought by the overthrow of Traoré in 1991 and the democratic election of President Alpha Oumar Konaré the following year. I revisited the ever expanding capital Bamako, the bustling riverport city of Mopti, fabled Timbuktu, and several Dogon villages precariously perched along the high Bandiagara escarpment.

One chilly winter evening in Dogon country, the rising full moon became slowly engulfed by what at first appeared to be the reddish haze of *harmattan*[5] dust blowing south from the Sahara. A clamor of children's voices and the rhythmic beating of drums escalated steadily through the village quarters of Sangha where I was staying, infusing the night air with a festive defiance. The chanting grew bolder, uniting in frolicking processions that took to the narrow streets and alleyways. Back and forth, across and around the village, bands of young children numbering a hundred and more circulated excitedly, chastising the sinister forces that veiled their moonlight. "Sun, give us back the moon!" they cried loudly in the local Dogon dialect, all the while banging pots and tin cans with hands and sticks. Others demanded that the "cat" release her, believing the animal had sprung from the earth into the heavens and trapped the moon like a mouse. Waves of children washed by me in a swirl of Qurᶜanic exhortations of "*lā ilāh illā Allah*"[6] لا إله إلا الله, invoking God's mercy. Enormous stamina and persistent musical refrains summoning animist forces and the powers of Islam ultimately prevailed over the cosmic mischief, and after several long hours the eclipse surrendered to the pleas of joyous children and balance was restored.

The renowned Scottish explorer Mungo Park remarked in the description of his late-eighteenth-century travels into the heart of West Africa that "an eclipse, whether of the sun or moon, is supposed to be effected by witchcraft."[7] More than 150 years later, in the final decade of colonial rule, Ligers introduced his three-volume publication on the Bozo people of the Niger River with a detailed account of the prescriptions issued by elders to combat lunar eclipses. Among other rituals, this included pounding water in mortars scattered throughout the village quarters.[8] During my own fieldwork, many individuals of various ethnic and cultural backgrounds in Mali claimed that children are the prime agents in restoring order during an eclipse. As illustrated by the example from Sangha, young Dogon children up to the age of twelve are ushered over the threshold by their parents and older siblings to join the boisterous and amusing processions. Although most adults were at least vaguely aware of a natural explanation for this planetary event through radio and television broadcasts, they nevertheless chose to stay safely indoors while the powers of childhood innocence routed the source of disequilibria.

Fortuitously, witnessing the eclipse and ritualized prescriptions in Dogon country threw into relief the harmonious coexistence of seemingly divergent ways of knowing the world, namely, belief in the supernatural, devotion to a monotheistic creed, and a scientific understanding of cause and effect. Each system is structured by its own internal logic that is regularly harnessed and forcibly reproduced in political and ideological struggles the world over. In Mali, animism, organized religion, and science exist, to a significant degree, in a relation of mutual toleration allowing individuals to creatively negotiate understandings and explanations for events, good fortune, and life's many hardships. At the same time that supernatural forces animate the land and waterways, Islam connects the nation's majority to a global community of shared faith; the natural sciences are a component in formal schooling, and Western-style reasoning about world happenings has become common parlance through modern media and communications. These occasionally competing, sometimes complementary, and often fused worldviews were also evident at the construction sites in Djenné where I worked as a laborer for the next two winter seasons, researching apprenticeship and traditional building-craft knowledge. In the everyday practices of Djenné's masons, so-called traditional black-African knowledge (*bey-bibi*), Islamic knowledge (*bey-koray*), technical know-how, and basic engineering principles are in constant dialogue with one another, configuring the craftsmen's individual practice, identities, and professional status within the community, and dynamically redefining the social meaning of the architecture that they erect and modify over time.

Through detailed ethnographic accounts of life and work among my fellow builders, this book illustrates the complex weave of different ways of knowing-in-practice. The book takes a broad and encompassing perspective on what constitutes knowledge, one that crucially moves beyond propositional forms of knowledge expressed in text and the spoken word to include, at the very least, the skill-based practices and performance enacted by the socialized and enculturated body of the craftsman.

Anthropologist as Apprentice

Like earlier fieldwork in Yemen, I employed an apprentice-style method throughout my stay in Djenné.[9] By laboring as a building-team member and assisting the masons with their chores, I gained invaluable firsthand experience of mud-brick construction, the sometimes treacherous site conditions, and the normally amicable social relations among the workers. Occasionally, contending religious practices and spiritual convictions ruptured the harmony, providing important insights into the nuances of the workers' Islamic identities and their beliefs in the supernatural. The constant rally of banter exposed divisions and alliances along ethnic lines and incited discourses of "blackness," as competing masculinities measured and monitored gendered comportment. Through daily discussions and listening to talk between masons and clients, I learned about the wider political and economic factors that were propagating change in consumer tastes for new building materials and living spaces, and that subsequently shaped the discourses of masonry practices within the professional community. Importantly, a direct and regular involvement in the work enabled me to establish a strong and lasting rapport with my fellow builders and to share in their daily lives.

This exchange of toil for ethnographic knowledge was smoothly accommodated within the local system of learning. Apprentices of all Djenné trades—including tailoring, embroidery, leatherworking, potting, blacksmithing, goldsmithing, or masonry—are expected to pay for the technical knowledge, trade secrets, and personal formation they receive in an appropriate manner. Payment is routinely made with the free labor supplied by apprentices throughout their training period, and in some instances this is supplemented with gifts of money, kola nuts, or foodstuff. I purchased hats for my colleagues to protect them against the intense sunshine, gave them articles of work clothing, and happily loaned out my shiny blue bicycle in return for the generous knowledge I reaped and the good friendships I enjoyed. Like my fellow common laborers, however, I was not privy to the masons' secrets. I was nevertheless free to make notes while they mumbled hushed verses, and they entertained my questions about the purpose and effects of their ritualized performances. Only apprentices who work closely with their masters, and over a period of many years, are taught the spells that guarantee protection and bring good fortune.

A schedule of long working hours and participation in what were often monotonous manual tasks allowed for scrutiny of the building techniques, and careful and repeated observation of the professional conduct, social interactions, and on-site communications of my colleagues. Not surprisingly, much work-related communication between craftspeople is nonverbal, commonly relying on an intercourse of gesturing and deictic pointing, as well as other sources of visual, auditory, and somatic information exchanged between acting bodies.[10] Daily immersion in this environment heightened my attentiveness to a multitude of stimuli that impact the making of both builders and buildings. An apprenticing role also made me acutely aware of the sensible and psychological phenomena that affect work performance, including the extreme climate and conditions of the Sahel; the sheer physical strain of labor; well-being and illness; hunger and appetence; the tedium of endless mechanical tasks; and the euphoria when a job is done. All these factors color the book's portrayal of the construction of "traditional" masons.

The use of the term *traditional* in describing Djenné's masons implies neither stasis in their professional practice nor temporal displacement in some imagined and romanticized past. Rather, *traditional* in this context qualifies their direct and un-alienated mode of production.[11] Building is normally realized without interference from architects or engineers, and all stages of construction, from foundations to finishes, are executed solely by masons. The only other trades with a hand in the making of houses are carpenters or metalworkers who manufacture doors and windows, and potters who throw the giant clay downspouts. Masons seldom use measured drawings, but recent commissions from foreign patrons and for government-sponsored restoration works have honed their abilities to work from plans. Even when basic drawings and specifications are furnished, the activities of design, problem solving, and construction unfold together, requiring an ongoing process of improvisation and subtle innovation. Space and form are conceptualized and realized through the mason's total involvement in building a house with his tools and materials. In contrast to the growing numbers of contractors in Mali's larger cities who build with concrete and steel, Djenné's masons continue to use mainly local materials. Dwindling supplies of palm timbers for roofing, however, means that most are now trucked in from outlying regions. Further, the palette of finishes has expanded to include imported paints, cement rendering, and glazed ceramic tiles.

Until the early decades of the twentieth century, the mason's principal tools were his long crowbar-type implement called a *sasiré*, the wooden-handled hoe (*kumbu*), and an adze for chopping palm wood. Mud mortars and plasters were transported in thickly woven baskets (*segi*) which laborers carry on the top of their heads. Though the inventory of tools remains sparse, a number of additions were made during the last century resulting in significant changes to local building practices and form. Recent importations include the wooden slip-mold for producing rectangular bricks, the plumb line (*guuru karfoo*),[12] spirit level, measuring tape (*mètre*),[13] and the trowel. A small and fine French trowel (*truelle française*) is imported for executing delicate plasterwork and sculpting decorative elements such as the projecting roofline miters (*sarafar*). A second, more robust trowel called *truelle kuuru-bibi* (literally, "black-skin trowel") is produced by local blacksmiths and used for spreading mortar and chopping bricks to size. The blacksmiths also manufacture heavy-weight hammers with a sharp axe-like blade on the opposite side (*daasi*). This multipurpose tool is used for breaking stones, chopping timbers to length, and driving pegs into the hard earth when setting out foundations. Both imported shovels (*pelle*)[14] and hoes are employed to dig the shallow trench foundations for houses.[15]

Heavy machinery and power tools have not yet found their way onto construction sites, but electricity has delivered a diversity of other technolo-

Italianate balustrade and satellite dish on a new home in the Bamana Quarter

gies to Djenné. In the years since I began fieldwork, the small number of land-line telephones in the town have been superseded by an inundation of mobile telephones and two Internet cafés. Communication technologies are not only altering social interaction and etiquette as elsewhere, but they are also plugging Djenné into events, products, ideas, and opinions that emanate from well beyond its familiar frontiers. The full impact of global communications and circulation of information on local masonry practices, consumer habits, lifestyles, and the built environment remains to be seen.

Significantly, the masons' traditional education remains entirely practice-based, and their transmission of knowledge relies on an apprenticeship system which they control and reproduce. Technologies and secrets are transferred and transformed in the confluence of generations. The introduction of structural or stylistic innovations to the existing repertoire is never an individual affair but requires carefully negotiated acceptance by peers and public. Innovations, moreover, only become legitimate when they are accommodated within standard building practices. For this reason, approval of novel craftsmanship is granted almost exclusively to older "master" masons (*barey amir*)—and often posthumously—who have earned status and authority through experience, prestigious commissions, and the training of many disciples. Young masons who are overtly creative are chastised for their conceit, though occasionally they are successful at opening spaces for divergent practices. During my stay, this was illustrated by young masons who, much to the consternation of some older colleagues, clad exterior walls with "modern" tiles and adorned rooftops with Italianate balustrades. Internal debate breeds consensus and discord within the trade community, and ultimately serves to regulate change within a framework of continuity. By strategically assuming positions in the overlap between discourses of modernity and tradition, masons can improvise and introduce innovation to decorative vocabularies, their use of materials, and structures while still asserting that their practices, technologies, and buildings uphold local tradition and reproduce Djenné's special sense of place.[16]

An Anthropology of Place-Making

Although this is a book about building, architecture is not its central focus. Architecture, instead, provides the backdrop to a detailed depiction of craftsmanship and the agents responsible for physically producing and reproducing Djenné's unique *style-Soudanais* houses and its grand mosque.[17] A handful of scholarly works including those by Prussin, Maas and Mommersteeg, Blier, and Bedaux et al. offer comprehensive analyses of the town's architectural history, its built forms and spatial planning,[18] but these are weighted in favor of the building as cultural object rather than the builder as social subject. This book addresses this imbalance and complements the existing corpus of work by positioning the masons and their laborers at centre stage. LaViolette, in her writings on Djenné potters, likewise emphasizes the social relations and cultural behavior of the women artisans, noting that most studies on the topic concentrate on "the minutiae of the production process to the virtual exclusion of the women at work, as if the pots make themselves."[19] Jansen, too, in his research with Mandé *griots*, makes the point that although the recital of a historic or genealogical text is the most tangible cultural artifact produced by these bards, vocalization of the "correct" text is a minor aspect in learning to speak properly. Aside from merely transcribing their stories and praises, Jansen's ethnography grapples with the inculcation of broader and less tangible social skills that make a successful *griot*.[20] My study of masons similarly centers not on analyses of the material artifact but on its producers and the processes of their production.[21]

During fieldwork, I did not conduct surveys on the lives and training of all Djenné's masons, nor did I carry out in-depth ethnographic research on the town residents. The principal unit of my investigation remained the groups of builders with whom I formed intimate associations while churning mud plasters, hauling sun-dried bricks, and preparing tools. Alongside my thorough accounts of these builders' training and trade knowledge, I have woven my own apprenticing experiences into the narrative. As a work team, our practices were formed and constantly transformed in relation to one another. Individual progress and group coordination evolved (or regressed) in correspondence with the tasks at hand and with the physical evolution of a building through its various stages of construction. Learning and knowledge were recognized to be situated within an ever changing context of social actors, tools, materials, and physical parameters.[22] My anthropology of architecture may therefore be more accurately described as one about place-making, since it converges on the skilled interaction between sensing, learning bodies and the dwellings that they make.[23] In short, masons' practices are not only responding to and creating a physical environment, but, more important, they are *making* their own spaces and places of learning.

The next section explores the recent history of the masons' unique professional association and its enduring hierarchy in order to describe the social, political, and economic parameters within which my fellow builders learned and operated.

The Masons' Pecking Order

In her study of Djenné's craftspeople, LaViolette's grading of builders correlates closely with my own field observations.[24] The ranks, in ascending order, include, first, the apprentices (*dyente idye*), who are in long-term contractual arrangements with mentors; the officially validated masons (*barey*), who are entitled to accept commissions and build independently of their master(s); active senior masons with a secure clientele and with control over much of the town's construction work; and master masons (*barey amir*), who have retired from active building but continue to be prominent decision makers in the community and whose expertise is highly regarded. This gerontocracy also corresponds to Monteil's early colonial account which records that the corpus of masons was subdivided into age sets.[25] From as early as the late nineteenth century—and long before that date according to local oral histories—Djenné's professional community of masons have been organized as a guild-like association known as the *barey ton*.[26] The Mandé term *ton* refers to an "association" whose membership is defined either by a professional or age-set grouping.

A chief, the *barey bumo* (literally, "head mason"), presides over the *barey ton*. During my stay Sekou Traoré was the acting *barey bumo*, elected by the senior members of the association to succeed his father, Babèr Traoré. The patronymic Traoré is Mandé in origin,[27] but the family claims a *koyra-boro* identity signaling their established residency in urban Djenné.[28] Despite the strong majority of ethnic Bozo in the building trade, descendants of the Traoré family have long occupied the post of *barey bumo*. Indeed, the head mason who oversaw the reconstruction of the town's great mosque in 1906–1907 was Ismaila

Facade of the Maïga family's Tukolor-style house,
the residence of Djenné's chief (*Djenné wéré*)

LEFT Mason Sekou Traoré, chief of the masons' *barey ton* association

Traoré.[29] The *barey bumo* at that time was chosen by the traditional town chief (*Djenné wéré*), a Maïga of Songhay descent. In his keen observations Monteil relates that "the chief of the corporation of builders is chosen by the traditional chief of Djenné from among the most intelligent and capable candidates: he is a sort of local architect who is generally highly skillful. He is obeyed and listened to by the other builders who undertake no work without his instructions."[30]

For much of the twentieth century the *barey ton* firmly controlled all building works and the reproduction of Djenné's distinct architectural heritage. During the catastrophic droughts that afflicted the region in the 1970s and 1980s,[31] however, significant numbers of young males, including masons, migrated to Bamako, Dakar, and Abidjan in search of work.[32] Many never returned. This period, defined by severe economic hardship, witnessed a serious degradation of the town's built environment and a general assault on the traditional authority of the *barey ton* that endured well into the final years of the century. Masons old enough to remember claimed that, prior to the long drought, the *barey ton* was strong and well organized. Some recollected that the *barey ton* once operated a central fund supported by regular contributions from individual masons. The fund was drawn upon to provide pensions and financial security for retired or injured masons, and to assist younger builders with the costs of their wedding celebrations and festivities for newborn children.

Before the drought, wages, too, were fixed by the *barey ton*, and masons were duly rewarded for their services. In the 1930s Monteil recorded that clients typically provided their masons with all necessary building materials and "a proficient master mason received a daily wage of 400 cowry shells; the mason who prepared the mortar was paid 200 cowries and the laborers each received 100."[33] When the French arrived, cowry shells were the standard local currency throughout much of the Sahel and remained in circulation well into the twentieth century.[34] Their use at Gao was noted by Ibn Battuta as early as the mid-fourteenth century, and cowries have been recovered in other contexts by archaeologists at more ancient levels of strata. The most popular variety of the shell was imported from the Maldives via North African markets, demonstrating the existence of long-distant trade links that crisscrossed the continent.[35]

By 1970 the *barey ton* set the mason's wage in monetary terms at the near equivalent of 750 CFA (Communauté Financière Africaine francs) per day, and clients regularly supplied their team of builders with breakfast and lunch on-site.[36] Gifts of kola nuts were also part of the daily remunerations made to the chief masons. Economic instability by the middle years of that decade, however, meant that wages were no longer stable. Payment for work consisted

Moroccan-style merchant-trader houses close to the central marketplace

only partially of cash and was supplemented by a bartering of grains, food, and clothing articles for labor. Some clients were accused of manipulating the situation to their own advantage by bargaining down their masons' salaries. Builders, many of whose sideline practices of fishing and agriculture were detrimentally affected by the droughts, competed with one another for the few commissions on offer and grudgingly accepted lower dues. One mason recounted that the "foreigners" (i.e., Malians from other regions) who settled in Djenné during these decades were ignorant of the customary etiquette between masons and clients, and were responsible for corrupting the existing wage structure and diminishing the masons' status. The practice of supplying daytime meals was gradually phased out; masons' incomes plummeted; and the structure and authority of the *barey ton* largely collapsed.

The latter years of the 1980s delivered steadier rains, and an improving economy translated into building activity. Historic bonds between masons and patron families in the old town survived, and fresh contracts were forged with new households in the expanding quarters at Djenné's perimeter. These mainly single-storey constructions were laid along rectilinear grids of roads, and the designs of some facades borrowed eclectically from the existing repertoire of decorative elements.[37] The *barey ton* slowly reconsolidated its professional network, but the association faced uncertain recovery of its former authority and power. Their once familiar scope of practices was confronted by a rapid encroachment of imported building materials and new technologies including cement breezeblocks, corrugated steel sheeting, and the use of formwork, poured concrete and steel reinforcing bars. Masons returning from abroad with newly acquired construction skills were adept at working with the "modern" materials that increasing numbers of clients desired and could now afford. Widespread neglect of the old mud-brick buildings and progressive abandonment of their distinctive styles and forms prompted national and international concern that Djenné's architectural heritage was under siege.[38] At its meeting in Brasilia, in December 1988, the United Nations Educational, Scientific, and Cultural Organization (UNESCO) declared the town a World Heritage site and the Malian government established a Cultural Mission at Djenné to promote its protection and conservation.

At the national level Djenné's heritage became more firmly enmeshed in questions of Malian identity, and was linked to plans for developing the country's tourist industry and luring foreign aid. Growing international awareness and direct intervention in conservation strategies stirred prickly competition over issues of "authenticity," "correct" building practices, and sustainability. Bedaux et al. remark that Djenné's so-called *style-Soudanais* architecture "has practically become a symbol of national identity," but local- and national-level constructions of identity will inevitably differ and become a possible source of conflict over heritage-resource management.[39] Within this climate, the *barey ton* grossly profited from the surge in building activity and conservation work, and was soon able to reinstate the mason's fixed daily wage at 1500 CFA. They further inflated this figure to 2000 CFA by the early 1990s, but, despite the rising prosperity of individual trade members, the association's former sense of camaraderie remained weak as did its ability to implement cooperative building work.

In 1995 scholars and government officials from Holland and Mali coordinated their efforts to produce a detailed plan for the rehabilitation and conservation of Djenné's architecture.[40] The Dutch-funded project was divided into three phases over a seven-year period, terminating in 2002. Among the project aims was the need to foster grass-roots interest and expertise in heritage conservation, and establish a lasting schedule of annual building maintenance.[41] Both the *barey ton*'s authority and the renewal and reproduction of traditional building-craft knowledge were therefore deemed vital to the project's success. The planners judged that many young masons lacked an adequate formation and experience, and were incapable of calculating the cost and quantity of materials and labor. By employing them in the controlled rehabilitation of selected Tukolor and Moroccan-style houses, masons would gain firsthand knowledge about traditional spatial configurations and proportioning, palm-wood ceiling construction, mud-plaster decoration, and decorative forms. Through practice, this knowledge would become part of their skill set and would ideally be transmitted and learned by successive generations of apprentices. The project also required masons to work with fixed budgets, thereby preparing them to operate more effectively within Mali's money-based economy. Masons who hitherto built without drawing had occasion to become literate in reading the measured plans drafted by the project architects and technicians. Although most local masons did not use drawings on their own commissioned works, the skill qualifies them to work further afield where plans are integral to the building process.

Prior to the Dutch-Malian venture, government-sponsored projects in the region typically employed contractors from Bamako and Mopti with proven track records of working with fixed budgets and with reinforced concrete. Plans for a new Djenné hospital in 1998, however, opened a window of opportunity for the town's masons to assert their budding independence and display the diversity of skills acquired by the community—especially by those who

The *barey ton* masons making benedictions after re-plastering the mosque

had worked abroad with concrete and formwork. The *barey ton* convened a meeting and, though they agreed to labor alongside the assigned masons from Mopti and Bamako, they insisted that local masons take the lead. Similarly, as the Dutch-sponsored restorations progressed, the *barey ton* asserted its decision-making powers to act without direct influence from outside interests. In view of the large sums of foreign capital targeted for these works, the masons raised their wages again, fixing the daily price for a mason and a laborer at 2500 and 750 CFA, respectively. A mason's wage was now considerably higher than that of the average civil servant, and Djenné's government workers groaned over the disparity, arguing that their schooling merited better remuneration than artisans who work merely with their hands. Those at the helm of the restoration project worried that salary demands had surpassed market thresholds and would be untenable once injections of funding ceased. Justifiably, they feared that few local patrons could support such fees; unless wages returned to sensible levels, many buildings would again be abandoned to neglect and to the corrosive effects of rain, sunshine, and *harmattan* winds.

The *barey ton*'s recovery brought a revival of its meetings. In theory, these are held on the last Sunday of every lunar month at the home of the *barey bumo,* Sekou Traoré. All qualified masons are welcome, but many young members rely on senior colleagues to inform them about important events or relevant news. Some masters elect to send their protégés to the meetings in their stead. Generally young masons do not speak but listen and report back. The total number in attendance depends on the season and individual availability, but, on average, between thirty and forty of the town's more than two hundred masons are present.[42]

Barey ton meetings are customarily launched with words from a senior mason, and then the floor is opened to all participants wishing to speak. The typical seating arrangement segregates junior from senior members, and the power to make final decisions is respectfully deferred to masters. In jury-like manner, the masters reach consensus usually through lengthy negotiations. A centrally positioned intermediary plainly repeats all questions and statements, and reiterates the *barey bumo*'s responses and declarations for the benefit of all those in attendance.[43] In the past the intermediary was a Horso slave who, devoid of status, could neither truly offend nor be offended by any freeman.[44] Descendents of this former servant caste continue to act as intermediaries, and Horso are socially sanctioned to cast jests and criticism in a manner not possible for other individuals.[45]

Barey ton meetings are convened primarily to organize the division of labor for building large public projects such as the hospital or new schools; to mediate conflicts between masons and clients; to settle disputes between masons over territory and resources; to discipline rogue practitioners; and, most important, to organize the annual re-plastering of Djenné's Mosque. This "awesome, messy, meticulous and fun" festival takes place each spring and requires the cooperation of all townsfolk.[46] The *barey ton* arrange the date, organize the labor, and secure all necessary materials and equipment. In return, prominent townspeople furnish gifts of grain, rice, millet porridge, and money, and these are divided among the masons. Masters normally give a proportion of their share to former pupils, who in turn present small gifts to their own apprentices. This formal hierarchy is reproduced in everyday social interactions between masons and trainees, both on- and off-site. Regular meetings of the *barey ton*, it is argued, nurture solidarity that enables the trade community to quickly diffuse internal conflict and to act as an effective political lobby in defining its professional status and negotiating working conditions for its members.

Apparently, according to early sources, masons formerly occupied a low status in the twentieth century. As Monteil records:

> The masons come primarily from the Inland Niger Delta (referred to by the Bozo as the "Pondo"), and they are typically from the region of Djénnéri and Pondori. Regardless of his social class, a local person may become a mason; but, though masons are freemen and not part of a caste group, it is unlikely that those from families of good standing would choose this trade since masons are regarded with the same low esteem as all artisans.[47]

Prussin, too, suggests that, although Djenné's masons are freemen, they are also accorded low esteem.[48] This seems a fair assumption since, for example, masons were responsible for emptying the night soil of their patrons' toilet towers (*nyégé*)—a task commonly denigrated in Islamic cultures. In later work, however, Prussin queries her evaluation of their status, recognizing that masons are commonly addressed by the venerable Arabic title *mallam* reserved for learned men.[49] LaViolette, in her study of artisans, records that Djenné's masons are fully intermarried with free and undifferentiated populations of fishers and farmers, and that their social status is akin to that of "elite businessmen."[50] During my fieldwork I, too, observed that all Djenné's masons are town residents, and most are from family lines with long-established roots. Some occupy the middle classes economically, and socially are highly regarded for their technical expertise and potent trade secrets that combine *bey-bibi* (black-African knowledge) and *bey-koray* (Islamic knowledge).[51] Though many masons are illiterate with little or no formal education and minimal Qurᶜanic training, others have managed to complete secondary school; still others are versed in the religious scriptures and can accurately recite full *suar*.[52]

Like any aspect of identity, the social status of the profession is vulnerable to change and must be constantly negotiated. In order to retain the respect they enjoy today, masons will have to accommodate new forms of knowledge, practice, and learning that are responsive to larger transformations around them. This may one day necessitate the inclusion of computer-aided design skills, power-tool training, and abilities to work with a more varied and complex palette of materials compatible with, and sensitive to, Djenné's earthen architecture.

In summary, Djenné's building tradition has survived centuries of political, social, economic, and environmental change and continues to play a determining role in the town's postcolonial identity. The *barey ton* and the masons' apprenticeship are fundamental to the maintenance of this heritage. Together they produce experts who are not merely technically competent in their craft but are moral agents and artisans with defined duties and obligations to their public.[53] Secrets, spells, and benedictions, as well as ethnic lore and professional identity, are inculcated in trainees from their earliest days at the construction sites. As I demonstrate in the following chapters, this rich and complex learning engenders a distinctive comportment of body and mind characteristic of Djenné's masons, and is exemplified in the noble and resilient persona of its trade masters.

Outline of the Book

The ensuing chapters explore the situated learning and personal formation of Djenné's builders through detailed portrayals of their daily work, social relations, and sometimes difficult living conditions. That Mali is one of the very poorest nations on earth must be underlined, and survival in the arid Sahel is a challenge for even the most fortunate of the region. Life expectancy at birth is less than fifty years; only 35 percent of the population is literate, and the country consistently ranks at the bottom of the UNDP (United Nations Development Programme) human poverty index.[54] Masons fortunate enough to secure steady employment are positioned, economically, in the lower and middle classes, and at the time of my research a few could afford to purchase small motorbikes, build their own modest homes, and marry more than one wife. The vast majority, however, receive insufficient commissions from their handful of patrons and, like the rest of the town's more than ten thousand residents, are forced to seek alternative occupations as farmers, fishermen, and traders.

Throughout this ethnography I record not only the masons' progressions and achievements but also the many hardships that regularly afflict their positions and livelihoods. Of necessity, their life strategies have to be both flexible and resilient to cope with occupational injuries and serious illness; the overshadowing menace of regional drought, low river levels, and crop failure; and the fluctuating demands for building work and maintenance that surge and plummet with the volatile economy. Despite these ever present hurdles, the masons' commitment to their professional craft identities and to creating a safe and meaningful living environment is unwavering. Their buildings convey a tremendous pride of place, steeped in the town's rich cosmopolitan heritage and ancient urban history.

The principal narrative of life and work is interleaved with the chronological sequences of raising a mud-brick house, from foundations to finished plaster and ornamentation. In doing so, I offer a comprehensive account of the construction process that includes technical and structural information about these massive two-storey mud dwellings; the nature of the tools and materials used; and deep insight into the relation between building activity and social life in Djenné. Briefly, once a property is acquired and rights are granted by various local chiefs, construction begins. First, benedictions are made to protect the site against evil *djinn* (spirits or genies) and shallow foundations are excavated. Suites of rooms, arcaded verandas, and courtyards are configured and modified as the building activity proceeds. Thick mud-brick partitions and exterior walls rise together in tandem, buttressed by slender pilasters that extend the full two-storey height of the house and divide the facade into well-proportioned bays. The placement of doors complies with the distribution of structural loads, and the height of window openings is determined in relation to the erect human body. An array of geometric ceiling patterns are constructed with successive layers of palm-wood beams, gently elevated toward the center to create a shallow dome-like effect. Decorative displays of *sarafar* miters and projecting wooden *toron* crown the parapet of every noble rooftop, and when the house is complete all surfaces are caressed with a smooth protective coating of fine mud plaster. In relaying how these tasks were accomplished, I highlight the decision-making processes, improvisations, and problem-solving strategies at each stage, as well as the subtle innovations introduced and creatively negotiated by the masons.

The book is divided into two parts, reflecting my consecutive periods of fieldwork and the different teams I worked with. Several key laborers and masons are present throughout, and accounts of their lives and changing circumstances unfold during my five years of frequent visits up to 2005. In that short span of time, some men stumbled from steady work to destitution; one blazed a new and lucrative career path as a self-styled contractor; and others built sturdy reputations as excellent and honorable craftsmen.

Upon arriving in January 2001 I settled comfortably at the government's Cultural Mission and was soon acquainted with mason Bayeré Kouroumansé. In the 1980s Bayeré had worked closely with the architect Pierre Maas and the anthropologist Geert Mommersteeg during their respective studies of Djenné's architecture and planning, and its Islamic practices, and he was now the appointed mason overseeing site works for the Dutch-Malian restoration project. His local knowledge and trade connections would prove invaluable, and he quickly identified a site where I could begin my independent fieldwork. The property was located outside town on the banks of the Bani River, and the new house was being built for an expatriate Dutchman. The situation presented me, as an ethnographer, with a number of unforeseen advantages. The vast majority of commissions in town are for repairs and alterations or, at best, for second-storey additions. The riverside house, in contrast, provided a rare opportunity to engage in a new construction from the foundations upward, starting with the consecration of a virgin site. Daily labor allowed me not only to record the social interactions between team members as well as their professional practices and learning strategies, but also to examine the interface between local building traditions and foreign intervention. Although the client subscribed wholeheartedly to regional styles and construction methods, instances of miscommunication and tension highlighted the ways in which Djenné's architectural tradition accommodates outside influence and change. Such negotiations have been ongoing since the early colonial period and, arguably, long before because of the constant influx of populations from far-flung regions arriving with their own cultural perspectives. A recurring theme of this book is that tradition is dynamic and always situated at the confluence of continuity and change.

The chapters in part 1 describe the rudimentary principles of building and the social structure of the trade. In illustrating the processes of acquiring land, blessing a site, laying foundations, and erecting the mud-brick walls and ceilings, the mason's kit of essential tools, techniques, and secrets are gradually introduced. I detail the division of tasks and responsibilities between masons, apprentices, and laborers, and in so doing explore their lives and personal relations on- and off-site. The team I worked alongside during my first season included a large number of laborers from Dogon country who had traveled to Djenné to study at its many prestigious Qur'anic schools. These men are seldom contracted as apprentices; local laborers who are not descendants of established mason families likewise find that access to the higher rungs of the trade is impeded. Intense inter-ethnic banter is used to regulate the hierarchical relations between Bozo masons and their Dogon subordinates and also to control the reproduction of trade knowledge. In situations when banter turns to aggression and discussion to confrontation, self-appointed intermediaries usually intervene. Mediators simultaneously appease and gently rebuke both opponents in turn, thereby leveling tensions and brokering an agreement without the casualty of humiliation. This social mechanism for synthesis is frequently employed on-site and is a catalyst in resolving disputes over design and operational issues. If, however, threats by a would-be usurper are deemed serious, defensive magic is harnessed and religious *marabout* scholars may be consulted for their cache of ritual procedures, benedictions, and amulets.[55]

The integral function of rituals, incantations, and protective amulets in building activity was plainly evident. Masons take regular precautions to ensure the safety of their workforce, and to guarantee the structural integrity of their buildings and the well-being of their patrons. In addition to the Islamic knowledge (*bey-koray*) they possess, masons incorporate traditional black-African knowledge (*bey-bibi*) into secret passages that summon the authority of Allah and powers of animist forces. A mason's secret knowledge is not about total concealment but rather about strategic revelation. Numerous episodes illustrate how the performance of benedictions is intrinsic to the entire process, from start to finish. Secret knowledge is knitted into the weave of trade skills, and its inheritance and mastery are the measure of a competent mason.

On my return the following season, I joined a new building team to work on projects in the densely populated quarters of the old town. These projects presented me with opportunities to engage in the later stages of house construction, and thereby advance my technical experience from the year before. The events described in part 2 unfold against the final stages in making a house, including the challenge of constructing mud-brick arches, erecting staircases and narrow toilet shafts, sculpting well-proportioned assemblies of decorative elements, and applying sweeping layers of smooth mud plaster. During this second season I worked under the yoke of the talented al-Hajji Kouroumansé, an artisan who balanced technical judgment with aesthetic creativity to sensitively expand the repertoire of elements. Like other masons, al-Hajji's most important tools were his hands and body. Heights were measured against his torso, and dimensions were paced off, and sizes calibrated, by his fingers, hand spans, and arm lengths, all resulting in spaces responsive to human posture and movement.[56] My training under al-Hajji afforded me precious insight into a mason's apprenticeship. For young men entering the trade, this long and rigorous education forges their identity as members of Djenné's historic *barey ton,* and instills a deep knowledge of their social position, professional responsibilities, and power within the broader community. If possible, junior masons continue working under their masters for several years or longer with the benefit of continued mentoring. Some, however, have difficulty securing work and are left with little alternative but to pursue new trades.

The chapters in part 2 portray in detail my apprentice and mason colleagues, their aspirations to succeed and struggles to survive. Outside the short building season from January to April, masons face few employment opportunities. Some fish the rivers or cultivate fields, and others take up petty trading, selling trivial items and dry goods from their homes or at the Monday market. Scant precipitation in recent years has further weakened the regional economy, adversely affecting demand for building and consequently the welfare of many masons. Case studies of individual trials and tribulations open a window onto masons' household economies, family life at the hearth and in the courtyard, and domestic relations. The tales in these final chapters reveal the men's passion for their craft, their rivalries and vulnerabilities in the building trade, and, in the case of one apprentice, his desperate determination to escape the grueling work of masonry and abandon Djenné's stifling, conservative community altogether.

Ultimately my story reveals that Djenné is a living, changing town. Citizens and masons take pride in its World Heritage status, but a host of obstructions continue to frustrate full-fledged conservation efforts. Weak governmental and local leadership, abetted by fragile economics and conflicting development initiatives, have impeded long-term planning for conserving the mud-brick houses and staunching the pillage of treasures from nearby Djenné-Djeno.[57] At the same time Djenné's population has courted outside intervention cautiously, tactically resisting the imposition of rules and regulations on their living environment. The residents, masons included, struggle to participate in Mali's national project for progress and plug into the global arena of information and future prospects. Perhaps more than any other town in the country, Djenné maintains a strong sense of continuity, but, as this book will show, its builders demonstrate that tradition and continuity are necessarily couched in a relation with modernity and change. My argument, reinforced in the epilogue, is that the tradition most worthy of support and conservation is the apprenticeship system itself. This rounded education endows young men with complex skills to innovatively reproduce an urban landscape that is meaningful to their fellow residents. Ultimately ownership of Djenné's architectural heritage must be entrusted to those who make its buildings and keep it a living place.

Part 1 · Elementary Lessons in the Art of Building

Building laborers in the payload of a truck on their way to Sanuna

1 · Back to Work

Start of the Season

Crisp light, an unblemished pale-blue sky, cool temperatures, and no breeze— these early morning comforts would soon evaporate like a mirage in the scorching white heat of the Sahel.[1] By noontime temperatures would soar, and prevailing *harmattan* winds[2] and whirling *djinn*[3] would blanket the flat land-scape with heavy clouds of dust and sand. I stood by the silent roadside with my daypack slung over one shoulder, and under the shade of my baseball cap I kept an anxious eye on the western horizon for a white pickup truck. Ar-rangements had already been made for a lift with the driver. A young boy dressed in a ragged over-sized Florida State sweatshirt and short pants trotted past on a mule and gave a tiny wave. Two farmers with hoes in hand strolled by next, heading to their fields outside of town. "Bien dormi?" they inquired in a routine manner. Their casual greeting soothed my jittery stomach—a familiar mix of anticipation and excitement that accompanies the start of new fieldwork.

The pickup arrived at 8:20 AM. The cabin was cramped with men, so I climbed into the back payload and squeezed myself between other bodies. My eager greeting elicited a few faint smiles and subdued responses, but most of my fellow passengers stole glances through sleepy eyes—not unfriendly, mainly inquisitive. The truck sped off before I could get properly seated on the back panel, and those next to me grumbled and elbowed at the others nearer the front to make room. The wind picked up, and heads retreated like turtles inside the stretched necks of sweaters. January mornings were considered cold by local standards. After five kilometers on the tarmac road headed in the direction of the ferry crossing, we turned right onto a rough dirt track running parallel to the river. The building site was several hundred meters ahead through sparse bush and past stands of stunted acacia trees. It was an isolated and peaceful spot on the banks of the Bani River, with a fine view over the slow moving waters. The dry scrubby terrain was littered with hundreds-of-thousands of pottery shards, revealing its ancient connections with the vast archaeological site of nearby Djenné-Djeno.[4]

The driver of the truck was the patron of this new house construction. Tony had retired after selling his film production company in Holland and was fully invested in realizing his dream to live in Africa. He briskly introduced me to the masons who had been seated up front in the cabin, and then proudly guided me around his property while the men prepared their tools and materials for today's work. The Dutchman walked me through the plans for his ambitious project, animatedly describing his visions for a grand two-storey Tukolor-style house, a small house for a guardian, a kitchen garden, and a large plot of papaya and various other fruit trees. A property wall would eventually surround his private land and keep out the grazing herds that passed along the shoreline. Building activity commenced shortly before my arrival in Djenné. The masons were making walls for the guardian's house and laying stone foundations for the property wall. Construction on the main house had not started. Finishing the guard-house at the property entrance was the first priority in order to install a guardian to keep full-time vigil over the premises.

Tony led me circuitously back to his truck. He had something to show me, he said, and opened the cabin door. He groped under the driver's seat for a dusty cloth sack and from inside he pulled out the long jawbone of a horse (*bari*). The teeth rattled in the desiccated jaw as he held it up teasingly to my face. An older laborer nearby looked on disapprovingly and reprimanded Tony for his seeming irreverence, reminding him that these bones should remain hidden and that "sacred objects were not for everyone's eyes." Chastened, Tony obligingly wrapped the bones back in the cloth. With more solemnity, he went on to describe how the horse bones had been blessed by a powerful *marabout* who issued instructions to bury them in strategic locations along the property boundary. This, he explained, would secure protection for his health and his home against malevolent forces. I soon realized that

RIGHT Mason Baba Kouroumansé

I had received my first important lesson about the dynamic fusion between Djenné's building practices, Islamic knowledge and occult prescriptions.

A total of four masons were on-site, including one named Baba Kouroumansé who was in charge of daily operations. The remainder of the team consisted of a young apprentice and eleven laborers. My strategy was to spend this first day merely observing the pace of work and studying the different skills and tasks involved. I hoped to establish an amiable rapport with the men and gradually be permitted to work alongside them for the remainder of the season. After Tony departed I joined two masons who were raising the mud-block walls of the guardian's house. Bamoy[5] and Hasey[6] Kouroumansé were the younger brothers of Baba. They were polite but slightly wary of me, perhaps speculating that I had been hired by the European client to monitor their work. In their view, "Why else would a *tubaabu* [white man][7] choose to hang around a construction project?" I tried voluntarily to clarify the issue by explaining how I came to Djenné to learn about masons and the building trade, emphasizing that I had no contractual ties to their employer. For the time being, however, they remained averse to my assisting the laborers in any way. Bamoy insisted that I sit nearby and observe him and his *petit frère*, Hasey. He mockingly warned that their work was far too dirty for a *tubaabu* and I would soil my clean white T-shirt. Initially I complied, but as the day wore on and suspicions eased I tactically engaged myself with the team in passing along materials.

The linguistic and ethnic mix on the building site was quintessentially "Djenné" in character, as was the mutual tolerance and relative ease of social relations. Those native to Djenné spoke among themselves in mainly Djenné-Chiini, an indigenized version of the Songhay language prominently used along the northern reaches of the Niger bend and in Gao and Timbuktu.[8] The lingua franca between all builders, however, was Bamanankan interspersed with French, both the official languages of Mali. The sixteen-member team represented various places. All four masons (*barey*) and the apprentice (*dyente idye*) were native to Djenné and claimed a Bozo identity. The Bozo are thought to be the earliest inhabitants of the territories of the Inland Niger Delta and are a people largely defined by their traditional occupation as fishermen, moving with the catches along the Niger and Bani rivers.[9] In Djenné and its hinterland, Bozo also constitute the majority of building masons and therefore wield the greatest power and influence in the trade. The laborers (*mina bara*), on the other hand, came from diverse locations in Mali and neighboring Burkina Faso. There were several Dogon from the Bandiagara region east of Djenné; a local Bozo resident and Somono fisherman; and a couple of Mossi, a Bissa, a Marka-Dafing, and a Bobo-Djiula all from across the border in Burkina Faso.[10] Most of the young laborers had the status of *talibé*, or students of the Holy Qur'an. Some had ventured great distances to study at one of Djenné's numerous Qur'anic schools under the direction of a *marabout*.[11] *Marabouts* regularly send their students out to work in order to pay for lodging, meals, and studies. The remainder who were not Qur'anic students were either local or migrant laborers from outlying villages who sought temporary employment between crop cycles or when river levels were low and fish stocks depleted. My own foreignness to Djenné seemed a fitting addition to this eclectic blend of languages and cultural backgrounds.

My Welsh name "Trevor" proved nearly impossible to pronounce, much less remember. It provided amusement for a short while as the men tried to vocalize the strange conglomeration of harsh-sounding consonants, until one laborer asked me to choose a "Malian" name. I readily proposed "Abu Bakr,"[12] the name bestowed upon me in Northern Nigeria nearly ten years earlier and which I answered to throughout my stay in Yemen. "Abu Bakr Sadiq!" ("The companion of Prophet Muhammad") another exclaimed, and this recognizable name, an instant crowd-pleaser, was immediately adopted. In Mali the Arabic name Abu Bakr is frequently shortened to Boubacar, Boucar, and Boucari. The nickname Bayeré is a further derivative of these. I quickly accustomed myself to respond to these unfamiliar variations. Several masons who became close acquaintants and friends over the course of my fieldwork also conferred their surnames upon me, charitably welcoming me as an honorary member of their families. Sportingly, my own French surname, Marchand ("merchant"), was translated at one point to *Djiula*, an appropriate Mandé term for a "merchant trader."

The Division of Labor

There was a straightforward division of labor on the guardian's house. A young Dogon named Sedou manned the well and transported buckets of water twenty or so meters to a mound of earth shaded by a cluster of small thorny acacia trees. Sedou worked alone and in complete silence. He was a recent arrival in Djenné and spoke only his regional dialect, making communication difficult at best, even with his Dogon comrades who came from villages dispersed along the Bandiagara escarpment, the plateau, and the Seno plain. Boucari, the older laborer who had chided Tony about the horse bones, was in charge of mixing the raw earth and water with an added dose of poison. Cypermethrin, a noxious smelling potion sold locally in tiny brown glass bottles, was used in mortar for

the first eight courses of brickwork to keep termites from making the finished building their future mound.[13] With his trouser legs and shirtsleeves rolled high, Boucari trampled about in the pile of thick red mud-mortar breaking up the dry mound with a hoe and kneading it with his stomping feet and bare legs. He was small and wiry, and a truly effervescent character with a tendency toward aggressive provocation. He periodically abandoned his station to grill me with questions aimed at measuring me against his blatantly negative image of "the white man." He also had a great deal to tell me about himself. He boasted that at forty-four years of age he had worked half his life in the building trade and that his formidable experience would prove valuable to my study. In overhearing Boucari's tales, the two masons pronounced him a liar and sternly ordered him back to work. He retreated theatrically to his station, provoking laughter from the others, and in a short while was back again for more. Boucari was unabashedly the site clown and was more intent on rabble rousing than work.

Two other laborers—one a Burkinian Qur'anic student and the other a young Djennénké[14] boy—carried mud in thickly woven shallow baskets on top of their heads to where the masons were working. They sprinkled a fistful of fine, dry soil inside the baskets each time before filling them, swirling the dust around to coat the interior surface and discharging the excess. This prevents the wet mortar from sticking, making it easier to dump the load at its destination. The mud was shoveled in, transported, and plopped on top of the brick coursework at a spot indicated by Bamoy or Hasey. The masons then spread the mortar in a thick, generous layer with their large trowels. Another two pairs of hands supplied them with a steady flow of rectangular sun-dried mud bricks. They were also Qur'anic students from Burkina Faso. One collected the bricks with a wheelbarrow from a large stack, and both unloaded them, either stacking the blocks or laying them in rows along the ground. On cue, the second young man passed them along hand-to-hand or tossed them directly to the masons who caught and placed them in the bed of wet mortar. Each course overlapped the one below in a standard, staggered bond to produce a solid wall construction. Signals between masons and their helpers were sometimes spoken: "Noo ay see ferey!" ("Pass me a brick!") the mason commanded softly and repeatedly, rhythmically controlling the timing between his actions and those of the laborer. Much of the communication, however, relied on eye contact and simple, slight gestures of the head, hands, and forearms. Conserving energy was a priority in this midday heat, and was achieved by minimizing all superfluous efforts.

The four rooms of the single-storey guardian's house were set out in a linear arrangement along the property line. The kitchen (*futey*) was located at the far

LEFT Sedou, Qur'anic student and Dogon laborer from Djialassougou

end and separated from the living quarters (*hu*) by a storeroom (*dyiney dyisi do*). The typical double-room living quarter was positioned adjacent to the entrance of the property and contained a parlour (*galiya*) that gave access to the sleeping room (*tasika*). The walls of the building were being constructed in sun-dried mud bricks on top of shallow foundations of the same material. All walls, including the exterior walls and the three interior partitions, were one brick-length thick. The sun-dried bricks were being manufactured a short distance up river and measured 36 centimeters long by 18 wide by roughly 8 centimeters high (plus or minus a centimeter in any dimension owing to shrinkage). The two long exterior walls were supported on foundations of one and a half brick-lengths in width, and the shorter walls stretching perpendicularly between them rested on foundations equal to their own thickness. Walls were not built in tandem; rather, a single wall was arbitrarily selected and erected to a chosen height and then another was built up. The use of a standard staggered bond between brick courses enabled the builders to later connect adjoining perpendicular walls in a secure, stable fashion.

Before initiating any new section of wall, the two younger Kouroumansé masons summoned their brother, Baba, from where he was building the property boundary walls with the help of the fourth mason and the apprentice. Baba measured out the correct lengths for them with his tape measure, neatly marking where the brickwork should begin and end by slicing a line into the foundations with his trowel. For each successive brick course, the end bricks were set into place first, and a plumb bob (*guuru karfoo*) was carefully lowered down their faces to verify vertical alignment with the courses below. Next, a blue nylon cord with nails tied to each end was tautly drawn between the outer faces of the two end bricks and fixed in place by winding it around the bricks and temporarily inserting the nails into the wet mortar. The cord served to align the outer faces of all the bricks in the row which now could be laid quickly between the two carefully placed ends.

Enough thick mud mortar was spread to lay four to six bricks at a time. One by one the bricks were tossed along to the masons who, in one fluid motion, caught them and set them in place. Since there were slight differences in the height of the bricks, the masons had to quickly scrutinize each brick and discard any that varied significantly with the average height of the course being laid. Bamoy and Hasey moved their palms and fingertips rapidly, almost sensually, over the brick surfaces, checking for irregularities or serious defects. With a gentle twisting motion, those that had been approved were married into the bed of mortar. Each brick in the course was later tapped into place with the butt-end of a trowel to line up evenly with the nylon cord, and the plumb bob was lowered down along the wall at various locations to verify verticality. The oozing mortar between courses was fingered along the crevices to fill gaps, and any excess was smoothed over the wall with a trowel.

As the walls rose in height, Bamoy and Hasey rendered the exterior surfaces with a layer of rough mud plaster to protect the brickwork against wind erosion. Bamoy explained that it was also good practice for deterring vermin, especially scorpions (*dontoni* or *noor-foo*) and snakes (*ganda-karfoo*) from nesting in between the coursework. Sedou, the young Dogon laborer, had recently decapitated several long slithering snakes near the site well with the blade of his hoe. The men feared snakes, and these reptiles were mercilessly exterminated whether venomous or not. People knew that locally produced antivenins were risky and pharmaceutical serums were not always available, so the swift elimination of any snake seemed the best precaution.

Brick Making

Salif Toulema, better known as Salifou, was the chief brick maker for the project. He was somewhere in his forties and had come to Djenné ten years earlier from his village in the Dogon region. He had a gentle, thoughtful face with mournful eyes that intimated a difficult past. Occasionally I strolled along the river to rest under the big gnarly shea tree (*Butyrospermum parkii*) that shaded his workspace, and we engaged in casual chitchat. Brick production commenced in early October, several months before the start of the actual building season, and Salifou set up shop on the riverbank a hundred meters or so beyond Tony's property. A couple of teenage boys from Djenné sometimes assisted him when faced with a pressing quota, but he mainly worked by himself—a situation he seemed to prefer. Salifou arrived early each morning by bicycle, usually by 7:30 AM, and finished after 3:00 PM. In a single day he alone could produce nearly 150 bricks. Tony purchased these at the standard unit price of 10 CFA. Since the bricks were conveniently produced nearby, he saved on the usual transport fee of 5 CFA levied on each brick by the town's cart-and-horse drivers.

The earth for the bricks was systematically clawed away from the riverbanks with a hoe and gathered into tidy piles with a crater hollowed at their centers. A well-worn path led down to the river's edge, where water was drawn with a bucket. This was added to the earth, along with chopped straw and dung readily supplied by the cowherds that pass up and down the banks grazing on the stubble of untended winter fields. The tensile strength of laterite[15]

Salif Toulema (aka, "Salifou"), the brick maker

is negligible, so the soil must be reinforced with vegetal matter. Straw not only reinforces the tensile properties, but it also provides capillary channels for moisture to escape from the interior of the drying bricks.[16] The mixture was first worked with a hoe and then churned by bare feet and legs until the consistency was moist, thick, and even.

The rectangular wooden mold was made from four pieces of sawn timber with attached wooden handles. It measured 9 centimeters high with interior dimensions of 36 centimeters long by 18 centimeters wide. This was laid flat on a dry patch of ground cleared of small stones and loose earth. The brick maker grasped a large clump of the prepared mud with both hands and slapped it firmly into the mold, pressing it down with his palms to remove air pockets and to fill the entire volume from corner to corner. The upper surface was smoothed by hand and made level with the top edge of the wooden sides before slipping the mold up and off. The mold was placed on the ground adjacent to the fresh brick and then the next was made, and so forth. These rectangular bricks have been coined *tubaabu ferey*, or the "white-man's brick," because Europeans are thought to have introduced the quick-and-easy slip form to the region in the early 1930s.[17] Prior to this, a smaller, denser cylindrical brick, shaped and pre-stressed by hand, was uniquely used and referred to as the *djenné ferey*, or "Djenné brick." Although contemporary masons insist that the old-style brick is more resilient, many claim that once an historic construction becomes unstable and the walls buckle, repairs are impossible and it must be demolished. In fact, no one produces or builds with *djenné ferey* any longer, and the specialized knowledge is quickly disappearing with the grey-bearded generation of masons.

The introduction of the wooden brick mold represents perhaps the most critical transformation in local building form and practice. Because of their regularity in size and planar surfaces, *tubaabu ferey* can be laid quickly and efficiently, and more courses can be raised daily compared to using bricks of the *djenné* type. Not only has wall thickness been reduced, but walls are now straighter and architectural lines crisper than in the past. Nearly perfect verticality has been further guaranteed by standardized systems of measurement, plumb lines, and levels. These changes in building form are lamented by architectural historians and conservationists who see the molten contours of surviving *djenné-ferey* buildings as characteristic of the town's distinctive style.

Salifou's bricks baked in the hot Sahel sun for a couple of days before they were neatly stacked and left to dry out further. Stacks of mud bricks were the favored hangout for an assortment of small lizards that basked on their hot surfaces and took refuge in the dark cool spaces in between. When transferring bricks from these piles by hand, workers needed to be wary of snakes nesting in the cracks and crevices. Sun-dried bricks are large and heavy compared to the standard kiln-baked variety. Their bulkiness, as well as the sharp stalks of protruding straw, makes them awkward to toss, catch, and handle, and because they are brittle, they tend to break more frequently than their kiln-baked counterparts. But they possess superb advantages in terms of the straightforward technology required for their production and the availability of copious supplies of raw materials. Curing is solar powered and therefore requires no timber or other precious fuel in the preparation. Mud bricks also have ideal thermal properties as a building material, absorbing heat in the daytime to keep interiors relatively cool, and radiating their stored heat throughout the chilly night to maintain fairly constant indoor temperatures. And, when left to decompose, mud bricks, almost poetically, return to the land from which they came.[18] One potential problem is that as brick makers claim turf along the riverbanks to harvest the mineral-rich soils, they widen and alter the riverbed and thereby accelerate the erosion of fields and settlements along its course.[19]

Lunch On-Site

Lunch (*tjirkosé*) for the entire team was prepared daily by a Somono woman whose family set up residence in a well-shaded grove of trees along the riverbanks.[20] Their small encampment was situated immediately adjacent to Tony's land near the new guardian's house, and the family was able to generate a supplementary income from the basic services they provided him. Her eldest son, Hussein, worked alongside his father as a fisherman, and their catch provided the staple in their diet and featured regularly on the work team's lunch menu. When time allowed, Hussein also labored on the building site. He hoped to save enough money to buy a battery-operated radio to keep him company in his *pirogue*[21] while fishing, or to hang from the handlebars of his bicycle when riding about town.

With a signal from Baba, work was interrupted at 1:30 PM, and the men quickly washed their hands with the supply of water kept in an oil drum next to the well. Everyone gathered in a small clearing among the thorny shrubs and bushes, out of the direct sunshine. Rolling up shirtsleeves and impatient to eat, the builders hurriedly took seats on stool-sized stones arranged around the covered bright-blue plastic tub of food left by our Somono neighbor. The men fidgeted and some elbowed for a good position. The circle was tight, and we sat close to one another, all sixteen torsos twisted in the same direction with right

Masons performing communal midday prayers by the Bani River

shoulders leaning inward, ready hands within reach of lunch. Two of the bodies parted like a gate to make way for Baba, who stepped into the circle. There was momentary silence, with all in position like sprinters in the starting block. Baba removed the lid, reserving it for his own private platter, scooped out several handfuls of rice with sauce and a couple of tiny fish, and moved back out of the circle to let his team members have their share. A flurry of fingers and hands shoveled the sauce-soaked rice out of the tub and firmly squeezed it into balls. The balls were fed into mouths on flat outstretched palms, using the right hand only. It took some practice on my part not to burn the tips of my fingers on the steaming hot rice. It was always a tasty meal spiced with hot chilli peppers and tiny fish that seemed more bone than flesh.

During the rapid feeding frenzy, not a word was spoken, and the plastic tub was scraped fastidiously clean. Except for Baba who stood off to one side, daily lunch was a communal affair that echoed the mostly non-authoritative expression of hierarchy and relaxed social relations among the team members. There was no privileged seating arrangement among the other masons, the apprentices, or the laborers, and everyone engaged fully and equally in the competition to get their fill. If it was apparent that someone was not getting enough, more room was made for him at the edge of the bowl. At this

particular building site, so far from town, it was logical that the client provided the team with a lunchtime meal since no other eating options were
available here in the bush. Lunch, and even breakfast, as well as a daily allow-
ance of kola nuts, had once been part of the standard contract between clients
and masons, but this practice has waned since the decades of drought in the
1970s and 1980s when contracts became more strictly cash-based.

After eating, the men moved individually away from the circle to wash up at
the oil drum, and some ventured down to the river's edge to make ablutions
(*walaa*). They discreetly found shady spots in the vicinity and prayed alone or in
small groups.[22] Baba persuaded them to pray this way rather than as a large assembly, since this took less time and they could get back to work more quickly.

Afternoon Heat

Building resumed at a more leisurely pace in the afternoon. Baba made the point
that Djenné masons worked *kayna-kayna* ("bit by bit") and meticulously—
never with haste—and they were highly regarded for their fine, patient craftsmanship. I spent the rest of the afternoon passing materials to Baba where he
and a younger mason were constructing the stone-and-concrete foundations
for the perimeter wall. Stone-and-concrete foundations are a recent intervention in the toolbox of local building practices. In the not-so-distant past, mud-
brick houses were supported on foundations of the same material. A small
number of new reinforced-concrete structures, including the hospital and several schools, serve as prototypes despite Djenné's World Heritage status, which
prohibits the use of such materials. Masons have acquired the know-how for
erecting formwork and mixing concrete from their work experience in the capital and abroad, and a growing clientele with resources are requesting such
modern and, in some instances, more practical materials. At Sanuna, by the
river's edge, the masons resolved that stone-and-concrete foundations were the
best solution for ensuring that the house is not washed away.

The second mason, clearly junior to Baba, was Konamadou Djennepo.
Baba happened to be married to one of Konamadou's older sisters, and the
two men regularly worked together. Konamadou was an affable character
with an infectious laugh and a gift for gab. Over the course of my fieldwork,
Konamadou remained a steady source of news and information, and he became my dearest friend in Djenné. He introduced himself on that first day by
recounting a short story about his clan.

The Djennépo family, along with the Tennépo and the Kayentao, were said to be the original Bozo inhabitants of Djenné's territory. The traditional Chiefs of Djenné (*chef du village* or *djenné wéré*), like the present one, Ba Hasey Maïga, were Djennénké descendants of a noble family of Songhay settlers. On each New Year's Day of the Islamic calendar, the traditional Chief presents a sheep to the patriarchal head of the Djennépo family (presently Komamy Djennépo) in recognition of his people's autochthonous status, and as a sign that his northern *Koyra-boro*[23] people who arrived as occupiers in the fifteenth century continue to seek peaceful relations with the Bozo. The Head of the Djennépo clan ritually slaughters the sheep and shares the meat with the Tennépo and Kayentao families. Also, throughout the year, all the town's families make offerings of grain to the Head Djennépo. Quantities vary from a handful to a sack-load of grain. When the Head of the Djennépo deems that a sufficient sum has been collected, he performs benedictions that guarantee peace and prosperity for the entire population, and the grain is then distributed between the same three original Bozo families.

Like many Bozo family names, Djennepo is derived from the Bamana language, translating to "the girl is dead." Djennepo was the patronymic of the virgin Tempama who, it is said, was interred long ago in the city walls. Konamadou explained that the sacrifice rid Djenné of the devils that once inhabited the place. The legend recounts how the council of elders deemed a virgin sacrifice the only possible way to fortify the town's defensive earthen ramparts and guarantee prosperity for the settlement. Tempama's burial place is signposted at a spot close to a now vanished city gate on the watery edge of Yobukayna quarter, next to the boundary with Kanafa.[24]

The stone and concrete perimeter-wall foundations were being constructed using formwork made from long planks of timber. A shallow trench was dug, and the planks were lined up lengthwise along each side. The planks were stood on their edges and braced in upright position using short sections of steel reinforcing bars that the masons pounded into the hard, dry laterite soil. Two laborers transported stones by wheelbarrow from a pile delivered to the site by truck.[25] Another group of laborers prepared batches of concrete with cement and granular sand brought from the river's edge by horse-drawn cart (*wotoro*). The two masons, assisted by the apprentice, arranged the stones carefully in the shallow formwork, placing larger ones at the bottom and using smaller ones to fill gaps. Once a length of formwork had been filled in this manner, concrete was shoveled in and prodded with crowbars and trowels to release trapped air pockets and ensure that the binder made contact with every stone. Stones protruding above the top of the formwork were crudely chiseled down to size with a large, heavy hammer. The hammerhead repeatedly disengaged from its flimsy wooden shaft. The apprentice made several studied attempts at remedying this situation by dipping the top end of the shaft into wet concrete to provide resistance, then cramming it back through the hole in the iron hammerhead. This was not altogether successful, unfortunately, and nearby workers had to be wary of hazardous projectiles.

The word for "apprentice" in Djenné-Chiini is *maale-banya*—literally, "the slave of the master"—but this term has been largely replaced with *dyente-idye*.[26] The apprentice on this site, Diabaté Yonou, was a member of a well-respected family of Djenné masons. Officially he was being trained under the guidance of the elderly master mason (*barey amir*)[27] Mama Kourani, who, according to many, was the town's greatest living builder. Presently, however, Diabaté was under the yoke of Baba, who was also revered for his mastery in the trade. It was regular practice, especially for elderly retiring masons, to send their apprentices to train with younger colleagues in order to acquire work experience and broaden their exposure to different building techniques and problem-solving strategies. When working for someone other than his own master, an apprentice was entitled to a daily wage, which made this arrangement attractive to the trainee. Diabaté was a burly, powerful young man with a full face, broad toothy smile, and hands like paddles. He had minimal schooling and spoke Djenné-Chiini with a smattering of Bamanankan and a small vocabulary of French. According to Baba, his apprentice was probably fifteen or sixteen years old at most, but by Diabaté's own guess he was closer to nineteen or twenty. Like many men on-site, his age was not known with certainty and he likely exaggerated the figure to boost his status and gain autonomy.[28]

Diabaté, the only apprentice working on this building site, was also the only one with the advantage of being of the right ethnic identity and, more importantly, having family connections to ever become a full-fledged Djenné mason. The majority of hired laborers were "foreign" students deprived of any formal training or long-term investment in the building profession. Those laborers who were Djenné-born and not Qurᶜanic students were fully aware of their own limited access to the higher rungs of the trade and were largely resigned to this lower status. The rules and the hierarchy were plainly evident, and both reflected the perpetuation of a tenuous social cosmology that, historically, equates certain ethnic and group distinctions with corporate identities defined by a shared professional activity.[29] In reality, the mapping of ethnicity and occupation is in perpetual flux, responding to shifting power regimes, economic forces, and environmental conditions, and Mali's postcolonial era has witnessed new opportunities for social mobility and transformation, albeit few in number. But shared imaginings of tidy ethnic and social-class–based divisions stubbornly linger, and these are reified in everyday discourse as I address more thoroughly at the end of this chapter. This partially explains the absence of truly hostile competition between young laborers to excel in the trade and the generally fluid social interactions between all ranks and across ethnic boundaries.

The afternoon schedule was short. By 3:00 PM the heat was nearly intolerable, and in the coming winter months the landscape would be parched by the *harmattan* winds and temperatures would climb. Tony, frequently accompanied by his chief mason, Bayeré, returned by truck in the late afternoon to ferry the team back to town. Bayeré was there to make his end-of-day inspection and to discuss with Baba any issues that arose, to schedule deliveries, and to plan the future phases of the project. Bayeré was also a member of the Kouroumansé family and a paternal cousin of the three mason-brothers on-site. He rarely engaged in actual masonry work anymore and had settled into his responsibilities for overseeing the project and acting as a general contractor of sorts.

On Sunday afternoons Tony and Bayeré paid the workers in cash. Sunday marked the end of the six-day workweek, and the builders needed money to purchase food and other necessities at the Monday market.[30] A mason's standard wage (*bana-hay*) in Djenné was set at 2500 CFA per day, and a laborer, as noted earlier, earned 750 CFA. Fees were determined by the masons' professional association, the *barey ton*. On this project, Tony paid just above the standard daily wage and offered a midday meal as an incentive to keep his men committed to working at a site inconveniently located so far from the town center. The laborers and apprentice were paid 1000 CFA, and Baba, as chief of the site operations, was paid 3000 CFA (250 and 500 CFA, respectively, above the normal wage).

When they returned home in the late afternoon, the men spent time relaxing their aching muscles, praying at the mosque, taking care of children and family needs, or visiting friends. Visiting plays an important part in the social schedule, and people gather together to exchange news, listen to the local radio station, or watch evening television. Some masons take on additional, less labor-intensive commissions to plaster (*kreepi*) walls or make repairs to client's houses. Others operate small convenience stores from their homes, selling basic food provisions and small items to neighbors. A hearty early evening meal after sunset typically consists of more rice and sauce but in larger quantities than lunch. The student-laborers do chores for their *marabout* teachers and then resume

Qur^{c}anic studies and recite *suar* late into the evening by the glow of kerosene lamps.

Bantering and Trade Boundaries

One afternoon, early in my fieldwork, Bamoy suddenly asked me in a serious register to more fully describe my reasons for studying Djenné's masons. At the time I was squatting on top of the rising walls of the one-storey guardhouse with him and his *petit frère*, Hasey, and carefully observing how they placed the diagonal roof beams over the interior of the first room. The process involved a great deal of concentration and largely silent cooperation, with Bamoy handling one end of the heavy palm trunk and Hasey struggling with the other. I responded frankly that I was here to learn about local building techniques, and to understand the masons' building-craft knowledge and the ways that it is controlled, disseminated, and changed. While shifting the beam ever so slightly, keeping his eyes and hands focused on the task, Bamoy calmly and flatly declared that I should give them a *cadeau* (a gift) for the valuable information I was receiving. His tone was grave. The laborers at ground level were silent.

Among the Bozo, and in Mandé cultures generally, knowledge is not something freely and democratically available to individuals but instead is a privilege one pays for either with money, gifts, or some sacrifice.[31] Aside from more immediately recognizable practices of bloodletting or millet porridge offerings, the forfeiture must also include a self-sacrifice that entails physical, emotional, or spiritual hardship as illustrated in Brett-Smith's study of blacksmiths (*numuw*).[32] I feebly protested to Bamoy that I had indeed offered a *cadeau* in the form of free labor that I provided daily. He retorted cuttingly that my labor was a *cadeau* for the project patron but not a gift for them. Bamoy was absolutely correct. The contract for this project was based on a daily wage, and salaries were paid out weekly by the client. Thus any savings made from my contribution of sweat remained in Tony's pockets without increasing Bamoy's or his brothers' earnings. When I conceded defeat and asked him what sort of gift might be appropriate, he chuckled playfully and said that he was only joking. A surge of laughter issued from the laborers below. During this season and the next I learned a great deal not only about knowledge, both guarded and displayed, but also about the role of banter in socializing individuals, reproducing inter-ethnic social relations, and maintaining trade boundaries.[33]

Control over the reproduction of the *style-Soudanais* architecture in

Djenné constitutes a prestigious form of cultural capital, and, for some, becoming a mason is a desirable choice and a privilege worth defending. Bantering relations were frequently invoked to entrench the hierarchical divisions between masons and their team members on-site. The most historic and highly developed form of banter is that between the Bozo and Dogon; to a lesser extent, banter peppered with nationalist overtones was exchanged between Malian laborers and those from neighboring Burkina Faso.

Anthropologists across Africa have recorded the existence of so-called joking relationships that bind ethnic and socio-economically differentiated groups, as well as kin by marriage.[34] These relationships, more than occasional teasing, exhibit a highly formalized discourse that the parties regularly, and predictably, engaged in. The repertoire of jokes, often in the form of insults, is restricted, and limits of abuse are carefully observed. Like other anthropologists who have addressed this social institution in their studies, I was curious about its function and performance as a form of both cooperative and antagonistic communication and entertainment. The results of my inquiries—though somewhat confirming Radcliffe-Brown's universal conclusion that joking relationships serve to organize and stabilize a system of social behavior, and also many of Griaule's more relativistic observations about the Bozo-Dogon alliance—demonstrate specific and highly strategic employments of inter-ethnic banter.

More specifically, I discovered that bantering relations were manipulated to control access to the building trade; to maintain clear professional boundaries and hierarchies that reflected ethnic divisions; and, most important, to create opportunities for individual resistance and accommodation. All the masons I worked with throughout my fieldwork were Bozo, as were two of the three apprentices. The Bozo, as noted, have traditionally been the fishermen of the Inland Niger Delta,[35] and they remain the most prominent group in Djenné's building trades. The Dogon, on the other hand, have historically inhabited the dry plateau, cliffs, and plains of the Bandiagara escarpment, and many Dogon residing in Djenné came to the town to acquire an Islamic training that, aside from expanding their religious knowledge, would boost their social standing when they returned home. Many laborers were Dogon Qurᶜanic students, and the majority were determined to leave Djenné when they completed their several years of education.[36]

The rallies of insults (sing., *mootey*) between Bozo and Dogon on the building sites were predominantly jovial and aimed to inspire laughter from both sides as well as from spectators. The remarks, which were often obscene,[37] overtly challenged social status, masculinity, intelligence, and, occasionally, the other's myths of origin and ethnic identity. Griaule, challenging Radcliffe-Brown's all-encompassing structural-functionalist theory of what he terms "joking relationships,"[38] proposed the term "cathartic alliance" (*alliance cathartique*) to more accurately describe this specific type of insulting relationship that he and Paulme[39] recorded between the Dogon and the Bozo in the 1930s and 1940s. With reference to Dogon accounts of the importance of twinship, and to their myths of origin and popular oral tales about the source of the alliance between them and the Bozo, Griaule described how a portion of the vital force (*nyama*) of each had passed into the other during long-ago events, and thus every Dogon has a part of the Bozo, and vice versa, residing in their livers. In brief, the alliance primarily serves a need for mutual purification and is manifested in an exchange of insults intended to act on that portion of the self in the other, expunging impurities from the livers of both parties and restoring a balance in the spiritual order. Separated, a Bozo or a Dogon is incomplete, but face to face and acting on that part of themselves in the other, their vital energy becomes whole.[40]

Griaule's entire argument relied heavily on the concept of *nyama*, and although the concept is apparently common among most Mandé cultural groups,[41] some have contested its importance or even its existence among the Dogon.[42] My work with Bozo and Dogon builders confirms that neither group recognized or employed the word *nyama*, nor could they map an equivalent term from their Djenné-Chiini or Dogon languages to the definitions I supplied. Rouch defined the Songhay concept *biya* in terms similar to those used by Mandé scholars to describe *nyama*.[43] *Biya* was indeed understood and used by Songhay residents who recently came to Djenné from Timbuktu and Gao but, curiously, not by native Djenné-Chiini speakers. Regardless of the absence of a specific term, the special status of the bantering relation between Bozo and Dogon was universally acknowledged, and all builders shared the conviction that "energy of action,"[44] equivalent in description to *nyama*, infuses all living and nonliving things. This vital force can be tainted, unbalanced, or ruptured by behavioral or verbalized transgressions, and such violations require actions of purification in the form of prayer, secret incantations, ritual procedures, the preparation of *gris-gris* (or *baka*, amulets), or the ingestion of African medicines. The concept of *nyama* is revisited in the next chapter in a discussion of masons' secret knowledge.

Although they worked exceedingly well together on the building sites, Dogon and Bozo laborers neither shared residence nor spent a great deal of social time together outside working hours and Friday prayers at the mosque. The development of close friendships between Bozo and Dogon men was often impeded by language barriers, as well as by cultural differences marked by such straightforward issues as food preferences, pastimes, and occupational skills (i.e., fishing versus cultivation). Nevertheless, a special connection between the two populations was recognized, and my masons occasionally recounted similar versions of the alliance myth recorded by Paulme, sometimes reversing the ethnic roles of the rescuer-chief and starving child. This popular story about the origins of the alliance between the cliff-dwelling Dogon and the Bozo of the Inland Niger Delta tells how the two ethnic groups came together cooperatively during a great famine. At this time, both groups were living along the banks of the Niger, and it was decided that while the Bozo journeyed along the river to fish they would leave their children in the care of the Dogon. During their absence, one of the Bozo children was on the brink of starvation. The Dogon chief revived the child by cutting a piece of flesh from the calf of his own leg, roasting it, and feeding it to the young Bozo, and thereby instantiating a lasting blood tie between the two peoples.[45]

Paulme suggests that this blood pact is comparable to a marriage in that it creates a new alliance and a framework of social relations tempered by joking-type relationships, such as that recorded between a Dogon man and his wife's sisters and their daughters.[46] The Dogon consider the alliance with the Bozo as their most sacred bond, and it is the model on which other inter-Dogon alliances are based. Further, because of the importance of this blood pact, Paulme points out that it precludes intermarriage between the two ethnic groups in the same way that marriage alliances among the Dogon also imply exogamous relations between the succeeding generations.[47] Indeed, my fellow workers explained the prohibition against marriage between Bozo and Dogon as a mere consequence of the blood-based alliance.

Bantering is the most prominent public expression of the Bozo-Dogon alliance. The exchanges in Djenné were conducted mainly in Bamanankan[48] and only occasionally in French.[49] Exchanges between builders on the construction sites were typically initiated when a member of one group fumbled with their task, causing an obvious disruption in the team's working rhythm and thus inviting ridicule or reprimands. Spectacles of bravado such as moving heavy stones or carrying exceptionally large loads of building materials were read as a challenge to others, often resulting in amusing competitions involving feats of strength and verbal banter. The content of the bantering and the nature of the performances I witnessed were almost identical to that recorded by Griaule more than fifty years ago. The insult themes included all three categories of obscenities described by Edmund Leach in his discussion of taboo: "dirty

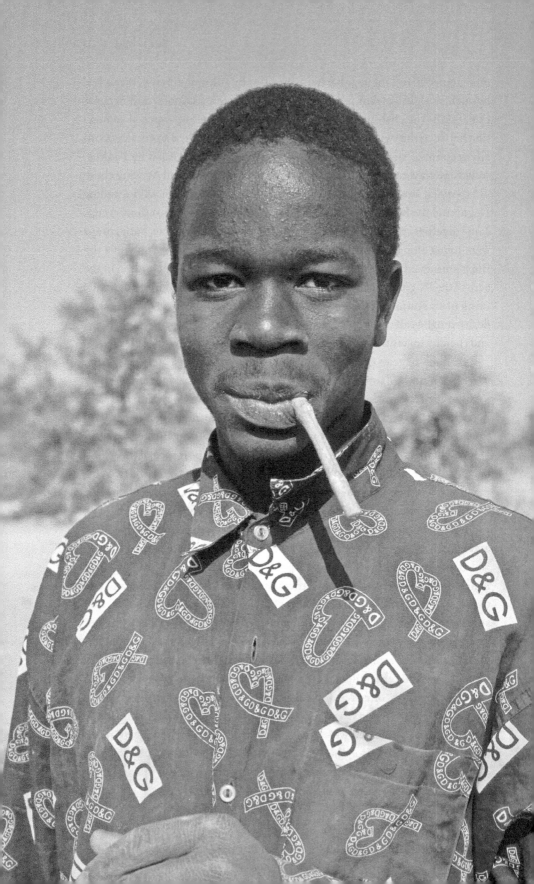

words—usually referring to sex and excretion; blasphemy and profanity; animal abuse—in which a human being is equated with an animal of another species."[50] Griaule noted that, following normal greetings, a barrage of obscenities was unleashed that usually identified the sexual organs of the other's parents—"The penis of your father!"; "The vagina of your mother!"—to which the other responded with analogous statements. The rallies turned to mockeries, breaching the borders of the other's sacred beliefs and practices. Bozo ridiculed the principal foods of Dogon, namely, millet and crocodile meat, as being fodder for horses; Dogon retorted that the Bozo was a fish that walked on land (alluding to the vulnerability of a species forced outside of its normal habitat); Bozo accused the other's spiritual chief of never washing and being licked by a snake (referring to the Lebé cult); Dogon cursed the Bozo as being that "dirty thing of the water" that has made the water *djinn* impure.[51]

One morning, while hauling stones by hand from a pile to where the masons were laying the new house foundations, Hamidou Guindo, a young well-built Dogon, playfully challenged some of us to lift heavier and heavier stones. Strength and muscle mass were regularly associated with consuming meat, and discussions about diet often emphasized eating the heads of animals—especially those of sheep, cows, and fish—thought to be an ideal breakfast to fuel up for a hard day's work. In provocation, I loudly praised Hamidou's strength so that the masons could hear, and suggested that he was the best worker on the site. Hamidou enjoyed this but was bashful. "No, no!" objected the Bozo mason Konamadou Djennepo, shaking his finger. "The Dogon are *petit*. The Dogon are the sons of the Bozo!" Konamadou's kinship metaphors asserted hierarchy and a demand for respect. A great burst of laughter issued from those standing nearby. Hamidou, waving his finger back toward the mason and shaking his head, looked to me with a broad smile protesting that this was a lie. "The Bozo are the sons of the Dogon!" he retorted. Konamadou interjected "The Dogon don't know how to achieve anything by themselves, and we Bozo must teach them everything." There were more protests from Hamidou and his Dogon colleagues who were outnumbered and outranked in this context. "Dogon didn't come from Allah," said Konamadou, "They fell directly from the sky like stones" (alluding to the celestial ark in the Dogon myth of origin). A more vocal Dogon laborer chimed in: "Yes, well the Bozo was born from fish!" Konamadou retorted "When a Dogon sees a car coming towards them on the road, they run and hide amongst the rocks. They might hide for three or four weeks without emerging or even eating!" Here he was referring to the seclusion of Dogon

LEFT Hamidou Guindo, Qurᶜanic student and Dogon laborer from Bankass

villages and their historic resistance to outside intervention. Typically the exchange would peter out, and we would all resume our tasks.

A Dogon laborer whom I worked with during my second building season cultivated a very different relation with his Bozo superiors. Youssuf was pompous, boisterous, and very strong. He was also a Qurʿanic student in Djenné but had acquired construction-work experience as a migrant laborer in Ivory Coast. He was quite exceptional among both the students and laborers for having not only one but three wives and six children. Of necessity, his meager wages were supporting more than his studies. Youssuf regularly chided the other laborers for being bachelors (sing., *koosow*) and living together in rooming arrangements, and he bragged constantly about his virile potency and that he had a wife here in Djenné to cook his meals. Nothing in his demeanor was remotely charitable. The men soon began to address him as *kado*, an ethnically derogatory Fulfuldé-language term for the Dogon.[52] This ambiguous term, which could be read as either an insult or a jocular term of endearment, was suitably employed by the other builders to express their dislike for Youssuf without being entirely candid about it. His familiarity with construction work also made him cocky with the senior builders.

At one stage while the mason and his apprentice were plastering the interior wall surfaces of the house, Youssuf picked up the mason's trowel from where it had been set down and applied a splotch of plaster onto the wall. If this bold act had been executed by any other laborer the mason would have taken little notice, but he was plainly irritated by Youssuf's lack of reverence for his tools. A mason's tools were almost sacred, and new tools were presented to an apprentice when he had succeeded in various stages of his training. The mason cursed: "If you handle my tools again without permission your genitals will swell to an enormous size!" gesturing simultaneously with both hands at his crotch. I initially thought that this might be a sought-after curse, and that if larger genitals were an undesirable attribute here perhaps I had stumbled upon a fascinating cross-cultural difference in male perceptions of their bodies. I soon understood, however, that the mason meant Youssuf would be struck with elephantiasis, a truly debilitating and potentially fatal disease most commonly found in Africa. This was not merely banter; the mason was threatening to exercise his power to punish.

Djenné's masons are alleged to possess a power of speech associated with secret knowledge (*bey-bibi* and *bey-koray*). Their daily incantations provide protection for their work teams, the building, and their clients. Words can also be used destructively. Powerful masons can put curses upon those who meddle in their affairs, "steal" commissions, or engage illicitly in the trade. These curses can cause debilitating injuries or trigger structural collapse. Though the mason who cursed Youssuf was not yet a trade master, he was widely regarded as a potent healer. His capacity to mend was presumably equal to his ability to contaminate, and it was with this possibility that he threatened Youssuf. Youssuf bullied the laborers, competed with the apprentices for attention, and took liberties with the masons' tools, and he needed to be put in his place. By forbidding him to touch the tools, the narrow limits to which he was permitted to participate in this profession were fixed, and this boundary line was defended by a curse.[53]

A great deal of teasing was also exchanged between the Malian and Burkinian workers who accused one another of having *une tête noire* or *une pensée africaine.* Such racially loaded allegations suggested "thickness" or "slowness" in thinking and actions, and implied that the other was stifled by pre-Islamic, black-African traditions. Builders who wore what was deemed to be an excess of *gris-gris* or protective amulets on their bodies also took the brunt of this sort of teasing that overtly challenged their faith in Allah to do the protecting, and thus was effective in coercing a narrow vision of religious conformity.[54] Laborers also launched aggressive, jocular attacks on the Bozo masons with similar connotations of being "black" and dim-witted. The Bozo are popularly regarded as the darkest-skinned people of the region, and there is widespread social commentary on degrees of "blackness" and "whiteness" throughout the Sahel. Bamoy Kouroumansé occasionally pulled rank by reminding them with a stern look that he was the mason and they were just *petits.* Moments later his angular expression would soften, and the playful exchange of insults would resume. Limits were observed, however, and both parties normally steered clear of making truly offensive remarks. Comments that transcended the limits would fall flat, and the chorus of laughter would fade to a few nervous giggles or, worse yet, complete silence. In this sense, the rules of conduct and limits for bantering were mediated between the various parties largely through the tenor of their response. As members of the audience, and in their occasional participation, younger men learned what was appropriate and tolerable; what successfully provoked the heartiest laughter; and the importance of timing and rhythm in the exchange.

The content of the insults and banter exchanged on-site was neither rigid nor static, nor was it the exchange of a single genre. Rather, factors on-site, including professional hierarchy, individual aspirations, and emotions, shaped the form and content of the dialogue, and were reciprocally shaped by it. As Brennies noted in his study of language and disputing, "Language is not an epiphenomenal reflex of other relations; indeed it often creates and shapes those relations."[55] In addition to providing a vehicle for the exchange of insults, banter should also be recognized as a way to manipulate outcomes, relations, and identities. Many themes recorded by Paulme and Griaule remain unchanged, including the use of banter to impute hierarchy with kinship terms; with obscenities, blasphemies, and animal categories; and through attacks on myths of origin and other sacred institutions. On building sites, attacks on intelligence, adeptness, and masculinity are integrated with jocular exchanges, as are the derogatory references to blackness, backwardness, and un-Islamic practices. The content of banter and the style of delivery reflect and create new perspectives and beliefs in Malian society. Such exchanges, Parkin suggests, "present opportunities to those who are creative enough to articulate such meanings into new combinations, and so, through what is culturally interpreted as licensed abuse, to defy the existing restraints."[56] Players carefully navigate from a position of spectatorship to one of participation. Individual creativity is manifested in practice, and the limits of abuse are negotiated in the online exchange between actors.

Bantering on construction sites brings underlying tensions to the surface. As illustrated, the banter is not uniquely a competition between Bozo and Dogon identities, but it also encodes a stark hierarchical division of labor that is closely entwined with ethnic politics. Dogon builders could not move beyond the lowly status of laborer, and ambitions to do so were curtailed primarily with jests. It may have appeared to an outsider that a certain degree of equality (as described by Griaule) was expressed in the bantering exchanges that set these occasions apart from the normal hierarchical relations on-site. In fact, the senior Bozo builders reserved the last word for themselves and regularly used their authority to draw things to a close. When trade-status boundaries were threatened, obscenities and blasphemies turned into real curses. The Bozo hospitably offered their Dogon cousins employment that enabled them to make a living and finance their studies and activities while residing in Djenné, but the Bozo also had a vested interest in keeping them off the higher rungs of their time-honoured profession and maintaining full control over the reproduction of the town's famous mud-brick architecture.

Defending professional trade borders is, arguably, crucial to maintaining distinct group identities where, historically in this region of Africa, vocational specialization has been an integral component of ethnic identity.[57] Bantering suitably fulfills the dual and seemingly contradictory function of wedging two groups apart while keeping them together: jocular expressions of competition and aggression produce and reproduce the dividing lines between Bozo and Dogon, while the special status of the bantering relationship defines a unity that excludes all others. Bantering, therefore, is not a straightforward "border-making language" in the sense of performatively bringing into being places (and identities) where commonality abruptly ends.[58] Bozo-Dogon bantering draws, and is enacted upon, ethnic and professional borders, while simultaneously creating spaces along those borders that accommodate communion between members of the two groups moderated by hospitality and tolerance.

"Sudanese-style" colonial administrative building in Segou

2 · Staking a Claim

Alluring Djenné

Tony retired from the film industry, sold his company in Amsterdam, and set off for Africa in search of a new way of life. After aborting his efforts to settle in Namibia, he journeyed to West Africa. Mali had long held a special place in his imagination. As a young man Tony spent time in the company of a Spanish Surrealist and was deeply impressed by the artist's worldview and his vivid descriptions of Mali's architecture. The fantastic molten forms of towering mud and amorphous pinnacles crowned by giant white ostrich eggs undoubtedly appealed to surrealist sensibilities. Many artists of this movement would likely have enjoyed their first introduction to this exotic place through the writings of Michel Leiris. Leiris had participated in Marcel Griaule's Dakar-Djibouti mission (1931–33), which took him to Mali and inspired his first major book, *L'Afrique Fantôme* (1934).

Tony's choice to settle in Djenné was equally influenced by an architect friend who was a self-described enthusiast of "vernacular architecture." He told Tony that traditional masons, like those in Mali, are both the designers and makers of their works, and that their intimate understanding of local materials combined with straightforward building methods reliably yields aesthetically pleasing results. The architect shared a popular belief that vernacular builders possess an innate sensibility for balanced composition and proportion, and that their know-how is uncontaminated by Western industrialization, technology, and mass production.[1] Such views concord with those expressed by the so-called Master Builders[2] of twentieth-century Western architecture—namely Le Corbusier, Mies van der Rohe, and Frank Lloyd Wright—all of whom paid homage to the "uncorrupted reason and instinct" of primitive man as builder.[3]

This Western reverence for what might be described as "primitive" or "organic" architecture in "traditional" societies (those typically identified with the pre-industrial past) can be traced back along the threads of Western philosophy through the developments of European Romanticism to, at the very least, its origins in Rousseau's noble savage (1762). Marc-Antoine Laugier authored one of the earliest architectural treatises evoking Rousseau's view that "one should go back to the very beginning of human history and find there the norm by which the present can be guided, and, if necessary, corrected."[4] The frontispiece in the second edition of Laugier's *Essai sur l'Architecture* (1753) displaying Eisen's famous engraving of a primitive hut "is not a curious illustration of a distant past or a factor of an evolutionary theory of architecture but the great principle from which it now becomes possible to deduce immutable laws."[5]

Nearly a century later Viollet-le-Duc, author of the most eminent architectural treatise in nineteenth-century France, extolled the virtues of building materials readily available in nature.[6] Viollet-le-Duc's rationalist theory, derived from his structural studies and restorations of French medieval cathedrals and fortresses, espoused the notion that style should be a product of the climactic conditions of a place, the nature of the available materials, and the customs of its creators. His rationalism, argues Prussin, was rapidly adopted by the students at the École Centrale and the École Polytechnique, who were to become the future administrators and engineers of the French colonies. Some of these men would also have a hand in fashioning the hallmark colonial style of architecture for the French Sudan.[7] Prussin's research advocates the importance of a cross fertilization of ideas between Europe and colonial Western Sudan in the nineteenth and early twentieth centuries. In relation to early modernist architecture, she suggests that Auguste Perret's innovations in reinforced concrete, Antonio Gaudi's design for Barcelona's church of the Sagrada Familia, and Le Corbusier's design philosophy may have been inspired by Sudanese architecture in a manner similar to the way earlier French colonial architecture in West Africa was inspired by the rationalist ideas of Viollet-le-Duc.[8]

Across the English Channel, and nearly a decade before the first publication of Viollet-le-Duc's treatise, John Ruskin, too, advocated the value of using local materials in a manner sympathetic to the surrounding natural environment.[9] He esteemed the medieval Gothic for its reverence of nature and natural forms, and promoted an "organic" relation between builders, their materials, and the environment. In his celebrated manifesto, *The Seven Lamps of Architecture* (1849), he wrote that the creations of architecture were "not essentially composed of things pleasant in themselves," but rather "depend for their dignity and pleasurableness in the utmost degree, upon the vivid expression of the intellectual life which has been conserved in their production."[10] In his discussion of beauty, Ruskin endeavored to "trace that happier element of [architecture's] excellence, consisting in a noble rendition of images of Beauty, derived chiefly from the external appearances of organic nature."[11] "Man cannot advance in the invention of beauty, without imitating natural form,"[12] claimed Ruskin, and surely "the Power of human mind had its growth in the Wilderness."[13]

Ideas that the origins of mind were rooted in wilderness propelled the quest for an unadulterated *pensée sauvage* well into the twentieth century. The articulation of, on the one hand, a temporal divide made between mechanistic modernity and a medieval mode of handicraft production, and, on the other, a conceived separation between the West and its imagined Other overlapped and reinforced each other. In anthropology, Levi-Strauss's structuralism posited a universal dichotomy between culture and nature that underpinned a host of oppositions constructed between body and mind; female and male; savage and civilised.[14] The cultural artifacts and social institutions of primitive societies were analyzed to identify the organizing principles of human thinking. In the realm of architecture and planning, these dichotomies were reflected in the polarity instituted between the organic and the rational. The category of organic was mapped onto the medieval town and most non-Western building traditions, like the mud architecture of the Sahel, relegating such productions and producers closer to nature. In studies of Djenné's residential quarters, for example, contemporary description problematically perpetuates the use of "rational" and "pre-rational" categories to differentiate Western town planning from its African counterpart: "The alleys and small public places resemble veins carved into the homogenous mass of the town. These labyrinthine and capricious veins form structures that differ from our rational methods of urban planning in the West. Such structures may be referred to as pre-rational."[15]

Reason, by contrast, was the defining attribute of Western-trained architects and planners whose spaces were conceptualised objectively with the mind as opposed to being made with the body sensually immersed in its environment. The modern architect's claim on rationality has its genesis in the Renaissance's rediscovery of Vitruvius and measured classicism, Brunelleschi's formulation of perspective drawing, and Alberti's *re Aedificatoria* that sundered form and function from the specificities of context. Later, Descarte's postulation of space as absolute, infinite *res extensa*, homogenized space and laid the landscape bare for the grafting of a human-centered order.[16] For many prominent architects of the last century, however, that primitive "Other" and creator of organic forms also represented the possibility of salvation. Rykwert writes that it was generally agreed that "if architecture was to be renewed, if its true function was again to be understood after years of neglect, a return to the 'preconscious' state of building, or alternatively the dawn of consciousness, would reveal those primary ideas from which a true understanding of architectural forms would spring."[17]

Theories of the savage mind and the primitive hut eventually prompted more direct interest in the study of vernacular buildings and human settlements. The latter half of the twentieth century witnessed a proliferation of publications celebrating the beauty and genius of non-Western forms and styles that, historically, had been relegated outside the canons of the architectural discipline.[18] Prussin argues that perhaps the most significant reason for the scholarly neglect of African architecture, for instance, was the shared attitude by architects and laymen that "building in sub-Saharan Africa is not architecture at all, but at most, building technology."[19] Prussin later added to her argument: "since no permanence, monumentality, authorship, materials of construction, building technologies, spatial articulation, or enclosure was visible to the Western eye," the existence of an African architecture was denied.[20] Oliver also noted that non-Western building traditions were equally ignored by anthropologists who were more interested in other social concerns.[21]

Djenné was at the forefront of the West's exposure to non-Western dwelling and architecture, and it constituted the central theme of Labelle Prussin's pioneering doctoral dissertation (1974). Almost two decades later, Maas and Mommersteeg published a comprehensive and erudite study of Djenné's urban growth, planning, and architecture. In a footnote they pay homage to the Dutch architect Aldo van Eyck, who published a series of articles during the 1950s and 1960s on Mali's vernacular architecture in the journal *Forum voor Architectuur en daarmee Verbonden Kunsten*.[22] Van Eyck's enthusiasm for Malian building influenced subsequent generations of Dutch researchers at Eindhoven's University of Technology, and, during my second fieldwork season, a sanitation project in Djenné was being piloted by engineering students from the Technical University in Delft.[23] Issues concerning the town's heritage and traditions were addressed by contributors to Bedaux and van der

Waals volume[24] and to Brunet-Jailly's volume,[25] and the contents of Bedaux, Diaby and Maas's more recent work is devoted exclusively to Djenné's now internationally recognized mud architecture.[26]

Djenné and its celebrated mosque—reputed to be the largest mud structure in the world—have featured in numerous publications devoted to what Bourgeois coined the "spectacular vernacular."[27] In critically examining his own use of the term, Bourgeois noted that the use of "vernacular" to describe monumental building traditions of the various regions concerned is inaccurate and "will probably be looked back on as having been naïve."[28] Publications on "vernacular" architecture nevertheless continue to raise general awareness about the diversity of local building types, and promote constructive discourse about the use and meaning of such terms as "architecture," "style," "tradition," "heritage," and "authorship."[29] Blier pays homage to Rudofsky's pioneering efforts in this domain of scholarship, noting that "most writers in the field now boldly identify the creators of these buildings as their architects."[30]

For many newcomers—including those seeking alternative lives, scholars of vernacular architecture, American and Japanese tourists, and visitors from sprawling urban Bamako—Djenné represents a place apart. Not dissimilar to the French medieval village, its winding alleyways, asymmetrical public spaces, and individuated buildings seemingly deny the regularity and homogeneity of the contemporary city and the sense of alienation that arise with mass production. The surfaces of Djenné's architecture are crafted by hand, and every house is shaped by a history of intimate negotiations between inhabitants, masons, and the harsh forces of the Sahel. Its proportions may be said to satisfy Le Corbusier's manifesto that architecture is based upon the human body,[31] and the building process ensures a direct engagement with raw materials and uncomplicated, human-powered technologies. Underlying the "pre-rational" planning and forms of Djenné's buildings is an immediately apparent logic of structure and scale that appeals both intellectually and aesthetically.

Acquiring a Site

Djenné's allure committed Tony to building there. His sense of wonderment toward the local architecture was tempered, however, by a strong aversion to residing within the confines of the densely populated island-town. Concerns about hygiene and his desire for privacy, open space, and a fine contemplative view over the Bani River instigated his search for a secluded building plot.

Acquiring land rights in this region is a complex affair. Bedaux et al. report that in Djenné there is "no adequate and official registration of the land." The local authorities therefore refuse to grant official construction permits, since these might "be used to claim ownership of a house or some plot of land." Litigation procedures are customarily dealt with by *marabouts* and chiefs.[32] Permission to settle, cultivate, and build outside town is equally problematic, and must be sought from both the official mayor and the customary chiefs. The mayor, as a representative of state, has the authority to award allotments, and the customary chiefs, who maintain historic entitlements to enormous tracts of land outside the town, have final jurisdiction over proposed plots on their holdings.

The chiefs trace their ancestral land rights to the early-nineteenth-century Macina-Fulani *jihad* and invasions led by Cheikou Amadou (1775–1844). At this time, the Fulani pressed into the area from the north and staked their claims to territories surrounding Djenné. Contemporary Fulani chiefs legitimate these claims through their possession of authentic Arabic *tarikhs*, which are written deeds and histories of ownership and inheritance. These precious documents are closely guarded and kept in private libraries or concealed in ornamental vessels (Arabic *hirz* حرز) worn as jewellery. According to relative timescales, the Fulani are recent emigrants to this once formidable trading center, but they quickly became powerful property owners within the town itself. Sedentary urban life has proven fruitful, and significant numbers of Fulani are leading *marabouts* in the ubiquitous Qurʿanic economy. This generates not only financial gain but also political influence over Djenné's religious identity. Many harbor superior attitudes toward their various ethnic neighbors, especially regarding religious scholarship, and they identify themselves as "white-skinned" and as having originated somewhere in North Africa, like the descendants of the Moroccan invaders who, for more than two centuries, dominated the town after their defeat of the Songhay Empire (1591 CE).

In observing local custom, Tony appointed an intermediary to speak and act on his behalf. He elected the mason Bayeré Kouroumansé to lead the property negotiations and to be the project's chief mason. First, Bayeré prepared an application for a one-hundred-meter square plot in the nearby village of Fokloré situated along a narrow branch of the river, west of town. This was submitted to the mayor, and together they paid a visit to the customary chief of the area, a Fulani of the Sidibé clan. They soon learned, however, of heated litigations over land rights between the village's Fulani population (represented by their customary chief) and the Rimaïbe residents (descendents of the former slaves of the Fulani).[33] The mayor was not willing to consider their application until this potentially explosive issue was resolved. Pressed to proceed, they searched for

RIGHT   Mason Bayeré Kouroumansé

alternative options. At this point, the owner of a local hotel-café, Mr. Baba Maïga, informed Tony that he possessed the deeds for a piece of land that had been exceptionally allotted in Sanuna. The site was located several kilometers east of Djenné, on the banks of the Bani River.

Originally the plot had been granted on a usufructuary[34] basis to an influential Bozo family by the regional military commander during the early years of President Moussa Traoré's dictatorship (1968–91). The accompanying documents, signed and dated in 1971, described a plot measuring eighty by one hundred meters bordered on the east by the river, on the west by a rice field, on the north by a millet field, and on the south by a ruined house and property of the Nasiré family. The original Bozo owner was by now deceased and his heirs had not developed the land. According to customary laws, the land must be *mettre en valeur*, meaning either put to agricultural use or built upon in order to maintain the property rights and transfer it to a third party.[35] Despite having never built there, the eldest son sold his inherited usufructuary rights to Baba Maïga for a small sum. Baba hoped to construct a hotel, conveniently located close to the main ferry crossing and with magnificent river views, but the project never materialized. When the opportunity arose, he therefore opted to transfer the rights to the Dutchman in exchange for a financial loan to buy a *pirogue* as part of his more modest plans to exploit the tourist market.

With the papers in hand, it remained for Bayeré to obtain consent from the mayor and a blessing from the Fulani chief in order to validate Tony's rights in the eyes of both the state and customary apparatus. Only after this was achieved could he initiate construction on the house. An application was submitted describing the Sanuna allotment. The mayor was apprehensive about authorizing a project that risked entangling the two systems of government, but Bayeré's persistence prevailed and he next organized a meeting with the customary chief. The chief's vast territories stretched some ten kilometers along the Bani to the village of Diabolo. Both Tony and the customary chief attended the meeting, but all negotiations were enacted by Bayeré and the son of the original Bozo owner of the deed. The son was designated as the chief's intermediary and he was also the representative of his deceased father who was still recognized by customary law as the rightful owner since the land had not been put to use. After lengthy protocol and discussion, the chief expressed willingness to allow the foreigner to live on his land, and Tony offered him the *prix de thé*—an offering of money for "tea leaves" that solemnizes pacts and fortifies relationships. A contractual document was drawn up granting Tony the right to build and occupy, and this was signed in turn by the Bozo son, relinquishing his family claims. In effect, however, the land would always belong to the customary chief and therefore could not be owned outright by a second party.

A subsequent meeting was convened by Bayeré with Baba Maïga who was represented in the discussions by an elder family member. The son of the original Bozo owner of the deed was also present. A document was drawn up stipulating that Baba would transfer his rights accordingly and a detailed genealogy of ownership was included in order to curtail the possibility of future conflicts. Jubilant at having navigated their way through the process, Tony was eager to announce his plans to start building. "But wait!" everyone objected, "Not so quickly!" It was explained that, first, the son of the original owner had to put the land to use in order for the chain of ownership to be validated. It was agreed that Bayeré would also act in this instance as the mason on behalf of the Bozo family, and he was commissioned to erect a small one-room, mud-block structure on the site and to supervise the digging of a well. Bayeré instructed Tony to give the Bozo son the *prix de thé* for participating in these formalities and for making appearances at the site during this initial stage of construction. The spectacle had to be witnessed publicly, and there had to be unanimous acknowledgment that the procedures prescribed by the customary laws had been observed. "Tu es garanti là-bas!" ("You are guaranteed there"), the men and women in Djenné proclaimed when they greeted Tony afterward, affirming that his rights were recognized. As the new tenant, he was required to periodically visit the customary chief to offer the *prix de thé* and sustain his guarantee.

Blessing the Site

The totem (*kabi*) for all masons in Djenné is the *m'baaka* (*palandi* in Fulfulde), a small lizard common throughout West Africa.[36] The male of the species (*m'baakahar*) has an attractive, bright yellow-orange head and can be regularly spotted sunning itself on rocks and on the heat-drenched walls of buildings, sporadically performing energetic sets of tiny "push-ups."[37] The *m'baaka* is used by many ethnic groups in the preparation of medicines to cure various ailments from coughs to male impotence. It is unlawful for builders to harm them, however, and children caught vexing these amusing little creatures are severely reprimanded: "Ils sonts les amis des maçons" ("They are the masons' friends"), claimed one builder. Masons are believed to share the *m'baaka*'s agility, balance, and capacity to cling to, and scale, vertical wall surfaces. Harming these lizards can compromise their own mortal powers and instigate danger or lure malicious forces. When the dusty *harmattan* winds blow hard in the winter months, severely reducing visibility and rendering site conditions treacherous, it is evident why the builders aspire to the *m'baaka*'s sure-footedness.

Masons take regular precautions to ensure the safety and well-being of their entire workforce, and to guarantee both the structural integrity of the buildings they erect and the protection of their clients. It is advisable that new works, like any journey or life project, begin on an auspicious day.[38] In his detailed discussion of building a *sâho* (a communal house for unmarried Bozo boys), Ligers recorded that the village chief sent an intermediary to a mason from the Djenné region to request that he arrive for work "dans un mois, le cinquième jour de la nouvelle lune" ("in a month, the fifth day of the new moon").[39] According to mason Bayeré Kouroumansé, a *jaari benté* (auspicious day)[40] in Djenné is calculated by the project's chief mason based on, among other things, the lunar calendar and constellations. His choice is then considered by a neighborhood network of wise elders that might include his own trade master, the patriarchs of his family, and *marabouts,* and these men also warn him against *jaari futu* (inauspicious days). When the mason arrives at the correct choice through these consensual procedures, they congratulate him: "Tu as bien calculé!" ("You have calculated well!"). The initiation of work on a chosen day might include nothing more than hoeing a shallow furrow at a spot where foundation trenches will later be excavated. This was indeed the case at the Sanuna site along the river. Following a simple initiation of turning the soil, Bayeré returned several days later to erect a small, one-room mud-brick structure. This was built in the name of the original Bozo owner, as agreed, to set the process of *mettre en valeur* in motion, and it would be eventually dismantled and recycled in making the actual house. In his role as chief mason, Bayeré also arranged for a specialized team to excavate a deep well on-site. This project, too, began on an auspicious day calculated by the head of that work crew.

Prior to commencing full-blown construction activity, Bayeré and his mason-cousin Baba Kouroumansé visited the site with a woven basket of mixed grains. The basket was put to one side, and the men carefully selected four melon-sized stones from a pile delivered by truck. In turn, each mason muttered benedictions over the stones that comprised a mix of Qurʿanic verses and potent incantations made in Djenné-Chiini. Barely audible levels ensured that the masons kept their individual "secrets" (*sirri*) hidden, while at the same time providing a public spectacle of their power and expertise for anyone who might be watching. Secrets were not about absolute concealment but rather about strategic and partial revealing.[41] After speaking the mysterious words, Baba, squatting down in front of the four stones, raised his right hand to his mouth and spat into it, then rubbed his open palm over the stones in a clockwise direction. He repeated this several times, thereby transferring the power of his benedictions to the stones themselves.[42] Words, as Stoller remarks in his study of the Songhay, "are not merely neutral instruments of reference…[but] can be dangerously charged with the powers of the heavens and of the ancestors."[43] During his late-eighteenth-century travels, Mungo Park witnessed a similar transfer of powerful words to stones:

> The attendants insisted on stopping, that they might prepare a *saphie* or charm, to insure us a safe journey. This was done by muttering a few sentences, and spitting upon a stone, which was thrown before us on the road. The same ceremony was repeated three times, after which the Negroes proceeded with great confidence; every one being firmly persuaded that the stone (like the scapegoat) had carried with it everything that could induce superior powers to visit us with misfortune.[44]

At the Sanuna building site, the masons blessed the basket of grains (*attaam*) in the same manner as the stones. The chief mason reasoned that the grains were not a fetish associated with pre-Islamic animist practices because the grains came from God.[45] Bayeré said that "God created man. But in order to procreate, God gave humankind the capacity to do so. Likewise, God also bestowed upon certain individuals the power to perform rituals and benedictions which should always be made in His name." The grain mixture consisted of cottonseed, sorghum, millet, maize, *fonio*, and rice.[46] It was explained that the first provided us with the things we wear, and the others gave us nourishment, and therefore the placement of grains in the house foundations and at the corners of the property ensured prosperity and abundance of food for the inhabitants. "If the benedictions are made correctly," said the mason, "then God will lend His assistance. On the contrary, if they are not, God will end the work." Both Bayeré and Baba proceeded to dig four shallow holes at the four corners of the property with their hoes. In each they placed one of the blessed stones,[47] and over these they sprinkled a little of the grain mixture before backfilling the holes by hand. A generous reserve of the grains was kept on site for sowing into the foundations as the house progressed.

Sometime later, when recounting the event, Bayeré informed me that these rituals combined two types of specialized knowledge. In addition to the Islamic-based knowledge, *bey-koray*, masons also incorporate elements of traditional (non-Islamic) black-African knowledge, *bey-bibi*. The standard French translations of *bey-koray* and *bey-bibi* are, respectively, *magie blanche* (white magic) and

Bayeré Kouroumansé burying a protective *gris-gris* in the house foundations

magie noire (black magic). Indeed, the Djenné-Chiini term *bey* might be correctly glossed as "magic" since it is made manifest in the form of incantations, spells, and rituals that have the power to transform, protect, and sometimes harm. *Bey,* however, does not refer specifically to the performative actions or to the occult powers they unleash but rather, more abstractly, to the secret knowledge that one possesses for enacting and achieving these outcomes. A more precise translation of *bey* is the French term *connaissance,* and since this term and the French word *secret* were used by the masons in describing it to me, I use the term "knowledge," sometimes qualified by "secret." The adjectives *koray* and *bibi* translate as "white" and "black," respectively, and refer in the first instance to the white-skinned Arabs associated with bringing Islamic knowledge to the region in the eleventh century CE[48] and, in the second, to the black-skinned people of sub-Saharan Africa. Practitioners can employ either *bey-koray* or *bey-bibi* for both good and evil purposes, and thus the categories do not neatly conform to conventional Western associations of white magic with innocuous spells and black magic as harmful.

Bayeré placed his cousin Baba in charge of overseeing the daily operations on-site so that Bayeré could attend to other building projects in town. Baba was highly competent and a well-respected member of the *barey ton,* but Bayeré would nevertheless retain his position as Tony's chief mason. Every household in Djenné has a chief mason responsible for its building work. The mason executes the projects himself, or, if he is unable to do so, he organizes the materials and schedule, and delegates the building work to other trusted masons. These ties of patronage are historical, and the affiliation between a client family and their associated family of masons is maintained through successive generations. Again referring to the building of the *sâhô,* Ligers recorded that the village elders came to inspect the completed work of the invited mason, and the chief of the *sâhô* society declared:

> Effectively, you have worked well and we thank you. Every time that the *sâhô* needs repairs, such as when a decorative column is crumbling, we will call upon your services. Likewise, when we want to re-plaster the building, we will commission you.[49]

According to Ligers, the elders paid the mason the agreed upon fee and offered him an additional sum of money "pour les noix de kola." Like the *prix de thé,* this additional gift initiates and sustains future bonds of patronage between client and mason.[50]

Many masons in Djenné, and especially those regarded as masters of their trade, are believed to possess secret knowledge and extraordinary powers, and this is further reinforced by their Bozo identity. Maas and Mommersteeg note that other ethnicities popularly attribute occult powers to the Bozo.[51] Large numbers of Bozo are itinerant fishermen whom Rouch referred to as "les anciens maîtres des eaux," and it is therefore not surprising that many of their secret powers are associated with water, including their ability to remain submerged for long periods and swim astonishing distances.[52] Bozos make special benedictions to the water spirit Bafaro before entering any body of water to either fish or swim.[53] Imperato noted that the Bozo, though Muslims, "retain many animist practices, especially those related to the river and fishing,"[54] and de Grunne wrote that they "represent the ancient inhabitants of abandoned *toguere* of the delta by a python that watches over the land."[55] In referring to Bozo myths of origins such as the account of their ancestor's emergence from holes in the earth along the Niger River, or the sacrifice of the virgin Tempama at the founding of Djenné, McIntosh questions whether such autochthonous myths have not served to "bolster claims to ritual authority over the land and the right to minister to the land and water spirits of the Middle Niger."[56] I noted the importance of the public, sometimes theatrical nature of the masons' rituals, benedictions, and incantations made at the building site. In addition to being expressions of their belief system, these performances of benedictions and incantations are a vital component in the construction of identity in competitive bids for power as a corporate group of professional craftsmen.

Urbanized Bozo in towns such as Djenné, Mopti, or Segou have adopted other occupations either in place of, or in addition to, their traditional fishing practices. These include, most notably, potting, blacksmithing, and masonry.[57] Prussin has recognized the interdependence between these three crafts in West Africa's mud-building tradition, whereby smiths forge the masons' tools and potters produce the kiln-baked downspouts for roof drainage.[58] Among the various Mandé cultural groups that includes the Bozo, as well as among many other peoples of West Africa, blacksmiths are segregated as a corporate caste (*nyamakala* in Manding)[59] and thought to possess powers associated with transformation,[60] the skills of mediation,[61] and the capacity to control *nyama*.[62] Mandé blacksmiths, like Djenné masons, are often "linked to a 'host,' or *jatigi* family" over many generations whereby the blacksmith's first loyalty is in the service of their host.[63] It is also common that smiths' wives are potters,[64] a craft also qualified by processes of transformation with fire, turning raw clay into cultural artifact.

In the realm of building, senior master masons (*barey amir*), like the blacksmiths described by Brett-Smith,[65] accumulate secrets and power with age and experience. They possess the ability to bring misfortune to disloyal patrons or, more typically, to masons that patrons might employ in their stead and without their consent. It is suggested that poisons are sometimes used to make rivals ill, but, more commonly, Djenné's masons transmit their powers through secret invocations and even everyday utterances. When a senior colleague strolls by a building site and casually inquires to those working there "Wor na goy?" or "Ça va le travail?" ("How is your work?"), it is wise to give the old mason a present, or else his words may cause injury to someone on-site or trigger the structure to fail and collapse. The most frequent injuries sustained in this way are cuts from thorns or shards of glass concealed in the soft, wet mud plaster. Potentially debilitating wounds to hands and fingers can damage tendons or become infected, resulting in missed work and financial loss. Though such injuries are normally attributed to a curse, the accidents are not necessarily blamed on a specific individual. In most instances, the old mason harbors no grievance toward the victim, but the power transmitted by their words can cause harm. Younger masons therefore periodically offer the *prix de thé* to these senior craftsmen in order to appease them, and, more important, to disarm the latent powers of the old masons' words through the positive power of the gift.

This is similar to practices throughout the Mandé region of making small offerings or sacrifices at crossroads, shrines, or altars to ward off *nyama*,[66] or "splashing" praise singers (*jeli*) with bank notes against their perspiring brows while performing in order to counteract the potency of their lyrical recitations of genealogies, histories, and deeds. The Manding word *nyama* (*doni fi* in Bamanankan) is not used in Djenné (at least not in this sense), and most residents are unfamiliar with the term.[67] The town is a cosmopolitan confluence of several cultural groups including Mandé, Songhay and Fulani, and the dominant language, Djenné-Chiini, is a dialect of northern Songhay.[68] The associated concept of *nyama*, appropriately translated by Bird as "energy of action,"[69] is, nevertheless, commonly understood but seemingly not named. Like their Mandé neighbors to the south, many Djennénké people believe that, when a person or animal dies or is killed, a vital force or energy is released into the world that requires skillful manipulation and control. Killing a living thing therefore incites a chain of events that will somehow return in time upon the perpetrator, and even possibly upon future generations of that person's family. Words, too, are infused with force and can be dangerous, because, once released, they actively shape social and political circumstances.[70] Mandé individuals describe *nyama*, more concretely, as the force that instantiates the consequences of one's words and actions, and such a causal force is also popularly recognized in Djenné.

Mason Konamadou Djennepo insisted that the power of the masons' secret knowledge was transferred through the act of speaking. As he explained, he gestured gracefully with his right hand, moving his tightly bunched fingertips outward and away from his lips, and spreading his hand open like a blossom into the air in front of him. It is not the particular words or sentences that masons know he assured me but rather the act of directing speech toward another individual, a building, or some other object. Konamadou made it clear that I, too, have powers, because I know how to write and speak French. My literacy means that I have been schooled and possess the sort of knowledge prized and rewarded by the modern Malian state, and French, the language of the former colonial power, continues to dominate high-level political and economic discourses that impact the livelihoods of everyone in the country.[71] In discussing the powers of literacy more than two centuries ago, Mungo Park noted that "all natives of this part of Africa consider the art of writing as bordering on magic; it is not in the doctrines of the Prophet [i.e., Islam], but in the arts of the magician that their confidence is placed."[72] Jansen also records, in his study of contemporary *griots* (*jeli*) in southwest Mali, that, for the older generation, writing is above all a sacred act and not a means of regular communication.[73] On the topic of Hausa-Fulani architecture, Prussin writes that "the sacred quality of Arabic script is manifested in the oft-cited Fulani proverb that 'those who write are magicians,' and it is the holy men, the *torode,* who write the talismans that are both worn and attached to buildings."[74]

When produced by a recognized subject in the right context, the written and spoken word is deemed capable of acting forcefully upon the world and transforming it. Hoffman, in her study of Mandé griots, writes that "nothing [is] more dangerous, more feared or more respected and admired than spoken language," because it has the power to persuade, anger, and calm, and "to invoke the silent forces in humans, beasts and spirits that enable the powerless to do great things."[75] "In Djenné," Konamadou continued, "people have knowledge of the leaves and the trees for making poisons, medicines, amulets, and *gris-gris,*[76] and masons possess the power of words. They know secrets and incantations. Every person in Djenné knows some secrets, and we masons have the power of speech!"

A Blessing from the *Marabout*

In his study of Songhay religion, Rouch determined that the *marabout*'s services are summoned in all human activities, and one of the *marabout*'s main occupations is the production of amulets imbued with protective properties, including the protection of houses.[77] Maas and Mommersteeg similarly define the practice of *maraboutage* as "the various magical-religious practices such as performing divinations and making amulets."[78] Protective amulets prepared by marabouts in Djenné are referred to as *alhijāba*, derived from the Arabic word *hijāb* (حجاب), meaning "cover" or "screen," and *al-hijāb al-hājaz* (الحجاب الحاجز), meaning, more specifically, "amulet." *Marabouts* control not only religious knowledge and its capacity to heal, protect, and transform, but they also manage personal knowledge about their clients from the immediate neighborhood and beyond. Men and women visit *marabouts* in search of cures and solutions to their problems, and also for protective devices and potent benedictions for their life projects, personal relationships, and affairs.[79] In return, they make payments of money, kola nuts, and other material goods. Their holy man may instruct them to purchase a kola nut, specifying that it be red or white depending on the deed, and to offer it to an elderly or needy person. Red kola nuts frequently have gender associations with men, and white ones with women, and the nut itself is said to be an aphrodisiac. A gift of kola incites a chain of benevolent acts, and the goodness of the deed eventually returns to the giver as fulfillment of the benedictions made.[80] The production of amulets and the performance of benedictions is a steady business, and, not surprisingly, *marabouts* are perceived to be financially well off, and a few are very wealthy indeed. In the early 1990s more than 13 percent of the town's population were employed in this profession.[81] As one of my mason colleagues remarked sardonically, "In principle, there are two professions here in Djenné: the job of the tout, and, when one grows up, the *marabout*'s profession."[82]

A second round of ceremonial blessings was choreographed at the Sanuna building site by the distinguished *marabout* Modi Adou Sidibé. Marabout Sidibé served as a *muezzin* (*almujun* in Djenné-Chiini) for the town's mosque, and his amplified voice frequently called the faithful to prayer. As a Fulani, he strategically traced his family's ancestry in Djenné to the nineteenth-century *jihad*s led by Cheikou Amadou, and thereby to the advent of "true" Islam in the region. In his younger years he and a business partner imported consumer goods from Senegal and other neighboring West African countries into Mali for a handsome profit, and he spent his share of the proceeds to build a house and establish a Qurʿanic school. The school buttressed his *marabout* identity and brought him paying students.

I met Sidibé at his home, and, in deference to his elevated position, I grasped my right forearm with my left hand as I reached to shake hands with him. He was a compact rotund figure with greying hair and immensely kind eyes. I was accompanied on this visit by Tony, and Sidibé invited us to join

Marabout Modi Adou Sidibé

him in a small room on the ground floor where he was conducting a Qurʿanic lesson with one of his students. The room was connected by a small passageway to the inner courtyard of his house and had its own door providing direct access to the street so that students could enter and exit without disturbing the family's privacy. We were directed to bamboo armchairs propped up against one wall, and Sidibé sat on a dilapidated chaise lounge positioned along the adjacent wall in the light of the open door. The student sat crosslegged on a reed mat in the opposite corner of the windowless room, patiently waiting for his lesson to begin. Numerous tiny wooden *walaa* boards[83] were neatly lined up along the base of the mud-plastered walls, their surfaces inscribed with *suar* painstakingly handwritten by the *talibé*. The black ink was made from the soot of cooking pots dissolved in water, and the writing utensils that students used were reeds with whittled nibs. Lessons could be easily washed away and the boards used over and over again. At one time Sidibé operated a large school, but he professed that he was too old now and only had energy to teach, at most, forty students.

The *talibé*, a young man in his late-twenties, was blind. Marabout Sidibé began reading a long *sūra* from an open page of the Qurʿan he held on his knees, and the student rhythmically repeated the passages in tow, following closely behind his teacher by just two or three words. Sidibé's reading acted purely as a mnemonic that set the recitation in motion. The young man was soon steeped in concentration, fully engulfed in his oral performance. At one point Sidibé's wife entered the room to interrupt her husband for lunch, and later a young vendor appeared in the doorway boldly advertising the wares she carried in an oversized basket balanced on her head, but the student steadily continued his recitation, taking no notice of the interruptions.

Boys from many families begin their Qurʿanic studies at the age of seven or younger. They must first learn to make proper ablutions and to pray, and slowly, through focused repetition of these practices, they come to know Allah. "Without knowing God," said Sidibé, describing the stages of a religious education, "they can know nothing." "Through the Qurʿan—through the Word of Allah—the boys learn to translate the essence of mankind." They learn Arabic, starting with the script and phonetics of the individual letters. They then proceed to write, read, and memorize the shorter *suar*, beginning with the *Fatihah*. Those who are serious and continue with their studies may eventually complete the entire Holy Book, and, as its title suggests, be capable of reciting it possibly by rote.[84]

After the lesson Sidibé led us upstairs onto a shaded veranda to join him for a lunch of rice, sauce, and fish. In addition to operating the Qurʿanic school, he

A Qur‛anic student copying verses from the Holy Book onto a *walaa* board was also a herbal doctor and produced amulets, some of which were purportedly prepared with a combination of written Qurʿanic verse and bees wax. During a visit to the patch of land in Sanuna prior to construction, he identified three trees that he forbade Tony to fell. Two of these were *daarey* trees, which yield a small round yellow fruit mildly tasting of baked apples.[85] The building laborers warned me not to eat too many *daarey* fruits because, though tasty, in quantity they can cause an upset stomach. The leaves and the bark of the *daarey* tree are used in the preparation of fertility medicines for women and therefore have an economic value. The third tree, with thick, round waxy leaves, produced clusters of tiny green flowers with a most intoxicating perfume, and, in season, its small berry-like fruit is said to be delicious. The leaves and thorns of this *garboy honno* tree (wild date)[86] are boiled in water and the vapors inhaled to relieve headaches; the fruit is used to relieve constipation. Aside from their medicinal properties, Sidibé also insisted that these trees were the abodes of good spirits who keep *shaytan*s (an Arabic term for devils) away. He informed me that there were once many devils that lurked in the vicinity of Djenné, but a great number of them have left for *Misr* (Egypt) because they resented the onslaught of movement and frenetic energy caused by cars, airplanes, and factories in modern Mali.

In discussing the *marabout* profession, Sidibé described his own secrets and power as being firmly embedded in his Islamic knowledge, and claimed that many of the amulets he produced involved the writing of Qurʿanic verses on pieces of paper that he concealed within packages, leather wallets, or other vessels. The sacred space of all benedictions, whether written or oral, is opened with "b'ism Allah" ("In the name of God") like the beginning of all but one *sūra* in the Qurʿan. The Word of Allah provides protection, he contended, and he was merely a specialized agent who possessed the "secrets" for effectively transferring that power of protection to people, their future plans, and their possessions. Sidibé acknowledged that other groups, aside from *marabouts,* also have "secrets" related to their trades, including blacksmiths and fishermen. Masons, too, he said, have secrets, but theirs differ from those of the *marabout*, and, curiously, he added, "they are not Islamic." When I inquired further about the nature of the masons' secrets, he admitted that he could not describe it, but he assured me that they are special and unique. Sidibé reasoned that, since many of the masons are illiterate and receive only elementary religious training, they rely on spoken words and spittle to transfer force. He considered them to be powerful nevertheless, pointing to the fact that some masons command failing walls to stand upright, and he warned against certain old masters as they could indeed cause harm. He asked for the names of the builders I was working with, and then approved them as being fine men with honest intentions.

Marabout Sidibé performed an especially powerful benediction for the Sanuna site that would bring further protection to the land and good fortune for all those who might live there. He summoned Touré, the chief of Djenné's *donso ton* association of hunters, to find and retrieve the bones of a horse from somewhere outside town. Touré returned with ribs and a lower jaw full of teeth, and Sidibé blessed these and presented them to Tony in a sack, instructing him to bury them on his property margins. Horse bones were chosen, Sidibé said, because the horse (*bari*) is a powerful animal with an important role in West Africa's Islamic history. It was on swift horseback that the nineteenth-century Fulani cavalry delivered a "pure" version of Islam in waves of *jihadist* campaigns that stretched from Senegal to Hausaland where Uthman dan Fodio established the Sokoto Caliphate. In Hausaland, horses continue to be associated with wealth and noble status, and the so-called big men of Zaria, Kano, and the other Hausa Emirates proudly tether their horses in the *kofar gida* (men's court-yard) on prominent display for any passers-by who might peer through the open doorway of their *zauré* (entrance vestibule) into the family compound. The horse signals their readiness to rise up in arms at a moment's notice for their Emir and to be lead into battle under the green banner of Islam.[87]

At the start of construction, Bayeré and Baba Kouroumansé buried some bones at the northwest corner of the property, near to where they had earlier buried a blessed stone. The bone was laid at the bottom of a shallow hole, and a rock was gently placed on top before backfilling the hole with soil. Three other burials were made nearly two months later, and in close succession of one an-other. These were carried out at the center points along boundary lines rather than at the corners: the first along the north side, adjacent the entry gate to the property; the next below the stone foundations of the east embankment on the river; and the last along the southern perimeter. Baba excavated a small hole, and Bayeré placed a rib inside running lengthwise parallel to the boundary, and the two masons covered it with a double layer of mud brick and *banco* (mud mortar), covered over with dry earth. Following an opening "b'ism Allah," no further words were spoken during the quick and rather unceremonious ritual. Baba explained that this was "because the bones had already been made pow-erful by Marabout Sidibé."

The following day Bayeré prepared another *gris-gris* to be concealed in the foundations of the embankment wall, directly above the spot where the horse bone had been interred. His *gris-gris* consisted of a half-page inscription in Arabic, handwritten in ballpoint pen on a sheet of loose-leaf paper. Bayeré allow no one to read it, nor would he say what it comprised except that it was a passage of Qur'anic verse woven with *bey-bibi* incantations. He carefully folded the paper into a small rectangle then bound it tightly with masking tape. The masons buried it among the stones and covered it with concrete. Again only the customary Qur'anic *fatihah* was pronounced, because the device itself contained the power of written words. Afterward, Bayeré boasted that he could "guarantee" that the house was safe and firm and that no harm would ever meet his client there. His declaration carried with it the intention to publicly stake out his mason's expertise. He had secured not only the technical skills of his trade but also a corpus of occult knowledge that lent his work credibility and social prestige.

As we stood up from the mat, Sidibé cupped both kneecaps in his hands and complained about his arthritis. Tony helped the old gentleman to his feet, and Sidibé hobbled into a dark room off the veranda. The *marabout* returned shortly with a package of analgesics in one hand and held out a bottle of anti-inflammatory pills to Tony with the other. He asked Tony to read the microscopic print on the side of the bottle to verify their place of manufacture. Imported medicines are valued alongside local traditional ones, and medication from Europe is thought to be more effective than drugs manufactured in the Middle East or India. These were from Germany. Contented, Sidibé requested that Tony bring him back more of this type the next time he flew home to Holland for a visit. Not all ailments are curable with herbal medicines, Islamic texts, and animal parts or preventable with talismans and benedictions; people in Djenné, and in Mali more generally, exploit both systems to their greatest advantage. Pills and local cures are not perceived as incongruous with each other but as complementary and as providing an array of options for individual conditions and budgets. I again shook hands with the old *marabout* as we took our leave, slipping a stash of rolled bank notes into his palm for the *prix de thé*. Evidently pleased with the gesture, Sidibé warmly invited me to return again soon.

Bamoy Kouroumansé laying brick coursework

3 · Magic and Mortar

Throughout my field studies I stayed at the government's Cultural Mission in Tolober[1] situated one kilometer outside Djenné. My accommodation consisted of two rooms in a plain, one-storey mud-brick structure furnished with a slim foam mattress and a mosquito net. I stored supplies in wall niches and hung my clothing from a line rigged across the width of a room. A standing tap in the courtyard supplied fresh water for the household, and a pit latrine and bathing area were located in a more substantial two-storey building where the director stayed. In addition to reading material, notebooks, and pens, my essential field equipment included a battery-operated reading lamp, a camping lantern, plenty of candles, and wooden matches. At that time there was no electricity in Tolober, but the Mission had a petrol-operated generator that supplied power to the house for a few hours each evening. The Mission also owned the only television in the quarter, and after dark the courtyard filled with the laughter and sighs of our neighbors who came regularly to watch Brazilian soap operas on the black-and-white screen. Supper was prepared for the staff and the handful of visiting researchers who came and went during the winter season by a tiny but resilient Rimaïbe woman. Malado pounded grain, washed vegetables, and butchered meat in the courtyard, and cooked for endless hours over a fire in a windowless kitchen blackened by soot. Supper was taken together in the open air seated around a low Formica-top table. When the television audience dispersed and the hum of the generator was cut, I climbed to the roof terrace over my bedroom, stretched out on my back, and meditated by the infinite stars that pierced the plush inky blackness.

I purchased a royal-blue "iron-horse" (*guuru-bari*)[2] from a shop on the market square. The sturdy Chinese bicycle was equipped with a lamp and clanging bell, and each morning I set out to Sanuna to join the work team at the house by the river. The tarmac road followed a meandering creek to the Bani. Its rustling reeds were populated by grey herons, squeaking jacanas, and hundreds of great white egrets. The turquoise plumage of rollers flashed among tall dry grasses; stands of acacia squawked with pied crow; and black kites circled overhead in the fresh morning air. As winter wore on, the dusty *harmattan* winds blew harder and hotter, and the creek gradually dwindled to a trickle.

Most of Djenné's building activity takes place in these few dry months squeezed between the final winter harvest and the spring rains. Labor is in short supply at the start of the building season, when town residents are still in the fields gathering crops of millet and rice, and again in late March and April when average daytime temperatures rise to intolerable levels. The battering combination of intense heat and relentless winds topples immune systems and introduces a festering assortment of illnesses and bronchial infections. The rains following the dry season typically last into October, submerging the good-quality clays below high river levels until December. Mud-brick production is therefore impossible for much of the year. In response to the seasonal cycles and fluctuating levels of precipitation, people in Djenné are necessarily practiced at several occupations.[3] Masons, too, engage in alternative economic activities including agriculture, fishing, and petty trading, but their professional identities remain proudly vested in the practice of building—even in cases where masonry constitutes a small proportion of their work. A fortunate few manage to secure enough commissions to carry them through the year. Building work during the rainy periods include standard repairs and maintenance, interior plastering, and occasional decorating with paint or tiles. For most of the town's two hundred or so masons, however, building work is confined to the dry winter months.

This chapter starts with the foundations for the main house at Sanuna. This was a brand new house and therefore differed from constructions in the old town that were typically erected on existing foundations or built above extant structures. Local use of the Arabic term *al-hāit* (الحائط meaning "the wall") to describe foundations indicates that their use was borrowed from the Arabic-speaking world, and likely from North Africa.[4] The house at Sanuna gave me the opportunity to participate in a project that began from the consecration of the ground and continued through the subsequent building phases. Shallow trenches were first excavated following the outline of a drawn building plan and then were carefully filled with stones and concrete. The use of stone and concrete was increasingly popular with patrons who could afford these materials, and in the case of the Sanuna riverside site, the chief mason deemed them necessary for making foundations that could withstand rising ground-water levels and possible flooding. Before setting out the stones and pouring the concrete, the trenches were first sprinkled with a mixture of grains that would protect the structure and its dwellers from misfortune. In Djenné, the importance of benedictions, amulets, and blessed objects in the construction process is equal to, if not greater than, the mortar that binds bricks.

The use of plan drawings for this project was somewhat novel. Historically, houses in Djenné are laid out according to spatial configurations that exist in the mind's eye of the master mason and that are progressively realized in dialogue with actual site practices. Growing numbers of builders, however, are able to read basic architectural drawings. This skill is typically acquired while working on bigger building sites in Bamako, Mopti, or Kayes, but drawings are now being employed more frequently in Djenné as well. I explore tensions on-site that arose as a result of the sometimes unconventional practices at Sanuna, including the use of drawings and the overt role played by the client in managing the day-to-day operations. This made the riverside site and its European patron especially pertinent to my study of Djenné's changing architectural tradition, its dynamic building practices, and the ever shifting ground of authority and expertise.

Significantly, Tony was a contemporary agent in a long history of external forces that have actively shaped the town's architectural tradition, extending back at least to the early colonial period. Foreign influences have been the rule and not the exception throughout Djenné's long cosmopolitan mix of resident traders, scholars, and craftspeople. Today, vested interests in Djenné's built environment are more numerous and diverse, ranging from the heterogeneous aspirations of its resident community to the preservation dictates of the government's Cultural Mission, the concerns of international scholars and conservationists, and the expectations of growing numbers of tourists who come in search of a timeless African city. The confluence of these discourses impacts the aesthetic tastes and consumption patterns of homeowners, as well as the working arrangements on building sites and the hierarchy of control over projects. Conditions at the Sanuna site and the client's visibility at all levels of decision making alludes to emerging trends in the region's building trade, as clients with access to national and global networks of information and resources appropriate greater roles in the planning, stylistic expression, and selection of materials for their new buildings. This shifting balance in authority over reproducing the built environment alters relations between masons and patrons, as well as professional relations within the association of masons. Bayeré's transformation of his own traditional role of chief mason into a modern contractor clearly demonstrates these altering relationships.

The role and status of the Qur'anic students, or *garibou*, who worked on site, are discussed in the second half of the chapter. Though they form an integral part of the local economy, both in terms of supporting the large number of *marabout* teachers and in supplying a steady pool of manual labor in all sectors, these boys and young men are socially marginalized and denied access to proper apprenticeships in the town's traditional trades. Rare cases of *garibou* being offered a mason's training took place in the decades of drought, the 1970s and 1980s, when many local youths moved to other regions and countries as migrant laborers. It also occurred more recently, when classroom-educated sons of masons have opted for less strenuous careers forcing their fathers to cast more widely for new recruits. At the Sanuna site, one *garibou* in particular stood out from the others for his diligence and acute intelligence. Samadolo Anasse was awarded increasing responsibility, and the masons half-seriously enticed him to join their trade. Anasse's sights were decidedly set, however, on a future as a Qur'anic scholar, and he planned to return one day to his village in Burkina Faso and set up his own school.

After completing the foundations, the masons began raising the mud-brick walls of the house. The chapter describes this work and the careful calibration of palm-wood lintels over door and window openings, before concluding with a discussion about the configuration of palm-wood ceiling structures. Overexploitation of the ronier palm[5] has made this tree a scarce resource in the Sahel, and its timber is the most costly material used in traditional Djenné constructions. Not surprisingly, selecting good stocks and determining its most appropriate use are serious considerations for both clients and masons.

Foundations for a House

Masons Baba Kouroumansé and Konamadou Djennepo were starting the stone and concrete foundations of the main house at the site in Sanuna, while Bamoy and his younger brother Hasey continued erecting the guardhouse at the entrance to the property. The plan of the main house consisted of six large rooms arranged linearly and parallel to the riverbank. A ground-storey veranda with

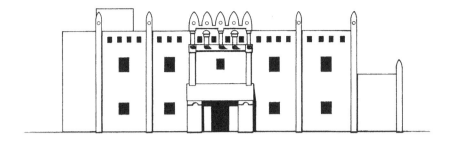

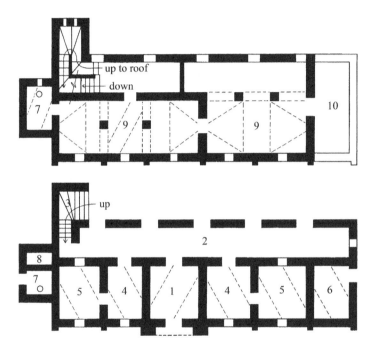

1. vestibule
2. arcaded veranda
3. stair tower
4. parlour
5. sleeping room
6. store room
7. toilet/bathroom
8. nightsoil tower
9. open-plan accommodation
10. roof terrace

(*Top*) Front elevation of the house at Sanuna, facing the Bani River. Ground-floor (*bottom*) and first-storey (*middle*) plans of the house at Sanuna (with reflected ceiling plans).

wide arched openings ran the length of the building, linking the rooms and looking inland to the vegetable garden and fruit trees. Arcaded verandas and arch constructions seem to be recent features in Djenné's architecture, introduced from North Africa by the French colonial administration in the twentieth century and integrated into the vocabulary of the *style-Soudanais*.[6] The sequence of rooms included a centrally positioned vestibule (*sifa*) that served as a breezeway between the river and garden; two sleeping room (*tasika*)[7] and parlour (*galia*) ensembles, and a storeroom (*dyiney dyisi do*). No kitchen (*futey*) was planned for the main house, as food would be prepared in the guardhouse kitchen.

The second storey would eventually consist of two long open-planned rooms with access at the far end to a roof terrace (*soro*) built over the storeroom, and a corridor constructed directly above the veranda. These rooms looking out over the river would be private spaces for the patron to conduct work, and therefore served the same purpose as a traditional *har terey hu*, designating the room reserved for the household patriarch.[8] An enclosed staircase (*kali kali*) would link the two storeys and give access to the roof where it would be protected by a small enclosure (*kali kali sunduku*).[9] A separate tower of vertically stacked toilets (*nyégé*) built at the far end of the house would service both floors.

To complete the project, a grand Tukolor-style facade (*potigé*) with its distinctive covered portico (*gum hu*)[10] would majestically address the sweep of the Bani River. Beyond its protruding entryway, however, the layout inside this building bore no resemblance to the older, compact Tukolor-style homes. The small rooms of these two-storey dwellings were typically clustered around an interior courtyard (*batuma*) with the principal living spaces situated on the second storey. A popular explanation among local residents for the protruding *gum hu* element is that, during the period of Tukolor political domination in the nineteenth century (1862–93), slave-raiding horsemen galloped directly into houses to take innocent captives. The hooded vestibule with its low entrance was allegedly devised to prevent the horseback intruders from entering. Prussin has advocated a more pragmatic reason for the *gum hu*, suggesting that the vestibule afforded protection from sun and rain.[11] The last of these houses was thought to have been constructed prior to the rebuilding of the Mosque in 1906, after which the so-called Moroccan-style became the facade of choice among the city's elite.[12]

A simple house plan was devised by Tony in coordination with his chief mason, Bayeré. The drawing was pinned to the ground with small stones, as the two site masons measured out the width and length of the foundations with a

Mason Konamadou Djennepo with a basket of blessed grains

tape. According to the plan, the house would measure twenty-two meters in length by seven wide. Baba and Konamadou traced these rectangular dimensions onto the site by driving steel bars into the soil at each corner and tautly connecting the bars with blue nylon cords to indicate the exterior and interior perimeters of the fifty-five-centimeter-wide foundations. After verifying that the spacing between the parallel cords was consistent, they proceeded to replicate the outline onto the earth with their hoes (*kumbu*). While the masons paused for a rest, the apprentice Diabaté and a Dogon laborer were ordered to hoe more deeply into the hard ground, staying carefully between the lines, and a third worker removed the loosened soil with a shovel. The shallow trenches were excavated in three successive layers reaching a total approximate depth of twenty-five centimeters. The masons then meticulously chiseled the sides with the flared end of their crowbars (*sasiré*) to produce perfect rectilinear channels.

The heat and physical exertion required the men periodically to replenish their energy with a ladle of *garsi*, a thick white porridge made from pounded millet and either fresh or curdled milk (*waa gani* and *waa-kutu*, respectively). *Bita* was another popular millet-based porridge consumed with a ladle, and, like *garsi*, it was sometimes referred to by the French terms *crèmie* or *bouillie*, meaning gruel. Both were prepared by the masons' wives in the morning and stored in covered calabashes or plastic containers on the building site. They were said to restore vigor, and *garsi*, in particular, was thought to contain medicinal properties that enhanced the male sex drive and sexual performance.

Prior to placing the stones and concrete, Konamadou first scattered a reserve of blessed grains into the channels. The grains would protect the exterior walls of the house and guarantee prosperity and abundance for its inhabitants. Holding the woven basket in his left hand, the mason sowed the grains with his right as he slowly circumambulated the entire perimeter of the foundation. Only the foundations of exterior walls would be protected in this manner, because, as Konamadou explained, "it is those walls that are most vulnerable to evil spirits and to people's malicious wishes directed at those living inside." Not only did this practice protect against unwanted visitors, but it also drove out evil spirits, devils,[13] and destructive *djinn* that might be lurking on the site. These ubiquitous forces are popularly believed to inhabit rock formations, trees, bodies of water, certain narrow alleys of the town, and the rooms of some houses.

A host of innocuous spirits and supernatural creatures also reside in the landscape around Djenné. *Wakoloni*, for example, were reportedly tiny creatures that from a distance might be mistaken for children. *Wakoloni* come out at night to wander through fields on the outskirts of town, and they sport large hats and carry lanterns. Inside the dome of their hats they keep unimaginable wealth, and if someone is lucky enough to catch a *wakoloni* they could live in riches for the rest of their lives. *Wakoloni* were especially fond of grilled peanuts, and intrepid individuals might try to lure them by offering peanuts in one hand while snatching their hat with the other. One Djennénké man explained that the *wakoloni* are descendants of the Tellem population, who dispersed or were culturally assimilated after the arrival of the Dogon people on the Bandiagara Escarpment around the fourteenth or fifteenth century.

Konamadou's rite was performed with little pomp and ceremony. No words were spoken since the assortment of grains had already been blessed, and Baba later clarified that "seeds are the work of Allah and require no speech. They already contain force." Konamadou added that the reason for the rite is "hu a ma yakuba," meaning simply "for the house to have force." Following the scattering of grains, Baba performed a second rite. He squatted at each corner of the foundation and, holding a large stone with both hands, recited secret verses made up of *bey-bibi* incantations and Qur͑anic *suar*. Baba then spat on the stone and placed it into the trench. In doing so, the spittle effectively transferred the power (*alkuuwa*) of his secret incantation to the foundations of the house.[14] When he finished, the mason hollered for the laborers to start hauling stones from the nearby pile, and the construction work began.

The foundation channels were packed to grade with a careful arrangement of stones and in-filled with concrete mixed on-site. Horses delivered cartloads of sand from the river shores, and bags of Portland cement (*simaan*) were brought from the town. Four days later, once the mixture of large stones and concrete had set, a second course was added directly on top of the first to make up a total foundation depth of fifty centimeters. The formwork was made from long timbers measuring five by twenty-five centimeters in width, and these were carefully aligned with the edges of the first foundation course to maintain the fifty-five-centimeter width. Many of the boards were badly warped, and they were held upright against the steel bars and twisted back into shape by wedging their faces between large, heavy stones. In some cases, sturdy sticks were cut to length and braced between the two parallel boards to maintain an even width.

Diabaté stayed close to the masons throughout, assisting them to erect the formwork and position the stones. Although he was formally the apprentice of the master mason Mama Korani, Diabaté, like other trainees in Djenné, frequently worked with different masons to broaden his experience and, more important, to earn a wage that he would not otherwise gain when working for his own master. Baba took the necessary time and patience to show Diabaté how to tailor stones with minimal hammer blows so that they would not protrude above the height of the boards, and he repeatedly showed him how to arrange larger stones on the bottom with their sharp edges pointing upward, followed by a succession of medium to small rocks for filling the gaps. Konamadou Djennepo expended even more effort in mentoring. The younger mason closely monitored Diabaté's performance and ensured that the boy meticulously followed his example. When the concrete was poured from a wheelbarrow (*otoro*)[15] into the formwork and spread evenly over the stones, Konamadou demonstrated how to eliminate air pockets by prodding the runny mixture with a stick and the point of his *kuuru-bibi* trowel. While doing so, he generously explained that the exercise was crucial for strengthening the foundations.

That morning, a group of women and children arrived by horse and cart at the river's edge adjacent to the site. Two of the women were Konamadou's sisters, the eldest of whom was married to Baba Kouroumansé. Bozo rarely marry outside their ethnic group, and many of the Bozo families in Djenné are related by marriage.[16] This creates vast and often complex networks of social obligations, relations of patronage, and factional cleavages among them. A small number of Bozo masons, for instance, control the contracts for Djenné's prestigious houses, and this lucrative work is shrewdly shared out according to personal and family politics. The three Kouroumansé brothers relied heavily for work on their cousin, Bayeré, just as Konamadou Djennepo depended on his brother-in-law, Baba, to keep him employed.

Once the women finished doing laundry, they made their way up the steep banks, babies swaddled to their backs and toddlers in hand. They were colorfully dressed in wax-print cottons, and some were adorned with modest gold jewelry and beaded bracelets. The women had come to greet us and leave two of Baba's young sons to work with their father for the remainder of the day. They chatted casually with the masons for a few minutes and then Tata, Baba's wife, clutching her younger sister by the shoulders, playfully launched into a pitch directed at me. "Femme? Femme?" Tata auctioned boisterously, yearning to know if I would take her sister for my wife (*wandé*). My co-workers, including my fellow bachelors on-site, exclaimed repeatedly, "You're old!" "You must get married!" "You must have children!"

Being married and having children are crucial to achieving full adult identity. These duties are reinforced by Islamic teachings in the Qur'anic schools and the mosque, and by a socio-economic emphasis on the need for procreation. For most people in Mali, children continue to be the main source of security in the absence of a state welfare system and in such a harsh and unpredictable natural environment. Children are needed to work in the fields, to fetch water and gather firewood, to assist with the household chores and care for younger siblings, and to hawk foodstuffs and wares door-to-door and in the marketplace. A second and third wife not only bolsters male status but ideally increases the total number of surviving offspring in a part of the world where the rates of both infant mortality and maternal death are staggeringly high. Boucari, the "site clown," had two wives but no children, and his workmates sporadically took sweet revenge on Boucari for his pranks by mocking his impotence. Those who were single and of marriageable age, like myself and several Qurʿanic students, were taunted for missing out on the pleasures of married life.

After the women boarded the horse cart and returned to town, the two young sons hung close by their father waiting for instruction. Baba handed his trowel to Komar who was no more than nine years old, and the boy scrambled down the steep bank and ran along the dry riverbed, his younger brother trailing close behind. Komar washed the tool in the running water, removing caked concrete from the palette, and returned it promptly to his father. The two children lugged small stones to where Baba was filling the formwork, but they soon tired of this task and scurried away to the river's edge to play. Baba was not concerned by their lack of focus and said that little boys must be introduced to work gradually. According to him, a mason should start taking his son to sites when the boy turns seven, and training commences with minor tasks such as those he delegated to Komar. Responsibilities could be expected to increase with age, and by the time a boy turns ten more discipline is applied. Serious apprenticeship only begins at fifteen or sixteen years of age, when the individual is physically strong enough to handle the tools and materials, and when he is considered to have acquired a disciplined focus on his tasks and heeds instructions. Every so often, Baba would pause to glance toward the river's edge to make sure the boys were safe and not venturing into the water. "They're bound to catch cold if they get wet," he muttered, with furrowed brow and shaking his head.

A European Patron with Drawings

With the foundations nearly complete, vast quantities of bricks would be needed to raise the walls. At three brick-widths thick, each square meter of wall surface required almost ninety *tubaabu-ferey* bricks. To keep to the schedule and finish the first storey before the rains, Tony elected to employ four additional brick makers to assist Selifou along the riverbanks, and he paid them the standard 10 CFA per brick. As the project unfolded, the patron played a growing role in calculating the quantities and costs of materials and in scheduling the work. Though these responsibilities were shared with his official chief mason, Bayeré was often occupied with other contracts in town and thus his participation in the project was reduced at times to merely advising on structural and design decisions.

Building contracts in Djenné take one of three basic forms. As in the case of the Sanuna site, a client can choose to control the finances throughout the project and, with guidance from his mason, he remains responsible for purchasing all necessary materials and for paying all members of the building team a daily wage in accordance with those set by the *barey ton*. In this case, the apprentice receives a daily wage as well, even when working under the guidance of his own master, since payments come from the client's accounts and not the mason's working budget. Cash salaries are typically paid on Sunday, the last of the six-day workweek, before the Monday market. Alternatively, a client can retain all responsibilities for organizing and buying the building materials but arrive at a lump sum agreement with the mason for the total cost of labor prior to commencing work. In this scenario, the client issues one or more cash advances to the mason who is responsible for paying his labor force on a weekly basis. Finally, for an agreed-on price, the mason can be delegated total responsibility for materials and labor, and for the payment of his work team. In the latter two cases, the apprentice's salary is withheld and the young man is expected to labor in exchange for learning.

Periodically Tony consulted with Baba as the principal site mason to estimate quantities, but Baba experienced difficulty arriving at accurate figures. Although Baba was recognized by his peers as an accomplished and experienced mason, this project was replete with unconventional challenges. For starters, the project was exceedingly large, including not only the construction of the principal house but also a separate guardhouse, a lengthy enclosure wall, and a stone embankment along the river. This commission was for an entirely new house on virgin soil and therefore lacked the benefit of neighboring dwellings to dictate the size and shape of what could be built. Masons rarely, if ever, have the opportunity to erect houses on open lots unless building the simple one-storey courtyard houses that are laid out on a grid in the expanding reaches of the Kanafa quarter. In most situations, masons execute standard repairs and maintenance, or add rooms and possibly a second storey to an existing structure. Even when reconstructing a collapsed home, the defined urban site presents the mason with a recognizable set of spatial and historical constraints that serve to limit his choices and guide decisions. Defined property boundaries,

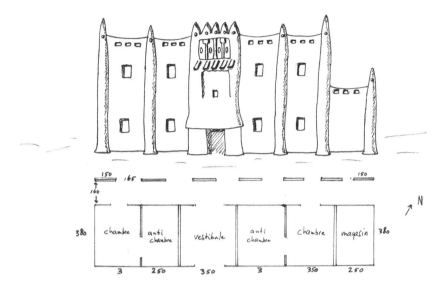

Client and chief mason's drawings for the floor plan and front elevation of the house at Sanuna. Drawn by the building patron Ton van der Lee and his chief mason, Bayeré Kouroumansé.

street edges, existing party walls, and extant foundations dictate design and planning to a considerable degree. A mason's customary responsibilities are therefore limited to calculating costs and materials for making specific architectural features or for erecting buildings of moderate size. Also, when working in town, suppliers and materials are close at hand and transportation is easily arranged, so precision in scheduling and long-term planning are less pressing issues than when working on an isolated and distant site.

That Tony was a European presented unique circumstances to those normally encountered between masons and clients. Local clients stipulate spatial and budgetary requirements, and possibly aesthetic and stylistic preferences at the start of projects, but their masons are typically granted full license to make the planning and structural decisions they deem appropriate. In many situations, interaction between a mason and his client is minimal during the construction process, and negotiations that do occur are concerned mainly with issues of money and scheduling. Tony, however, made daily site visits and played an active role in determining the planning and structural design of his house. He expressed an overt willingness for the masons to work autonomously, but he nevertheless intervened throughout the process. The client wanted a home that was both "traditional" and customized to suit his European sensibilities, and aspects of that synthesis were foreign to the builders' experiences.

The simple ground-floor plan and front elevation drawn on A4-size paper communicated the elementary design intent. Plans for the second-storey and the placement of crucial structural features such as the staircase and the large toilet shafts remained unresolved, however, until much later in the project. Tony initially believed that preliminary planning guidelines would form the basis for all subsequent decisions, invoking the innate expertise of the Djenné masons he employed. In fact, because the site masons had not resolved the layout themselves through their usual embodied engagement with the physical context and the materials, they lacked an overall conception of the building and found it difficult to partake constructively in the structural planning for the upper storey. The combination of supplying rudimentary drawings with the expectations that they would make their own decisions sent mixed signals to the site masons, confusing in their minds the boundary between following dictates and being delegated the sort of autonomous responsibility to which they were accustomed. Quarrelsome debates between the hierarchy of masons and the client erupted over the division of labor, and struggles for control over the work continued throughout the project.

After foundations for the exterior walls and the interior partitions were laid, the now ragged plan drawing was removed from the muddy ground and safely stored away, but all parties continued to refer to it when making planning choices. On separate occasions, however, Baba proclaimed, "I never use drawings when I build houses in Djenné." Pressing his index fingers to his temples for emphasis, and staring intently into the eyes of his audience, he added "The plans are in my head." Baba was not asserting that plans are conceptualized in his "mind's eye" as internalized images and mapped onto the physical context. Masons did not walk onto building sites and pace-off plans according to predetermined templates, in the same way that architects and artists do not mechanically reproduce visions on paper. Rather, design solutions and spatial configurations arise in the process of building or drawing, and are made manifest through an active hands-on engagement in creative production. As a trained mason, Baba's creativity was in direct dialogue with tools and materials, not pen and paper, and his composing resulted in dwellings, not drawings. Indeed, a mason's activities of designing and building are inseparable and unfold together, incrementally informing each other and in a manner responsive to multiple factors including the wishes and constraints imposed by clients, the qualities and limitations of materials, and the physical characteristics of the site. Building, like all craftwork, entails continual improvisation and problem solving in response to an evolving and changing context. The final plan or design is therefore the result, and not the generator, of the work.

"I've built from drawings in Bamako. That was in concrete," Baba told me, referring to his past experience in the capital. "I may not know how to speak French all that well, but I know how to build from drawings." His statement forged an intriguing correlation between French language and architectural drawings as foreign ways of knowing, and thereby asserted his ability to operate within alternative systems and in the wider world beyond Djenné. For Baba and other Djenné masons, drawings remain incompatible with local ways of knowing, because they make manifest intentions and ideas for something not yet realized. As artifacts, architectural drawings circulate without masons, and thereby separate ideas about planning and design from the physical processes of building. A mason's knowledge is embodied in his activities and is therefore conceived as interiorized and individually possessed. Like the secret knowledge of *bey-bibi* and *bey-koray,* trade knowledge should be carefully managed and selectively revealed. It is coveted as a precious resource that differentiates craftspeople from others, and its accumulation in the form of skilled practice and secret incantations promotes a public recognition of expertise and status.

In discussing local ways of knowing, another senior mason explained, "We didn't write in the past because we feared that if our knowledge was transcribed onto paper, it would escape us and others would steal it. It was safer to keep it all in our heads." He included architectural plans and drawings as part of the inventory of transcription practices, and made it clear that much trade knowledge remains secret.[17] "Now, in the modern world, we're confronted with so many things to know and so many problems to solve that we must write them down. There's too much for the head!" the mason exclaimed.

At a later stage in the riverside house project, a visiting foreign conservationist pointed out the absence of a traditional feature from Tony's drawing for the Tukolor-style facade. Tony subsequently asked his chief mason why he had neglected to inform him of this missing feature when they first drew the plans. Bayeré was incensed by the challenge to his expertise and responded agitatedly that the plans stored in his head far surpassed what was contained in the drawing. The mason haughtily reminded his client that he had plenty of experience building these houses and then proceeded to list other decorative features that would also be included on the final building that had not been identified by the conservationist. In doing so, Bayeré was not only publicly reaffirming his expert status, but he was also demonstrating that he possessed a more profound knowledge than the foreign expert.

Ferry crossing at the Bani River on the day of Djenné's Monday market

Monday Market Days with Konamadou

On Sunday evenings, seated comfortably on my rooftop and bathed in the tangerine glow of the sinking sun, I monitored the sluggish procession of trucks rumbling west along the tarmac road toward the spiky silhouette of Djenné. A blast of bass horns punctuated the continuous drone of engines, and a haze of thick black exhaust stained the air with an acrid scent. The convoys have journeyed from distant places, and every lorry is loaded impossibly high with goods, livestock, and people, all heading for the Monday market. The river barge works late into the night on Sunday, ferrying the cumbersome trucks across the shallow waters. Villagers from the surrounding region travel by horse-drawn carts festively painted in bright primary colors. In the dry season, most carts cross the water at a shallow ford situated within throwing distance of the police checkpoint in Tolober. Passengers disembark, roll up their trouser legs, skirts, and *boubous* and wade cautiously across, trailing behind their horse and carts and mindfully avoiding sudden dips in the riverbed. Those on bicycles dismount and lift them above their heads before gingerly stepping into the slow-moving current. Safely on the other side, the village travelers steer a well-beaten path that delivers them onto the main road some seventy meters beyond the checkpoint, and thus bypassing police spot checks and avoiding taxation.

Many of the town's masons recuperate on market day, but some work as petty traders selling foodstuff and small household items. Most building laborers pick up odd jobs, conveying merchandise for vendors and shoppers with pushcarts along the congested pathways that crisscross the vibrant marketplace. Many hundreds of tiny stalls cramp the square in front of the mosque, and scaffoldings made from thick branches support tarpaulin sheeting to shade the more fortunate ones. I found Konamadou seated behind a low wooden table selling bags of sugar, dry biscuits, candies, flashlight batteries, and boxes of matches. He was chewing kola nut and greeted me with a sheepish grimace of pulp-covered teeth.

Only the week before, Konamadou had vowed to quit chewing kola and called upon Baba and me as his witnesses before Allah. Baba adamantly denounced the habit, proclaiming it a waste of money and bad for one's health. The price of a kola nut had increased sharply over the past months owing to the worsening security crisis in Ivory Coast where the bulk of kola crops are harvested,[18] and it had reached 75 to 100 CFA per nut. Without provocation, Konamadou defended himself: "Allah approves of kola!"[19] I glared skeptically, and again he broke into an orange smile, adding with wavering conviction, "When you die, all the tobacco you smoked and chewed, and all the snuff you snorted during your lifetime leaves your body. But kola remains inside you because it is good and approved."[20] He also made a meek attempt to justify his frivolous expenditure: "If I become a successful trader, I can afford all the kola I can chew." Thoughts of escaping the drudgery of physical labor and becoming a trader fired Konamadou's ambitions, and, like so many people, he dreamed of being blessed with instant riches. "If I were a *tubaabu*" he once told me, "all I would do is sleep and wake up in the morning to find piles of money!" This fantasy reflected a pervasive notion that all white people are rich, and stemmed from the limited interaction most townspeople have with the groups of well-heeled and camera-laden Western tourists who traipse through Djenné on market day during the brief tourist season.

At noon Konamadou's younger brother, Bamoy, arrived to take over the stall. We wound our way through the clamor of the market, past a thicket of bristling horns in the cattle fair, and finally into the narrow streets of the Semani quarter.[21] At his family home, Konamadou's wife, Ainya,[22] was preparing lunch with her sisters-in-law in a shaded corner of the courtyard. Rice and sauce bubbled in blackened metal cauldrons over low fires, and the outdoor cooking area was littered with onion skins and scores of miniature desiccated fish skeletons. Bright red fire finches darted back and forth pinching morsels of food and grains of rice. A reception of children surrounded us, jumping up and down excitedly and covering us with a host of sticky fingers. Konamadou brought them to order with a script of idle threats and sent the young boys to wash their hands for lunch. We ate inside a room off the courtyard, shielded from the sun by a plastic woven mat rolled over the doorway. Konamadou's father, Baba, and four of the little boys joined us. The meal was shared from a large enamel bowl positioned at the center of our floor mat, and, characteristically, the ritual of eating was rapidly gotten over with. The boys scampered off, leaving Konamadou, his father, and me to a more tranquil chat. Baba was a pirogue builder, not a mason, and he told me of his frequent travels along the river to the village of Sirimou, where his third wife stayed. He also spoke about the decline in the pirogue-building business as a result of the years of poor rains and falling river levels. He expressed worries about the safety of his eldest son who was a migrant laborer in troubled Ivory Coast, and the family waited patiently for the badly needed remittances to arrive. Konamadou's younger brother, Bamoy, fished the Bani, but, like the pirogue industry, fishing reaped meager returns as waters vanished and catches dwindled.

Ainya delivered a bowl of water for us to clean our hands, and Konamadou thanked her graciously. They had been married for two years, and he was very fond of his wife. The single blemish on their relationship, according to Konamadou, was that they remained childless. Questions of virility, fecundity, and even future security dominated their worries. This was made more poignant by the pressures and expectations of family, and Konamadou's father kept an awkward silence throughout this discussion. The couple had consulted a *marabout* and were advised to be patient and rest their faith in Allah. There was little else to do. We rose to our feet, shook out creaking knees, and squinted our way back into the harsh sunlight.

In the courtyard the circle of seated women still ate, and Konamadou's mother had returned from the market to join them. His mother was tall and handsome, and a notoriously shrewd vendor who sold sachets of pulverized rock salt exported from Timbuktu by *pinasse*[23] along the Niger. Interior courtyards (*batuma*) are the hearth of Djenné's domestic life. Married women and girls of marriageable age spend considerable time there drying crops and fish for storage, preparing meals, doing laundry, caring for battalions of children, and socializing. Basic cooking implements consist of charcoal fires in three-pronged clay vessels or small metal braziers, heavy metal pots and cauldrons, and a host of stirring and straining utensils. Grinding stones and large wooden mortars and pestles for pounding millet and other grains are also

Woman making beaded bracelets (*kamba-hiiri*) in the courtyard of her house

kept in the courtyard. During the rains, cooking is done inside tiny purpose-built rooms off the courtyard or in cramped spaces under the flight of stairs. The mud walls and timber rafters of these windowless rooms are blackened with a velvety layer of soot, and the eye-watering smoke of charcoal fires billows through small perforations at the top of the room.

Many women in Djenné prepare cooked foods that are sold from the doorways of their homes or hawked in the streets. Goods are often individually packaged and imaginatively arranged on trays and in baskets that are carefully balanced on the heads of their young children who follow circuitous routes through their neighborhoods. Unlike the blacksmiths' wives who have well-defined socioeconomic roles as potters, most women in town do not have an ethnically or caste-prescribed profession. Bozo women in smaller fishing communities continue to be responsible for preserving the catches, which involves drying, smoking, and scorching, as well as the sale of fish,[24] but catches around Djenné are relatively small. In the past, Bozo women were also noted for weaving large baskets from palm fronds that were widely sold and used for storing rice, but these have been largely replaced by cheap plastic imports. Now, like so many women of the town, they make bracelets (*kamba-hiiri*) with thousands of miniscule, imported plastic beads painstakingly strung onto nylon fishing line. The women produce infinite combinations of glittering, colored patterns that are sold from home and at the Monday market.

Baba Djennepo retired to his room, and Konamadou and I conversed with the women, who resumed their playful scheme to wed me to the younger sister. We finally exited the house by an alternative route, passing first through a small storeroom where fishing nets and hooks were hung neatly from the palm ceiling beams, and then entering Konamadou's shop from the rear. The snug little room had a corrugated-metal door opening directly onto the street, and in the late afternoon the mason sold a limited variety of wares. He slowly saved earnings with the ambition of opening a bigger and better-stocked shop. On cool evenings, I pedaled my bike into the Semani quarter to visit Konamadou. The shop was crammed with children piled onto wooden benches and seated cross-legged on the floor, and every pair of eyes was fixated on the flickering blue light of the TV-screen. Like most of their neighbors, the Djennepo family had no electricity, so the appliance was juiced by an old car battery. When the children left, Konamadou sat by a kerosene lamp to study the Qurᶜan. The young and spirited *marabout* who lived across the road copied several short *suar* in elegant Arabic script on a sheet of lined paper as a gift for Konamadou. The mason could not read, but he practiced copying the shapes of individual letters and words with a ballpoint pen. The number of lines contained in the passage served as a mnemonic for reciting the respective *suar* that he had memorized as a boy in Qurᶜanic school. "I start each morning by reciting these *suar*," he told me proudly. "They protect me throughout the day."

On my night-time journeys back to Tolober, thick darkness filled the street passages squeezed between high windowless walls of mud, and splashes of warm light escaped from lantern-lit doorways. In vestibules scattered throughout the town quarters, boys sat late into the evening inscribing *suar* onto wooden *walaa* boards in carbon-black ink, and reciting verses aloud. The night was infused with the drone of a thousand discordant voices mechanically pronouncing the word of God. At the small bridge on the edge of town that connected Djenné to the tarmac road, gatherings of boys of all ages swarmed like shadflies under the white light of streetlamps to rehearse their lessons.

Garibou Laborers

My study principally addresses the lives, practices and professional training of the masons and their apprentices who reproduce Djenné's traditional building trade, but it is necessary to discuss the positions, roles, and personal ambitions of the Qurᶜanic students who labored for them. None of these young men whom I worked with was from Djenné and they were perceived as outsiders, as implied by the popular term for Qurᶜanic students, *garibou,* derived from the Arabic word *gharib* (غريب), meaning "stranger." This stranger's status qualifies their position in Djenné's social hierarchy and also within the town's tight-knit religious community. The city *marabouts*, especially those who consider themselves authentic *Djennénké* residents, maintain a social distance from their foreign students, and are normally reluctant to teach powerful secrets to anyone but their own sons and possibly Djenné-born students of reputable families.

The *garibou* also remain "outsiders" on the construction sites. Access to either permanent positions or higher status in the masons' trade is extremely limited, and though masons value the foreign students as a convenient pool of labor, they regard them as peripheral to the professional hierarchy and rarely train them as apprentices. Masons classify the *garibou* as part of the town's transient population that historically included scholars and traders, and they do not consider them worth the effort of training. They are also reluctant to reproduce potential competitors who may one day escape the structure and regulations of the *barey ton* and set up practice elsewhere. *Garibou* as young as seven and eight years old work on construction sites for a daily wage of 250 CFA, and

those who are older and deemed capable of heavier workloads earn 750 CFA. Several of the older *garibou*-laborers I worked with challenged conventional notions that equated marginality with a lack (or absence) of agency and power, and they frequently demonstrated strategic abilities to appropriate the margins, attempting to shift the boundaries in order to create their own discursive space and control the construction and representation of their identities.

Throughout West Africa, many consider that Djenné's *marabouts* are among the most powerful, claiming that the town's reputation as a great center of Islamic learning is recognized throughout the Muslim world, and as far away as Mecca. Parents from all over Mali and neighboring countries send their sons to study Qurʿan under the tutelage of the town's religious instructors. Boys are sent away from home at seven years of age, and sometimes younger, and studies may last many years depending on the level of knowledge pursued and the child's ability to survive the tremendous hardships of this mendicant existent. Some parents allege that being a *garibou,* with all its associated hardships and deprivations, disciplines the child's reasoning ability (Arabic ʿaql عقل); molds him into a responsible member of the religious community, and provides him with a potential career path.[25] Many of these children, especially those who are orphans or from severely impoverished families, become the custody of *marabouts* out of necessity or desperation. The young *garibou* beg door to door daily, reciting the Fulfulde verse *gido Allah garibou* ("Garibou, Friend of Allah"), and generous townsfolk offer food and money as alms (*saraa*) in accordance with Islamic prescriptions. The rice and porridge ladled into the tin pails they carry is their main source of nourishment, and the coins they collect, and sometimes steal, finance their lessons. Brenner reports that, in Mali, "this form of Qurʿanic schooling is widely accused of contributing to the rise of juvenile delinquency," since most of the young students end up on the streets without a trade and become beggars or worse,[26] a view echoed by concerned town residents.

Nearly all the older *garibou*[27] in Djenné seek temporary employment, bequeathing their entire salaries to the *marabouts* as payment for board and lessons. Many who labor six days a week throughout the building season also ply the Monday market to earn additional money. They solicit work from merchants and shoppers to ferry heaps of dried fish and other goods between vehicles and stalls, and they are sometimes permitted to keep these meager wages for themselves. With the pocket money, *garibou* buy cigarettes, tea, aspirin, and an occasional new article of clothing. It involves a great deal of toil and discipline to save for a journey home. Many boys and young men have no contact with their families throughout the entire period of study, and they rely on news and mes-

LEFT Seventeenth-century house and Qurʿanic school of Sory Baba Boucoum

sages carried by itinerant traders and traveling students who make the trip from Djenné to their distant villages. Often, any extra savings that they do manage to accumulate finds its way into the pockets of their teachers. Students are convinced that if they present their *marabout* with special *cadeaux* (French for "gifts") and demonstrate obedience, respect, and an aptitude for this religious vocation, they may be granted privileged access to certain trade secrets. These include verses and performances for producing incantations and benedictions, and the recipes for preparing herbal remedies, amulets, and *gris-gris.* Those who travel to Djenné to pursue serious studies with a prominent *marabout* can reasonably expect to return to their village after several years with a certain degree of status-by-affiliation, and, depending on the level of training received, they themselves might take up Qur'anic teaching and *maraboutage* as a profession.

When I began working at the building project by the river, I was stationed alongside a young Burkinian man. We were part of an assembly of laborers passing materials on to the two Kouroumansé masons who raised the mud-brick walls of the guardhouse. Samadolo Anasse was a Bisa in his early twenties who had ventured from his small village outside Bobo-Dioulasso to study in Djenné. He wore an intensely serious air, and though pleasant and polite, he initially monitored me with a degree of suspicion and judged the masons for their lack of religious knowledge. Anasse's first direct question to me was predictable: "Are you a Muslim?" he asked provocatively. "No," I replied frankly, leaving myself vulnerable to his full barrage of impassioned reasons why I must convert. One mason quickly intervened, strictly forbidding Anasse to preach religion on-site. They, too, sensed the challenge of his self-proclaimed moral authority. Without stirring up trouble, but hoping to provoke further exchange, I responded to his inquisition in Arabic. Although the many languages spoken in Djenné are sprinkled with standard greetings, exclamations, and sayings in Arabic, the vast majority of Qur'anic students and many of the *marabouts* cannot converse in that language. Arabic is considered to be Allah's chosen tongue for reciting the Qur'an but not necessarily a productive language to better interpret, understand, and discuss the writings of the sacred texts such as the *hadīth.* For many, oral and written Arabic remains a fetish and a powerful ingredient for producing amulets and spells. Anasse stared quizzically, "Is that Arabic?" he asked. "You study the Qur'an, don't you?" I taunted playfully. He cast a hard look, then laughed with amusement. Anasse and I became fast friends.

During the course of the season, several *garibou* laborers became noticeably proficient at their tasks, and though the Bozo masons frequently mocked and

Salam, Qurʿanic student and laborer from Waguia in Burkina Faso

bantered with their Burkinian assistants, they readily acknowledged that a few were indeed reliable workers. Salam, a Mossi from Waguia with an entertainingly naughty wit, told me that he was gradually learning the trade and perhaps he would abandon religious training to become a mason. But it was Anasse, in particular, who earned the greatest respect and was delegated increasing responsibility. He demonstrated leadership qualities and maturity, and his command of French and Bamanankan made him an important intermediary when conflicts arose between the different actors on-site. The masons regularly called down to Anasse from where they were working and asked him to judge the level of the palm-wood lintels they set over doors (sing. *hu-mé*) and windows (sing. *fúney*). He was also responsible for regulating the flow of materials from the stockpiles to the masons, and he was eventually put in charge of reporting the bad behavior and misconduct of fellow laborers to the head mason, Baba.

Toward the end of the season Bamoy exclaimed aloud, "Anasse should forget *maraboutage* and become a builder!" But clearly he was not encouraging Anasse to do so in Djenné. In fact, this career path is not a viable option for those born outside the town or without blood ties to the already established families of masons. As discussed previously, all households in Djenné are contractually bound to a mason, which makes it difficult, if not impossible, for anyone without arranged or inherited patron affiliations to find work.[28] Further, the possibility of usurping someone else's clients is curbed by the masons' secret knowledge of benedictions and curses. Masters are believed to possess powers to protect their interests and to harm those who threaten the established, Bozo-dominated order. Recognizing the existence of such limitations, Anasse paid little attention to the flattery and continued laboring to finance his studies and appease his *marabout*. He had an unwavering determination to become a religious scholar and *marabout*, and then return home.

Level Lintels

Hasey Kouroumansé arrived on site each morning, slung the plastic strap of his battery-operated radio over the branch of a tree, and tuned into Djenné's local station. Radio Jamana broadcast news and regional events, and a variety of music ranging from military marches to reggae. Popular tunes roused short bouts of merry singing, and rap music prompted some young laborers to mime the defiant postures and attitude they learned from music videos. Unlike the builders I worked with in Yemen, however, Djenné masons and their laborers do not sing together as a team. Work-songs (*hājl* هاجل) on Yemeni

RIGHT Bamoy Kouroumansé applying mud plaster around a door lintel

building sites are sung to better coordinate and synchronize tasks, to let off steam, and, arguably, to alleviate the monotony of repetitive physical labor.[29] No such formal device was used by my West-African colleagues, but laborers occasionally organized games whereby opposing teams competed in passing materials to the masons or carrying heavy loads. Like the songs, these competitions spurred activity and diverted thoughts from the heat and the dust, and the sheer tedium of the workday.

The height of the guardhouse walls had reached the top of the door and window openings. Bamoy and Hasey checked the evenness of the walls prior to placing the sturdy palm-wood lintels. To do so, Baba loaned them his prized spirit level made from lightweight aluminium and prestigiously imported from France. The two masons laid a cut segment of timber measuring five by ten centimeters over each aperture, in turn, and checked the horizontal dimension with the spirit level. In the case of one window, a significant discrepancy was discovered between the heights of the wall on each side of the opening. "Moroccan" windows had been commissioned from a carpenter. These windows, with their wooden lattice work painted red and green, were also called *koyra di fûney*, meaning "town window," referring to their use on the houses of Djenné's merchant-traders. Each one for the guardhouse would measure sixty centimeters square. The wall on one side of the opening currently measured sixty-five centimetres and the other was slightly less than sixty in height. Hasey removed the uppermost brick from the higher of the two sides and carefully reduced its thickness with his *kuuru-bibi* trowel. Holding the brick upward in his left hand, Hasey made systematic chops with the trowel blade, rotating the brick with light tosses until he had successfully removed the facing of brittle mud without cracking the brick. He smoothed the rough face and replaced it in the bed of mortar. The height of this side now measured a perfect sixty. Hasey then built up the lower side of the wall with the thin layers of facing just removed from the higher wall, embedding them in a cushion of fresh mortar.

The lintels were made from lengths of wood from the ronier palm (*sebe* in Djenné-Chiini), and a second layer of thick branches (*gar bundu*) harvested from deciduous softwood was placed above.[30] A toxic solution of water and cypermethrin was poured over the palm sticks to prevent termite infestation before spreading a thick layer of mortar on top.[31] The softwood branches were cut to size with a small axe (*daasi kayna*) at ground level, and then set snugly into the mortar to fill crevices between the palm-wood members below. This combination of elements produced a solidly reinforced lintel. At Sanuna, mortar (*banco*) was being manufactured from recycled bricks that

Reflected plans of a *fata-taki,* a *fata-hinka,* and a *dar-fo* ceiling showing the direction and layering of the palm-wood ceiling beams

had been used to erect the temporary building on-site that put the property into "official" use. The walls of the derelict structure were dismantled with *sasiré* crowbars, and the bricks were pulverized and mixed with water. Bamoy explained that it was acceptable to recycle mud bricks taken from properties where benedictions had been made by known masons, but it was risky to borrow materials from unfamiliar sites. Abandoned houses often harbor evil spirits and *djinn,* and it is highly possible that they will travel with the materials and defile the new building and harm its inhabitants.

Basket-loads of mortar were tossed along a line of men stretching from the freshly trodden pile to the masons installing lintels forty meters away. The empty baskets then traveled back along the same network of hands. One batch of mud was squarely rejected by Bamoy who scooped out a handful and crumbled the contents between his fingers. He vented at the laborer who passed him the basket, but his irritation was directed at Boucari who kneaded the mixture. Boucari had neglected to add sufficient quantities of water, and he was visibly more interested in pestering Sedou, the young Dogon who manned the well, than performing his tasks. Bamoy's ebbing patience was turning into anger, and Boucari sprung back into position on top of the soggy pile of mud and began stomping and churning rapidly with his hoe. Commands and reprimands were in order on building sites, but it was rare for masons to express extreme anger toward members of their team. Displays of rage and emotional outbursts are considered childish and convey a lack of reason (Arabic *ʿaql* عقل), which is a highly esteemed attribute in Islam, repeated throughout the Qurʾan. Though I never witnessed such displays from Bamoy, it was rumored that his good reputation as a mason had been compromised on past occasions because of his explosive temper. Masons and patrons alike agreed unreservedly that he was technically skilled, but self-restraint and reasoned judgment on and off the worksite were equally important qualities by which a mason's practice and persona were judged.

Detail of a *fata-taki* "four-winged" ceiling construction in the house at Sanuna

The Price of Palms

When I arrived the next morning, Baba and the client were already on-site discussing roofing options for the guardhouse. Palm trunks were becoming an increasingly precious commodity and they were now imported to Djenné from as far away as the district of Sefeto in western Mali (near Kita) and even illegally over the border from Burkina Faso. A priority in the efforts to conserve Djenné's architectural tradition and building practices is the need to promote and establish local, sustainable sources of timber. Regulated plantation and forestation projects could potentially supply mature ronier palms for *toron*[32] and ceiling construction, as well as various hardwoods for the manufacture of doors and Moroccan-style lattice windows at affordable prices. Quartered palm trunks sawn to four-meter lengths were selling at a unit price of 6000 CFA, making them the most costly component in the construction of a new building. Because of their exorbitant cost and the difficulty in securing a sufficient quantity of palm trunks in the marketplace, patrons sought the most economic solutions to their roofing problems. At Sanuna, Baba was instructed to reserve the best timbers for roofing the ground-storey rooms of the main house and not squander the valuable stocks on the guardhouse.

Baba sketched three alternatives on the sandy ground with the tip of his finger. His ceiling plans included only the geometric arrangements of vectors that indicated the linear directions of spans between invisible walls. The ends of each span were marked by bold fingerprints pressed firmly into the soil to indicate the points where the timbers rested on the tops of walls. The first option he produced was the symmetrical *fata-taki* ceiling[33] composed of diagonally placed timbers over the four corners of the room. The diagonal members supported two higher levels of spans over the center of the room that ran perpendicular to the walls, and created a shallow dome-like effect. This elegant solution was favored by the mason for both its aesthetic and structural properties, but it consumed the largest number of palm timbers. Baba next illustrated the *fata-hinka* ceiling[34] that consisted of palm trunks spanning diagonally over two opposite corners of the room and supporting a layer of timbers that stretched above them. This required fewer of the large palm trunks than the first option but more than the final alternative. The third ceiling arrangement, *dar-fo*, required two parallel palm-wood beams spanning opposite walls and dividing the ceiling space into three equal parts. Each third would be roofed by smaller timbers and branches laid perpendicular between the beams and the walls. Baba liked this solution least, arguing that it was not structurally sound. A compromise was eventually reached: all four rooms of the guardhouse would have *fata-hinka* ceilings.

I took a pause from work that same afternoon and strolled along the river-bank to the spot where Selifou molded bricks. He and two young assistants marched silently up and down the dry riverbed fetching pails of water while two others treaded the gooey mixtures that suctioned earnestly at their feet and calves and made moist sucking noises with each step of their dance. I seated myself on the roots of an enormous gnarled *karité* (shea-butter tree)[35] that clung to the eroding banks, and I gazed over the gently flowing river. The Bani changed with each passing day, and its receding waters were gradually replaced by grassy little islands that floated like bright emeralds on the calm murky currents. Fishermen in sleek black pirogues navigated the watery landscape, casting their nets like lassoes and drawing in wriggling bundles of tiny silvery fish that sparkled in the afternoon sun. The large *capitaine* that commanded handsome profits in the market had already migrated downstream to deeper waters. This river not only sustains life in the arid Sahel, but it also replenishes the villages and towns with building materials. Annual flooding delivers fresh deposits of mineral-rich silts ideally suited to making bricks, mortar, and plaster. Like the riverbanks, Djenné's houses are in a perpetual state of flux and change: eroding and collapsing, becoming modified and regenerated as families grow and diminish over generations. And, like the undulating course of the river, the soft contours of the region's architecture are forever taking shape.

Masons Bamoy and Hasey Kouroumansé positioning ceiling timbers

4 · Conflict and Resolution

Baba's Replacement

One morning, Baba announced to a disappointed team that he would depart for Bamako. He secured a month-long contract through his cousin, Bayeré, to labor on a new reinforced-concrete structure in the capital where he would earn a better salary and gain experience in "modern" building techniques. A replacement was hired straight away, and Baba spent a morning showing him the ropes before leaving.

Baba's replacement arrived promptly on his bicycle at 8:00 AM fully prepared to assume duties. The name of the new mason was Ibrahim Sao, but everyone called him "Tonton," a colloquial French term for "uncle." Tonton was a lean man in his late fifties with a striking grey moustache and beard, and some team members addressed him respectfully as *Vieux* (French for "Old One"). Much of his life had been spent abroad. Following the death of his father in 1962, he left Djenné and, in his words, "set out to see the world" in the exhilarating years immediately following Independence of the French West African colonies. Tonton first traveled to Burkina Faso, where he stayed for six years with an older sister who was married and living in Bobo Dioulasso. From Burkina he traveled to Ivory Coast (*wankiya*), making his way south by train. He stayed in Abidjan for nineteen years working as a laborer on high-rise buildings and various civil engineering projects, gaining valuable experience in reinforced-concrete construction. He regularly toted his trowel of French manufacture, pronouncing that it was presented by a government contractor for his fine workmanship on a concrete bridge. Though Tonton had no formal education beyond childhood Qurʿanic lessons, he acquired a good standard of spoken French in Ivory Coast, and he had an inquisitive mind matched by a cutting wit. His first wife and five children stayed behind in Abidjan when he returned to settle in Djenné at the end of the 1980s, and some years later he married a second wife in town.

From the outset it was clear that Tonton was both an amusing and complicated character. He launched into tasks with electric energy, and theatrically scaled walls and tiptoed around their narrow perimeters like a cat. He instantly resumed Baba's mentorship of Diabaté, monitoring the apprentice's work and conscientiously introducing him to new procedures. While correcting Diabaté's use of the plumb line, he turned to comment, "We old masons have all the building knowledge in our heads. Young masons haven't any and it's our responsibility to teach them." He confidently claimed expertise in both *béton et banco* (concrete and mud). Tonton also entertained his fellow builders with humor and charm, and often instigated the highly charged bantering sessions that erupted between Bozo and Dogon laborers. One lunch, while standing aloofly outside the ravenous circle gathered around the giant bowl, he expounded loudly on dining etiquette, comically rebuking those who grabbed greedily at the rice and allowed grains to fall on the ground about them. Despite his seemingly extroverted nature, Tonton also had a propensity to slip into dour moods of obstinacy and bitter sarcasm that lasted for hours, sometimes days.

On Tonton's first morning, both Baba and the client were on-site to oversee the transfer of command and acquaint him with the project. The three men stood together on the foundations of the main house, intensely discussing structural solutions for supporting the second storey and the roof. Second-storey walls were normally built directly above the load-bearing ones below, more or less replicating planning arrangements of rooms on both floors. However, Tony wished to create an open-planned space on the second storey, and this necessitated an alternative strategy. The maximum distance between supporting elements was restricted by the available lengths of quartered palm trunks.[1] Though some timbers were long enough, it was risky to span the 3.80-meter width of the space without intermediate supports. Tony favored a row of pillars aligned on the longitudinal axis of the room, and he traced his plan in the dirt marking each spot for pillars with an "X." This, however, required an asymmetrical positioning of the ground-storey doorways between parlor (*galia*) and bedroom (*tasika*) compartments, since the heavy pillars could not be erected above openings. Baba, on the other hand, argued for short sections of wall extending into the room from both sides. These would be built over the ground-storey partitions and would reduce the open span to 3.20 meters. He communicated his solution by walking it out over the foundations, gesturing the size and placement of the walls with his hands and arms, and pointing above to imaginary lines of the beams they would support. The advantages to the mason's scheme were that the *galia-tasika* doorways could be maintained in their usual symmetrical position, and, more important, the central aisle of the second-storey space would be unobstructed.

Tony thanked Baba for his suggestion, but he insisted on the pillars. Much to everyone's surprise, Tonton boldly interjected in support of Baba's option, chiding Tony for "not imagining the space correctly" and insisting that piers would impede the visual openness of the room. With animated authority, he arranged six mud bricks in the formation of a fifty-five by seventy centimeter pillar at the center of the foundation and stepped back for his audience to observe. He then proceeded to chuck them one by one back onto the ground, pronouncing, "Piliers, c'est pas bon!" ("Pillars, they're no good!"). Tony made several attempts during the first weeks to appease the strong will of his new site mason and establish congenial relations, all to little avail. "You have so much energy, Tonton!" Tony would say encouragingly. Without looking up from his work, the mason responded flatly, "Pourquoi ça?" insolently dismissing Tony's gesture and testing the fragile balance of power that existed between them. Tony tried again, complimenting Tonton on his efforts: "Everything is progressing so quickly now!" The mason retorted aggressively, "Why? Was it not progressing before?" subverting all praise. Tonton was determined to claim authority on his own terms, and he resented what he interpreted to be patronizing pleasantries.

Baba left the site at noon to attend Friday prayers at the mosque and prepare for his long journey the next day. A lingering discussion about possible solutions for the second storey continued between a group of laborers, but Tonton interrupted sharply "It's time to work now! Questions and discussion are for the evening." With Konamadou's assistance, Tonton resumed Baba's work on the main house while the Kouroumansé brothers roofed the four rooms of the guardian's building. Tonton ventured over to inspect Bamoy and Hasey's site several times in an effort to chaperon their work, but the two younger masons fiercely resisted any supervision. Initially Bamoy and Hasey politely pretended to heed the offers of advice or mildly defended their own procedures, but, as weeks passed, the tension between the camps heightened. By the end of the season the Kouroumansé brothers blatantly ignored him, and they began hijacking laborers from

Tonton's workforce to bolster their own. In Baba's absence the chain of command corroded, and the daily organization of men and materials loosened.

On reflection, Tonton's utter failure to preserve authority was not altogether surprising. The reality was that he had spent nearly half his life outside Djenné and was regarded as foreign in many respects and lacking the authentic formation that local masons received. Though he boasted about his competence with mud, most of his laboring experience had been with concrete and in a very different context. Tonton had returned to Djenné in the late 1980s to an economy severely battered by two decades of drought, and he found himself without any particular role in the community. It was he who branded himself with the endearing kin title "Tonton," spinning a history of intimacies and connection with the town's people. Tony once playfully hailed him "Le maçon de Djenné," but Tonton rejected this prestigious designation, saying "Non! Le maçon d'Abidjan." His correction, intriguingly, raised the stakes by pinning his status to one of Africa's largest and most flamboyant modern cities, while simultaneously disclaiming a high rank in Djenné's hierarchy. I soon discovered that any respect Tonton commanded on-site was mainly owing to his age, not his proficiency as a craftsman. Several colleagues even accused him of milking his "greybeard" role to manipulate his professional and social positions.

Constructing *Fata Hinka* Ceilings

A hefty shipment of quartered palm trunks was trucked illicitly from Burkina Faso and delivered to a prominent Djenné merchant. Fifty were sent to our site, and the client and masons were relieved at having secured sufficient stock for roofing the guardhouse and the ground storey of the main house before the rainy season (*kaydiya*). More timber would be needed for the second storey, but this expenditure could wait until the following year.

Before starting each morning, Bamoy performed a discreet ritual to guarantee good work and the protection of all team members from accidents and danger. Squatting on top of the walls next to a fresh dollop of mortar and a stack of bricks ready to be placed, Bamoy stared intensely into the open palm of his right hand and began murmuring rhythmic, barely audible verses while repetitiously touching the center of each finger with the tip of his thumb. He finished, paused briefly, and then picked up a brick to begin building. Bamoy regularly made a small spectacle of this ritual, but when I asked him to explain its content he shook his head laughing and pronounced my name "Abu Bakr!" with amusement. He said that he performed the counting on his fingers just twelve times and recited secrets that contained a mix of Qurᶜanic verse and *bey-bibi* incantations, but he refused to reveal any of the precise wording or significance. Bamoy told me simply that he learned this special secret from his deceased father and that he would teach it to his prog-eny.[2] The interleafing of familiar Qurᶜanic *suar* with esoteric phrases, and the combination of these utterances with prescribed series of postures, move-ments, and gestures, produces a purposely ambiguous communication. This ambiguity contributes significantly to the power of the masons' secrets. An observing audience, including patron-clients, attribute special abilities to masons that enable them to engage with occult forces. Since the general pub-lic is denied access to, or control over, this realm, they must put faith in the masons to protect their houses and built environment.[3]

Bamoy and Hasey began the *fata-hinka* ceilings over each of the four rooms. This style of ceiling construction involved covering two diagonally opposite corners of the room with closely spaced timbers and spanning the central area between with a perpendicular arrangement of wood. First, equal distances of ninety centimeters were measured with a tape from a corner along the top of its two adjacent walls, and marks were incised with the ma-son's trowel. This was repeated at the corner diagonally opposite the first. The marks indicated the outer limits of where the ends of the hefty beams would rest on the walls. The first two quartered-palms were hoisted by labor-ers to the masons who straddled diagonally across from one another. With coordinated effort and patience, Bamoy and Hasey placed the beams in their exact position and adjusted the horizontal level by wedging tiny pieces of rubble under their ends. Before placing the remaining beams to close the two triangles, the masons laid a course of bricks over the four ninety-centimeter segments of wall to raise these two corners and secure an even spacing be-tween the two parallel beams. They could then fit the remaining beams of decreasing length one next to the other, alternating thick and narrow ends until both triangular segments of the ceiling were densely covered over.

The span of the first beam was carefully determined by stretching a nylon cord between points on the top of the walls and marking the distance with knots. The cord was then passed down to the ground to Anasse and Salam, who were responsible for selecting timbers. Choosing good wood was a tricky task and timbers were regularly rejected by the masons as too thick or too thin, lacking straightness, or insufficiently dry. Once a selection was agreed upon, the laborers used the cord to mark the required length and Anasse

chopped the palm trunk to size with an axe. All the main beams were selected, measured, and cut in this manner, but as shorter ones were needed for
filling in the triangular spaces over the corners of the room, the laborers measured their cuts more casually. The length of each successive beam was shortened by a measurement equal to the span made between Salam's stretched
thumb and tip of his index finger. Most of his approximations were spot on,
and the task became a skill-challenging game of judgment and embodied
measurement.

The ends of the closely spaced beams were supported on the inner half of
the wall thickness. The tops of partition walls were divided equally to support
the ceiling timbers of adjacent rooms. In the case of exterior walls, an outer facing of mud bricks concealed the ends of the ceiling beams. Once all the beams
were in place, and the crevices and spaces between them filled with thinner
branches, the wood was doused with a nauseating solution of cypermethrin
poison. An orchestrated team of laborers then conveyed endless baskets of mud.
Two boys dusted the baskets with a coating of dry soil and Boucari shoveled
liberal helpings of oozing red mud inside. The full baskets were tossed along a
chain of hands to the final laborer who stood precariously balanced on an empty
oil drum next to the walls of the guardhouse. He passed the baskets on cue to
Bamoy and Hasey who plopped the mud cleanly out, like jelly from a mold, on
top of the trunks and branches. They gradually built up a bulky layer, constantly
spreading and smoothing the mud with their *kuuru-bibi* trowels. Emptied baskets were speedily returned along the same chain. When synchronicity peaked
and baskets flowed smoothly back and forth, eight loads of mud reached the
masons per minute. Such well-timed coordination, however, was short-lived.
The rhythm typically faltered if loads accumulated around the feet of the final
laborer or, worse yet, if baskets arrived at the same point from either direction.
Missed catches meant that full baskets splattered over the ground and up trouser legs, inevitably provoking a roaring ovation from the team.

After the two opposite corners of the room were roofed and the mud dried,
the space between them was spanned with thick tree branches. These branches
were supported on top of the triangular corners and ran diagonally over the
room. Like the corners, this middle section was also covered in a deep layer of
mud. The overall structural arrangement of sections layered one above the
other yielded a slight convex curvature in the roof's profile, and this served to
efficiently drain rainwater to the perimeter where it was evacuated through clay
downspouts (*handoro*). A low parapet wall neatly perforated by a series of *handoro* was later constructed around the top, and simple comb-like projections

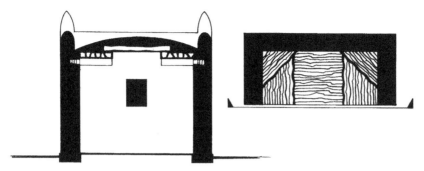

Section through a room roofed with a *fata-taki* ceiling; reflected ceiling plan adjacent

visually reinforced the four corners of the building. It now remained for the Moroccan-style windows and corrugated-metal doors to be installed, and for all wall surfaces to be plastered with a fine coat of mud mixed with rice husks.

Mud's vulnerability to erosion from the elements promotes creative experimentation with new protective finishes for wall and roof surfaces. An array of mud plasters—with names such as *laabu-bibi, laabu-tyirey, batakara, laabu-kuntur,* and *laabu-fumbu*[4]—are concocted with various grades of laterite and supplemented with quantities of chopped straw, dry rice husks, and cow manure; less commonly used are tiny pebbles, ash, earth from termite mounds, powdered *baobab* fruit (*koo*), or *karité* butter (*bulanga*). The added ingredients improve the mud's durability and water resistance. Most plasters are prepared and used immediately, but others are fermented in pits or piles for several days or weeks and command high prices. The breakdown of organic matter liberates colloid particles, and the fermentation strengthens the mud's cohesion and repellent properties.[5] In the process, the mud typically changes color from shades of ocher and red to dark grey. The smell of fermented mud such as *laabu-fumbu* is especially putrid, and this plaster is reserved as a final coat for interior and exterior surfaces.

Daytime temperatures were mounting, and the heavily dust-laden winds blew stronger. Bamoy was afflicted by a recurring infection that was progressively damaging his vision. Within a week, his reddened eyes were glazed over with an opaque film. He had previously consulted doctors in the larger towns of Mopti and San, but they failed to diagnose the illness and could only prescribe antibiotics. The accuracy of his work was suffering, and he missed several days of work. On an exceedingly hot afternoon, Anasse collapsed on-site from a soaring fever. His colleagues carried him into the shade of some bushes to rest. His fever soon turned to chills, and he moaned of an aching back. By the beginning of March, three more laborers succumbed, like Anasse, to acute bouts of malaria. Those who fell ill were responsible for finding a replacement during their absence. They lost all wages while out of work, and if they failed to find a trusted substitute, they also risked loosing their job permanently to a stranger. Some men began wearing disposable respiratory masks available from the town's shops as protection against the medley of viruses circulating with the *harmattan* winds. Copious quantities of dust triggered congestions and infections that wore down immune systems and made people susceptible to more serious and life-threatening illness.

Planning the Rooftop Miters

One Monday evening after the market, an enormous exhaust-spewing and overloaded truck drove recklessly off the end of the river ferry (*baki*), taking with it the winch that operates the access ramp. Djenné's link to the rest of the world was severed for almost a week while the ferry stayed anchored in the river's stream with the rear wheels of the truck still on deck, its nose fishing and its tail end pointing skyward. Market goods and supplies of Malian-produced "Castel" beer for the Chez Baba Café had to be paddled across in pirogues and taxied into town by waiting pickup trucks. From our riverside position at the construction site, we kept daily tabs on the mostly uneventful progress at the ferry.

Prior to starting the mud-brick walls for the main house, Tonton and Konamadou measured out the dimensions of the pilasters (*sarafar*) that would project from the Tukolor-style facade along the river. The pilasters would be aligned with the interior partition walls behind the facade and would extend above the height of the building, terminating in bold miter-like points. The name for the two "male" pilasters defining the ends of the facade is *sarafar har* and the "female" ones that frame the entranceway to the house are called *sarafar woy*.[6] In addition to breaking up the planar wall surface into horizontal sections and giving it rhythm, the pilasters also serve a structural function by acting as buttresses to counteract the lateral forces exerted on the exterior wall by the interior partition walls when they expand and contract with changing humidity. Tonton and Konamadou incised the fifty-five- by twenty-five-centimeter dimensions of each of the five slender pilasters onto the ground with the sharp end of a stick. An older Mossi laborer named Abdullahi and a Dogon named Hamidou Guindo excavated the shallow foundations with a hoe and scooped out the loose soil with bare hands. Hamidou was slight but powerful, and his proficiency with the hoe meant that he was frequently assigned this arduous task. Diabaté followed behind, sculpting the sides with the flared end of a *sasiré* crowbar; his work was subsequently checked by Konamadou and amended when necessary. Buckets of water were poured into the box-like holes to dampen the soil before filling them with stones and concrete.

When it came to planning the dimensions and placement of the two more substantial pilasters that would hug the main entrance of the house and support the overhanging hood of the *gum hu,* a focused discussion ensued between Tonton and Konamadou. The vestibule of a typical Tukolor-style house is narrow and this is expressed by a somewhat compressed arrangement of vertical elements and decoration over the *gum hu* as displayed by the house of Djenné's Chief (*Djenné wéré*). By contrast, the vestibule of the riverside house was wide, measuring 3.50 meters across its interior space. After adding the fifty-five-centimeter-thick walls on each side of the vestibule, the width of the resulting *gum hu* would total 4.60 meters. There was concern among the masons that these dimensions would result in squat and unattractive proportions.

The two masons then turned their attention to the number of spiky projections (*sarafar idye*) that would be needed to crown the roofline above the *gum hu.* They explained that their advanced planning of every element was essential for achieving a harmonious and well-integrated composition. In the absence of drawings, these decisions were characteristically worked out by masons on-site with tools and materials. Tonton marked the total 4.60 meter width of the vestibule onto the concrete foundation with chalk, and Konamadou cut a forty-centimeter length from a stick. Forty centimeters was the length of a standard *tubaabu-ferey* brick, and the stick therefore corresponded to the base of an average *sarafar idye* miter that was one-brick wide. They began by randomly choosing a spacing of twenty-five centimeters to separate each miter, and then proceeded to test this by alternating the cut stick with twenty-five-centimeter gaps, starting at one end and moving along the chalk line. This combination fell short of filling the total length, so they executed more trials, incrementally increasing and decreasing the spacing each time until they got it just right. The masons finally arrived at a configuration of eight *sarafar idye* evenly separated by intervals of twenty centimeters to fill the 4.60-meter length.

I was at first perplexed by their seemingly cumbersome exercise. I had quietly worked out a solution in my head with mathematical formulas.[7] But in using different methods, we arrived at the very same quantities and dimensions. In their trial-and-error method, a series of spacing dimensions were selected to determine the total number of miters needed; in my own mental calculation, a total number of miters was selected to arrive at a spacing. My colleagues were evidently numerate in a different way. They employed a method of calculation that simulated their own physical method of constructing the assembly of spikes. Research with athletes, dancers, and craftspeople confirms that knowing extends beyond propositions that are thought and expressed in words. Human knowledge necessarily includes ways of knowing that are thought and expressed in action and skilled performance.[8] Tonton and Konamadou's physical practice of laying out the sticks and gaps in sequence clearly expressed an embodied way of thinking about mathematical relations and proportions.[9] Embodied ways of calculating are also enacted in a wide variety of everyday spatial activities that require quick and accurate estimations of relative speed, distance, dimensions, and proportions. In the masons' exercise, the length of stick, representing the width of a miter, was held constant and the dimension of the spacing was introduced as a variable. The range of that variable was confined by what the masons knew from experience from this construction, so values that were either too small or too large were rejected outright. Ultimately Tonton and Konamadou's simulated layouts resulted in a configuration that covered the length of the chalk line exactly, beginning and ending with a *sarafar idye* miter at each end.

Their satisfaction at solving this problem was short-lived. Bayeré arrived by motorbike in the late afternoon to monitor progress. When he made his rounds to the main house, Tonton and Konamadou proudly shared their proposal to build eight spikes. "Eight!" Bayeré exploded, "There can never be an even number of *sarafar idye*!" The two masons protested that their calculations were made correctly and there would be room for eight, with a reasonable opening between each. "A Tukolor facade with an even number of miters," Bayeré declared sardonically, "That would ruin my reputation!" According to him, only incompetent masons made this error. "The total must be an odd number. There should be five, like on the drawing," he continued.[10] Tonton and Konamadou were apparently unaware of Bayeré's "odd number" rule. The older mason countered that the vestibule was unusually wide and five was too few. "Then possibly seven," Bayeré replied sharply, "but not eight." The chief mason then took hold of Konamadou's cut stick and repeated the exact same trial-and-error exercise, alternating sticks and gaps. After several determined attempts, Bayeré smugly concluded that there would be seven *sarafar idye* with thirty centimeter spaces between. His solution likewise fit the 4.60-meter *gum hu* perfectly and satisfied his wish for an odd number. Later, he would in fact return to the original design for five by increasing the width of each miter to sixty centimeters and the gaps to forty.

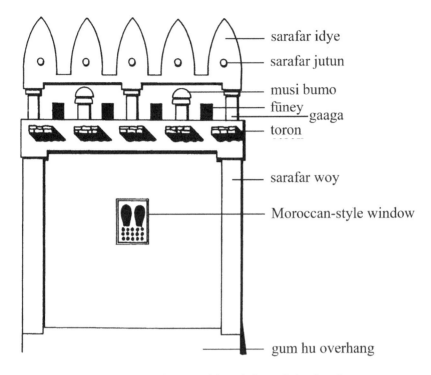

sarafar idye

sarafar jutun

musi bumo

fūney
  gaaga

toron

sarafar woy

Moroccan-style window

gum hu overhang

Elevation plan of the decorative elements of the Tukolor-style facade at Sanuna

That evening I asked Bayeré to explain his insistence on an odd number of *sarafar idye*. In silence, he started by sketching out on the ground with his finger the decorative ensemble of elements along the parapet wall over the entrance, and moving upward from there to the spikes. Bayeré first drew the *sarafar woy* on each side of the entrance and capped the top with a horizontal line. The elements above began with two stumpy *gaaga* pilasters[11] resting directly on top of the *sarafar woy,* and a third placed in the center. A second horizontal line was etched above the three *gaaga,* and between them he drew squat vertical lines with mushroom-shaped hats that he called *musi bumo* (cat's head). There were now five evenly spaced elements between the two horizontal lines. Below each of these he pricked the ground with his fingertip to indicate where the palm-wood *toron* would project outward, and above each element he drew the outline of a tapering *sarafar idye*. When he had finished his illustration, he concluded matter-of-factly that it is the central positioning of a *gaaga* pilaster that determines the rest of the arrangement and necessarily results in an odd number of spikes. Like his mason colleagues, he employed a simulated process of using his body to demonstrate and verify the mathematical relation of components.[12]

At the start of the next morning, Tonton and Konamadou resumed their calculations from the day before. Konamadou laid the stick and Tonton alternately measured the gaps. When they reached the chalk mark delineating the end of the *gum hu*, they stood tall and proclaimed defiantly to me and the other laborers who waited patiently nearby that their own solution was right: there should be eight spikes! The issue was never openly debated again with Bayeré, but the masons' public authentication of their result evidently gave them a measure of satisfaction and partially restored their tarnished authority in the eyes of their work team. Contented, they began measuring the foundations for the bulky pilasters that would support the vestibule's protective hood. It had been collaboratively determined that these would project sixty centimeters outward from the wall and be a full meter in width in order to give the main entrance an air of gravity and importance.

Mediators

Tonton was soon convinced that I was not working in the service of his client or monitoring the quality and efficiency of their production in any way. He came to appreciate my objective to learn about the masons and their trade skills. He joked about working alongside a *tubaabu* but had no difficulty understanding my strategy of offering free labor in exchange for knowledge. All specialized knowledge, whether masonry or *maraboutage,* came with a price that was weighed in terms of the apprentice's unwaged toil and disciplined obedience or with gifts of money and small luxury items, and often a combination of the two.

Tonoton nevertheless schemed to make me the conduit between him and the client. Rather than approaching the project patron directly, Tonton came instead to me with his endless lists of requirements for the worksite. The mason first demanded a terracotta vessel for storing fresh drinking water, and then requested a new straw hat. He complained that the one Tony bought for him was too large, and he had to wear a wool cap beneath it to keep the brim from slipping over his eyes. He next asked for an extra metal pail for transporting well water, and he forcefully complained that there was an insufficient number of laborers to start building the mud-brick walls of the house. I merely listened to Tonton's petitions, resisting as best I could the role of go-between he urged me to play, and I tried to remain impartial in site politics. Tony also consulted me occasionally for an architect's opinion on design and structural issues, and

Abdullahi, laborer from Burkina Faso and resident of Djenné

again I refrained from offering advice. I repeatedly reinforced the idea that I was here to work for the masons and learn their way of doing things.

Just days after being repudiated by Bayeré for his miscalculation of the *sarafar idye* spikes, and facing growing insubordination from Bamoy and Hasey, as well as from several cheeky laborers, Tonton staged a protest. He arrived at the site, parked his bicycle in the shade of a tree and sat defiantly on a pile of bricks staring out at the river. Tony, who had delivered the work team in the payload of his truck, approached the old mason cautiously to inquire about the delay. Like a detonation, Tonton unleashed a list of demands conditional to continuing the project. "There are only four laborers. That's too few!" he erupted. Tony coolly corrected him, stating that there were sixteen men on-site and he refused to hire any more. "I have only four laborers" Tonton repeated stubbornly. Tony began naming off the members of the team working on the main house, "There are you, and Konamadou, and—" Tonton objected immediately, interjecting that he and Konamadou were masons, not laborers. The growing volume of the debate sparked the interests of Abdullahi, the Mossi laborer, and he moved in closer toward the event like a curious pied crow. Tony politely consented that they should not be counted as laborers, and he made a second attempt at a list "There is Diabaté and—" Again Tonton protested, "Diabaté is an apprentice, and almost a mason!" At this point Abdullahi skillfully positioned himself in the contest. He proffered an opinion, calmly shaking his head in agreement with Tonton and reiterating the mason's claim in a subdued voice. Diabaté's classification was always fascinating in these circumstances, since the inherent ambiguity of the apprentice's position meant that his status could be shifted in either direction depending on the aims of the argument.

Tony was becoming exasperated, but he quickly collected his composure and continued with his register "There is Abdullahi, Hamidou Guindo, Sulayman Sanu the Bobo, and young Mamadou." "Voilà!" shrieked Tonton, "There are only four." Tony shot back "Well, there are sixteen people on this site, and I'm not hiring more, so you had better gather the laborers you need from the available men." Of the sixteen, four were masons, one was an apprentice and the remainder were laborers. One of these, Sedou "the Dogon snake hunter," manned the well, Boucari prepared mud, and five were finishing the guardhouse with Bamoy and Hasey. This time Abdullahi shifted his stance to face Tonton and bobbed his head in full agreement with Tony, repeating the answer that there were already sixteen men.[13] Tonton paused for a moment with pursed lips, and then agreed "Fine, but where will my additional laborers come from? I must have seven." He enumerated the tasks and generously padded the required number of laborers to fortify his position. "You'll have to take them from Bamoy," Tony said, "and maybe work on the guardhouse will just have to slow down."

Tonton conceded to this plan with a fleeting smile, and then immediately laid into Tony about a lack of baskets. "How can I start brickwork on the house with so few baskets?" he demanded, waving an empty one at Tony. Tony struggled to remain calm. "Bayeré is my chief mason and he organizes these things," he said, with a detectable waver in his tone. The Mossi nodded, staring disapprovingly at Tonton. "I need five new ones to transport mortar and to keep some as reserves." Abdullahi swiveled to shake his head now at Tony. "You need to tell me what you need beforehand Tonton, not when we're here on-site and ready to start working," Tony scolded. Abdullahi's head bobbed back and forth like a spectator at a ping pong match. "What other things do you need? I don't want to drive back and forth to town." I interrupted to remind Tonton that he wanted a pail. "Oh yes! A pail!" Again, Tony objected angrily, "Bayeré should be supplying these sorts of things!" After more negotiations, an agreement was finally reached that satisfied Tonton, and Tony announced that he was going to town to fetch the mason's requests. "No!" insisted Tonton suddenly, "We'll make use of what's here and take laborers from Bamoy. The rest can wait." Tony laughed and shook his head in bafflement. Tonton replied with a mischievous grin.

Abdullahi frequently played the role of mediator (*almustasbi*) when disputes arose on-site. He was slender and handsome with kind sparkling eyes and a goatee beard of curly black hair. Abdullahi's tranquil disposition and maturity inspired trust. Though born and raised in Djenné, he proudly celebrated his Mossi origins and visited family relations in Burkina Faso annually. He was thirty-nine and the oldest of the laborers, with a great deal of experience on construction sites. Abdullahi understood construction and was regularly stationed at the side of the masons like an assistant or apprentice, though he never underwent formal training. He actively participated in the masons' discussions about design and structure, but, most important, he was drawn in as a mediator when dissenting stances polarized and horns locked. The use of mediators and intermediaries is widespread.[14] Such roles are institutionalized in associations like the *barey ton* or in wedding and circumcision rituals where members of Djenné's Horso community fulfill this function. It is typically the designated third party who oils negotiations behind legally binding contracts and transactions involving large sums of money. In everyday situations, nonpartisan bystanders commonly assume roles as arbitrators to referee conflicts sometimes between individuals with whom they have no previous acquaintance. The key role of mediators is to diffuse the intensity of the debate by simultaneously appeasing and rebuking the opposing sides, and ultimately leveling the tension so that an agreement can be reached. Most important, this social mechanism procures a settlement by letting off steam without the casualty of humiliation, allowing both sides to keep face.

Much to Hasey and Bamoy's annoyance, Bayeré consented to transfer two of their laborers to Tonton and Konamadou. When Tonton's elaborate plan of action was put into play, however, it proved to be a comedy of errors. After only fifteen minutes the activity had no discernable structure, and Tonton's supposed tidy division of labor fell to pieces. He and Konamadou could lay bricks only so quickly, and the number of men now exceeded the masons' need for materials. The laborers tripped over one another and kept swapping roles among themselves; even Tonton confused their assigned duties. Some of the boys stood idly on the sidelines puzzling over what to do. By lunchtime there was a small migration back to work alongside Bamoy and Hasey at the guardhouse.

Two weeks later Tonton led another mini rebellion, this time requesting that the entire team be permitted to quit at noon on Friday to attend midday prayers. Tony reluctantly consented, but Bayeré firmly refused, threatening that anyone who left early would have to make up for lost time. Tonton tried once more to negotiate a bargain whereby the builders could attend prayers every third Friday, but again his efforts were quashed by Bayeré.

House Walls

The start of brickwork on the main house was initiated with Tonton's utterance of "b'ism Allah" ("In the Name of God" باسم الله). Working at opposite ends of the long front wall, Tonton and Konamadou spread thick layers of smooth mud plaster over the foundations and laid the first bricks. Once the two corners were set, a blue nylon cord was looped around and tautly stretched between them to indicate the inner and outer faces of the fifty-five-centimeter-thick wall and guide the bricklayers. Diabaté initially handed supplies to Tonton, and Abdullahi assisted Konamadou to lay a single course of bricks along the foundation with both masons converging toward the center. To hasten the procedure, Tonton instructed Diabaté to lay bricks at the middle of the wall between the two masons, and I was delegated the apprentice's position at the side of the mason. In his finicky manner, Tonton insisted that I blow the dust off each brick before passing them so that it would not irritate his eyes. This was followed by a vocal complaint that the mortar was too stiff: "This is good for ceiling plaster, not laying bricks!" he grumbled. Tonton ordered the laborers responsible to stop making mortar from old discarded bricks taken from Bayeré's first structure, and instead use the red soil newly excavated from the foundation. The mortar for the first eight courses of brickwork was mixed with cypermethrin to prevent termite infestation. Two men churned the mud with their bare legs and arms. Sulayman Sanu, the Bobo, loathed this task and thoroughly cleansed his limbs with fresh water after each batch was prepared. Nevertheless, by late afternoon, his eyes glazed, his expression became blank, and his reaction time slowed.

Meanwhile, Diabaté had selected a random spot near the center of the long wall to begin his bricklaying. Tonton had chalked the location of the main door onto the foundations, but in his eagerness the apprentice paid no notice to the white lines and commenced a rapid progression of mortar and bricks between the nylon cords. The client, who was still on-site that morning, came to inspect and proclaimed encouragingly, "Diabaté is a mason today!" Tonton paused at the end of the wall to shake his trowel at Tony, "Non! On n'a pas dit!" making it patently clear that Diabaté had not yet been pronounced a mason by his master. Diabaté was deeply immersed in his activity and continued his section of the wall. A few moments later, Tonton glanced over to make sure the apprentice was keeping his bricks between the blue cords and realized that Diabaté was carelessly bricking over the entrance to the house. He hollered for him to halt, and after making a public display of his ineptitude, Tonton ordered the flustered young man to remove the bricks.

Once the first course of the front wall was complete, bricks were laid at the two remaining corners of the house and the cord was extended to demarcate all four interior and exterior faces. A single course of bricks was laid along the two side walls of the house, followed by the long rear wall, leaving gaps in the brickwork for the entrances to the various rooms. The first course of the five interior partition walls was laid next. The interior doorways connecting bedrooms and parlours (*tasika* and *galia*) were not centrally positioned. This asymmetry was a deliberate response to the forecasted plans for the storey above. The client's wish for a vast open-planned second storey had been resolved earlier by the decision to support the roof with a central line of pillars running along the longitudinal axis of the space. These load-bearing pillars needed to be fully supported by load-bearing walls below. Like the exterior walls, the ground-storey partitions were fifty-five centimeters thick and solid.

The spatial planning for both storeys was now established and the configuration of ground-storey rooms was laid out on the foundations with a course of bricks. The remainder of work this season would be somewhat mechanical and monotonous. The ground storey would be raised in three vertical stages, each of eight bricks high. Tonton refused to use any grey-colored bricks for the exterior walls. He reserved these for interior partitions, declaring that all bricks on the exterior should be the reddish ones made from mud along the riverbanks. Not only did Tonton believe that the latter were superior in quality, but he also wanted the color to be consistent for aesthetic reasons even though the house would later be plastered with mud. The slender *sarafar* pilasters on the front facade were built in tandem with the walls and their brickwork was securely interlocked with the main structure. Bricks for the *sarafar* were chosen carefully, and only those that were well shaped with sharp edges and intact corners were used. This guaranteed that the vertical lines of the monumental facade would be crisp and well defined. The introduction of rectangular *tubaabu-ferey* bricks and plumb lines in the first half of the twentieth century produced straighter walls and harsh edges compared to the contours of older houses made from conical *Djenné-ferey*. This has altered the character of Djenné's architecture, but erosion from the sun, wind, and rain quickly softens the profiles.

Tonton permitted Diabaté to lay bricks for the first eight courses, and he anxiously put his budding skills to the task. The mason kept a close eye on the apprentice, correcting him when necessary and strictly reminding him to keep the brick faces aligned with the blue cords and to check them regularly with a plumb line. When the builders reached the fourth course, the zealous apprentice began slopping down mortar and piling bricks before the two corners had been set and the cord adjusted to the next level. Tonton harshly reprimanded Diabaté for his recklessness, and a group of laborers nearby snickered nervously. With head hung low, Diabaté silently assisted the masons in raising the cord and then continued his work more attentively. As the height of the walls progressed, the team found that its rhythm and materials flowed smoothly. An average of 1,100 bricks were laid each day, and Bayeré now had eight dedicated brick makers producing daily quotas of a 100 to 150 bricks to meet the project's requirements. This total would decrease as the walls got higher and the masons had to balance gingerly on top of the walls to work. When all walls were built to eight courses high, Konamadou assembled a low platform inside one room equal to the height of the finished floor level. He then asked the client to stand on top in order to gauge the height of the windowsills in relation to his body. Tony was a tall Dutchman and the house would be tailored to his measurements. After briefly discussing the matter, a mid-chest height was selected so that Tony could gaze comfortably out the small square apertures to the river. The human body was the yardstick for many building dimensions.

Konamadou's assistant Abdullahi was diligent and well prepared. Abdullahi selected bricks of appropriate quality, and he kept a reserve of half-bricks and assorted broken pieces for when the mason needed to fill odd gaps in the wall. Diabaté, on the other hand, was assisted by Mamadou, a teenage Bozo laborer from Djenné who was roughly Diabaté's age. Mamadou was a highly unpredictable character and displayed an aggressive tendency toward his fellow workers. Quite out of the blue, he decided that he wanted to be a "head laborer," like Abdullahi, and have a more direct involvement in the masonry work. Rather than helping Diabaté, Mamadou interfered persistently with the apprentice's efforts. He spread mortar with his bare hands and intercepted bricks being delivered to Diabaté in order to lay them himself. If the apprentice or masons put down their trowels, Mamadou swiped the tools to work on his own little patch of wall. In an attempt to imitate Konamadou, he held bricks in one hand and awkwardly flipped them over from one edge to the next, sometimes dropping and breaking them. Konamadou nimbly flipped bricks in his hand in order to assess their geometries and contours, but the young laborer was clueless about the real purpose of this exercise. Mamadou was a nuisance and regularly aggravated the others, but he was rarely reprimanded, and in fact often ignored. All the masons recognized that there was something not quite right about the boy, and it was rumored that his father was an abusive bully. They almost conceived of Mamadou as a young child lacking a fully developed sense of reason (*hollo,* literally "crazy" or "foolish"), and therefore collectively determined that disciplining him wasn't worth the effort. Some of the men believed that he had "caught" his madness in the blowing *harmattan* dust. Certainly meningitis is contracted in this way, and the disease can cause both deafness and brain damage.

There were intermittent periods when the *harmattan* winds died, the dust settled, and we were exposed to intense sunshine and baking heat. I bought every team member a wide-brimmed straw hat for protection like the one the client gave Tonton. When the steady winds returned, the men tied straps under their chins to keep their hats from blowing away. The Qurʿanic-school laborers had no money to buy a change of vest and trousers, and their clothes became ragged with the passing months. One lunch, Sulayman Sanu sat on a stack of bricks mending a trouser leg he had snagged on a branch. Using an

Rising walls of the main house at Sanuna

acacia thorn as a needle and a twisted length of plastic carrier bag for thread, he carefully stitched the plastic through small holes that he punctured in the fabric on each side of the long tear and tied knots at each end to keep the mend in place. Unfailingly the winds returned, blowing with renewed force and masking the sun with a heavy blanket of grey. Thick dust stung our eyes and blinded our lovely view to the opposite banks of the river.

The walls of the house were now approaching two meters and it would soon be time to install the palm-wood lintels over doorways and windows following the same procedures as those at the guardhouse. At this height only the two masons continued laying bricks, and Diabaté reoccupied his former position on the ground passing materials to Tonton. Powerful gusts swept across the river, threatening to topple the masons from their perches on the walls. They caught their balance each time, crouching low and shielding their eyes with their hands until the wind subsided. The full significance of the masons' special relation to the agile little *m'baaka* lizard was made plain in these circumstances. In the midst of one dusty squall, Tonton stood up straight, faced the wind head-on, and loudly proclaimed that it was "le caca des Dogons!" This provocation incited one of the many good-humored rallies of bantering between Tonton's Bozo comrades and the Dogon laborers.

End of the Season

The foreign client took a long trip home to Holland to escape the soaring temperatures and blowing dust of the Sahel. Truck transport therefore ceased, and those without bicycles were forced to make the long journey on foot taking nearly an hour each way. It wasn't long before more men found bicycles to borrow, and they charitably transported their colleagues back and forth to the site.

After the guardhouse walls were plastered and its doors and Moroccan-style windows installed, Bamoy and Hasey took over work on the main house, and Tonton and Konamadou began building the masonry embankment along the river. Constructing the embankment wall followed the very same procedures as those for making concrete foundation footings for the boundary wall and the buildings. The concrete and stone embankment would protect the land from flooding and erosion when the river breaks its banks. The footings were dug more deeply than the house foundations to keep the wall from toppling and washing away, and vast quantities of stones and cement were used. The laborers' tasks were tedious, involving mostly sheer strength and little skill. For entertainment we organized contests to determine who could carry the heaviest stones or toss them farthest. "National" teams were represented by Dogon, Bozo, and a single Canadian. The young men were highly conscious of their physical fitness, and they firmly correlated strength and muscle bulk with eating red meat. In these discussions, a particular emphasis was placed on eating the heads of various animals for strength and power. Some of the Qurᶜanic students moaned that they had scrawny arms and could not carry heavy stones because they could not afford meat and ate only a steady diet of steamed rice and sauce.

The earlier wave of illness was superseded by a spate of minor injuries. Konamadou deeply sliced his index finger on the edge of his trowel. It became horribly infected, so he applied a fine black powder that he kept safe in a metal pillbox. The powder was prepared by a *donso* (hunter) from burnt medicinal leaves and was meant to reduce the swelling. Three days later Konamadou stayed home from work with debilitating pain that spread through his left hand. He was replaced temporarily by a tall Horso mason named Traoré, and only after a course of antibiotics and much rest was Konamadou able to return to the site. Anasse, who had fully recovered from malaria, was ailing once again, but this time with tetanus. He punctured his heel on a rusty nail and resisted a visit to Djenné's hospital for a vaccination until he spiked a fever. One afternoon I visited him at his *marabout*'s house where he shared a tiny room with seven other young men. The dreary space was cramped and windowless, lit by the cold glow of a fluorescent tube. The men's scanty belongings were draped over lines and hung on nails driven into the thick mud walls; there were no mattresses or other furnishings. Anasse lied shivering on a woven mat trying to stay warm under a thin woolen blanket. Beads of perspiration soaked his forehead, and he could not eat. Fortunately his Mossi friend, Salam, took leave from the building site to perform tasks around the house for their *marabout*. Salam kept watch over Anasse until he recovered. Like most *garibou*, they had only each other for support and security.

Konamadou and Anasse recuperated and returned to the building site before my final day of work. After sharing lunch around the giant bowl, my colleagues invited me to join them in prayer by the river. I politely declined the offer but followed them down to the receding edge where they made ablutions in its slow-moving waters. A majestic black kite circled overhead, and in the distance, a Fulani, shaded by the enormous brim of his hat, shuffled across the grassy riverbed trailing his herd of long-horned zebu. The serene beauty of this place is matched equally by its hardship. Later that evening I visited Konamadou to bring him a pair of training shoes and a T-shirt. In return, he presented me with a generous gift of beaded bracelets to take to the women in my family and a box of biscuits for my long journey home.

Part 2 · Portraits of Life and Work in Djenné

Rear elevation of the house at Sanuna with ground-storey arcaded veranda

5 · Master and Apprentice

The Start of a New Building Season

In January 2002 Mali proudly hosted the "African Cup of Nations" (CAN 2002) football tournament. The event kicked off near the start of the building season. The crimson, green, and gold of Mali's flag fluttered throughout the country, and there was a general air of excitement as people huddled closely around televisions to watch the evening matches. The only television in Tolober village was the black-and-white set at the Cultural Mission where I stayed. It was powered by a small and noisy generator that supplied the Mission with a few hours of electricity every evening. The director maintained an open-house policy regarding evening television viewing, and during the football season the TV was placed on a table at one end of the open-air courtyard to accommodate the larger crowd of neighbors who came to watch. The other hugely popular program was a French translation of a Brazilian soap opera about Sao Paolo's fabulously wealthy. All eyes focused intensely on the flickering screen, and not a peep was heard except for an occasional empathetic sigh for a forlorn lover or a hiss at a callous villain. The moment the program ended there was a burst of applause, and animated chatter filled the crisp night air as young men, women, and children exited, exchanging opinions and forecasts for the next episode. A quarter of an hour or so later the houseboy switched off the generator, leaving the night to the soft serenade of chirping crickets and croaking frogs.

On my first morning back to work I found many changes awaiting me at Sanuna. Salif Toulayma, the former brick maker, spotted me from a distance as I pedaled over the bumpy, dusty road to the site. "Abu Bakr!" he bellowed, waving his arms high in the air in an uncharacteristically gregarious manner. Salifou recounted how he had abandoned his former backbreaking occupation as a brick maker and was now installed as Tony's house guardian, taking up residence in the small building adjacent to the gate. Tony regarded him as mature and highly trustworthy, and the appointment clearly boosted Salifou's spirits and self-esteem. He now held a respectable job, and the steady income had enabled him to take a wife. His wife was roughly half his age—a real live wire with a hearty laugh and jolly sense of humor. She clearly amused him, and the worry in his eyes seemed to have vanished. As the new woman on-site she had taken over the duties once performed by the Somono neighbor, and she was now in charge of preparing daily lunch for the work crew. That day, Salifou was pressed to run errands in town, so he interrupted our brief exchange and sent me in the direction of the main house where the team was working.

A group of laborers preparing materials at ground level had already announced my arrival to the others, and faces poked one by one through open windows as I made my way to the house. The project had advanced markedly since I was last here. The second storey walls had been completed and masons were now finishing the roof structure and building stairs in the tower situated at the far end of the veranda. Cow horns, whose hollow interiors harbored secret handwritten benedictions, protruded from the wall surface above several doorways, warding off evil spirits and mal-intentioned visitors. The series of impressive arched apertures along the second-storey veranda had been built, and the large openings would remain sealed up with the brick formwork until heavy construction had ended. When all the main structural work was finished, many tasks would still remain. Stacks of bricks were scattered about and piles of earth lay waiting to be trampled into mortar and plaster. Moroccan-style wooden windows and doors had been installed in the ground-floor rooms but had not yet been fitted into those above. The grand *gum hu* over the entrance of the Tukolor facade had not been started, nor had the sculpted roofline parapet and pinnacles that would ultimately lend the house its monumental presence and distinctive, vertical grace—the hallmark of Djenné's architecture. Nevertheless, the house was already impressive for its enormous volume and spectacular location commanding sweeping views of the river.

There were fourteen laborers to start the season, but this number would decrease as the project neared completion. Several faces were new, replacing laborers who had either left town, found new work, or been dismissed for slacking. Only two masons were hired back this year, as the operational budget had been trimmed and all efforts were now focused on the one building. I climbed the unfinished staircase to the roof to greet the masons working there. Baba had returned from Bamako and resumed his duties as head mason, assisted by his brother, Bamoy. Baba was always a perfectly poised gentleman with thoughtful, engaging eyes, and his tranquil confidence softened Bamoy's somewhat confrontational edge. They reported almost immediately that their youngest brother, Hasey, had contracted a dreadful illness and had been bedridden since last summer. A raging fever had seized him, and the constant pounding in his head made him delirious and aggressive; often he could not recognize people. Hasey's case remained undiagnosed by doctors who treated him, and neither African nor Western medicines, purchased at considerable cost to the family, had any effect. They hoped that with time and rest their young brother would recover. An uneasy quiet hung in the air, so I made an attempt to change the subject by inquiring about Tonton and Konamadou Djennepo. The conversation then took another awkward turn. Bamoy's silence deepened, and he squatted back down to continue arranging the twiggy branches that spanned the palm wood beams in the ceiling below.[1] "Tonton and Djennepo aren't working here anymore," Baba responded almost sheepishly. He was clearly uncomfortable about the issue. When I gently persisted to find out why, he advised that it was best to ask the chief mason, Bayeré.

Finding a New Site

Apart from Tonton and Konamadou, another key player missing from the team was the apprentice, Mama Kourani's young trainee, Diabaté. He had not been available when Bayeré rounded up the team to recommence work on the Sanuna project, and so he was now employed on occasional jobs with other masons. At the present time Diabaté was earning a daily wage at another of Bayeré's building projects in town—one being supervised by the fourth of the Kouroumansé brothers whom I was soon to meet.

Building activity in Djenné was plentiful that season. Neat rows of drying bricks skirted the water's edge, and piles of red laterite obstructed the narrow streets of the old town. Rains had been generous during the past two years, yielding abundant harvests, verdant pastures for livestock, and a steady supply of fish in the nearby rivers. Many residents had sufficient money to pay for necessary repairs and maintenance to their homes, and in some cases they commissioned new rooms, an additional storey, or even the complete rebuilding of their danger-ously deteriorating houses. In newer town quarters and in the outlying village of Tolober, several one-storey houses had pilasters and pinnacles pretentiously at-tached to their street facades in what amounted to crude attempts to emulate the monumental style of the urban elite. Two-storey houses in some of Djenné's historically poorer quarters, like Djoboro, were being erected in the traditional Moroccan style (and, less frequently, in Tukolor style) that was once the preserve of wealthy and established merchant-traders and distinguished *marabouts*.

Upcoming stages in the construction at the riverside house intrigued me from a technical perspective, especially the building of the *gum hu* and the care-fully calculated arrangement of roofline miters. But the absence of an apprentice on-site seriously frustrated my objective to understand the training and trans-mission of knowledge and expertise to younger generations in the trade. I there-fore opted to join another team of masons, this time working on house projects located in the heart of the historic town. The switch to this new team was facili-tated once again by Bayeré, since it was also one of his projects. Though still young and tremendously energetic, Bayeré rarely engaged in any actual ma-sonry work anymore, but had fashioned a more lucrative and less physically demanding role for himself as a sort of contractor/project manager. He catered to an assortment of clients, from the handful of ex-patriot Europeans who took up residence to local *marabouts* and regular Djenné residents whose contractual relations he had inherited from his father and uncle, both masons themselves. Bayeré was also responsible for monitoring the restoration of houses financed by the Dutch. With a long pale-blue Touareg scarf turbaned around his head, a denim jacket, dark-tinted sunglasses, and a cigarette coolly dangling from his bottom lip, Bayeré scooted around town on his moped, calling in on clients, sites, and suppliers. He commonly had numerous projects on the go, and in the evenings he balanced budgets, calculated materials, and formulated schedules. He moaned, theatrically, that his managerial tasks were far more taxing than the physical labor of the masons whose day ended at 3:00 PM, but he clearly relished the challenges that his work offered.

The site mason in charge of both the houses I would work on that season was an exceedingly amiable character named al-Hajji Kouroumansé. Al-Hajji was the most extraordinary talent I would work with in Djenné, and my own apprenticeship under him occurred jointly with the training of two younger men he was molding in the trade. Al-Hajji was the brother of Baba, Bamoy, and Hasey, and he was the second eldest. There was also a sister born between Baba and al-Hajji, and another between al-Hajji and Bamoy. Bayeré was their paternal cousin, and the four mason brothers profited from his wide network of patrons. The jobs he farmed out provided them with vital sources of income. When I met al-Hajji on-site, he warmly welcomed me to his team and instructed me to show up at 8:00 AM the next morning. We agreed that I would not be paid a salary, but rather, like an apprentice, I would earn my training and knowledge through dedicated physical effort. Like the Sanuna project, this arrangement more directly benefited the client or Bayeré who controlled the budget and paid the salaries, but al-Hajji was content to have me onboard since he had come to know about me through his brothers. Al-Hajji's team was currently reconstructing a two-storey house with a monumental street facade in the Moroccan style, and a small courtyard at the back. The Dutch government was financing the project as part of a cooperative effort with Mali to preserve the town's architectural heritage. This particular house project originated as a restoration but eventually transformed into a complete reconstruction. The house belonged to a *marabout* named Sekou Haydarah, who, as a *sharif,* traced his descent to the prophet Muhammad. The historic house was situated in Yobukayna, an old quarter west of Djenné's mosque.[2]

Flu prevented me from keeping my appointment the following morning, and I only got back on my feet two days later. There wasn't a soul around when I arrived at 8:00 AM, and the big wooden door of the house was bolted shut. I initially thought the starting time had been postponed, so I paid a brief breakfast visit to Konamadou Djennepo who lived in the Semani quarter across town. When I returned at 8:30 the door was wide open, but the site was strangely quiet. A current of dank air filled my nostrils with the odor of freshly wetted soil. I stepped into the darkness of the large vestibule (*siifa*) with ears perked and followed the faint rhythmic reverberations of a slapping noise coming from a room somewhere to the left. The sound grew louder as I approached, and inside I found a young builder teetering on a narrow, bowing timber plank that spanned the tops of two oil drums. He was busily applying a coat of mud plaster to the ceiling with only the light from a tiny window to illuminate his task. In a graceful arcing motion, he scooped the oozing mud from a basket balanced at his feet, swept his torso upright and slapped the mixture firmly against the palm-wood ceiling beams with his right hand. Using the same palm, he smoothed it out in broad sweeps over the irregular contours. He introduced himself to me by his nickname, "Yappi." His full name was Konamadou Konsinantao, and he was the older and more experienced of al-Hajji's two apprentices. He hopped down from his perch to tell me the whereabouts of the other builders, but he was eager to engage me in a chat. He immediately impressed me as an intensely ambitious and outgoing character: rather tall, a broad smile of perfect white teeth, long curling lashes, and round bright eyes that he fixed on me as we spoke.

Yappi told me that there had been a sudden change in the work schedule. The team was working on two projects in tandem: one was the reconstruction of this house and the other the construction of a large new house for a French ex-patriot who had acquired land in the heart of the Djoboro quarter. "Rather than working simultaneously on both projects," Yappi explained, "al-Hajji chooses to focus his efforts on one at a time, alternating between the two and transferring his entire team with him." The mason's choice of which project to work on at a given time necessarily juggled client pressures to complete their respective works, and also responded to the availability and stocks of building materials. A frequent short-age in the supply of palm trunks necessary for the construction of ceilings and roofs meant that building often came to a standstill once the walls had been erected to full height. Consequently, construction would resume at the alternate project. Al-Hajji periodically sent Yappi to spend the day plastering the com-pleted interior rooms at the dormant project. Such tasks delegated a certain de-gree of autonomy to the young man, and he was placed in charge of the hired laborers who assisted him. Both house projects had been started the previous building season and were nearing completion. They offered me an opportunity to participate in the later phases of house construction and expand the technical know-how I had already gained from the earlier stages of setting foundations and erecting walls at the riverside site in Sanuna. Over the next months I would learn about mud-brick arch construction and, more important, the sculpting of deco-rative elements. I would also meet a whole new cast of characters who would deepen my understanding of personal and professional relations.

Before pedaling off to join the rest of the team in Djoboro, Yappi seized the occasion to brief me about his own life situation, and, certainly, to probe what potential use I might be to him. Over the next months he would reveal himself to be a highly complex and strategic character. He was an individual who con-tinually prompted me to reassess my ideas of what it was to be a mason's appren-tice, or even a citizen in this remote Islamic town of the Inland Niger Delta. Yappi was twenty-seven years old and strongly believed he was too well educated for this line of manual work. He had not elected to become a mason. After the death of his father, his mother and older brother had decided to put him into the build-ing profession. While extracting tiny wood splinters from his palm with his muddy fingernails, he protested in a mildly arrogant tone that his intelligence was being wasted. He conceded to having performed poorly in his final school exams two years ago but thought he deserved a second chance. His ambition was to become a civil engineer and abandon Djenné for better prospects in Bamako or even abroad. But the family had foreclosed further schooling options, and he would remain trapped unless some compassionate soul could help him escape this drudgery. His narrative was well rehearsed, and I was starting to feel uneasy. "Life in Canada must be great! Could you sponsor me to get a visa for Canada?" he pressed all too predictably. I had faced that request countless times in Mali. I harbored no romantic notions about the hardships people faced here, and I entirely sympathized with his ambitions to leave, but I also knew that I was powerless. For someone like Yappi, with only a limited education and no money or political connections, getting into Canada as a legal immigrant would be exceedingly difficult. He was nevertheless determined to leave this town, and he would later return to his agenda in a highly unconventional and daring guise.

Djoboro was a densely populated maze of narrow streets and alleyways. It was said to be the oldest quarter of town, first settled by the early Islamicized populations leaving Djenné-Djeno in the twelfth century.[3] Like its neighboring southern quarters, Djoboro's residents were largely tradesmen or from the poorer artisan, laboring, and farming classes. Open trenches running down the center of its muddy streets overflowed with fetid sewage, and piles of rotting garbage collected on abandoned properties and at roadsides.[4] A barrage of different odors infused the air with a mix of sweet frying plantain, the rank smell of goats, and the stench of decay and human excrement. Djoboro contained few monumental houses; the new one al-Hajji was constructing was a notable exception.

Navigating the route from Yobukayna that first morning proved tricky and I lost my way on several occasions. Yappi's brisk instructions of "lefts" and "rights," interspersed with an array of landmarks to look out for, had become a soupy jumble in my head once immersed in the thicket of streets. As I pedaled, I glanced fleetingly down alleyways and between walls in search of familiar sights while keeping an eye on the degraded condition of the road beneath my tires. Several times I carried my bicycle over wide channels of thick slime. Through a crevice between buildings I caught a glimpse of the clay spikes (*sarafar idye*)[5] that identified the Brunet-Jailly house in the distance. It rose distinctly above the surrounding buildings of the neighborhood. A group of women gossiping at a communal water tap gave me my final clues, and I found my way around to the rear of the house and into the courtyard.

The Brunet-Jailly house, owned by a French professor working at the Institut de Recherche pour Développement in Bamako, was situated on a large lot that had been abandoned by the original owners and was now occupied by a

Rimaïbe family. The professor had purchased the land from the proprietors and offered the squatting residents employment as caretakers for his property. There were two entrances to his new home: one through the grand, south-facing Moroccan-style facade situated along the border of a narrow street, and a back entrance accessed through a twisting alley that led into a substantial courtyard dominated by a north-facing Tukolor-style facade. At the time of my study it was the only house in Djenné that united these historically distinct local building styles—Moroccan and Tukolor—in a single edifice. According to Amadou Tahirou Bah, a founding member of the Djenné Patrimoine group,[6] the exemplar construction of Brunet-Jailly's house would inspire others to maintain their grand residences and sponsor the building of new ones in traditional styles. The elegant interior, with its tasteful locally made furnishings and fabrics, recesses in the mud-block walls framed by softly sculpted relief patterns, and wall and ceiling surfaces rendered in mud plasters of various rich hues, effectively demonstrated that an earthen abode could provide a stylish and hygienic living environment. The project had begun one year earlier, and the builders had worked beyond the normally short building season through the month of August to complete the main house. By the time I joined they were constructing the second storey of a narrow auxiliary building extending from the southwest corner of the house along the southern edge of the courtyard.

Al-Hajji and the other builders were already at work, and two young boys were unloading a fresh delivery of red earth from a mule-pulled cart. I greeted everyone loudly and parked my bike in the shade beside the house. One laborer anxiously inquired where I had disappeared to since first meeting them at the *marabout*'s house three days ago. I explained, apologetically, that I had been tucked beneath bed sheets with the typical sort of throat infection, flu, and fever that plagues the Sahel during this dry, dusty *harmattan* season. I climbed the stairs in the courtyard to the second storey of the auxiliary building to greet al-Hajji and Bamoy Sao, the second mason assisting him. The three massive towers of the Djenné mosque created a dramatic backdrop to the jumbled roofscape that spread before us from the second-storey workstation. House plans in the densely populated heart of town conform to the irregular geometries of plots. Many are two storeys and inhabitants make use of their roof terraces for drying millet and chilli peppers, or for outdoor sleeping during the hottest months. Dwellings built in the newer quarters along the town's edge are aligned with the orthogonal grid of wide streets. These mainly single-storey buildings are planned around interior courtyards, and their boxy features lack the decorative embellishments and grandeur of the old houses.

Like my first day at the riverside site the year before, I spent most of this day observing and establishing relationships with the builders. I was immediately struck by how much closer they worked together as a team and by how casual their interactions were. The two masons, both Bozo, had a history of collaboration, and all the laborers were town residents, mainly of Djoboro. Unlike the previous corps I worked with, none were full-time Qurʿanic students. The team was also comparatively smaller. There were only six laborers including the two apprentices, and three of the young men were siblings. Each of the Bouaré brothers had radically distinct personalities, and as the season progressed I would learn how they all played significant roles in the entangled social connections between the team members.

This first day of work was cut short by the midday call to prayer. Friday was the only day of the week when work halted at 1:30 rather than 3:00 PM. The men filed down the stairs into the courtyard and washed up with clean water from an oil drum before heading home to make proper ablutions and don a *grand boubou*. Shortly after the *muezzin*'s voice beckoned to all the faithful, the streets of Djenné turned to rivers of vivid colors, the currents converging in kaleidoscopic formations on the same focal point. Wafting perfumes and spicy scents filled the air for this eventful moment each week. Robes of fine cotton floated elegantly on limbs that carried them swiftly and silently to prayer. Solid oranges, purples, and blues embroidered with spiraling lines and magic squares rubbed shoulders with brazen wax-print patterns of arabesques, geometric shapes, and amoebic swirls. Most men of the town, young and old, congregated for the Friday prayers: residents from the northern and southern quarters entering the soaring waxen structure of the mosque by their respective doors. When the prayers finished, like gravity reversed, the colors flowed back along the same routes from whence they had come.

Al-Hajji Kouroumansé

Al-Hajji's real name was Lasine, which was his father's name and also the name he gave his second-born son. Lasine was born in 1964 and later received the nickname al-Hajji in honor of his paternal grandfather who had made the pilgrimage (*hajj*) to the Holy Arabian Cities of Islam when he was just thirty-three years old—a considerable economic and religious feat for so young a person from a distant and impoverished West African nation. When the original bearer of the title died, it was common practice in Djenné for a younger member of the family to inherit the title "al-Hajji," thereby transferring the prestige associated with fulfilling this fifth pillar of the Islamic faith to a succeeding generation.

Al-Hajji Kouroumansé and his three brothers were all masons. Their father, Lasine Kouroumansé, had also practiced masonry in the past but his interests were primarily devoted to trading, and he regularly journeyed to Mopti where he bought and sold fish. Lasine's wife, Hawa Yonou, wanted all her sons to be fully invested in a proper Djenné-based trade. She felt that fish trading was not sufficiently reliable and discouraged her sons from this pursuit. With her husband's consent, Hawa made an agreement with her paternal cousin, Sulayman Yonou, to take on al-Hajji and his older brother, Baba, as apprentices. The Yonous were a well-regarded family of masons in Djenné. Sulayman's father, Sekou Yonou, and Hawa's father, Baba Yonou (brothers born of the same mother and father), were masons, and both had sons who followed successfully in their footsteps. Hawa's brother, Beré Yonou, though too old at the time of my study to actively engage in much heavy building, was highly esteemed in the profession not only for his mastery of trade skills but also for his pious demeanor. A mason's persona was judged both by the competency of his hands and his moral constitution. Beré Yonou's pilgrimage to Mecca further augmented his status within Djenné's influential religious community, and he was occasionally responsible for broadcasting the call to prayer from Djenné's mosque. Hawa had chosen to place her first two sons under the tutelage of her cousin, Sulayman, however, rather than her brother, Beré, to avoid the accusation of nepotism in her planning. Her decision was calculated to preserve a balance of power in the Yonou family while sustaining a sense of cohesion among her kin.[7]

Al-Hajji began working for his uncle, Sulayman, in 1970, at the age of six. Like other young boys working on building sites, he was delegated small duties which consisted mainly of carrying materials and supplies to the masons.[8] Reminiscing about his early training, al-Hajji recounted, "When I started, I was so small that I couldn't even carry a single mud brick. I hauled so many baskets of mud mortar balanced on top of my head that I lost the hair on my crown!" He lifted his woollen cap and bowed his head forward to show me the lasting bald patch. As al-Hajji and his brother Baba grew older, their uncle gave them increasing responsibilities, and they began to work more closely at his side learning the skills of the trade. That privileged position introduced them to the mason's bag of principal tools—the plumb line, crowbar, "black-skin" trowel, "French" trowel, tape measure, string level, and "French" level.[9] Assisting, observing, mimicking, and practicing honed their building techniques, and listening versed them in the mason's lore. They were a captive audience to negotiations with clients, disputes with suppliers, the management of a labor force, and the often politically charged interactions between masons. Both their father and uncle taught them to recite secret incantations (*sirri*) and to perform rites that protected them from harm, warded off potentially harmful spells cast by other masons, and guaranteed the structural integrity of their edifices. Together, all these factors forged the young men's identity as members of Djenné's building community, and ultimately instilled knowledge of their social position, professional responsibilities, and power within the broader community of craftsmen. In the case of these Yonou and Kouroumansé men, their identity as masons was also tightly entwined with the ethnic history of their Bozo people, who continue to play a prominent role in this trade.

Baba, as the senior of the Kouroumansé brothers, was declared a mason before al-Hajji, and he subsequently took charge of training their youngest brother Hasey. Bamoy, the third son, was placed under the guidance of his maternal uncle, Beré Yonou. Sulayman Yonou declared al-Hajji a mason in 1985, ritually presenting him with trade tools and offering benedictions (*albarka*) for a prosperous future. Sulayman, abiding by his obligations as a master mason, began delegating independent building commissions to his former apprentice and thereby transferred some of his established client base to al-Hajji. When I worked with him in 2002, al-Hajji was already an accomplished mason in his own right and was gaining recognition from his peers. Despite his success and his commitment to the profession for more than thirty years, he declared that he had no desire for any of his sons to follow his lead into the building trade. "The work is too difficult and the pay too little," he said. "Baba has eight children and doesn't send them to school. His sons will probably become masons, but not mine. I will send all three of my children to school. It's very important to read and write, and to learn French. I never had the opportunity, but my children will." He had two sons born of his first wife and a young daughter from his second. His eldest son, Abdullahi, now eight years old, had contracted meningitis as an infant, leaving him with permanent hearing and speech impairments. Though al-Hajji ideally hoped to keep him in school for as long as possible, he recognized that the boy's career options would be limited in a place like Djenné, and thus determined that he would send him to apprentice with a tailor (*taa-koy*).

Training Apprentices

Masons frequently take their sons to work with them, and those who are in school tag along when they have no class. If old enough, they are given small duties such as cleaning their father's muddy trowel or fetching water or a cup of tea. Mostly they watch the older men work, and, when their attention lapses, they wander off to play or take short naps in the shade. In the eyes of other neighboring children in Djenné, the rising walls of a new house are re-imagined as an extension of their urban playground, and little boys and girls scurry about largely unnoticed by the work team. A favorite activity is mold-ing tiny toys and figures from the soft clay and leaving them to bake in the hot sun.[10] For other young boys, construction sites present potential employment opportunities. As previously discussed, masons commonly hire students from the town's numerous Qurʿanic schools, especially boys who come to study from towns and villages outside Djenné. Local boys—usually those who have dropped out of school or have never been enrolled in the state edu-cational system—are also hired. The youngest on the sites are often under ten years of age, and they struggle to transport baskets of mud mortar. Older boys are hired as full laborers and can be expected to bear a heavier workload.

For the most part, none of these boys ever rises through the ranks to be taken on as an apprentice. Masons waste no effort in passing on technical skills, and they certainly never share trade secrets. The boys are either considered "foreigners," or their families, even if local, have no connections to the building trade. Their role at the site is therefore limited to performing necessary manual tasks such as unloading materials, fetching water, mixing mud mortar, preparing plaster, cutting palm wood, stacking bricks, and relaying all these materials in assembly-line fashion to the masons and apprentices who do the actual building. Masons repeatedly assert that only boys from the town's stock of building fami-lies will be taken on as apprentices and that the trade will remain dominated by Bozo. Though they trace the history of Bozo domination in the trade to three original mason families—the Nassiré, Yonou and Salamantao[11]—present-day access to the profession seemingly transcends ethnic boundaries, social classes, and castes. If heterogeneity is indeed a recent phenomenon, then it likely resulted during the decades of drought in the 1970s and 1980s. At that time, many Bozo masons deserted the region to seek commissions elsewhere, and when building activity resumed in Djenné, the trade, of necessity, absorbed outsiders to fill the vacuum. There has been evidence of ongoing diversification in the local building industry, indicating that boundaries to the trade continue to be porous. This contradicts what masons often reported. Al-Hajji Kouroumansé, for example, had trained several apprentices since he became a mason, some of whom were ethnically non-Bozo including a Horso (who left the trade before completing his apprenticeship) and, most recently a young Bamana, Ali Bouaré.

The Bouaré family were Bamana farmers from the village of Kéké who set-tled in Djenné less than two decades ago. The father opened a Qurʿanic school

RIGHT Apprentice Ali Bouaré

in the small house they rented in the Djoboro quarter, but the *marabout* Bouaré died in 2001, leaving behind his wife, four sons, and a daughter, with no other family members in the town to look after them and lend support. Ali was the third son and the couple's first Djenné-born child, and his mother now considered him old enough to earn a living and contribute to the household. Ali's mother was tactical in deciding to find her son a respected urban trade that would secure his, as well as her own, financial future and social status in the town. She approached the young mason al-Hajji Kouroumansé, who was a neighbor in their quarter, and asked him to take on her son, Ali, as an apprentice. Al-Hajji agreed, and Ali's two older brothers, Abdullahi and Sulayman, were made part of the deal to work as building laborers when not occupied with farming the family land in Kéké. Ali fully accepted that his own ambitions would remain secondary to his mother's wishes. He had no real decision-making power in matters regarding his career, but, when he began his apprenticeship, he set out to learn his trade with great determination in order to become a mason.

In Djenné, parents commonly make career choices on behalf of their sons, and, in trades such as masonry, carpentry, pirogue building, tailoring, embroidering, and shoemaking, parents arrange for their child's training under the guidance of a suitable mentor usually known to the family. Elder siblings also make such decisions for their younger brothers in the absence of a paternal household authority. Regarding other skilled groups such as blacksmiths and their potter wives, children most often follow their parents' career path, and usually marry endogamously within the trade group,[12] although, in Djenné, blacksmiths also marry outside, notably with Somono fishermen and farmers.[13] Other studies of apprenticeship have noted that, for various social and economic reasons, mothers and fathers are usually deemed inappropriate teachers.[14] Among Djenné's masons, however, there are no clearly defined rules prescribing specific social relations between master and apprentice. In the building profession, only some, and perhaps none, of a mason's children may take up the trade. If they do follow their father, it may or may not be he who steers the apprenticeship. Many boys in Djenné born into either a paternal or maternal line of masons acquire their skills from an extended family member, and regularly an uncle. Alternatively, they might receive their education from a craftsman of a different bloodline altogether. In fact, many apprentices circulate between several different masons during their lengthy training period, which includes kin and non-kin members. A master sometimes sends his apprentice to work under the direction of another mason, especially during periods when he has little or no work of his own or if he is traveling. This arrangement has the benefit of rounding out the curriculum by exposing the novice to varying expertise and strengths. Significantly for the young man, he earns a laborer's salary on these occasions (750 CFA per day), which he normally would not receive when working for his own master.

The agreements negotiated between a mason and the apprentice's guardian(s) are verbal, with no written contracts. In exchange for the transmission of skills and expert knowledge, the apprentice reciprocates with respect, obedience, and free labor for the duration of his training, which typically lasts several years. In Mandé culture, it is conventional to pay for knowledge and especially "secrets" that are either related to a specific trade or for making incantations, benedictions, and spells. Several masons reported that, in the past, apprentices customarily made regular payments to their masters in the form of small gifts of kola nuts or money (*le prix de thé/kola*). Though this seems to no longer be the case, junior masons do give small gifts to their former mentors and to Djenné's recognized master masons. They explain that the gifts constitute an outward sign of respect, and also secure lines of patronage whereby older masons can be expected to pass on commissions and extra work to younger ones. As already noted, it is also believed that some master masons possess considerable stockpiles of secrets that can be potentially harmful. Even the simple daily greetings they issue to fellow masons when passing a building site, like "Ahaabaa?" ("How are you?"), have the power to cause injury or a structure to fail, and must be guarded against. The *prix de thé* in this case serves to counteract any potentially malevolent force carried by the master mason's words.

An apprentice receives no payment from his master for his work, but he is given small gifts of money, usually during Ramadan and *Tabaski* (*eid al-kabir*), and he periodically receives a new article of clothing or other similar necessities. A master can also be expected to buy the medicine for a sick apprentice, and he may even pay for a doctor's consultation if the illness is deemed serious enough. Wedding arrangements and expenses are the responsibility of the boy's parents, but the mason will lend assistance depending on the family's financial situation. Apprentices under one's tutelage connote prestige and public recognition of one's qualifications. It also allows a mason to secure direct control over the reproduction of his trade knowledge and to perpetuate his craft through successive generations. It is therefore important to foster amicable, even paternal, relations with the young men one has trained and sent out into the profession. A mason may loan his apprentice to another project in order to render a good deed or pay for a favor. The young builder's labor is thereby harnessed as an extension of the mason's piety. For example, al-Hajji sent Yappi, his most senior apprentice,

Mason Bamoy Sao and apprentice Ali Bouaré constructing a lintel

to assist with the plastering of his former Qurʿanic teacher's home where he had studied as a boy. On this occasion Yappi was not paid by the *marabout*'s family; instead, his services were understood as al-Hajji's gesture of respect to the teacher's surviving kin.

Yappi was several years older than Ali Bouaré. His father had been a mason of the Djoboro quarter, and his older brother also practiced in the trade but had few clients of his own. The brother was a close friend of al-Hajji, and so he felt that his younger sibling would be better molded by al-Hajji's hands. At twenty-five years of age, Yappi, like Ali, initiated his apprenticeship at a relatively late age, but he had already accumulated considerable experience on building sites by assisting his father between studies. He was thus accorded a higher rank and delegated greater responsibility than was Ali, who, notably, was neither Bozo nor from a family of masons. When Yappi was sent to do plasterwork at the alternate project, Ali assumed the position of principal apprentice, working beside both al-Hajji and Bamoy Sao. Ali was consistently serious and attentive in this role, preempting the masons' needs and passing on their materials and tools in a timely manner. If al-Hajji left the site to attend to other business or to order materials, Ali assisted Bamoy directly with the building processes, positioning himself symmetrically in relation to the mason. In clear view of each other and working in tandem, Ali could observe and mimic Bamoy, receiving both his verbal directives and visual cues, and, similarly, Bamoy could easily monitor Ali's work and immediately correct any mistakes and miscalculations. When Yappi returned, however, Ali was once again demoted and usually forced to assume a role working with the laborers.

Junior (and sometimes senior) apprentices normally work with the laborers and perform the equivalent manual tasks. From a practical stance, there is often insufficient room at the mason's side for more than one apprentice at a time, especially if they are teetering on the top of a wall laying courses of bricks or aligning ceiling beams. More significant, perhaps, working with the laborers also immerses the apprentice in the basic activities of the building process and therefore, over the long term, broadens his understanding of the organization and mechanics of a construction site; introduces him to the nature, preparation, and handling of the materials; and instills a sense of discipline in his thoughts and actions as a member of a team. With this discipline comes a strict inculcation of recognition and respect for the hierarchy on-site and, more generally, within the trade, thus preparing the apprentice to approach his tasks and learning with diligence and concentration. Nevertheless, Ali's morale inevitably slumped when, with Yappi's arrival, he was knocked back down the hierarchy. Certainly, compared to learning and honing new skills at the side of a mason, relaying baskets of mud mortar and bricks was monotonous. The tempo and rhythm of his work faltered noticeably, and he would start whining about a sore back and feeling unwell. On these occasions Yappi was quick to chime in, loudly, that Ali wasn't sick or sore but simply lazy. Clearly, the intent of the more senior apprentice was not only to usher Ali back into line as a productive member of the team but also to publicly reaffirm his own senior position at the expense of his colleague. Critical comments about the other laborers, and especially those concerning Ali's slackness, evoked the competitive discourse and banter that exists between apprentices to win the recognition and favor of the masons and jockey for promotion.

"Come over here and watch carefully," al-Hajji would pronounce, summoning his apprentices to observe him perform a new task or to amend their poor habits and mistakes by way of example. A few verbal cues directed their attention to salient aspects of his performance, and he would ask them to repeat the task so he could monitor and make corrections. He spoke and gestured calmly while exercising his authority, fostering a mutual respect between himself and the young men, and simultaneously defining and maintaining the master-apprentice hierarchy. For example, Ali was instructed to plaster a wall surface resting directly above a doorway. When Ali had completed the task, al-Hajji returned to examine Ali's efforts, patiently pointing out the general unevenness of the finish and the sloppy plastered edge between the doorway lintel and the mud-brick wall. As al-Hajji took up his trowel to make the needed repairs, he turned to me to say, matter-of-factly, "It's clear he's still an apprentice. He has a lot to learn." Ali silently scrambled to the top of the wall and crouched down adjacent to the door opening so that he could better watch his master at work. Another time Yappi was stationed at his master's side, and the two were engaged in building up the parapet wall at the roof's edge. The parapet would be punctuated at equal intervals by small *fūney* apertures, and Yappi took the initiative to span the top of one rectangular opening with short palm-wood sticks. After spreading generous layers of mortar on each side, he mindfully embedded the sticks one beside the other to create a flat, perfectly horizontal lintel. Al-Hajji watched as his apprentice worked and interjected only at the very end to make minor adjustments. The mason was pleased with his apprentice's efforts and congratulated him by calling him *bey-koy* (expert). Such playful exaggerations were spoken periodically and in this case offered reassurance that Yappi was on the right path.

Becoming a Mason

The apprentice's major test is when his master asks him to construct a brick wall on his own, demonstrating that he can do so without flaws. If errors are made, he is instructed to dismantle the structure and begin anew. When he finally succeeds in erecting a perfectly vertical and structurally sound wall, and can do so repeatedly, the master presents his apprentice with a plumb line, the cost of which depends on the grade in quality. Neither Yappi nor Ali had earned their plumb lines yet, but al-Hajji promised that when they did, he would present them with the highest grade 9 plumb lines, costing approximately 5000 CFA each. Although the plumb line augments the apprentice's status, he will not necessarily be promoted to the rank of mason for some time. Final judgment rests with the master. When he deems that his protégé is fully qualified to be officially recognized as a mason in Djenné, he announces his decision at the next meeting of the *barey ton*. The apprentice himself is not present, as it is customary that only full-fledged masons attend *barey ton* meetings. The community of builders can be expected to accept the mason's decision without objection, and no official committee-based discussion seems to be necessary regarding access to the trade.

RIGHT Flared end of a *sasiré* crowbar, a principal tool of the masons

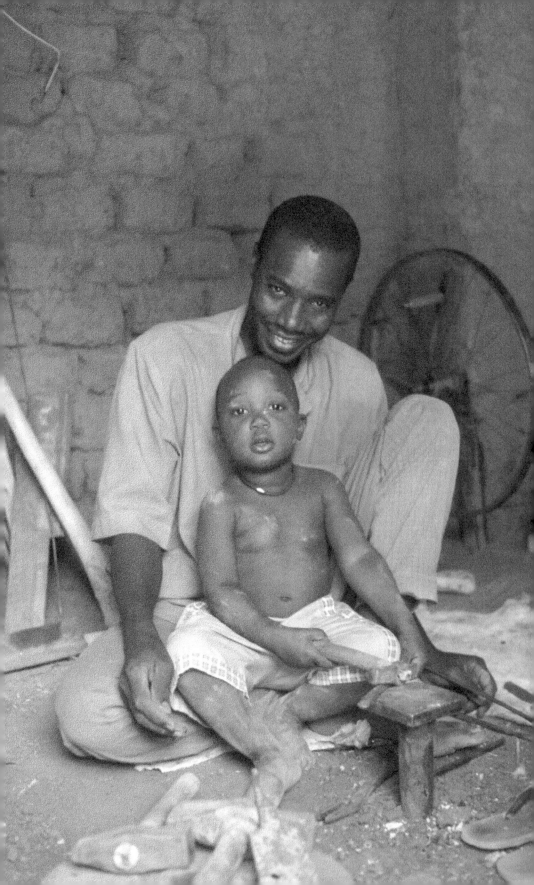

Negotiations do occur, however, but, arguably, in a more covert manner, one that emphasizes social, moral, and professional reputations. Because the apprentice circulates during his training period to work on different projects and in cooperation with various masons, the members of this close-knit trade become familiar with the young man's conduct and his trade-related skills. A mason, effectively, would jeopardize the reputation of his own professional judgment, and perhaps of his skills as well, were he to champion the promotion of an incompetent initiate. Poor judgment calls can mean a loss of face among peers, and more tangible repercussions can be experienced in the form of exclusion from cooperative projects organized by the *barey ton*. This may also explain why boys are often turned over either to an extended family member or a non-related craftsman for their training, even when the father himself is a mason. This defends against possible views from fellow members of the *barey ton* that the boy's promotion is purely nepotistic. Favoritism of this kind can call into question the mason's proficiency at reproducing the trade's skills, securing the craft's survival, and maintaining the esteemed reputation that Djenné's masons enjoy throughout the Sahel.

After the mason has informed the *barey ton* of his decision to initiate his apprentice as a full member of the trade, he delivers the good news to the young man's family. In a rather unceremonious manner, the mason and the boy's guardian (ideally his father) then make benedictions (*gaara*) for the boy's prosperous future as a craftsman. The benedictions typically comprise Qurʿanic recitations but also include incantations that mix *bey-bibi* and *bey-koray*. Subsequently, the mason presents his pupil with a *kuuru-bibi* trowel ("black-skin" trowel) and a *sasiré* (flared-end crowbar), effectively completing his kit of basic trade tools. Both tools are manufactured by the town's blacksmiths and cost approximately 2,000 CFA and 2500 CFA, respectively, at the time of my fieldwork.[15] The gifts, coming from the master, officially and publicly validate the transformation of the boy's many years of sweat and toil to his new professional status within the community. Al-Hajji avowed that "becoming a mason is a hard-earned privilege. Some boys will become masons quickly and others take a long time, while others will never be recognized as sufficiently competent."

The young builders I knew who had recently been declared masons continued to work with their masters or with members of their immediate and extended family in the trade. They were paid a mason's daily wage (2500 CFA), either directly from the client or from the senior mason who employed them and oversaw the project. Unless their master is deceased or retired and they inherit his clientele, they remain dependent on him for work, and this situation potentially per-

LEFT A blacksmith and his infant son at the anvil in the Semani quarter

sists well into their career until they manage to establish their own client base. During the early years in his new role, a young mason will work at the side of his master (or another senior mason), assisting more directly in the actual building processes than he did as an apprentice. By doing so, he hones his skills and learns new tasks with the benefit of continued direction and mentoring. He also learns by way of example to communicate effectively with clients and translate their requirements into spatial planning and buildings, negotiate contracts, calculate costs and budgets, schedule work, estimate quantities and order materials, and manage a team of laborers. Eventually the junior mason can expect to be allotted sizable tasks and even small project commissions to execute on his own with a team of laborers under his sole supervision. Though this work will still be moni-tored by the senior mason(s), his new autonomy is an important stride toward having complete responsibility toward his own clients.

The progress of some young masons is severely hindered, however, when their master does not have enough work to pass on to them or has retired from active building without leaving them a sufficient number of clients. Patron contracts are often willed to an earlier generation of the master's trainees, or to those who may have been better favored for one reason or another. Some young masons have no choice but to abandon the building profession and take up new trades. Konamadou Djennepo had apprenticed under his pater-nal uncle, Beré Yonou, who was also the maternal uncle of the four Kourou-mansé brothers. Beré Yonou was an older half-brother of Konamadou's father, Baba Djennepo, whereby both were born of the same mother, different fa-thers. When Konamadou was declared a mason in 1992, his aging master had just returned from a pilgrimage to Mecca and was slowly retreating from ac-tive building. A decade later Beré Yonou had very little work to pass on to his former apprentice, and Konamadou was forced to look for additional means to support his family. He began petty trading, initially selling a limited range of dry goods from his family home, then acquiring a small location in the Monday market next to his mother's stall and expanding his stocks to include Chinese-made rubber flip-flops. Konamadou proudly showed me a picture taken of him and Beré Yonou standing side by side against a backdrop of the mosque while its annual coat of plaster was festively applied. He revered his master but lamented the lack of building work. Konamadou kept faith that opportunities would arise and that perhaps Baba or al-Hajji, with whom he had often worked in the past, would land a commission and include him in the team. Meanwhile he was compelled to rely on his new and not tremen-dously profitable commercial ventures.

In conjunction with describing the various stages of house building, the next chapters explore apprenticeship training in Djenné and the intense social and professional relations that exist within the masons' community. Some masons, like al-Hajji, excelled in their craft, expanded their clientele, and introduced successful innovations to their method and design. Other competent masons, such as his brother, Hasey, and Konamadou Djennepo, suffered serious setbacks that threatened their livelihoods and jeopardized their future in the trade. Al-Hajji's apprentice, Yappi, was characteristic of those who recognized the barriers and limitations imposed by Djenné's pervasive patriarchy and conservatism, and willfully sought a means of escape. Indeed, the region's isolation, harsh climate, fragile ecosystem, and steeply fluctuating economy continues to pose a perpetual threat to the entire building industry and, with it, the persistence of the apprenticeship-style education and the town's unique architectural tradition of buttressed facades and towering mud miters.

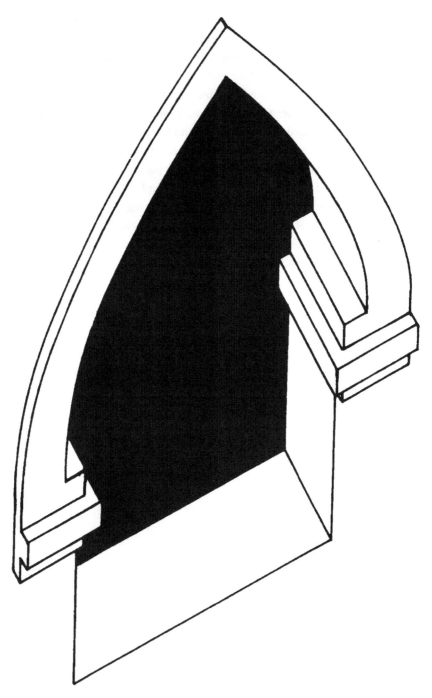

Axonometric view of Al-Hajji's spring-line detail for the arched openings on a veranda

6 · The Michelangelo of Djenné

Perou Cissé was the first to greet every member of the team each morning when we arrived for work at the Brunet-Jailly house in Djoboro. He was a sinewy, middle-aged man with an enormous, welcoming smile and eyes sparkling with good-natured mischievousness. Perou was the guardian and lived with his wife, their five young children, and his mother in the two ground-storey rooms of the new auxiliary building attached to the house. The family had been living in a dilapidated building on this site when the Frenchman purchased the land, but they were not the owners. Rather than evict them from the premises, Professor Brunet-Jailly offered them employment as the live-in caretakers and guardian. Perou had several years of schooling, spoke excellent French, and possessed a remarkable thirst for knowledge. He liked to talk, asking all sorts of well-informed questions about life in Europe as well as my native Canada. He had traveled in West Africa to Ivory Coast and Togo, and had been especially impressed by the vastness of the ocean. His questions were usually carefully formulated to demonstrate what he already knew about a subject, as much as they were posed to extract new information. He also had an astonishing capacity to retain the particulars. He was a Rimaïbé (the former slave caste of the Fulani), but al-Hajji and the others teasingly called him Peul.[1] He was very adept at teasing back, and when it came to banter, he was the master of ceremonies. Perou had expansive knowledge about the different cultures and ethnicities of Djenné, and about the gossip and colorful characters that populated the town, including the builders' individual families.

Combined with a quick wit and sharp tongue, he employed it all strategically to launch his amusing and always harmless assaults. The men appreciated the comic relief he provided during the grueling workday, and he frequently lent assistance by preparing materials and tools for the masons.

I arrived at 8:00 AM, and again no one else had arrived yet for work. Only Perou and his family were there having a breakfast (*tjirkaarey*) of *alfinta* cakes[2] and tea.

"They won't be here for a while yet. Come join us," he called over to me.

"Al-Hajji told me yesterday to be here at eight."

"Yes, but it's too cold this morning. Come." And he poured me a glass of tea.

"Cold" was not the word I would have chosen to describe temperatures hovering around 20°C (80°F). "Fresh," perhaps, was more apt. It was 8:45 before the others arrived, all wearing pullovers and some with hoods. Al-Hajji even wore a jacket over his multiple layers of T-shirts and sweaters. The masons, in particular, complained about having to handle the cold, wet mortar in the morning, saying that it stiffened their joints. Rounds of morning salutations and inquiries ensued about a good night's sleep, "Bien dormi?" and work commenced almost immediately. Curiously, I did not witness al-Hajji or Bamoy Sao make any sort of benedictions before starting off, so I asked about this. Both masons confirmed that they performed recitations each morning privately before leaving home. Leaving out specifics, al-Hajji said that his consisted of verses from the Holy Qurʿan and other secret incantations, but he could not reveal them to anyone. Bamoy interjected grandly, with a sweep of his arm over the landscape of sunlit roof terraces before us: "The benedictions we make are not just for the building site and our workers, but for the entire neighborhood where our projects are situated." The building foundations had been blessed in the beginning with a mixture of grains and nuts including *fonio*, millet, sorghum, cottonseed, maize, rice, and peanuts. Cowry shells were also thrown in, al-Hajji told me, "because they were once used as money and they would bring wealth and prosperity to the inhabitants." The Djenné-Chiini term for cowry shells is *noor koray, noor* meaning "money" and *koray* meaning "white."

Arches and Innovation

For the next nine days we would work on the second storey of the auxiliary building, directly above the rooms occupied by Perou and his family. This seemed to me not an altogether secure setup, considering that five children played and two women regularly cooked in the trajectory of potentially falling bricks, loose hammerheads, and rolling crowbars. Because benedictions had been made, no one else viewed this as a problem. A small water closet, standing like a lone sentinel's box, had already been erected at the top of the stairs leading up from the courtyard. Its floor and interior wall surfaces had been fitted with white porcelain tiles, and the plumbing was functional. The partition walls of two small bedrooms located off the veranda would have to be built, and, most important, the veranda wall with large arched openings overlooking the courtyard had to be completed prior to roofing the building.[3] A substantial section of the veranda wall, starting at the intersection with the main house and extending approximately 4.5 meters, had already been bricked to full height last season. It contained two arched openings that remained blocked up with mud-brick formwork, alternating with two slender arrow-shaped openings pointing skyward. We would add the final length of the wall with an additional arched opening. The program proceeded first by dismantling the existing parapet wall, and then removing the thick top layer of plaster and two courses of bricks. This was done to achieve a sturdier integration between the existing masonry work and the new wall construction that would extend above. With Yappi stationed across town at the *marabout*'s house, Ali directly assisted the masons by removing the bricks that Bamoy loosened gently with his crowbar so that they might be reused.

Professor Brunet-Jailly had given al-Hajji a photocopied page of black-and-white photographs of a rather dark interior. The interior displayed a gracefully executed arched doorway with finely sculpted detail at the base of its spring line[4] that was just barely discernible in the photos. The bold and simple detail was reminiscent of a classical dado-line molding. Its geometric profile comprised three successive layers of stepped projections that wrapped around the three faces of the wall. The client hoped that his masons could replicate this in the arched openings of the veranda. Al-Hajji and Bamoy stood side by side in the courtyard studying the photos, periodically shifting their gazes upward to the second storey where they were building. A strong gust of wind blew from around the corner into the courtyard, lifting a swirling cloud of dust into the air and fluttering the sheet of paper in al-Hajji's hand. The *harmattan* had been blowing hard during the past days and many of the builders had congested sinuses, snorting out the contents of their nasal passages onto the ground and into the mortar they were mixing. Bamoy sneezed. The two masons puzzled over how this stepped detail might be achieved with regard to the standard-sized bricks they worked with. They could visualize a solution of two-dimensional projections that articulated the inner surface of the opening, but they were having serious difficulties imagining a result that actually wrapped three-dimensionally around all three faces of the wall. I could only conjecture that this was partially because of the poor quality of the photocopy; more significant was that they were not in fact accustomed to reading drawings or studying photographs in this way and for this purpose.

Al-Hajji was clearly enjoying the challenge. He sent Bamoy up the stairs to try out experimental arrangements of bricks placed on top of the low right-hand section of wall that had been built up to the height of the spring line. Al-Hajji continued pondering the photograph, sporadically issuing instructions to his colleague to try stacking the bricks in such-and-such a way or like this-and-that. At that point Bayeré rolled in on his moped and self-assuredly tried to resolve the matter, but with no immediate success. Scratching his head as he contemplated the picture, Perou chimed in, mockingly, "Le pirogue n'est pas arrivé!" making a clever correlation between Bayeré's failure to receive inspiration and the literal definition of his family name, "Kouroumansé," which, in Bamanankan, means "the pirogue hasn't arrived."[5] Tonton soon joined the party, having wandered into the courtyard to pay a social visit. Tonton, or Ibrahim Sao as he was truly named, was Bamoy's paternal uncle, and he, too, began commandeering his poor nephew, who was becoming visibly agitated. It was al-Hajji who finally formulated a solution that was acceptable to all members of what had now become a committee. The three-stepped projection would protrude in relief from the exterior facade and from the inner face of the opening, but not from the interior surface of the wall. I was uncertain as to whether his decision not to continue the detail onto the third, interior side was because he deemed it would be concealed from public view and therefore not worthy of the effort, or, more likely, because the back side of the wall in the photograph was not visible to the viewer and therefore he had no reason to believe that the detail extended there. In any case, al-Hajji adjourned the consultation session and wasted no further time in joining Bamoy to resume their task.

The end of the completed veranda wall delimited the left side of the opening they were about to frame. A generous notch had to be made in the thickness of the wall along its edge so that the detail could be built into it, and above which the radius of the arch would extend. Bamoy squatted down facing the end of the mud-brick wall and began delicately chiseling out a three-course-high indent with his adze. As he proceeded to do so, the large section of wall above became unstable and slowly began to cave in on top of him. His removal of the few bricks had created weakness at the base, and a sizable mass

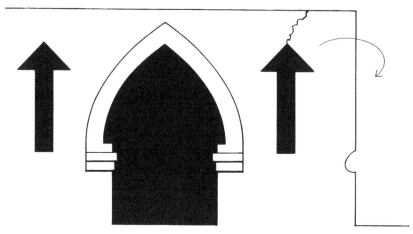

Elevation plan of an arched veranda opening with *sasiré* apertures on each side. The crack line above the right-hand aperture indicates the location where the wall began to fall away during construction. The failure was halted by the mason's benedictions.

of masonry split away from the rest of the wall, cracking along the narrowest segment at the top of the arrow-like aperture. Realizing this, Bamoy sprung upward, firmly placing his right hand and forearm along the wall's edge and shoving the heavy component back into place with all his strength while muttering some barely audible incantation. Al-Hajji quickly scrambled to the top and straddled the adjacent section of wall, also reciting powerful words, and pulled the unstable section back in toward him. He immediately began dismantling it course by course, from the top downward until he reached the level of the notch. The power of their words, they later told me, passed through their arms and hands and into the structure. According to al-Hajji, he relied on *bey-bibi* either to avert oncoming accidents or put a stop to difficulties already in progress. He called upon *bey-koray*, on the other hand, to make benedictions and provide protection and guarantees. One was used counteractively, the other proactively. He had unshakeable confidence in the logic of their use and their effectiveness, but I still shuddered at the possible scene of that bulky wall twisting and tumbling onto one of Perou's children below.

Working in close cooperation, the two masons built up the basic form of the details in brick on each side of the opening. Al-Hajji then spent considerable time shaping each one with generous layers of plastering mud applied with his small, pointed French trowel. He labored over them like an esteemed pastry chef putting the finishing touches to a competition piece. With tremendous patience and precision, he gave the stepped tiers crisp rectilinear lines and rendered the planar

surfaces perfectly smooth. When he finished, al-Hajji descended the steps to the courtyard so that he could stand back and critically assess his artistic endeavor. He summoned Ali to pick up his trowel and carefully guided him from a distance in making a final adjustment, shaving the inside edge of one of the details ever so slightly. I delighted in watching al-Hajji work. He remained consistently calm and fully focused on his task, rarely speaking but always engaged with the mood and workings of his team. I sensed that, as a tradesman, al-Hajji was more than a technically competent mason but rather an artist of sorts capable of balancing his reasoned judgments with imaginative creativity.

In Djenné, the formwork (*gabriyyer*) for constructing arches (*santal*) is typically supported on thick branches that span temporarily between two small ledges that project from the base of the wall into the space of the opening. The height of the ledges is equivalent to the arch spring line. Once the wall or building is completed and the formwork removed, the overall effect is vaguely reminiscent of a horseshoe arch but without the fluid curved lines that marry the vertical sides of the arch with the horizontal planes of the ledges. In the case of this arch, however, it was felt that the heavy weight of the formwork on a girder of branches would damage the newly crafted details positioned directly below, so it was decided that the formwork would rest directly on the ground and be built, as usual, in dry construction. The formwork would also protrude by two centimeters beyond the front face of the wall in order to support the slightly projecting placement of the *voussoirs*. The idea was to raise the arch itself in relief off the facade and embolden the geometry around the opening. At the level of the spring line, the formwork measured a total of six brick widths across. With each successive course, the overall width of the formwork was reduced by at first three and then later four finger widths on each side. By the eleventh course it had been reduced to a single, angular-cut brick placed centrally on top. At this stage the assembly appeared to be more of a triangle than the curvaceous outline of an arch. Its curved profile was subsequently crafted by the two masons who worked in tandem, each slowly building up their respective side of the formwork with thick applications of mortar and small pieces of brick to achieve the rounded contours of a pointed arch. Ali and his brother, Abdullahi, were asked to stand in the courtyard below and guide the masons, judging and amending the symmetry of their work by eye.

As discussed earlier, the use of the body to measure building components, like the use of finger widths just described for calculating the diminishing dimensions of the formwork, is characteristic of Djenné masons. Placement of windows and heights of ceilings are measured against the mason's erect body

LEFT Al-Hajji Kouroumansé building the protruding spring-line detail of an arch

Basket of thick mud mortar and baked clay tiles

and upheld arms; room dimensions are often paced off; parapets and balustrades are measured to the knees and waist; and the lengths of certain components, and the intervals between them, are calibrated by fingers, hand spans, forearms, and strides. At one point al-Hajji determined that he needed a thick wood branch the length of his forearm to the tip of his middle finger in order to span a small window opening. He asked Perou to cut it for him, demonstrating the required length by gesturing with his left hand along his stiff right forearm, from the elbow to the tips of his outstretched fingers. When Perou returned with the cut branch, al-Hajji discovered that it was too long and complained, holding the wood against his own arm to compare. Perou promptly replied, "Well, my arm isn't the same length as yours, is it al-Hajji?" The mason laughed good-humouredly at his own presumption and handed back the piece to be shortened, this time indicating the length with a notch from his trowel.

The regular, boxy mud bricks were employed in the same fashion as *voussoirs* of stone masonry would be used in constructing the arch. Each was tailored with the mason's adze to be set on a bed of mortar above the preceding one, following the curve of the formwork. A keystone brick wedded the two sides where they joined at the apex. It was carefully sculpted with angled edges for a tight, perfect fit that would brace the structure. Next, the wall was built around and above the arch, and the arch itself was plastered with mud on all sides to seal the joints and further strengthen it. This was the first time that either of the two masons had constructed this style of protruding arch that stood off the planar wall surface in relief. Its appearance differed from the arch in the photograph, but they were clearly pleased with it nonetheless.

They were quick to credit Master Mason Mama Kourani with its invention, like many of the innovative design and decorative features they employed.[6] "Even though there are other great masters in Djenné," al-Hajji declared, "none are as remarkable as Mama Kourani." Many masons and citizens alike supported this view. He no longer did much building, but Mama Kourani was reputed as a craftsman who worked patiently and meticulously, producing exquisite results.[7] Masons commonly attributed new and innovative design solutions to other individuals with already established authority, or even to deceased masters. This act may be construed as a strategy to qualify the masons' own practices or the architectural features they produced. By pointing to already validated persons, younger or lesser-known practitioners absolve themselves from the need to negotiate public approval and professional accreditation, seeking legitimacy, instead, as mere reproducers of an established practice or form, even though this may not be entirely true.

The question of whether Mama Kourani was indeed the original author of al-Haji's arch surround, or of any other architectural features ascribed to him, is not of the utmost importance. The main issue is that recognition and appreciation for a certain quality of creativity exists within, and even outside, the trade. This creativity is not one that reacts against and surpasses Djenné's so-called *style-Soudanais* but rather one that remains responsive to it. It expands and embellishes the repertoire of possible expression by producing its own articulation within existing boundaries of the discourse on traditional architecture. Such creative ingenuity grasps tradition as a responsive and dynamic resource, not as a static code of predetermined possibilities. Figures like Mama Kourani, real or imaginary, are integral to the machinery that produces and reproduces the trade's history, strengthening its roots and fortifying its regional and global reputation.

The Labor Force

Bamoy loosened the drawstring on his white tool bag and pulled out two *kuuru-bibi* trowels; one for him and the other he handed to Ali. With the veranda wall nearing completion, and Yappi still on duty at the site in Yobukayna, Ali was given the task of plastering the completed partition walls in the second-storey bedrooms. He was quietly enthusiastic. Ali figured that he was somewhere in the vicinity of twenty years old, though I suspected he may have exaggerated this figure by a couple of years. Perou, al-Hajji, and others publicly acknowledged Ali's good looks, and he was confident about them without being smug. He arrived each morning squeaky clean and changed his clothing regularly, sometimes sporting a brightly colored new shirt. Most laborers worked a season and more in the same outfit, patching holes and mending tears. Ali's sense of style was a bit flashier. His favorite article of clothing was the tube-like hat that he wore, claiming it made him look like a Rastafarian. He and some of the other workers were Bob Marley fans, and they would ask me to translate the garble of English lyrics they picked up. Showing a gift for sartorial invention, his Rasta hat was actually made from the cut-off leg of a pair of corduroy trousers. As an apprentice, he was diligent and attentive, rarely speaking or fraternizing with the other laborers. This perfect demeanor changed, of course, when Yappi returned and Ali got bumped back down the hierarchy, where he need not be so highly focused. But when at the side of the masons, he made every effort to interpret their thinking and predict their needs.

Bamoy Sao joined Ali to plaster. The mason deliberately stationed himself along the same wall at the opposite corner from the apprentice. From this position Bamoy could illustrate his own technique to the young man, while simultaneously monitoring Ali's progress. Following a quick study of the wall surface, Bamoy proceeded to lop off the glaring protrusions, irregularities, and dried excess mortar with the edge of his *kuuru-bibi* trowel. With trowel in hand, he then scooped the dark, smooth plaster from the basket set down in front of him, slapping it vigorously onto the brick surface, and smoothing it evenly with broad sweeps from left to right. Bamoy's covering neatly progressed by sections, working in meter-wide strips from top to bottom of the wall, and moving in the opposing direction to Ali so that they would meet at the center. Ali's method was notably less skillful. He haphazardly distributed splotches of plaster across the wall surface, moving from one area to the next and back again. The strokes of his trowel spread mud up and down, and in all directions. After a short while, Bamoy called Ali's attention over to his own work. Without specifically telling him what he was doing wrong, and offering no explanation about how he might get it right, Bamoy merely continued plastering, emphasising the side-to-side direction with the trowel by slightly exaggerating that gesture. Ali stood back a little from the wall to get a better view. He watched for a minute or so before continuing with his task. He now consciously tried to manipulate his trowel in a more controlled manner, but he had evidently taken no notice of the mason's section-by-section logic.

Mud plaster for interior wall surfaces is called *laabu-bibi*, literally, "black mud," because of its dark-grey color. It is prepared with earth that comes from pulverizing old walls and bricks, and is not considered strong enough for use in mortar. It is squeezed repeatedly through the hands and fingers to remove lumps or bits of debris before plopping it into a basket to send up to the masons. The less refined red-colored mortar is called *laabu-tyirey* (*tyirey* meaning "red"), and it is made from the same laterite used by brick makers, quarried from along the water's edge around town or the riverbanks and delivered by donkey cart. Although the laterite is very hard and crumbly, water turns it easily into mud. Al-Hajji teasingly commented that the *laabu-bibi* is black like Bozos, and the *laabu-tyirey* red like me, the *tubaabu*. The laterite excavated near town tends to contain a high content of refuse, and this makes its way rather directly into bricks and gets churned up in the mortar. Shards of glass, rusting tin cans, plastics, packaging, rags, cigarette cartons, dried animal dung, discarded batteries, bones, and even old bicycle chains are encased daily in Djenné's new walls. For obvious reasons the garbage poses a particular threat to the builders, and one must be wary when trampling, mixing, passing, catching, and applying materials. Every so often a laborer is sent to the local hospital for a tetanus booster.

The division of labor on-site was largely unchanging. It was grounded in some unspoken agreement that, with time and through habitual reenactment, had become more or less acceptable to all. Sulayman, the oldest of the Bouaré brothers, put his agricultural skills to task in preparing the mortar and plaster. This strenuous job involved breaking up the rock-hard laterite or old bricks into granular uniformity with a hoe; arranging the soil into shallow mounds with a hollowed cone at the center; adding water and blending the mixture first with the tool and then trampling the mud with bare legs to achieve an even consistency. Sulayman was not endowed with his younger brother's charming looks, or with a great deal of physical prowess and stamina. There was something not quite right about Sulayman, and I couldn't help but pity him. He did not catch on to things swiftly and often appeared to be daydreaming in a distant world, hiding beneath his oversized winter woolen cap. Between stints of work, he would find a shady spot, often in full view of the rest of the team, and nod off to sleep. He was polite and pleasant, and the physical contribution he made to the team was valued. That quiet tolerance of oddities, shortcomings, and disabilities typified Djenné. Everyone who respected and lived by the laws that shaped everyday life in Djenné had a place in the community.

Sulayman's middle brother, Abdullahi, and a second laborer, also called al-Hajj (but without an "I" at the end) shoveled the prepared mud mixtures

Laborer Sadio Traoré (aka, al-Hajj "the tea-maker")

into shallow woven baskets. These two were also responsible for executing various odd jobs that included stacking and arranging new deliveries of materials, and being part of the chain-like assembly that passed on materials from the courtyard to the masons working above. Al-Hajj's real name was Sadio Traoré, and he proudly defined himself as authentically *Djennénké.* His pilgrim's title was inherited from the *grand frère* of his paternal grandmother. His former schoolmates knew him as Sadio, but locally, in the neighborhood, he was "al-Hajj." He had more schooling than the other boys on-site, having completed the sixth grade, and he was also the youngest member of the team. He thought he might be fourteen or fifteen years old. His height made him appear older, but, on closer inspection, he carried the lankiness of adolescence. For more than half a year he had been apprenticing with a tailor, and he did this work for a few hours each day after finishing up at the site. The job as a laborer was merely to earn additional pocket money for smokes and tea while he meandered misguidedly through his apprenticeship. Al-Hajj con-

Passing building materials from the courtyard to the roof

fessed that he really did not want to be a tailor (*taa-koy*), but, like so many of the town's young men, he dreamed of becoming a trader (*maambala-koyni*), believing it would deliver instant, easy wealth. Djenné's heyday as a formidable center of trade and commerce, however, was long over. Aside from arranging, preparing, and passing materials, al-Hajj was also responsible for making tea, a ritual in which he invested his greatest pride, claiming that his bittersweet concoction of *whisky Africain* was the best in town.[8] When necessary, the masons disbursed a small sum of money to replenish his stash of charcoal, loose tea, and sugar. Over a low flame, he brought the thick, saturated beverage to a perfect boil, pouring it back and forth between the tiny blue enameled teapot and the single, thimble-sized glass to achieve the optimal strength. When ready, the sticky glass was passed hand to hand and everyone took a few sips of al-Hajj's restorative brew.

The final member of the labor force was Omar Sounfountera. Omar's typical position was to stand on top of an oil drum, acting as the vertical intermediary in the chain that passed materials from the ground to the second storey, and back down again. In quiet periods, when the masons were not demanding a rush supply of bricks and mortar, he assisted the other three in their tasks, most frequently joining Sulayman knee-deep in cool, oozing mud. Like al-Hajj "the tea-maker," Omar was an apprenticing tailor and labored on the building site to earn a living, but he was much more earnest about this pursuit than his colleague. He was, in fact, a competent tailor and rented a stall in the Monday market located somewhere in the midst of the endless row of other tailors where he set up his pedal-operated sewing machine and jostled for clients. Omar's father had been a tailor but quit the profession to become a kola nut trader. Unlike the other team members who were all residents of Djoboro, Omar lived in Yobukayna, a quarter equally populated by mason families. His paternal line was Fulani, and his maternal lineage was Bozo.

It is extremely uncommon for a Fulani to work in the building trade, and none from that group, to the best of my knowledge, could be counted among the town's masons. This traditionally pastoral, fervently Islamic population deemed the building profession, or any other involving the handling and manipulation of soil including pottery and agriculture, as below their stature. Historically, Fulani who had settled in Djenné aligned themselves professionally with the *marabout*'s craft or commerce. Young Omar had no such pretensions, and he was a popular member of the team. His Bozo ancestry exempted him from Fulani restrictions, and that his maternal line was the Salamantao, a revered family of masons, made his participation in the building trade all the more probable.[9] As a baby he had contracted meningitis and, as a result, suffered a complete loss of hearing (*lutu*). He had no formal spoken language per se, but he vocalized a remarkable range of sounds that enriched his signing with intonation and infused it with emotional force. He was an extremely effective communicator. When he was in high spirits, Omar's voice, more than any other, could be heard on the site. He had a wry sense of humor and reveled in matches of playful teasing with his workmates. He was treated as an equal and was well attuned to their daily conversations and to current events in the town. Sadly, hearing impairments are common in Djenné largely as a result of the virulent strain of meningitis that plagues this region when winds transport fine atomized mixtures of dust, germs, and assorted fecal matter. Most local people therefore possess at least an elementary ability to sign that they append with an expanded series of gestures, and some, like Abdullahi Bouaré, are highly adept at nonverbal communication.

Bamoy the Healer

Mali had been victorious in yesterday evening's African Cup of Nations football match against Algeria with a score of 2–0. People were visibly pleased, and some men wore a blissful, almost vacant smile for most of the following day. There was a Bozo player on Mali's team but no one at the site, including our Bozo masons, could think of his name. They certainly did not qualify as true football fans but rooted proudly for their country in this African showdown.

Work had hardly begun that morning when a commotion erupted in the alleyway just outside the courtyard. A hefty woman came scuttling in, flip-flops dragging up dust, shouting for Bamoy. There was a panicked exchange of information. Bamoy quickly rummaged through his tool bag and darted out, the rest of the team following on his heels. By the time I turned the corner, he had a full-grown sheep gripped firmly by its snout and was yanking the animal's four legs out from beneath it to bring it to the ground. While someone held the legs, he pinned it with full weight under his right knee from behind and, still clutching its snout, arced the animal's head back offering its elongated throat to Mecca. With his free right hand, he deftly and deeply slit into the animal instantly activating a bright red gush that shot out almost a meter onto the dusty road, splattering for a few moments in its own puddle. As the fountain subsided to a trickle, the animal's squirming body released its last life. The dozy sheep had wandered into someone's courtyard from the street, nuzzled open a sack of rice grains, and helped itself to a generous feeding. It was a blessing that it had been caught. The uncooked rice would have expanded in its stomach, bloating the organ until it exploded—a cruel, tortuous death. It was better to slaughter and butcher the animal immediately to salvage its valuable meat before stomach acids poisoned the carcass.

Al-Hajji was in Yobukayna checking up on Yappi and Diabaté. Ali assisted Bamoy in constructing lintels over the two second-storey bedroom doorways of the auxiliary building. Setting lintels is a long and delicate procedure. The lengths of cut palm wood (*sebe tyen*) must fit snugly, one next to the other. Their irregular wedge-shaped sections make this somewhat difficult, and the prickly, fibrous nature of the wood makes it unpleasant to handle. The builders' palms were riddled with tiny splinters. Pieces of palm wood are often thicker at one end than the other, and have to be rolled over in place, from one side to the next, in order to find the most stable position. The flat assembly of palm wood spanning a window or door is made as level as possible, and this is determined by eye. It is common for the wall on one side of the opening to be slightly higher than the other. The differential is corrected by either modifying the height of the uppermost brick with a trowel or building up the lower with small fragments of brick, shards of pottery, and mortar. The masons constantly tap the palm wood beams into place with the edge and butt-end of their trowels, every so often lifting one out of place and repositioning it to improve the level. Bamoy and Ali, straddling the wall on opposite sides of the doorway from each other, worked together in a symmetrical arrangement. This enabled Ali to mimic and learn from the mason while engaging pragmatically in the building process. Al-Hajj "the tea maker" and I handed them wood and mortar which they used to secure the sticks in position and to evenly cover the top of the finished lintel. The mud-brick wall could then be continued above. Al-Hajji normally verified the work before the walls were raised further, and made any necessary corrections in a discreet and humble manner.

Abdullahi Bouaré had temporarily replaced Omar on the oil drum to pass materials. He enjoyed playing the clown and performed with a well-timed sense of slapstick humor; he also had a rubbery face that produced a myriad of practiced contortions. I stood in one of the arched veranda openings at the edge of the floor plate, catching the basket loads of mortar that Abdullahi launched upward, often without looking to see if I was there. A series of baskets were coming along in quick succession, and, as I twisted to toss the one just received onto al-Hajj "the tea maker," Abdullahi catapulted another at me. The basket hit me squarely in the shins, dumping its entire slimy contents all over my trouser legs and seeping into my shoes. He winced theatrically as I bellowed in English, "You big dummy!" Perou, who was standing nearby, thought that this was the funniest thing he had ever heard, and plucked that phrase from the air like a piece of ripe fruit. He blurted it out repeatedly to Abdullahi, perfectly mimicking my heavily stressed intonation, and each time killing himself with laughter. Whenever a team member fumbled, missed a pass, dropped something, or showed signs of wavering energy, Perou especially seized the opportunity to unleash a barrage of teasing. Historically the Rimaïbé were slaves of the Fulani and, like the former servant class of Horso, they were expected to make witty and insulting remarks. Freemen and nobles were expected to take no offense. If they did get angry or retaliate against their subordinates, they risked losing status and respect. Perou kept that privileged practice of his former slave ancestors alive and well. His playful taunting usually took the form of fairly innocuous, patronizing comments about "not eating enough breakfast"; "being fed only sugar and water rather than honey"; "being too poor to eat meat"; "not getting enough rest"; or "not having a woman to lie next to at night." The latter was pointedly aimed at the laborers and me, all of whom were still bachelors. Marital status, the number of wives, and virility (demonstrated by heads of children) were dominant issues of both serious discussions and jokes, and the men were markedly more interested and concerned about the fact that I was unmarried than about my nationality or religious affiliation. Perou endlessly amused himself by reminding me in an almost sadistic tone that I was all by myself in Djenné with no one to sleep beside me. He even teased al-Hajji for producing only half the number of children that he had, and with double the wife power!

Most of the men worked barefoot and some wore tattered flip-flops or molded plastic shoes. The bright-blue, green, or pearly white shoes were imported from China, and the flimsy plastic provided no real protection for their feet. Al-Hajj "the tea maker" picked a brick up from the pile with one hand to hoist up to Bamoy. The brick suddenly split lengthwise in two, and half of it fell hard onto al-Hajj's big toe. The toe immediately puffed up like a dark purple plum, and the boy fought hard to hold back his tears. Bamoy scrambled down the wall to attend to the injury, sternly directing the laborer to sit on the ground and he knelt down in front of him, taking the damaged foot in his hands. He summoned Ali to fetch the little blue teapot, and he proceeded to pour the remainder of its hot contents over the toe while caressing it gently. Bamoy professed to be curing the injury with secrets, and within ten minutes the swelling abated and al-Hajj "the tea maker" was back at work. Others in the neighborhood confirmed that Bamoy Sao was well recognized for his healing powers, and people came to him with breaks and sprains, but he modestly claimed to know only "*kayna kayna*" ("a little, a little"). He alleged to have learned his secrets from his father, and adamantly asserted that they were of the *bey-koray* variety, not *bey-bibi*. This application confounded al-Hajji's earlier explanation that *bey-koray* was used preventatively and *bey-bibi* counteractively. All individuals, in fact, had their own somewhat varying personal accounts about how and when these forms of secret knowledge were used, and it largely depended on the dispositions their teachers handed down.

Bamoy's deceased father, Sekou Sao, had also been a mason and was responsible for teaching his son the trade and putting him through school up to the sixth grade. Bamoy wished he would have had the opportunity to further his studies, but his already considerable level of literacy and education was quite rare among masons of his generation. Historically the Bozo had resisted administrative and institutional procedures imposed by the French, and following Mali's independence they continued to rebuff the state schooling system and the national adoption of the French language. Some parents still believe that state-run *madrassahs* and schools corrupt their children's minds with foreign thinking and strange ideals. They fear that the young will become spoiled and impolite.[10] For these reasons Sekou Sao, like many other Bozo parents, removed his son from the system. Many of the town's Bozo children were never sent to school, but most (if not all) of the boys received at the very least a smattering of Qurʿanic lessons from the local *marabouts.*

In contrast to the itinerant Bozo fishermen who resisted foreign incursions and state projects of conformity, many of the formerly pastoral Fulani have reaped impressive political rewards through their tactical compliance: a zealous embrace of "pure" Islam launched the nineteenth-century jihads that established new capitals at such places as Hamdullahi (Mali) and Sokoto (Nigeria), and bestowed dominant and long-lasting positions in West Africa's religious community. Later, a strategic submission to the colonial government and engagement with education meant that Fulani individuals were able to assume positions of wealth and power within the state apparatus. Bamoy's recognition that schooling provides opportunities, and his avowal to enroll all five of his own children, including his daughter, in the state system, represents changing Bozo attitudes and perceptions about their place in wider Malian society.

Bamoy, born in 1960, was named after his maternal grandfather, Muhammad Djadjé. He was given the typical Songhay nickname "Bamoy" following his grandfather's death in order to protect the deceased's name and spirit. Bamoy was his mother's only son, and he taught his younger half-brother to build once he himself was declared a mason. Presently he had just one apprentice, Caramogho Toma, who was a young Somono man from Tolober village.[11] His apprentice did not work with us on the two houses because Bayeré gave priority to his cousin al-Hajji's regular team members. Meanwhile Caramogho, like many apprentices, patiently waited for work experience and the chance to establish a career in the trade. Bamoy and al-Hajji had cooperated together on several projects over the past years. They first worked together under the direction of Mama Kourani installing kiln-baked terracotta tiles on the grand mud-brick gate structure of the Sory Thiocary School built over the site of Cheikou Amadou's nineteenth-century mosque. Bamoy boasted that he had assisted Mama Kourani in building three village mosques in the vicinity of Niono, in the direction of Segou. Like his uncle, Ibrahim (alias "Tonton"), he was agile and athletic, and basked in the theatrics of an occasional high-walking performance along the top of a wall. Generally Bamoy was a jovial, upbeat character, but he could also become inexplicably irascible from time to time, withdrawing from the group conversations. He was acclaimed for his cache of secrets, and, aside from the benedictions he made each day, he also wore a blessed silver ring (*korbo*) that lent further protection.

The rings worn by men in Djenné come in various designs, including plain or twisted bands of copper, silver, or gold; bold sculptural designs; delicately worked filigree metal; and stone settings of carnelian, agate, jasper, and turquoise. *Korbo* are blessed by *marabouts* and imbued with powers that protect the wearer against evil intentions. Other types of *gris-gris* are also worn on the body but often in a more concealed manner.[12] *Kamba baakawal* are armlets worn high on the upper arm, usually beneath the shirtsleeves; *baakawal* are worn around the waist, against the skin; and *tira* are hung around the neck.[13] Some individuals insist on removing their *gris-gris* when engaged in impure activities, such as defecating, to avoid profaning them. *Gris-gris* are typically composed of twisted or woven strips of shiny black-tanned leather that secure a tiny pouch of the same material containing potent Qurᶜanic inscriptions. Omar, our Fulani-Bozo colleague, was perpetually mocked by the other men for wearing such a large number of these protective devices. He carried several *kamba baakawal* on his arms, a *baakawal* around his waist, and a *tira* dangling from a string around his neck like a Catholic with so many saints' medals. Al-Hajji confidently informed Omar that he did not need these, that the benedictions the masons made each morning were enough to keep him safe. The Bouaré brothers warned that, as a Muslim, he should have more faith in Allah's plans for him. In these discussions, however, it was never a question of whether one should or should not wear *gris-gris,* but more a matter of the quantity that adorned one's body. Ali lunged skyward to toss a brick to Bamoy straddling the wall above. His shirttails lifted high, revealing a sleek black-leather band around his waist. He staunchly defended his *gris-gris*, stating that he needed only one amulet as opposed to the many charms covering Omar's body. Omar had seemingly tipped the acceptable balance between spiritual conviction and faith in material fetishes, but this balance was perpetually in the process of social negotiation.

Djenné's Michelangelo

One morning I accompanied al-Hajji to the *marabout*'s house in Yobukayna to check on the progress of Yappi and Diabaté's work. We found them assiduously plastering the ceiling of the main vestibule, applying an initial layer of *laabu-tyirey*. This resilient, thick gooey plaster made from red laterite, chopped straw, and rice husks (*modu*) adhered well to the irregular surface of palm-wood rafters and branches. When this was thoroughly dried, a second layer of *laabu-bibi*, made with the darker soil of the old bricks and rice husks, would be added. Three hired laborers prepared vast quantities of mud and passed it on to the apprentices where they stood elevated on a plank of timber spanning two oil drums. Diabaté, who was a good hand shorter than Yappi, poised himself on a precarious stack of bricks to lift him closer to the ceiling. They picked clumps of the straw-saturated plaster from baskets that balanced beside them, and slapped it with force (*sanfa*) against the surface to ensure that it penetrated the spaces between wood members and held fast. Once several daubs hung closely like a colony of swallow's nests, the builders would then smooth them out by hand into a sensuous covering that revealed the bumpy contours of the structure. Plastering ceilings was a messy, time-consuming procedure. Yappi looked to al-Hajji, wiping globules of mud from his eyes and mouth, and complained of a sore neck and aching arm muscles. The mason called both boys down to take a break and to show them something new. He squatted down to the earthen floor and, with his finger, proceeded to sketch out the soft curvilinear forms of a *handu koray* ("white moon" or "full moon") detail. This detail comprised two superimposed crescent moon shapes whose contours melded into the lines of the *fata-taki* ceiling. Al-Hajji explained that a *handu koray* would later be sculpted in the niches of the ceiling pattern over the main door and the window opposite, and explained to the apprentices in sufficient detail how this would be achieved. These generous offerings of new information stimulated the minds of the young men and motivated them to look beyond the drudgery of their currently repetitive task to more creative endeavors.

The following day al-Hajji resumed crafting details at the Brunet-Jailly house, but this time for the arched openings that had been completed last season. These two arches would have to be stylistically amended to match the newest opening in the veranda wall. He used his crowbar to bore two holes through the base of the second-storey wall, one on each side of an arched opening. A thick branch of wood long enough to cantilever approximately forty-five centimeters over the courtyard was then fitted through the holes. A counterweight of bricks was loaded onto the branch lengths that extended across the floor on the interior side of the wall. Yappi and Diabaté had returned earlier with the plank of timber they had been using at the *marabout*'s project, since this was the only sturdy piece of sawn lumber owned by the team. Al-Hajji laid it across the two protruding branches and secured it with a piece of cord. This platform would serve as his suspended workstation for executing the details. Watching with amusement as the mason eased his way out onto this risky-looking contraption, Perou enthusiastically recounted how Bamoy once lowered himself by rope from a rooftop to make repairs to a second-storey window, all the while standing perfectly upright on his crowbar. The circulation of these exaggerated tales of bravado and superhuman feats effectively promotes the mystique and power of Djenné's masons, and bolsters the public's confidence in their constructions.

With the sharp point of his trowel al-Hajji scratched a measured outline of the spring-line detail into the wall plaster on each side of the opening, equal in dimension to the already completed decorations. The guiding marks were made on both the inside faces of the opening and the exterior wall surface before he began to carefully chisel away the surface with his adze. He carved out the wall to a depth of nearly ten centimeters, and then perfectly squared the perimeter edges of the hollowed-out areas. The three-tiered, spring-line details were built up in layers using flat kiln-baked tiles and mud mortar. The tiles were made by the potter-wives of the blacksmiths and measured 11.5 × 20 × 2 centimeters thick. They were typically used for tiling floor and stair surfaces, and at times more problematically for covering mud-brick walls. Once al-Hajji had achieved the basic form of the decoration, he encased the protrusion in a thick coating of the binding mud mortar and sculpted the surfaces with great finesse using his French trowel. It was an extremely effective solution for integrating these details into the wall surface without having to make major modifications to the existing structure. The arch surrounds would be added in the same way.

I watched al-Hajji with great admiration for his skills and creativity, playfully hailing him "Michelangelo" as one of the greatest compliments I could pay him. Unfortunately neither he nor anyone else on-site had the faintest clue about who

Michelangelo was. And why should they? I tried to briefly describe his accomplishment as one of the greatest painters, sculptors, inventors, and architects in European history. Al-Hajji was clearly flattered by the comparison but typically humbled himself as only *un petit maçon*. Bamoy interjected with the speculation that Michelangelo must have been *un diable* (a devil) to have possessed so much knowledge. He then exclaimed: "Even the great master masons in Djenné who know everything about building, like Mama Kourani, are also *diables*!"

7 · *Vulnerable Craftsmen*

Konamadou was doing a brisk trade in bars of laundry soap. Every Monday he set up shop along with a myriad of other temporary, rickety stalls that filled the vast open market space in front of the mosque. The dusty square was transformed weekly into a sea of rippling tarpaulins that shaded merchants and goods. Viewed from the crenulated rooftops of adjacent houses, the crush of hawkers and shoppers looked like shoals of brightly colored fish maneuvering in file passed one another beneath and between blue plastic waves. Konamadou's younger brother, Bamoy, also peddled soap, slowly plying a wheelbarrow of the large ocher-colored bars along the congested passageways and returning every so often to restock. The astringent smell of lye mingled with the concoction of other market odors: pungent dried fish, sweet mangoes and ripe papayas, chilli peppers, sour milk, the factory smell of brand-new rubber flip-flops, cooking oil, frying cakes and plantains, spicy perfumes and aromatic incense, fishy balls of stock flavoring, reeking sheep and goats, donkeys' manure, and the tang of human toil in midday heat.

I regularly sat with Konamadou in the cramped space behind his make-shift counter to spend a leisurely market-day morning people watching. We took turns between sitting on his frayed deck chair and a wooden box, chatting during the long intervals between sales and beating the forever accumulating dust off his merchandise with a flywhisk. "There are five kinds of work here in Djenné," Konamadou asserted confidently, while making change for a Fulani customer elaborately adorned with gold and with a mouthful of teeth filed to sharp points. "One either makes a living as a builder, a farmer, a fisherman, a *marabout*, or a trader. And it's common for most people to take up more than one occupation in order to survive." Except during the winter months of the region's brief building season, Bozo masons typically fish, assist with cultivating and harvesting family fields, and some, like Konamadou, are petty traders (sing., *marba*) selling trivial items and dry goods at the Monday market or from their homes. Similarly, many *marabouts* tend crops, and the farmers and fishermen who hire out their laboring skills are involved in petty trading or pirogue repair. The only townspeople in a position to have a single profession are apparently the successful large-scale traders, who own proper shops, and also the highly esteemed *marabouts* who attract numerous students and clients for their *maraboutage* practices. Some of these men are also large landowners. Konamadou's concise inventory of Djenné professions had excluded government officials and civic administrators; the city's craftsmen such as the blacksmiths, potters, leather workers, tailors, embroiderers, a handful of jewelers, and the mud-cloth dyers who produce *bogolanfini*,[1] as well as the throngs of women who bead bracelets and sell homemade foodstuffs. His list, however, accurately depicted the narrow set of employment options one faces in the town's preindustrial and rather isolated economy.

Building laborers also work the market on their one day off to earn a little extra money to buy necessities and small luxuries like an occasional kola nut or cigarette. This year, however, Djenné's market was providing fewer and fewer work opportunities as the winter wore on. Anasse came by to greet us at Konamadou's stall and reported that his job had been eliminated because of the seriously depleted fish stocks. For the past few years he had loaded and unloaded the huge woven baskets of stinking dried fish that came in by truck and horse-drawn cart. The last rainy season had yielded scant precipitation, resulting in lower water levels on the Niger and the Bani, and thus far fewer fish. Bozo fishermen had been moaning since January about tiny catches. I had also noted the dramatic change from the previous year. Last February, working at the Sanuna site by the Bani riverbanks, I watched the fishermen in pirogues adroitly casting their round nets into the low waters and moments later hauling in a writhing silvery bundle. This year there were markedly fewer boats, the Bani was already dried out and impassable in sections, and nets were coming up empty. A plate of succulent *hamkoray*, the renowned Niger *Capitaine* (a large species of Nile perch, *Lates niloticus*), was harder to come by, and fish prices had shot up in general.

Predictably, insufficient rains would also have negative repercussions for the region's masons. The hive of building activity this season was mainly owing to profits earned the previous year from abundant crops and fish stocks. Farming continues to be a significant generator of income, as reported by Maas and Mommersteeg more than a decade ago when it accounted for nearly a quarter of Djenné's economic activity, and fishing at that time tallied just over 6 percent.[2] The region's fertile soils, normally abundant aquatic life, and access to the main waterways made this location a prime choice for settlement. Saad, quoting al-Sa'di, argues that Timbuktu's existence and growth from the twelfth century on relied heavily on the established trade and economy of its sister city upriver.[3] Although commercial trading enriched Djenné throughout its long history, the importance of this activity was greatly diminished when the French made Mopti the regional center at the turn of the nineteenth century. The main asphalted road through the country connecting Bamako to Gao bypassed Djenné, and the town's watery location was only accessible by ferry. Trade was therefore circumscribed to a local and regional level, and the quantities of exchange have remained fairly moderate. Therefore, as in other drought periods during the twentieth century, sharp declines in agricultural production, ebbing fish stocks, and poor pastures for livestock resulted in fewer circulating francs and a reduced demand for market goods, crafts, and construction. A senior member of the influential Maïga family who owned large tracts of agricultural land outside the town complained about his paltry harvests: "Rice and grains are our staples. Without good harvests there's simply no money! We all suffer. It's up to the will of Allah to grant us rain."

Despite the healthy commissioning of works in town, Konamadou found no employment as a builder. Since being sacked from the Sanuna site, he had worked on just two small projects in Tolober. Next year's building season was destined to be even tougher for him, when Djenné's fragile economy would be battered by the full impact of the winter's poor crops and most projects would come to a grinding halt. His self-esteem was deflated, as well as his savings, but he remained mildly optimistic that something would come along and he would resume his professional work as a mason. Konamadou believed that he had been the victim of messy site politics between Bayeré and Tonton. According to Bayeré, on the other hand, both masons had slacked off repeatedly and chose not to heed the several warnings he had issued. From my own experience working alongside Konamadou, it was difficult to fathom that his exemplary diligence had changed suddenly to indolence after I left Djenné. I suspected, instead, that Konamadou's version was correct and that as difficulties mounted between the client, Bayeré, and Tonton, the young mason, who had been teamed up with Tonton on the house project, got caught on the wrong side of the fence. Al-Hajji and Baba Kouroumansé, for instance, continued to think highly of Konamadou, and the brothers vowed to bring him onboard at the first opportunity. This would remain difficult for the moment, however, since both depended heavily on sub-contracts farmed out by Bayeré. In an act of careful diplomacy, they never raised their cousin's name on those few occasions when they discussed their colleague's dismissal. Meanwhile, Konamadou would have to support his family with the small revenue he generated from commercial trading.

Konamadou's finances were indeed stretched. He and his wife lived in his mother's house in the crowded Semani quarter together with his younger siblings, his older brother's wife, and her six children. His older brother had departed many years ago to work as a fisherman in Ivory Coast but failed to send back remittances. In his last correspondence the brother announced that he had taken a second wife and had no intention of returning to Djenné anytime soon. This negligence plainly irritated Konamadou, and he and the others assumed responsibility for feeding and clothing his brother's family. His own father, Baba Djenneppo, could make only nominal contributions to his first wife's household. Baba had three wives and eight children of his own, and garnered a modest salary from repairing pirogues. His peaceful workshop was set up in the shade of a *ramada* at the entrance to town, where he and several men mended the long black wooden hulls. His first and second wives resided in Djenné and the third lived in the riverside village of Sirimou, where he periodically traveled to repair damaged boats. Sirimou's population is a mix of Marka and Bozo, and subsistence is based on farming and fishing. During the winter months, Konamadou's wife and his mother also spent long periods in Sirimou frying *alfinta* cakes that they either sold or bartered for rice grains. The rice was stockpiled for the household reserves, and what they collected was made to last until the next harvest. Each Monday the two women journeyed back together to Djenné with their combined proceeds, and his mother sold small quantities of salt from her stall at the market. She was a Bozo woman of imposing stature who exuded pride and confidence, and she had worked many years as a vendor in the Monday market. It was thanks to his mother's influential negotiating that Konamadou was able to transfer from his formerly peripheral location in the market to a more central one next to her where, at least in theory, sales benefited from greater traffic.

After three years of marriage Konamadou and his wife were still anxiously anticipating their first pregnancy, and this delicate topic caused a considerable degree of consternation. His wife, Ainya, was a beautiful woman with a full, silky complexion of ebony skin and her smile revealed beautiful white teeth. Konamadou would not permit her to work the market, and, while in Djenné, she spent

Konamadou Djennepo with his younger siblings, nieces, and nephews

most of her time inside the house and courtyard with her sister-in-law beading bracelets for sale. When working in Sirimou (which she did out of financial necessity), Ainya was chaperoned under the watchful eye of her mother-in-law, and in Djenné her public movements would remain highly restricted until she produced a child—a public sign that her marriage to Konamadou had been consummated. Konamadou explained that she was undergoing a necessary period of "socialization" with his family, and it was best that she remained indoors until this process was completed. The couple lived in a two-room suite comprising a bedroom and parlor that was accessed through a second courtyard flanking the main house. This smaller courtyard was shared by a group of young Qur'anic students whom Baba Djennepo benevolently lodged in a spare room adjacent Konamadou's suite. Ainya's dowry of decorated enameled pots was proudly displayed behind tall glass cabinet doors set against the back wall of their bedroom. The other piece of furniture in the tidy room was a double mattress laid directly on the floor. The mud floor had been finished with a smooth layer of concrete and was covered by plastic-reed matting. A poster of the Great Mosque at Mecca was mounted on the wall above their bed, and on another wall hung a photo calendar of fluffy kittens and a colorful woven Fulani wedding blanket.

I was well known to the family and whenever I came to visit, the women socialized freely and comfortably with me. Receptions at the Djennepo household were always warm and animated, and invariably the army of little children that clambered up my legs and arms to greet me left me sticky with gooey handprints. Mealtime, by contrast, was a strictly gender-segregated affair. The men and boys typically ate first, and the women, girls, and infant children followed, eating what was left over and usually supplemented with a reserve of rice and sauce they kept for themselves. Though young Bamoy occasionally returned from the river with a small *Capitaine* perch or catfish in his catch,[4] these fish typically went straight to market and the family subsisted on the smaller bonier fish that got dragged in with the nets. At times when the men and women of the household ate simultaneously, it was invariably from separate bowls and in different spaces. Konamadou and I sometimes lunched together on the floor of his bedroom, and Ainya would eat next door to us behind a curtain that separated the parlor. During the meal, the couple communicated somewhat awkwardly, though affectionately, through the thin fabric barrier.

On all days but Mondays Konamadou operated his shop from a tiny room of the house with its own corrugated sheet-metal door that opened directly onto the street. In the evening he occasionally hooked up a small black-and-white television to an old car battery, and his younger siblings, nieces, and nephews would pile onto a wooden bench or pack together tightly on the floor to watch an episode of the Brazilian soap or a French translation of the 1980s American TV series *Different Strokes*. He sold the same wares that he did from his market stall: bars of laundry and beauty soap, sachets of Omo detergent powder, rice, cans of tomato paste, sugar, Lipton's tea bags, individually wrapped candies, dry biscuits, batteries, candles, matches, lighters, single Rothman cigarettes, ink pens, and a little palm oil that he measured out from a metal can with a cup and poured into small plastic bags sealed with a knot. This inventory pretty much encapsulated the available variety of goods sold by any of the scores of identical convenience stores scattered through the back streets of Djenné. There were smaller and larger versions of convenience stores differentiated only by the quantities they carried rather than by the variety or quality of their stock. For those who wanted to try their hand at trading, this was accepted as the foolproof recipe, and no one ventured to risk marketing anything else or introduce a special twist. The one novel item in Konamadou's store was a game: children paid 10 CFA to open cardboard windows on an illustrated panel, winning brightly colored balloons that corresponded to the printed numbers. It was popular with a handful of neighborhood children, but it wasn't making him rich.

Sitting together one afternoon in his store, Konamadou described the urgency of his situation. His older brother was not sending back money; the younger brother, Bamoy, was returning each morning from his nighttime fishing expeditions with fewer and smaller fish; his aging father could no longer provide sufficient support for his troop of wives and children; the mud walls of the house were in dire need of repair and new bricks would have to be purchased; and, more immediate, there would not be enough rice to get the family through the dry season. They would have to purchase additional sacks of rice at the already inflated market prices. Worried and humiliated by the situation, he reluctantly asked if I would give him some money. He had made a plan to buy additional stock for his store, and, if well selected, he could hope to make a comfortable profit. Like many young men in Djenné, Konamadou imagined that if one succeeded as a trader, life would be sweet and simple. From his careful market observations he had calculated that the trade in rubber flip-flops presented a golden opportunity. This reasoning was not based on a view of demand exceeding supply, but rather he reckoned that because so many vendors were displaying flip-flops these days, they must be a sure-bet sale item.

With the money I gave him plus his own savings Konamadou ordered a cardboard crate of flip-flops from a wheeler-dealer operating near the mosque. The delivery contained six hundred pairs of the Chinese-made footwear. He paid 100 CFA per pair and planned to sell them for the usual market price of 600 CFA set by other merchants. I met him at the stall on Monday morning to assist him with unpacking the merchandise and to set up his display. Konamadou decided that it would be most attractive to sort the flip-flops by color and arrange them in neat rows along the countertop. To draw attention to his new commodity he dangled a pair of each color to the awning ridge above: blue, green, yellow, red, and brown, each permeating the air with the synthetic smell of new rubber. As I removed the pairs from their individual clear plastic wrappings, I soon realized that all the shoes in the box were either size ten and a half or eleven. These would be far too large for the mainly female cliental he could hope to attract in the Monday market. This glaring discrepancy between the size of flip-flops and the feet he aimed to shoe did not seem to trouble him. Equally disconcerting for me (but seemingly not so for Konamadou) was that the man seated cross-legged on the ground in the neighboring stall not only flogged handmade flour sifters but also ran a flourishing sideline business repairing broken flip-flops for just 5 CFA a shoe. By late morning he had already amassed a profitable pile of worn and weary sandals for mending. Meanwhile, Konamadou had sold several bars of soap, some sugar, a lighter, but no flip-flops. We would just have to sit and be patient, Konamadou assured me: "Business always picks up later on, after the midday prayer when the country folk (*gens de la brousse*) have finished selling their fruits and vegetables and have some money to buy things to bring back to their villages."

A taxman working for the city hall made his rounds, stall by stall, with his booklet of receipts trying to extract 50 CFA from every merchant. The exercise appeared futile. Like most of his fellow petty traders, Konamadou protested mildly that he had not earned enough money and, without further objection, the taxman compliantly moved on. A few moments later a Bozo woman appeared in front of the stall, holding out two pots in each hand. The pots contained an odd assortment of small dried fish, *daarey* berries (jujube), other small food items, and a few coins. Without exchanging any words, Konamadou silently reached into the small wooden box that he kept by his feet, took out two 10 CFA coins, crossed his forearms, and dropped a coin in each pot. The woman had given birth to twins and was soliciting offerings. "You must put equal amounts of whatever you choose to give in each pot," he explained, "and by crossing your arms you make a benediction for the welfare of the children."[5]

A few more bars of soap were moved, but the flashy new footwear was attracting only casual window-shopping types. Several browsers paused to inquire about the price but moved along when they heard the standard "600 CFA." Feeling almost guilty at disseminating the values of corporate globalization, I made vague attempts to explain the rudiments of capitalism, pointing out that if he undercut his competitors by, say, 50 CFA or more, he would still reap a handsome profit per pair and, better yet, would drive up his revenues by increasing the volume of sales. After working out the math several times on his calculator, carefully keying in all the numerals, Konamadou finally resisted the scheme saying that he wasn't willing to risk earning fewer total gains than his fellow merchants who clung steadfastly to their 600 CFA price tag (and who also seemed fated to take most of their shoes home with them). Not until shortly after one o'clock in the afternoon did he triumphantly sell his first pair of flip-flops. A towering Fulani woman, bedecked with hammered golden lobed earrings that hung to her shoulders and striking tattooed lips and gums, christened a pair of size elevens in green with her formidable feet. Predictably the pace of sales immediately ground to a standstill. Business was most certainly slow this season, and with diminished supplies of fish and grains all the traders were feeling the pinch. On a typical bustling Monday, Konamadou could count on bringing home about 40,000 CFA, but in the last few weeks he would be lucky to bring home half that amount.

A medicine man (*safari-koy*) was seated on the ground in the full sunshine opposite Konamadou's stall, just two meters away, with elegant posture, legs crossed in lotus position, back erect, a long slender neck, his gaze transfixed on some point far beyond the hustle of the noisy market. I estimated him to be rather young. Thin, with delicate limbs, long hands, and chiseled features offset by the silver loops that pierced his ears, he was almost exquisitely handsome but at the same time had a wild, unpredictable air about him. His long, ragged, mud-cloth shirt was perforated with small leather pouches containing amulets and talismans made from animals' tails, teeth, and horns. An orange bandana was wound tightly around the base of his close-fitted cap, and this, too, was covered in *gris-gris*. His stillness would break periodically, and his eyes would then rove purposely over the crowds of women gathered around him. Like a Mandé hunter, the medicine man was referred to as a *donso*.[6] *Donso* were associated with the bush, and they possessed powerful knowledge about the healing and poisoning properties of plants and trees. They were also capable of harnessing and channeling the potentially volatile forces of nature and the spirit world, recasting them in either beneficent or malevolent forms. The medicine man sat with his paraphernalia scattered on the ground in front of him: various types of twigs and leaves, tree bark, black powders, red powders, shiny stones, and other forest findings. His range of potent medicines ranged in price from 5 CFA per dose to many thousands for the upper-end range of *gris-gris*. The element that made each one especially effective was not so much the physical composition; more important were the secrets, or *bey-bibi* and *bey-koray*, with which the *donso* endowed them.

The medicine man trekked a circuitous journey through the Inland Niger Delta, visiting numerous towns and rural markets and, from time to time, returning to the forests to replenish his stock of ingredients. He would only stay in Djenné for a few weeks longer before moving northward. Konamadou decided that it would be wise to invest in a special *gris-gris* of his own that could be concealed in a pocket of his clothing to lure customers. After some negotiation, he arrived at an agreement with the *donso* to pay 1530 CFA for a powerful amulet that would be prepared for the following market day. Konamadou had full confidence that the amulet would work, as this reputable *donso* possessed true *bey*.

"Some are amateurs or tricksters who only have *albida. Albida* is also a kind of secret knowledge, but its effects aren't guaranteed like *bey*," he told me. In fact, *albida* is derived from the Arabic term *al-bid'a* (البدعة), meaning innovation, even heresy.

On the following Monday the medicine man was perfectly poised once again under the sweltering sun. By noon the temperature had climbed to almost forty degrees Celsius, and beads of perspiration trickled down his forehead, around the contours of his face, and down his neck. The *gris-gris* he had manufactured for Konamadou was called a *yerkoy naarey*, meaning approximately "pray to God." Unfortunately, however, its magnetic powers appeared to have no grip on the day's shoppers. The buzz of the market wound down early, and both Konamadou and the deserted *donso* sat for long periods without making a single sale. In the neighboring vicinity, the only vendor drawing a steady trickle of business was the ever silent flip-flop repairman. The medicine man made sporadic attempts to conjure up his own activity by speaking loudly into the end of his wooden flute like a microphone, announcing the cures he had for sale in a creepy, almost hypnotic voice. He then proceeded to blow forcefully into the instrument, releasing a staccato of short high-pitched blasts. The curious spectacle achieved its desired effect each time, and within moments a circle of gawking spectators gathered around. Most, however, had been enticed purely by the entertainment and had no real interest in purchasing what he had to offer. With lowered head, I cautiously voiced my skepticism about the bushman's powers to Konamadou. Rather than questioning the efficacy of the *gris-gris* he had purchased or of the myriad adorning the *donso*'s body, he patiently explained to me that "in commerce, God determines whether one will have a profitable day or not. Even if one has many *gris-gris*, one won't receive customers unless Allah shows his benevolence." In short, the secret knowledge and *gris-gris* that people possessed were tools to assist them fulfill desires and achieve goals, but their potency was ultimately determined within an Islamic framework presided over by God.

A Visit to Hasey

When I finished work one afternoon, Konamadou joined me to pay a visit to young Hasey Kouroumansé. Hasey remained confined to his widowed mother's small home in the Djoboro quarter and had so far shown no real signs of recovering from his mysterious illness. The tiny courtyard of the one-storey house was crowded with several of Hawa Yonou's daughters-in-law who dutifully spent the daytime with her cooking, beading bracelets, and looking after the throngs of their own young children. Konamadou's older sister, Tata, who was married to Baba, was also there. Despite the bustle of regular household activities, the mood was somber. Hawa Yonou's long period of caring and agonizing over her youngest son had left the pitiable woman drained and weary. Her long almond-shaped eyes nevertheless retained a glint of sparkle below their heavy lids, and it was plainly evident whom her four sons took after in appearance. She greeted us with a frail outstretched hand and led us quietly to a bedroom doorway on the courtyard. Hawa Yonou slipped behind the long curtain to inform Hasey of our visit, while we waited outside on a wooden bench against the wall. At first his mother could not persuade him to sit up and he refused to come out of his dark room, remaining curled beneath the heavy covers on his bed and whimpering like a wounded animal. With further coaxing he finally emerged, walking unsteadily to the doorway supported on his mother's arm, and then slowly collapsing onto a low stool. The waft of air from inside was stale and heavy. I would never have recognized this man before me as that wiry, feisty, and sometimes aggravating mason whom I worked with last season. Hasey had grown small and frail. The whites of his eyes had turned dark yellow and were shot through with blood vessels. Clearly, he was also a bit mad.

For seven months now, Hasey had suffered splitting headaches, a loss of memory, and bouts of aggressive behavior, sometimes lunging violently at family members. He was terrified to leave his room, tossed restlessly at night, and shrieked wildly at the phantoms that tormented him. The combination of doctors' prescriptions and African remedies from the marketplace were apparently having no affect. He babbled incoherently to Konamadou and me about ghoulish spirits who were prying their way through sealed windows to get inside. His mother left him gently slouched against the doorframe and went to fetch an enameled pot from the dreary room. She crouched back down next to him and drew forth a small tea-glass of the murky liquid. A *marabout* had prepared the medicinal water by washing away inky Qur'anic verses from a writing board and collecting the holy fluid in a receptacle. The power of the written word in the West African context was poignantly elucidated by Mungo Park in his eighteenth-century description of producing a *"saphie"*[7] (protective verse) on a writing board:

> I . . . wrote the board full from top to bottom on both sides; and my land-lord, to be certain of having the full force of the charm, washed the writing from the board into a calabash with a little water, and having said a few prayers over it, drank this powerful draught: after which, lest a single word should escape, he licked the board until it was quite dry. (1983 [1799], 180)

This holy medicine infused with Qurʿanic writings was locally called *nasi* in Djenné-Chiini.[8] Hawa Yonou struggled with Hasey to help him drink, and Hasey managed to dribble most of the contents down his stained T-shirt. With a second glass he weakly rinsed his eyes and washed his face. He was completely exhausted now and returned to bed. I left his mother with a heavy heart and a small gift of money to buy medicine.

Hasey was just twenty-three years old and had planned to marry a young Bozo woman from the town. Arrangements had already been under way, and money had been sent to the girl's family just before he was struck by the strange illness. Wedding preparations had since been suspended, and his young fiancée continued to wait for his recovery. Like most single men his age, Hasey had been living away from home in a small room he rented from a family in Djoboro. Boys in Djenné commonly leave home when they reach sixteen or seventeen years of age and move into a nearby dwelling until married. Many households reserve a small room (*kani hu*)[9] and lease it, free of charge or for a nominal sum, to the neighborhood's adolescent males and bachelors. These rooms are often window-less and have their own separate entrance from the street, but without access to the rest of the house. Lodgers share cramped quarters with age mates, and some older boys are able to secure a room of their own. Typically these small, con-gested abodes are used for sleeping and socializing, and the boys eat most meals at home with their families where they also assist with daytime chores.

This practice of providing young men with a communal dwelling derives from the Bozo institution of the *sâho*. Until recently, *sâhos* were erected in all Bozo villages and were generally the most elaborately decorated mud buildings displaying complex facades of geometric brickwork and pilasters, and some had columns. At the time of my fieldwork, a few fine examples survived in villages along the river,[10] and others were being restored with funding from the Dutch government, including the elaborate *sâho* in the nearby village of Sirimou. In temporary fishing encampments along the Niger, Bozo communities continue to set up grass huts for adolescent boys, and these tend to be separated from the long, narrow line of dwellings.[11] The *sâho* was a space where boys learned to be independent from their parents, to organize themselves cooperatively within their own age group, and to mature sexually. In relative privacy, young men could court girls free from the watchful eyes of parents. Liberal sexual attitudes and premarital relations, however, have clashed with the Bozos' Islamic conversion and the adoption of a more conservative ideology. The *sâho*, regarded as a tradi-tional institution and associated with an animist past, has largely disappeared, replaced by the more modern and socially acceptable rooming arrangement.[12]

RIGHT A surviving *sâho* in the village of Kotaga along the Niger River

The door to Hasey's rented room opened onto a narrow alleyway known to be haunted by the spirit of a *marabout*.[13] Every Friday, the gargantuan specter comes out late at night and sits waiting, filling the entire breadth of the street with his girth. This *marabout* dons an enormous white *boubou* and carries a heavy chain of luminous white prayer beads. Hasey and his family firmly attributed his illness to a horrifying confrontation with this *diable*. The ghosts of *marabouts* and other holy men are usually referred to as *waliju* ("saints"),[14] and many doubt that these normally pious spirits would cause harm. Indeed, people invoke the benevolent powers of *waliju* to assist with daily troubles and crises. Other stories circulated, however, about wicked spirits belonging to deceased *marabouts*. Some men suggested alternatively that illnesses like the one plaguing Hasey were inflicted by evil *djinn* called *aru-kuru* in Djenné-Chiini (*kama limba* in Bamanankan). *Aru-kuru* gloat in the sadistic pleasure of punishing those they catch wandering the dark streets late at night in search of illicit love. "These nasty *djinn* are attracted to people and places that are 'dirty,'" said one Songhay friend, using the Djenné-Chiini term *jiibi-térey* to describe impurity rather than unwashed. "Men and women can't take each other home to make love where either their parents or spouses might be waiting. So, after covertly talking and flirting in the streets and market during the daytime, they arrange for a secret place to *rendez-vous*. They meet in the middle of the night amongst the piles of garbage (*dandara*) and debris at the edge of town, in alleyways or in abandoned houses. These are the places where *aru-kuru* hang out." Perhaps, correctly, I understood the *aru-kuru* to be playing the causal role in a narrative about promiscuity and sexually transmitted diseases, and all told within a moralistic framework that ultimately laid blame on the transgressors of proper etiquette and good behavior. I hoped that Hasey had not befallen such a fate.

Masonry Work for Konamadou

By late February prospects were slowly improving for Konamadou. He wasn't going to revolutionize the international flip-flop trade, but he was now earning a small and steady income from his shop and weekly market stall. The *gris-gris* certainly had not reeled in the anticipated hordes of shoppers, but Konamadou, with unshaken faith, calmly assured me that the power of the *gris-gris* would accumulate "*kayna kayna*" ("slowly slowly"). "Besides, if things don't pick up before the *donso* quits town," he said, "I'll exchange it for a better one or ask for my money back." In the past week he had also started laboring on the house of a childhood chum who still lived in the quarter. The project was a favor and he earned no money, but Konamadou enjoyed practicing as a mason once again.

During the day, when he was away from home, one of the student lodgers in his mother's house watched the shop. The student was a responsible Fulani boy whom Baba Djennepo had spotted herding cattle in Koutiala. The young teenager suffered from a painful, crippling disease that had stunted his growth, contorting his spine into an exaggerated hunch and raised his bony shoulders level with his ears. Baba took pity watching him wield a stick to chase cows. He convinced the boy's parents that their son was not suited for this work and arranged to bring him back to Djenné where he kindly provided room and board, and paid for his Qurᶜanic lessons with a neighborhood *marabout*. Initially the boy could not speak a word of Djenné-Chiini, but within a year he had become conversant in the language and proved to be a loyal assistant and productive member of the Djennepo household.

Konamadou was Baba's only son in the building trade. As a young boy, Baba had turned him over to his mason uncle, Beré Yonou, to work as a laborer, and his actual apprenticeship started some time later, lasting a full ten years. Though Baba had received several years of formal schooling while Mali was still under French administration, he, like many Bozo, resisted submitting his own children to the system. In recent years the older generation's staunch position against state schooling has relaxed somewhat and younger Bozos, like Konamadou's half-brother and nephew, were enrolled in classes. Konamadou's age group, however, had missed out and many remained illiterate with only a very basic level of spoken French, if any. Aside from manual labor and fishing, other sorts of employment opportunity were remote. As a young man Konamadou held steadfastly to the prospect that he would become a mason. He recalled earning a weekly salary of 250 CFA during his years of training (i.e., 10 percent of his current daily wage as a mason), and he was obliged to make regular small gifts to his master. In 1992 Beré Yonou made a pilgrimage (*hajj*) to Mecca and Medina, and prior to departure he released Konamadou from service to temporarily join his older brother in Ivory Coast and earn some money fishing. Konamadou stayed away for half a year, and when he returned to Djenné he resumed the final stages of his training. He was presented with his trowel and crowbar later that year, and Beré Yonou and Baba Djennepo made benedictions for his prosperous career as a mason.

In early 2001 the Dutch-Malian preservation committee overseeing the restoration of selected houses awarded Beré Yonou a medal for outstanding craftsmanship. Though still recognized as one of the town's most accomplished masters, Beré Yonou's volume of work was slowing to a trickle as he edged toward retirement. Most of his client contracts had been transferred into the hands of former pupils, and, sadly, little was left to pass on to Konamadou. Though Konamadou's maternal grandfather of the Sekré family had also been a Djenné mason, he had long ago switched to trading and nothing remained of his former client connections. Konamadou relied mainly on other masons, like the Kouroumansé brothers, to include him on projects. During the 1990s he had worked with Baba Kouroumansé on several concrete building sites in Bamako, and he regarded Baba as his *patron de béton,* as opposed to Beré Yonou who was his esteemed *patron de banco.* Now, however, Konamadou was the oldest remaining son in Djenné to care for his aging parents, and he felt that he could no longer journey far from home to find work.

The work for his friend involved some interior plastering, but no actual masonry work. Since marrying, the man had moved into a two-room building in his father's compound and his new wife pleaded to have the bedroom and parlor walls rendered and painted. Konamadou confirmed with a knowing grimace that every married woman insists upon her rooms being properly decorated. Cement is used to finish walls and floors by those who can afford it, and some residents circumscribe their door and window surrounds with a coat of brightly colored commercial paint. Imported glazed-and-patterned ceramic tiles have also made inroads among Djenné's wealthy. These slick, mass-produced tiles offer the allure of resilient and easy-to-clean surfaces, and, like porcelain squat-toilet plates and washbasins, they are popularly associated with modern, urban, and Western lifestyles.

Konamadou's Bozo friend had spent ten years fishing in Ivory Coast, but when he returned to Djenné to marry, work was scarce and his savings were soon spent. The friend mixed the plaster in the compound courtyard and delivered bucket loads to Konamadou inside. The finishing plaster had the fine, liquid consistency of pargeting plaster. It was made by mixing *laabu-tyirey* (red mud) with a generous proportion of red, granular sand taken from the riverbed, and plenty of water. The ceiling had been completed to wonderful effect two days earlier, and Konamadou was now standing on top of an oil drum finishing the mud-brick walls. He covered section by section, each measuring approximately one square meter. The runny plaster was scooped from the bucket in a quick, fluid motion with the flat plate of his trowel and splattered onto the existing dry surface of coarser mud plaster. He then smoothed it evenly with his trowel. He bragged jovially of his ambidexterity, and playfully amused us by wielding the tool in either hand with equal competence. After completing half a wall's surface in this manner, Konamadou further smoothed and homogenized the surface with two wooden block-like pads that he gripped in both hands by handles nailed onto their backsides. He then gave the wall its final polished veneer by gently buffing it with a dampened chiffon cloth. The end result was truly impressive.

We broke for tea and peanuts.[15] Children hawked tiny bundles of locally produced peanuts that they wrapped in clear plastic and conveyed about the streets on broad aluminium metal trays. *Jiminta* (syn., *namti*) was another popular snack made by crushing peanuts, sugar, and chilies into a thick, fudge-like paste. *Jiminta* was prepared by women and sold from the front vestibules of their houses. "Peanuts contain vitamins and they're a good replacement for meat," the friend volunteered, while rolling a handful between his palms and carefully blowing away the skins. "While many people can't afford meat," Konamadou added, "they can buy peanuts for just 25 CFA a bag." The mason then asked confidently if his work was good, gesturing to the walls and finished ceiling with a sweep of his eyes. I confirmed that it was excellent and compared him favorably to al-Hajji Kouroumansé. "Oh, I am still just a little child," he responded with rehearsed bashfulness, characteristically downplaying his own expertise and effectively neutralizing the power of my praise. Words carried force that demanded cautious management.

Later that evening, while chatting together at his store in the glow of a kerosene lamp, Konamadou told me that if he had been paid for this commission he could have made a handsome profit. "Potentially, a mason can make even more money by controlling the budgets of his own individual contract jobs than he does if he labors for someone else for a flat rate of 2500 CFA per day," adding, emphatically, that "2500 CFA doesn't go a long way if you have a family to feed." Konamadou then revealed to me that he had taken on a young apprentice of his own late last season. He had kept this news secret, because he felt ashamed of not having been able to provide the boy with any trade experience this year. He had desperately hoped that the three of us would be working together again and that I would meet his apprentice in action. Konbakary Djennepo was a distant relative whose career, like so many other boys, had been decided upon by his mother and older brother after his father's death. They came to the usual agreement that Konamadou would provide the boy with a professional training in exchange for dutiful respect and free labor. Soon afterward, Konbakary assisted him on two brief assignments in Tolober, and had proven to be a bright and ambitious pupil. Konamadou was clearly thrilled by the prospect of seeing this young man through to his membership with the *barey ton*. That night in the blackness of my room I closed my eyes and wished hard for the skies to bring rain, for the harvests to improve and the fish to multiply, and for better economic times in Djenné that would permit a good mason like Konamadou to have a strong hand in shaping the future generation of this city's fine and resilient craftsmen.

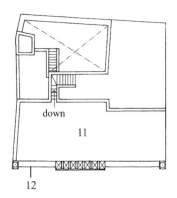

1. vestibule and Qur'anic school
2. vestibule
3. courtyard
4. sleeping room for garibou students
5. parlour
6. sleeping room
7. storeroom
8. kitchen
9. toilet
10. nightsoil tower
11. roof terrace
12. parapet wall and roof-line decoration

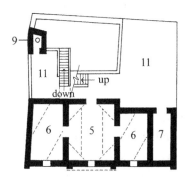

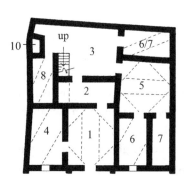

Ground-floor, first-storey, and roof plan of Marabout Haydarah's house in the Yobukayna quarter

8 · Cat Heads and Mud Miters

When the market shut down early Monday evening Bayeré sent a laborer around to Tolober to inform me that work at the Brunet-Jailly house would be canceled until further notice. The timber merchant was ill, and, reportedly, no other source of palm wood was available to enable us to continue roofing the auxiliary building. The *marabout*'s project in Yobukayna was also delayed while we waited for a supply of long, sturdy beams to construct the decorative *potigé* (facade) over the entrance to his house. I decided to take advantage of this break in the schedule to observe operations at other sites and meet with masons around town. I peddled off in the precious cool of the morning, and as I made my approach to the narrow little bridge spanning the stagnant shallow water surrounding Djenné, al-Hajji appeared suddenly, cycling over the top in the opposite direction. He paused to greet me, said he was on a search for wood and that he was determined to get his team back to work at the *marabout*'s house that very day. I had fully come to expect last-minute changes to the plan, so I re-routed my journey to Yobukayna where I found Bamoy and several laborers already gathered. I was excited to learn that we would begin constructing the *toron*, the cat heads and mud miters that accentuate the roofline of the *potigé*, lending the house its distinctively Moroccan features. This stage was crucial to the project. I would need to observe the technique and division of labor carefully, since the work involved focused craftsmanship and precise calculation of every element. The *potigé* is the architectural component that most visibly distinguishes Djenné's houses from West Africa's other mud building traditions, heralding the socioeconomic position of its inhabitants and the proficiency of its masons.

Reflections on Bozo Identity

Al-Hajji returned from his mission to the outskirts of town with an important tip. He had learned from another mason that a fresh supply of palm timbers had been delivered to a merchant at the edge of Yobukayna, next to the water and not far from the building site. He summoned all to follow him on foot through the labyrinthine passages of the quarter. Yobukayna is a wealthier neighborhood than Djoboro, populated mainly by farmers, merchants, and *marabouts,* and numerous two-storied homes and ostentatious pillared and decorated facades border its streets.

As we strolled, Bamoy volunteered his unsolicited reflections on the mainly Djennénké population that lived in this quarter. The term *djennénké* encompasses numerous ethnicities and designates all those whose families have been resident in Djenné for at least two or more generations. Though the Bozo form part of the ethnic mix that has populated the town since its beginnings (and are widely believed to be the autochthonous people of the Inland Niger Delta), they regularly distinguish themselves in conversation from the urbanized and heterogeneous grouping of Djennénké.[1] Supposed contrasting attitudes toward money and wealth typically highlight the distinction between the two, and the Djennénké are painted as miserly and frugal in the same way that that English satirically describe the Scottish. Bamoy, with a sneer, told me that "Djennénké people have piles of money, but they're forever whining that they have none. They hoard their earnings and won't even buy enough food to properly feed themselves. The Bozo on the other hand"— and here he perked up proudly—"spend what they have when they have it, and they'll always eat their fill! If a Bozo has 500 CFA they'll go straight to the market to buy rice and invite others to join their feast. If they find only 50 CFA, a Bozo will purchase a few Kola nuts and share them around." This sort of ethnocentric boasting capitalizes on prevalent beliefs in Djenné, and Mali more generally, that the Bozo are a kind and generous people. But it conveniently omits negative stereotypes and popular jokes about the Bozo's supposed feeble intelligence, narrow thinking, and superstitious ways.

Notably, when Bamoy discussed issues concerning his own cultural community he used the terms Bozo and Sorko interchangeably to designate the ethnic grouping. He, like others, claimed that both names referred to the same people, namely, his own related fisher folk of the Inland Niger Delta (or,

View from Yobukayna over Djenné's roof terraces to the mosque

more specifically, the riverine territory of the Pondo). When I pressed Bamoy to suggest a bozophone name for his people, he skirted the issue, claiming that he, like the majority of Djenné's urbanized Bozo, did not speak his ethnic language. This is not uncommon in Djenné, or in other urban centers where settled Bozo populations have been linguistically assimilated by the dominant Bamana-, Fulfulde-, or Songhay-language communities.[2] As noted by Blecke, Bozo identity cannot be straightforwardly defined by language.[3]

Bozo in the outlying region and along the river, however, typically use the term *tigué* to refer to themselves as a people. "The word 'Bozo' is a French term," Bamoy added, "and the *koyra-boro* call us *sorko*." The term "bozo" is, in fact, a French corruption of the Bamanankan *bo so*, meaning "house of bamboo."[4] This refers to the ephemeral brush and straw-mat huts erected by the Bozo in their *lakha* encampments when pursuing migratory fish stocks along the river, and it is the term Bamanankan speakers use to identify all non-Bamanankan fishermen of the Inland Niger Delta.[5] The *koyra-boro,* on the other hand, are Djenné's Song-hay residents who came from the north.[6] It is therefore not surprising that the *koyra-boro* would have identified the Pondo's fishermen as being the same as their own northern neighbors, the Sorko, whose similar fishing practices dominate the Niger bend between Timbuktu and Gao. It also seems entirely plausible that the mainly urbanized Bozo adopted the Songhay term *sorko,*[7] using it interchange-ably with *bozo* for self-identification, as the Songhay moved into the region in greater numbers and Songhay-based Djenné-Chiini became the lingua franca of trade and commerce.[8] The ambiguity connected with the name, identity, and ori-gin of the Pondo fishermen is exemplified in Ligers's title for his grand study of those communities: *Les Sorko (Bozo): Maîtres du Niger* (1964). His placement of *Bozo* in parentheses suggests that he interpreted it to be a secondary or sub-identity for these people, even though they occupy a different geographic region and possess a distinct language from the Sorko of the northern Niger bend.[9]

A question remains: To what extent did the Bozo have a cohesive group identity prior to the arrival of Bamana cultivators, Songhay merchants, and French colonialists. Daget, Konipo, and Sanankoua, for instance, wrote that "the Bozo never claimed to descend from a common ancestor, nor originate from the same region. Whereas some declared that their ancestors emerged from the earth, perhaps a way of claiming autochthony,[10] others declared unambiguously that they originated upstream from Mandé country, others from downstream, and others claim a Sarakolé origin."[11]

Despite communication divides by dialect (and in some cases entirely dif-ferent languages), competing myths of origin, and varying livelihoods and settlement types (from towns to migratory encampments), a strong sense of common ethnic identity exists among the Bozo people. For the most part, they have married endogamously within their group and have resisted integration with the constant procession of invaders and newcomers to the region. Though they share the waterways with the Somono fishermen, they still remain sepa-rate. Even in the dense cosmopolitan mix of Djenné, most Bozo families are concentrated in the modest quarters of Djoboro and Semani, where they have managed to maintain a distinct identity. Their professional pursuits remain narrowly defined, but as fishermen, fish vendors, pirogue builders, river trans-porters, and masons, the Bozo contribute to the local and national economies in important ways. As Islam encroaches increasingly upon ethnic and cultural forms of distinctiveness in Mali, and changing environmental factors render fishing a less viable option, it is difficult to predict how the existing Bozo identity will alter and transform in the coming decades.

On-Site Learning

When we finally arrived at the pile of timber outside the merchant's home, al-Hajji carefully selected several quartered palm trunks based on their length, straightness, and density. We then cautiously carried them back, two by two. Ronier palm wood (*sebe*) has a coarse fibrous composition that extends through the length of the trunk and provides high tensile strength and a satisfactory degree of termite resistance. The dense bundle of needle-like fibers easily pierce the skin when handling the wood, and some of my workmates sensibly kept a safety pin in their trouser pockets, and used it periodically to extract the deep and painful splinters.

Four slender mud-brick pilasters had already been integrated into the wall construction. They rose the full height of the two-storey facade and would serve to organize the arrangement of sculptural elements above the roofline. A single pilaster terminated each end of the planar facade, and two others framed the somewhat asymmetrically positioned entrance to the house. The clear span between the two pilasters framing the entrance measured 3.00 meters, and the width of each pilaster was 0.40 meters (equivalent to the length of a standard *tubaabu-ferey* brick), totaling 3.80 linear meters. Based on this measured dimension, al-Hajji determined that there should be a total of seven miters (*sarafar*) spread along the crest of roofline above the door. He patiently explained that the spacing between each element must be carefully calibrated with the use of a tape measure. "One small mistake means the whole facade will be spoiled," he insisted. Al-Hajji squatted down in the road in front of the house and proceeded to sketch two parallel lines in the dirt with his right index finger. These, he said, represented the two pilasters, and he capped them with a single perpendicular line to indicate the top of the parapet. He then made seven evenly spaced impressions above with his thumb that suggested the overall majestic effect of the miters. Worthy of note is that French is used to express the numerical values of linear dimensions, weights, and the time of day, arguably because tools such as metric tape measures, metric scales, clocks, and watches were popularly introduced during the colonial regime, and French vocabulary became fixedly associated with these scientific modes of European measurement. Quantities of items, however, such as bricks and market goods, are referred to in Djenné-Chiini.[12] Al-Hajji thus spoke of a span of *trois mètres quatre-vingt* ("three meters eighty"), crowned by *sarafar idye iiye* ("seven *sarafar idye*").

After delegating tasks, al-Hajji set off once again on his bicycle, this time

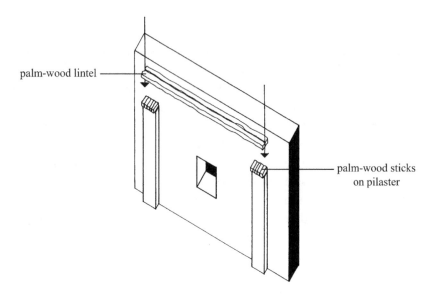

palm-wood lintel

palm-wood sticks
on pilaster

Small sticks of palm wood are placed on top of the mud-brick *sarafar woy* pilasters to distribute the weight of the heavy palm-wood lintel above. The lintel will support a decorative assembly of *gaaga* pilasters and *musi bumo* half-columns with *sarafar idye* above.

in search of African medicine. His youngest son's temperature had spiraled during the night, and the young boy suffered from aching, swollen limbs. Abdullahi Bouaré had been instructed to chop the palm trunks into specified lengths on the road outside the house, while the other laborers prepared large quantities of *banco* mortar in the courtyard and transferred supplies of bricks to the roof. Yappi had been sent on an errand to arrange for deliveries of laterite soil, thus allowing Ali to take up the apprentice's position alongside the mason. To begin, Bamoy Sao and Ali dismantled a 3.80-meter-long section of parapet wall stretching between the outer edges of the two pilasters that framed the entranceway. The low parapet had been constructed along the top of the completed exterior walls at the end of the previous building season to protect the house from erosion during intervening rains. Using a crowbar Ali assisted Bamoy in carefully removing one course of brickwork at a time, until they reached the uppermost level of wood members that supported the multilayered *fata-taki* ("four-winged") ceiling of the second-storey room behind the facade. The intact bricks of the dismantled parapet were reserved for erecting the *potigé*. Construction throughout the region regularly involves demolition and rebuilding, and an irritant to conservationist is that restoration and preservation efforts of historic buildings like this *marabout*'s house in Yobukayna often entail partial or total reconstruction. Local masons fully exploit what might be glossed the "plasticity" of mud building, arguing that the original walls, usually composed of cylindrical *djenné ferey* bricks, have become structurally unstable.

Ali passed short, thin sticks of palm wood to Bamoy, who carefully aligned them one beside the other on the flat top of either pilaster. The sticks were set perpendicular to the facade, extending back to meet the exposed ends of the wooden roof beams and projecting outward to cantilever just a few centimeters beyond the front faces of the pilasters. This bed of wood members provided lateral support for the pilasters that would carry the weight of three heavy palm timbers spanning them, on top of which would rest the entire decorative ensemble of cat heads and mud-brick miters awaiting construction. I worked nearby, passing scoops of fresh mortar to Bamoy, who used the pasty mud to fix the sticks firmly in place.

Pausing a moment to scan the cubist patchwork of sunlit terraces and shaded courtyards, the mason generously offered those at hand an explanation of how the *potigé* would be erected, describing the many stages sequentially. Bamoy first pointed to the section of wall and roof that he and Ali had cut away, showing us the horizontal palm sticks that integrated the tops of the pilasters with the solidity of the wall and the ceiling structure behind. He then described the placement of the crossbeam, the *toron*, the miniature pilasters and cat heads above, and finally the pointed miters, all the while emphasizing the complex nature of the ensemble and the necessity of following an exact method. His well-formulated instructions meshed words and gestures, and demonstrated a considerable degree of firsthand experience. But clearly Bamoy was rehearsing the steps and simulating the procedures as much for himself as for our benefit. Building the *potigé* is one of the most demanding tasks the mason faces, and the one that most publicly proclaims his expertise (*bey rey*). Bamoy was therefore determined to take the time required and ensure that his work was both technically proficient and aesthetically beautiful.

The Power of Benedictions

When Yappi returned from his errand, he resumed assisting Bamoy to span the long, heavy palm timbers between the tops of the two pilasters. Ali, the junior of the two apprentices, was once again driven back down the ranks to work with the laborers, monotonously preparing and passing materials from the courtyard to the roof. He slacked off for the remainder of the morning, feigning fatigue and whining about a sore back. Predictably, Yappi seized the opportunity to taunt his competitor, bellowing accusations from the rooftop that Ali was idle and hadn't eaten a sufficient breakfast. Issues of food, sleep, and sex are conceptualized as forms of corporeal capital and strategically employed in the banter between builders separating those with plenty from those who are lacking. It was not in Yappi's interest to discipline the younger man and bring him back into line; instead, Yappi made his gain by drawing public attention to Ali's professional ineptitude. Al-Hajji's sudden reappearance on-site spurred Yappi's malignant purpose, and he competed for his master's favor with heightened bravado. The mason's apparent disinterest, however, soon quelled the young man's boisterous assault.

From street level, al-Hajji directed the cumbersome positioning of the quartered palm trunks with an economy of commands and gestures, and with his characteristic emphasis on precision. This span was two storeys above street level and would carry the full weight of the massive *potigé* decoration. When all the timbers were secured in place, al-Hajji again departed in search of more wood. Bamoy and Yappi then began building up a thick layer of mud and setting bricks on top of the span, as I handed materials to them on cue. When the first course of bricks was complete, Bamoy repositioned himself, squatting directly on top of the construction to start the next layer. Intuitively I thought this a bad idea, somehow feeling that this span was not altogether stable. Just as I had a premonition of the collapsing structure, it actually began to crumble beneath Bamoy's weight, crashing onto the street below. Bamoy had nimbly leaped back to the roof in an astounding display of *m'baaka*-like speed and agility, seemingly defying gravity! An eerie silence followed the jolting thud, and even the *harmattan* winds appeared to come to a momentary halt. Bamoy, Yappi, and I peered nervously over the edge into the street below to assess the disaster. All the bricks, the mud mortar, and the heaviest of the palm timbers had fallen, and the house entrance was now obstructed by the debris. Miraculously no one had been directly below at that moment. Neighborhood children played outdoors all day, frequently traipsing in and out of doorways along the street, and laborers working at ground level continually exited and entered the house to fetch deliveries of building materials. All were safe.

"Ce n'est pas possible," Bamoy muttered breathlessly, shaking his head in disbelief. "Ce n'est pas possible." Yappi turned to me, slightly shocked, and said that he had never seen this happen before. Quickly regaining composure, Bamoy interjected that accidents like this can and do happen from time to time. He paused, and then exclaimed with grand confidence that effaced any trace of shaken nerves: "No one was injured, of course, because I made proper benedictions this morning before work." The whole assembly, nevertheless, had to be rebuilt. The palm trunk was salvaged from the street and hauled back to the roof, but the bricks had shattered and would be recycled as mortar. By midday, two courses of brick had been laid above the reconstructed span of palm timbers, and we were ready to start building the *toron*.

Toron

Toron are the neat rectangular bundles of short palm sticks that protrude perpendicularly from the walls of mud buildings, and are a characteristic property of the *style-Soudanais* mosques. In Djenné's houses, *toron* typically extend from the base of the parapet wall at the level of the roofline, and serve many functions. They act as a built-in scaffolding system that the masons use to construct and repair the decorative *potigé;* they partially shade the surface of the facade from the midday sun, thereby helping to keep interior temperatures cool; and they supply decorative relief.[13] On the *marabout*'s house, there would be seven evenly spaced *toron,* and these would align with the seven *sarafar* that would eventually be constructed at the top of the assembly.

Al-Hajji returned and joined Bamoy in building the *toron.* The old mason, Koto Salamantao, strolled past and politely assumed control from street level, guiding his two younger colleagues in the careful construction of the fifty-five-centimeter projections. Bamoy explained that this task required a third, experienced party to oversee the work from a vantage point where the composition, projections, and spacing between the *toron* could be properly assessed. Koto Salamantao verified by eye that the projections were even, and that the bundle of timbers in each *toron* was held together in a solid, rectangular section. Much attention was lavished on the facade and its decorative detail, since these constitute the most prominent display of household status and the masons' skill. Respectfully, Bamoy and al-Hajji addressed the senior mason as *patron* and were cautious not to utter his proper name when he was present. Al-Hajji regularly gave Koto Salamantao kola nuts or small gifts of money (the *prix de thè*), as is customary in the profession. He and Bamoy claimed that an old mason's words, especially those spoken by a trade master, were extremely powerful and required the neutralizing efficacy of gifts. More specifically, the gesture of giving and receiving small gifts initiates and sustains relations of patronage. Junior masons stand to benefit from the distribution (or sharing) of new building commissions that the senior tradesmen

Marabout Haydarah's house under construction in Yobukayna quarter

control, and that are occasionally delegated through the gerontocratic network of the *barey ton*. More generally, they receive benedictions from the
older masons that protect and guarantee successful work.

The old mason continued on his way after the first two *toron* had been perfectly arranged. In contrast to Bamoy's reasoning that a more experienced
mason should direct the work, the laborer Abdullahi Bouaré was ordered to quit
chopping wood and pass judgment on the placement and composition of the
new projections. In fact, Abdullahi was frequently called upon for this sort of
task. The mercurial balance he displayed in his acrobatic antics evidently translated to his perceptual skills for assessing proportion and symmetry, and these
were recognized and valued by al-Hajji. Omar, too, had a chance to escape the
monotony of mixing mud, and he enthusiastically volunteered to put his hand
to the axe while Abdullahi guided the masons' work. While Yappi and I waited
with the masons for more palm timbers to be cut to length and sent up from
below, al-Hajji commented critically about the incomplete decorations on a
nearby house. Status and qualifications among Djenné's masons are subtly
negotiated and defined through a competitive discourse that most often takes
place backstage rather than as an open confrontation. Al-Hajji's critique maneuvered the focus of attention to his own craft expertise, thereby providing his
junior colleagues with a lesson on correct building. For starters, the mason
pointed out that the facade of the other house was disproportionately high, and
thus all the decoration was wrong. "These are masons who have no experience
building a proper *potigé*," he complained. "They're local masons from this quarter," Bamoy chimed in, "Everyone wants to build the traditional decorations,
but they lack the knowledge." When Bayeré visited our site the following day,
he, too, remarked on the unusually high placement of the *toron* at the neighboring house and criticized those masons for having constructed an even number.
According to his rule, there must always be an odd number of *toron* correspond-
ing to the number of *sarafar* spikes above. In the course of their coordinated
exposé, the three masons agreed that what distinguished a master's expertise
was his ability to construct a proper staircase (*kalikali*), a slender shaft toilet
(*nyégé*), and a well-proportioned *potigé* (facade) with all its elements. "If one can
do all three," al-Hajji concluded, "one is truly *un patron, un vrai maître maçon*."

Following the call to prayer at ten minutes past two in the afternoon, al-
Hajji and several other builders paused to pray. They descended to the courtyard
of the house and lined up at the steel oil drum to make ablutions with the water
stored there. Prayers were made individually, some men staking a spot in the
open sun and others in the cool empty rooms of the house, all orienting their

prostrations in the direction of the mosque's *mihrab* tower visible over the roof-tops. During the remainder of the afternoon we managed to finish the fifth of the total number of seven *toron*. We worked nearly an hour beyond the normal finishing time of 3:00 PM. There was no *harmattan* haze to protect us from the blazing sun that day, and everyone was fatigued. My sinuses were inflamed, my throat scratchy, and I had a dull throbbing in my inner ear. The grueling six-day workweek started at about half-past-eight each morning and, aside from young al-Hajj's preparations of restorative, sugar-infused tea, there were no formal breaks for resting or eating. All team members on this project, including the masons, were paid a daily wage, and there was no financial compensation for the overtime they frequently contributed.

The two remaining *toron* were completed the next morning before we began dismantling the stretches of parapet wall flanking each side of the decorative *potigé*. Yappi loosened the bricks one-by-one with a crowbar, and I removed them and piled them up for later use. He struck up a familiar ballad about the difficulties of this work and his fanciful desires to one day become a *commerçant* (trader). "You can't keep doing this when you grow old," he warned sternly. "Even though I make benedictions each morning for protection, they don't guarantee that my body will last." Yappi's benedictions, I was told, were wholly comprised of Qurʿanic verses that he had learned from his father. "I'll leave Djenné," he said with a sense of conviction, "and go to France . . . or maybe Germany or America where a trader can make a decent living." His desire to desert his country altogether for better economic prospects abroad was somewhat endemic throughout Mali. At the time of this writing Mali remained one of the world's poorest nations and, despite foreign aid and development programs, many Malians shared the perception that the country's economy had made no progress. Brenner noted this a decade earlier, writing that "development" in Mali "is open to the charge that it simply reproduces the political and social *status quo*."[14] For many aristocrats and farmers during colonial times, becoming a merchant meant becoming a Muslim.[15] Yappi and other young men in Djenné, however, did not conflate religious identity with the pursuit of commerce; rather, they were primarily attracted by the possibility of financial gain and the chance to escape into the wider world.

Once the existing parapet wall had been taken down to a level just below the roof surface, al-Hajji and Bamoy began measuring and marking out the sequence of alternating *toron* and *fūney* (window-like apertures) that would punctuate the newly constructed parapet. Forty-centimeter-wide *toron* were followed by thirty-centimeter-wide *fūney*, and so on, filling the entire length

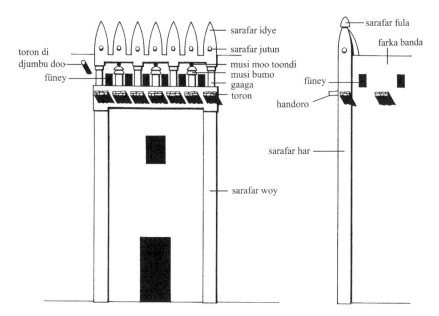

LEFT Elevation plan of the decorative elements of Marabout Haydarah's Moroccan-style house in Yobukayna quarter.   RIGHT Elevation of the *sarafar har* pilaster at the edge of the house facade, capped by a *fula*. The parapet wall along the roofline is punctuated with protruding *toron* and *fūney* apertures.

of the facade on each side of the *potigé*. Al-Hajji stood up when he reached the end of the building, straightened his posture, and let his tape measure recoil back into its case with a snap. He gestured with a nod of his head toward a house in the near distance looming larger and slightly higher than its neighbors. The grand house of Babèr Tawati was located a few streets over from *Marabout* Haydarah's house, and sat on a sizable plot of land. It was built at the turn of the century after the French administrators installed themselves in their *campement*, and Babèr Tawati, an influential member of the town's religious community, became the imam of the town's newly reconstructed grand mosque (AD 1906).[16] Several years earlier, al-Hajji had been commissioned by surviving members of the Tawati family to maintain their house, and he was in charge of reconstructing the weatherworn decorations along the roof. He directed my attention to the apertures (*fūney*) in the parapet wall, saying they were unevenly spaced. "I was still a *petit maçon* back then and had a lot to learn," he added. "But I also feared working on that house! Babèr Tawati's things are locked inside his room on the second storey."[17] He was referring to the room above the front entrance that overlooks the street and is typically the preserve of the household patriarch. "That room is haunted by his spirit," al-Hajji continued, "and nobody else can live in it." "If Babèr Tawati's spirit is angry with you, and you meet him face to face, there's no chance. You will die immediately! The kohl (*kalé*) around his eyes isn't the usual black . . . it's red like fire." Once more I was offered an account of vengeful holy men (*waliju*) whose spirits cause harm.

Cat Heads

When I arrived for work the following morning, the red, yellow, and green stripes of the Malian flag were fluttering from the rooftop in a proud display of support for the national football team. This evening's African Cup of Nations event would be the semi-final match against Cameroon, and an electric optimism animated Djenné's dusty air. Al-Hajji glanced down at me with a buoyant expression from where he and Bamoy were already at work. The two masons were carefully measuring the spacing and configuration for the decorative brick parapet that would be erected today.

This Moroccan-style composition would consist of six rectangular apertures (*fūney*), three bricks high, that would pierce the parapet wall above the level of the seven carefully arranged *toron*. Each aperture would be framed by alternating pilasters and half-columns. The squat pilasters (*gaaga*), four in total, would be terminated with bold rectilinear capitals supporting a span of long palm timbers running the length of the *potigé*. The three half-columns centered between the pilasters would be composed of semicircular drums carved from the brittle mud bricks with the masons' *kuuru-bibi* trowels. The height of the half-columns would equal that of the six apertures, and each column would shoulder two vertically superimposed spherical projections made from brick and sculpted with plaster. These pill-like protrusions were referred to as the *musi bumo*, or "cat's head." In the narrow space between the top of each *musi bumo* and the plastered span of palm trunks above, the masons would introduce an additional tiny round aperture which they called the *musi moo toondi*, or "cat's eye."[18]

Al-Hajji described how masons of the past did not know how to make the *musi moo toondi* until the now deceased and celebrated master, Mama Kourani, invented it. Since that time nearly two decades ago, al-Hajji continued, most of Djenné's accomplished builders had learned to produce this decorative feature that flaunts their skill and expertise. Bamoy heartily agreed with his colleague's account of the *musi moo toondi*, adding that Mama Kourani was also the author of other decorative and architectural features that have since been incorporated into the local architectural language.

Though Djenné's architecture has, for the most part, remained remarkably consistent over the past century or longer (arguably the result, at least partially, of the hegemony of colonial and postcolonial nation-state discourses on heritage and authenticity), the building tradition has by no means been static. As discussed earlier, an apprentice's long acquaintance with his restricted palette of tools and materials inculcates a practical knowledge of structural possibilities. His introduction to negotiations between mason and client concerning design and budget, as well as a growing familiarity with the practices of other masons in the community, shape his aesthetic sensibilities and his judgment of quality, proportion, and composition. In technical terms, a trade master is qualified by his ability to conceive of a project holistically—from design and planning to construction—and to coordinate all the resources and activities necessary for its realization. The combination of structural and aesthetic principles, together with an accretion of practical experience, enable master masons to creatively expand the existing repertoire of built forms and decorations in a way that is deemed both traditional and innovative by their fellow colleagues and public.

Innovations that have been successfully introduced thereby expand the discursive boundaries of tradition and reinscribe the town's architecture and spaces with contemporary value for its inhabitants. It is important to underline, however, that not all innovations by all masons are welcome additions to the stylistic canon. Young masons who might dare to challenge the limits would likely be labeled egoistic frauds, and older masons who had not earned a master's status would be regarded as pretenders and their creations ignored. Rank and privilege, as in nearly all social contexts, tends to reproduce itself. Career opportunities for an apprentice or young mason are largely tethered to the rising (or falling) position of his mentor. The rank of "master" in the trade—accompanied by the license to innovate—is based not only on technical know-how but also social accomplishment. This includes one's ability to win the esteem of other masons and perform eloquently at the *barey ton* meetings, establish a prestigious clientele and oversee notable commissions, and become a respected member of the religious community. In sum, it requires an aptitude to strategically negotiate one's position and identity as much as, if not more so, than peddling one's ideas as individual creations.

Displays of generosity and altruism, like *saraa* (Arabic, *sadaqa*) are choice vehicles for simultaneously practicing Islamic principles and promoting one's pious demeanor and good character in the public realm. The house across the road from where we were working was being replastered. Cartloads of dark grey, stinking oozing mud were being unloaded outside the building, and a sizable labor force of young *garibou* in ragged clothes had been assembled to take part in the work. This special, resilient mud plaster (*laabu-fumbo*) applied to exterior surfaces was prepared in a large pit by combining *laabu-tyirey* (red mud) with ample quantities of rice husks and water. The mixture was left to ferment for several weeks to a month, with regular intervals of stirring. The house being plastered was the family home of a now deceased *marabout* who had been al-Hajji's Qur'anic teacher when al-Hajji was a boy. Al-Hajji released Yappi from his present duties to assist with the task. The apprentice would receive no pay,[19] and his labor would be translated into a gesture of the mason's pious respect for the *marabout*'s surviving kin. Yappi was one of several plasterers working on the project, including Perou Cissé's younger brother who bore the family trait of incessant chatter and good-natured teasing. The army of *garibou* moved the mud in an endless procession of baskets-on-heads, from the sludgy heap to the plasterers on ladders who slopped it on and spread it by hand. It was a mucky and tedious affair that, ideally, should be rendered for all Djenné's buildings each year after the rains.

"A Real Mason"

Back on our own project, all the pilasters and half-columns had now reached three-brick-courses high, and al-Hajji and Bamoy plastered their outer surfaces with mud mortar to close the joints and smooth over incongruities. Bamoy referred to this layer as the *boubou de tjete*, or "the wall's *boubou*" (a *boubou* is the long, flowing garment worn by both men and women). At this point, lintels composed of short, thick palm wood sticks were spanned over the six *füney*, and the parapet wall was continued above. The boxy, projecting capitals of the four pilasters were built with pieces of cut bricks, but the cat heads required more attentive craftsmanship. Bamoy selected a mud brick without any cracks from the mound that had been piled on the roof. He then balanced it on the open palm of his left hand and began lopping off the four corners with his *kuuru-bibi* trowel, rotating it as he progressed. The force of his chopping eased as the brick took on a circular form, and he refined the edges with a staccato of sharp, calculated blows. Six of these circular bricks were made and passed one-by-one to al-Hajji who was perched on the projecting *toron* on the opposite side of the parapet wall. Confidently squatting there with his back to the two-storey free fall, al-Hajji proceeded to give the circular bricks a rounded shape, delicately sculpting them to produce six equivalent hemispherical forms. He then troweled a thick layer of mortar over the top of a half-column and set one of the pill-

Bamoy Sao sculpting the finishing details on a *gaaga* pilaster

like bricks firmly in place with its circumference slightly protruding over the edges of the column shaft. On top of this first rounded brick he placed a second so that each of the three half-columns carried a double-layered cat's head (*musi bumo*). Al-Hajji concluded the work by molding and smoothing each of the heads to an exquisite finish using fine mortar and his pointed *truelle française* (French trowel), while Bamoy guided his efforts from the street below.

The pace of work slowed for the laborers since few materials were needed to make the cat heads, and the young men congregated in the shade of the courtyard. A favorite topic of conversation was music, especially for al-Hajj "the tea-maker" and Ali. They all agreed that Salif Keita, Rokia Traoré, Ali Farka Touré, Habib Koité, and the other superstars of the Malian music world were top-notch, but some also listened to popular Western rock like Phil Collins and Dire Straits. The latter was alleged to be Bamoy's favorite band. Rap and its associated urban-combat dress code have made inroads in the last decade, and the country is pumping out its own performers of that genre. And, of course, reggae and the timeless rhythms of Bob Marley continue to appeal across generations. While Abdullahi pressed me for never-ending lists of new English vocabulary which he diligently recorded in ballpoint ink on mud-stained scraps of paper, young al-Hajj and Ali asked me to translate Marley's English lyrics to French. In the course of conversation that day, it struck me as odd that there was no talk of football or of idolized players despite the importance of the big match that would be televised that evening. None of the men owned a television, and most lived in rooms or houses without electricity and so might only tune into a battery-operated radio broadcast for the final results.

Al-Hajji departed before the midday call to prayer to arrange for materials at the Brunet-Jailly house in Djoboro, leaving Bamoy in charge for the rest of the afternoon. Ali was summoned back to the roof to assist the mason in constructing the tiny cat's-eye apertures (*musi moo toondi*) in the narrow space of the planar wall above each cat's head. The final steps in completing the *potigé* would be to span the final timber lintel across its length and, on top of this, erect the seven lofty miters aligned vertically with the four pilasters and three half-columns below. Bamoy was now balanced on the *toron* doing the building work, and my recollections of the near-tragic event two days earlier flashed through my mind. I subtly cautioned him to be careful, not wanting to offend his pride. He asserted with utter conviction that he would not fall, at which point Ali reinforced his statement: "If Bamoy falls, everyone in Djenné will say that 'Bamoy Sao isn't a real mason.'" "That's right," said Bamoy, exaggeratedly shaking his head up and down, "They would say I wasn't a real mason."

Ali Bouaré making bricks on the floodplain outside Djenné

9 · Yappi's Confession

Mali's national football team suffered a crushing defeat by Cameroon, three goals to one, and was eliminated from the final rounds of the 2002 African Cup of Nations. High hopes slumped, and Djenné's citizens were palpably morose for a day or more. Some cautiously mocked Djenné's *maraboutage* for its impotence but only behind closed doors, never daring to confront the *marabouts* face to face with such bold allegations. Most were more prudent, reserving their scorn for their fellow citizens, blaming one another, even themselves, for not offering the holy men sufficient *cadeaux* (gifts) to make the powerful benedictions that could "guarantee" national victory.[1] Because of this reasoning, popular faith in the *marabouts* and their craft was essentially left unscathed. Blame was transferred instead onto the miscalculation and mean-spiritedness of the patron population, thus opportunistically holding onto the possibility of getting it right next time. Simply put, far too many projects, plans, and aspirations were heavily invested in *maraboutage* to castigate this system of faith and fortune as defunct.

Site Visitors

At the building site, the morning hours were mined with strained silences that erupted in brief and boisterous squabbles. Considerable friction rankled laborer relations, impeded the flow of materials, and weakened overall cooperation. One of two new additions to the team, a Dogon named Youssef, was unquestionably a catalyst to the commotion. Youssef's pomp and arrogance made him immediately unpopular with the other men. The second, a Fulani named Musa, spoke no Djenné-Chiini but was pleasant and got on with work. Musa followed orders and wisely remained detached from the day's skirmishes. Both men were Qur'anic students and were hired temporarily during the final stages at the *marabout*'s house. The root of the trouble lay internally with the regular team members. Omar was especially obstinate, setting his own pace without regard for the others, and Ali, disgruntled to be laboring rather than apprenticing, was rife with mischief. Omar, poised on the top of an oil drum, threw a basketful of mortar without warning to Ali, who stood on the roof terrace above. The basket hit Ali hard in the shins and the contents splattered across his trouser legs. He fumed. When the next basket followed, Ali casually reached out with his hand, looked nonchalantly toward the blue sky, and flipped it over in midair. The full quantity came sliding out, and Omar recoiled from the plunging mud. It missed the top of his head by millimeters but covered his shoulders and back with cold mucky wetness. Tensions were rising.

With admirable timing, the water vendor sauntered into the courtyard unannounced and diverted the men's focus to other matters. A Rimaïbe woman with a penchant for sharp-tongued jest, she had a generous girth enhanced by the bulk of several babies swaddled to her corpulent body. As the guardian of the neighborhood's standing tap, she was officially responsible for collecting dues for water used at that source.[2] The tap was located at a place where the road widened to form a small public square and was one of fifty-two original public fountains installed in Djenné as a result of the severe drought conditions in the early 1980s. Reportedly more than six hundred faucets were now bleeding the town's piped supply,[3] but many houses were still without a connection and therefore relied on the public taps. Guardians, like the Rimaïbe woman, charged customers slightly higher rates than those paid by private households to the water board, and from these fees they earned a meager living. Typically she measured water consumption by the bucketful, but in the case of our building site, the supply was carried by a long rubber hose down the street and into the courtyard where it emptied into an oil drum. We were charged 70 CFA per barrel. While the water flowed, our guardian paid regular officious visits to verify that her valuable commodity was being delivered directly to the barrel where the volume could be accurately measured, and not being showered directly from the hose onto the piles of soil that lay waiting to be trampled into mortars and plasters.

Staking the width of the courtyard doorway, the Rimaïbe woman addressed the laborers in a low, cautious voice, piercing each in turn with a condemning stare. She lumbered across the courtyard, side-glanced over her shoulder into the filling barrel, and proceeded to proclaim everyone guilty without trial. Some of the young men squeaked protests, but the regular team members knew all too well that she tactically recited these hollow accusations to attract al-Hajji's attention. She stood at the center of the open space with hands folded on her waist and, glaring up to the roof, summoned the mason in a loud voice. The baby strapped to her back stirred from sleep with a whine. "You're a thief al-Hajji Kouroumansé!" she bellowed, followed by a shrill hiss. Al-Hajji grinned down over the edge of the roof. Her eyes lit up and she flashed a flirtatious smile, and then carried on full tilt with a barrage of condemnations. In the few brief lapses of her relentless rebuke, the mason retorted whimsically, further enticing her dramatized charade until the woman could no longer conceal her own amusement. "I'm coming back to check on you again, al-Hajji!" she said, now laughing boisterously and shaking her finger at him. "Don't you steal my water!" With these final words, she turned and exited with a confident swirl. The performance lightened the morning's anxieties, and the men, in teasing verse, exclaimed that al-Hajji was scheming to take the Rimaïbe as his third wife. He defended the innocence of his intentions half-heartedly, grimacing all the while like a flattered schoolboy.

Al-Hajji had two wives. The first and her two sons resided in the principal family house of the Kouroumansé located in the Konofia quarter. This house was presently owned by al-Hajji's uncle who lived in Mopti,[4] and al-Hajji shared the house with his older brother, Baba. Each of the brothers had his own parlor (*galia*) and room for sleeping (*tasika*). The second wife and infant daughter lived in a rented two-room accommodation for which al-Hajji paid 1500 CFA per month. This was situated in Djoboro, close to his mother's small house where he was raised. A year before we met, al-Hajji had secured a plot of land from the customary village chief of Djenné (*Djenné wéré*), Ba Hasey Maïga. The land was located near the water's edge in Kanafa quarter, and he was saving to build a house large enough for both his wives. Though he mused aloud about a third wife, providing adequate accommodation for his existing family was strain enough on the budget. Flirting with the idea and chatting up women like the Rimaïbe or his wife's younger sister who occasionally visited merely boosted his ego, at least for the time being.

The morning's next soapbox appearance, however, knocked the winds from al-Hajji's sail. A tall, slim, and powerful-looking man rode up to the house on a Vespa motorbike. He addressed the masons on the rooftop in a rumbling baritone voice, removed dark sunglasses, and assuredly made his way inside. He wore an embroidered regal white *boubou* and crimson felt skullcap over closely clipped silver hair. This older man had visited our site on previous occasions, always in the service of a certain Marabout Djennepo from the Konofia quarter. In a bullying tone he tried to persuade al-Hajji to abandon his current projects and carry out works for his patron. His manner was shockingly abrasive, and he was clearly accustomed to getting what he wanted by force. Al-Hajji covertly referred to him as *le gangster* and uttered under his breath that "he never asks, he commands!" The "gangster" was a Fulani who took up residence in town many years ago and made a small fortune as a trader; his eldest son was reportedly following suit. Because of his mercantile success, he insisted, somewhat pretentiously, that others recognize his full citizenship by referring to him as a "Djennénké," and not Fulani. He had come for another face-off with al-Hajji, but the mason stood his ground. "I'm too busy!" he asserted, "You can tell Marabout Djennepo that I'll come when I can." Their heated exchange was brief and the *marabout*'s intermediary (*almustasbi*) departed, clearly agitated. Al-Hajji turned to me with an exasperated look: "That man talks far too much! He thinks he's *le roi des farafines* (King of the Blacks)."

Al-Hajji had a number of small commissions concurrent with the *marabout*'s house in Yobukayna and the professor's in Djoboro, both of which were subcontracted to him through his cousin, Bayeré Kouroumansé. Several of the small commissions were for his clients, but others were for patrons with long-standing contractual ties to different masons. When I asked whether this stirred rivalries within the trade community, he answered in the negative. "If a mason knows that he isn't capable of making decorations, or some other part of the house, then he'll ask someone who does. . . . Even the patron might approach another mason directly, but it won't pose a problem. His mason will understand the necessity." Al-Hajji, for instance, had built an ensemble of *sarafar idye* and other roofline elements on a house in Djoboro, and this was executed at the invitation of the site's chief mason who admittedly lacked the know-how. Reportedly no hostile feelings or jealousies ensued. More recently, a gentleman from Yobukayna visited al-Hajji and requested that he cover the facade of his home in the terracotta tiles made by local potters. Again al-Hajji explained that it was standard practice for the client to employ a more competent, experienced mason for the difficult jobs, and that this does not result in conflict between a patron's mason and the one hired on a short-term contract. In recounting these stories of being brought in to complete tasks, al-Hajji was, in a sense, advertising his own expanding reputation as an expert builder, but he would only go so far before characteristically retracting with humility, claiming that he really doesn't know much since he's still only a *petit maçon*.

To my mind, there was a nagging discrepancy between al-Hajji's rendition of the problem-free relations between masons competing for patronage, and the widely circulating belief that masons employed the secrets of *bey-bibi* and *bey-koray* against fellow colleagues to curtail interventions in their long-standing contracts with households. Initial reflections on the matter led me to inquire whether a hierarchy of secret knowledge existed, whereby craftsmen with lesser powers dared not challenge those above them. This idea was flatly rejected by several masons, who described scenarios in which a third-party mason is legitimately invited to finish a job. They consistently emphasized the need for each mason to recognize his own abilities and limitations, and the importance of permitting those who are more capable to execute the complex tasks. Though such arrangements might reduce the mason's actual workload, and consequently dent his fee-earning potential, it effectively poses no real threat to the allegiance between mason and patron-household. The awarding of contracts to third parties is thus straightforwardly premised on a hierarchy of skilled competence and reputation. I was assured that virtuous masons only employ their secrets, or seek assistance from a *marabout* or diviner, when their status has been ostensibly marred by another person or if someone has tried to usurp their position in a clandestine manner. In fact, throughout my fieldwork I never encountered a mason who openly admitted to putting his secret knowledge to work in this way.

A Shot at Becoming an "Apprentice"

The remainder of the day was spent reconstructing the lengths of parapet wall that had been taken down on either side of the *potigé*. The long and elegant downspouts (*handoro*) manufactured by the local potter-women were first reset at the base of the parapet wall and angled slightly downward to quickly evacuate rainwater away from the terrace and into the street. Next, a series of small rectangular *fūney* apertures were inserted at regular intervals along the entire length of the parapet. Bamoy assisted al-Hajji in setting out the first course of the low mud-brick wall by eye, leaving centrally placed openings between the projecting *toron*. Al-Hajji then verified all spacing with his tape measure, making small adjustments to the layout of alternating brick sections and apertures as he went along. The tops of the *fūney* openings were spanned with batons of palm wood, and, on either side of the *potigé*, a thick piece of palm trunk was horizontally embedded in the wall, perpendicular to the wall surface, and prominently protruding on each side. This is called the *toron di jumbo doo* (literally, "the *toron* for descending"), and it serves as a scaffold for stepping up from the roof terrace, over the parapet wall, and onto the *toron* that projected over the street. The *toron di jumbo doo* is used by the masons each year after the rainy season to re-plaster and make repairs to the front face of the roofline decorations. The parapet wall itself was terminated with a rounded capping along its entire length, and the masons referred to this profile as the *farka banda* ("donkey's back"), slapping it almost affectionately with the palm of their hand as they hailed it by name.

As part of his daily meanderings, grey-bearded Salamantao stopped briefly to greet al-Hajji and Bamoy and engage them in friendly chitchat. His eyes sparkled as he looked up to the roof from beneath the wide brim of his straw hat. "Wor na goy?" he asked. "Na gonni," they replied politely.[5] Salamantao habitually dressed in a long, dark indigo shirt with matching trousers, and he carried around a trowel, plumb line, or some other tool. Like many tradesmen of his generation, he no longer engaged in much building activity, but he continued to keep tabs on former apprentices and offer advice and assistance. Building sites in Djenné are social spaces of sorts where friends and neighbors come to share gossip with the masons or to watch the work in progress. Some remain in the street, away from the construction, but others venture onto the sites, including neighborhood children seeking new adventures. Aside from the benedictions masons make to guarantee safety, no additional precautions are taken to ensure that the public does not get injured or to prevent them from interfering with the ongoing work.

Yappi was absent from the site for a second consecutive day to assist with re-plastering the house across the road. Rather than taking up the prime position beside the masons as he normally did, Ali had been instructed to prepare and pass materials with the laborers. This left me working alone alongside al-Hajji and Bamoy. Bricks, baskets of mortar, and pieces of palm wood cut to specified lengths were handed on by the assembly of laborers, and I stacked them and passed them to the masons on cue. Al-Hajji periodically called my attention to certain procedures in constructing the parapet wall, and he directed me, in particular, to watch as he carefully positioned the sticks of palm wood over the tops of the *füney* openings, firmly setting them in position and covering them over with a thick layer of mud mortar to create monolithic lintels. When greeting passers-by in the street below, he would bellow out proudly that I was his new apprentice, nicknamed "Mama Kouroumansé"—a flattering synthesis of the names of highly esteemed Mama Kourani and al-Hajji's own patronym. Mostly everyone knew that I had not, in fact, been taken on as al-Hajji's apprentice in any official sense. No long-term contract had been agreed on between us regarding an exchange of training for labor, and I made it clear to my building colleagues from the start that I had no intention of establishing myself professionally in their trade. Al-Hajji nevertheless took his role as my mentor as seriously as I took mine as pupil, and he made time in the work schedule to introduce me to the tools, materials, and techniques.

While raising the height of the parapet, al-Hajji summoned me to move closer to the wall and asked whether I knew how to use the plumb line (*guuru karfoo*). I nodded with shaky confidence, and he handed me the instrument to demonstrate. I pressed the edge of the square metal plate against the top of a newly laid brick, angling it so that the circumference of the weighty plumb bob touched the outer surface of the brick as I slowly, and nervously, lowered it down along the wall on its string. Al-Hajji watched patiently as it bounced and reverberated off the uneven surface of the wall, and when I finished he shook his head with firm disapproval and reclaimed his instrument. He then demonstrated the correct procedure, at the same time explaining that the plumb bob must not touch the wall surface but must fall directly in front of it, leaving a tiny gap. As he lowered the string, the metal weight came in contact with the course of bricks directly below, indicating that the newly set brick had to be adjusted, and the mason tapped it gently forward with the butt end of his trowel, and sunk the plumb line once again. This form of direct instruction comprising a mix of propositionally based directives with a physical performance of the skills is characteristic of the training method in Djenné's building trade. Apprentices can usually pose questions without fear of rebuke, and masons take on active roles as mentors with vested interests in honing their tutees' professional skills.

In comparison with the apprenticeship system that I studied among Yemeni minaret builders,[6] social relations between masons and their work teams in Djenné were notably more relaxed and informal. The men joked playfully with one another, and it was not uncommon for a mason to spend social time with his laborers or pay visits to their homes outside working hours. Many, in fact, were neighbors and their families maintained relations outside the work place. Unless the apprentice betrayed the mason's trust or acted truly reprehensibly, his position as a trainee was secure and his future stake in the trade was publicly recognized. In Yemen, by contrast, the position of the apprentice was seldom stable, and the young men competed sometimes ruthlessly for that privileged station next to the masons. Explanations and demonstrations were rarely offered, and most forms of questioning were dissuaded. Skills and professional comportment, therefore, had to be effectively stolen with one's eyes. The chosen laborer working at the mason's side was never overtly referred to as an "apprentice," and if he fell out of favor he was quickly replaced. The two-tier power structure that more rigidly divided Yemeni mason from laborer incited a certain degree of paranoia and suspicion among the ambitious members of the lower ranks who hoped to establish a career in the trade, and placed a considerable strain on social relations. This is not to suggest that competition was not present between apprentices, and even masons, in Djenné. A certain degree of back-biting rivalry was evident, for instance, in the daily struggles between Yappi and Ali. But both these young men were secure in their official status as apprentices, even though neither may fully know how long the training would last, who would be the first to be recognized as a fully fledged mason, or who would be granted the more prestigious contracts and eventually inherit his mentor's prized client relations.

Bamoy paused to wipe away the heavy beads of perspiration forming on his brow and ordered al-Hajj "the tea-maker" to fetch charcoal from the market to brew a pot of sweet, restorative tea. The temperature climbed steadily with the mounting midday sun. Throughout the morning, al-Hajj "the tea-maker" and I had been alone working with the masons on the roof terrace. As the penultimate member in the chain, al-Hajj's job was to stand at the roof's edge and catch the materials passed upward from the courtyard, which he then tossed along to me. My responsibility was to arrange and pass the required items onto the masons. When al-Hajj left on his errand, I found myself covering both roles. While the boys hollered that I assume the position at the roof's edge ready to catch a vertical onslaught of mud-filled baskets and bricks, the masons, who were erecting the parapet on the opposite side of the building, shouted out their own chorus of curt commands for more materials and such-and-such tools. Frantically I scurried back and forth between posts with full loads, dodging piles of bricks and debris, avoiding as best I could stray adzes and crowbars that could break my toes. I missed catches, helplessly watching as wasted deliveries of mortar oozed back down the wall from overturned baskets. Soon my hands and forearms were cut in several places from jagged bricks, and I incurred a constellation of splinters in my palms from the coarse bits of straw in the woven baskets. My T-shirt was drenched with sweat and I was quickly becoming dehydrated, but I desperately—and perhaps foolishly—wanted to prove to the masons that I could manage the task. After what seemed a tortuously long time, al-Hajji finally realized that someone else needed to assist, and he summoned Ali to lend a hand. By that time al-Hajj "the tea-maker" had also returned, and by then I, too, was in full need of a sugary infusion.

As usual, at the end of the day we gathered around the oil drum of water to wash the excess mud from our hands. I began picking at a splinter that had worked its way deeply into the fleshy base of my left thumb. Abdullahi Bouaré was standing nearby and leaned in for a closer look. Staring back up at me with a taunting grimace, he teased that "the *tubaabu*'s hands are too soft for African work!" and then waved his two hands provocatively in my face, daring me to compare. His hands were indeed like cured hides from his years of farm work and building construction. Also true was that many of my colleagues worked barefoot and seemed to feel no pain when treading across the hot, sharp, uneven surfaces. Perhaps this *tubaabu* had simply spent too many years at drafting tables and tapping computer keyboards. Al-Hajji brusquely interrupted Abdullahi's swaggering show of masculinity, and took my hand for closer inspection. The flesh around the splinter was swollen purple and sore to the touch, and the long dark strand of wood was clearly visible below the skin. The mason rummaged through the leaves of his wallet for a safety pin, which he carried around for this very purpose, and mercifully presented it to me. My self-directed micro-surgery took nearly twenty tedious minutes but effectively prevented a more serious infection. Just before departing, al-Hajji told me that he was highly pleased with my work performance and invited me to assist with the construction and sculpting of the spiky *sarafar* miters in a few days, insisting that it was crucial to my education. I had been eagerly anticipating this final stage of construction.

Ali's Brick-Making Enterprise

Despite aching muscles, I slept soundly that night, and the cool exhilaration of fresh morning air fully restored my enthusiasm for another day's work. My journey back and forth to the *marabout*'s house took me over bumpy, narrow streets in the Yobukayna quarter where I had to mindfully navigate my bicycle along the ragged muddy edges of open sewage gutters. Astonishingly, like clockwork, when I arrived each morning at one particular and challenging passage squeezed between the high walls of two residential compounds, a toddler from that neighborhood had unfailingly deposited a fresh, steaming bowel movement in the center of the path. This morning the mess in the midst of my tracks was not so tiny or tidy, unhappily leaving me little choice but to cycle straight through it.

One of the first to arrive, I ventured through the open door, abandoning my bicycle in an empty room off the vestibule, and made my way upstairs to the roof. Al-Hajji was already there with an older gentleman donned in a long emerald green *boubou* and a delicately embroidered skull cap. Standing at the unfinished section of the *potigé* looking out over Djenné, the two were discussing the building progress. Apricot light bathed the creviced surfaces of the silent town. Al-Hajji introduced the gentleman as Marabout Haydarah, the owner of the house we were reconstructing. He and his family were staying with relatives in a nearby quarter until the work was completed. Al-Hajji described for him the seven *sarafar* miters he was planning to build, gesturing their approximate placement and height with his arms. The *marabout* was evidently pleased and said he would return periodically for updates. Meanwhile, my fellow laborers were arriving, and the first splash of water was doused over yesterday's pile of mud mortar, soon followed by the rhythmic churning of the hoe to loosen the mixture.

Ali, proudly sporting a new shirt to work, removed it before taking up his duties and left it neatly folded in the swept corner of an empty room. He worked in a sleeveless vest and, while passing bricks to the masons, peered now and again at his left and right arms, admiring his biceps. Traces of adolescent narcissism lingered in Ali's early manhood. He indulged himself with new articles of clothing when he could but had to scavenge for extra earnings to afford them. "I make bricks by the water every evening," he boasted. Al-Hajj "the tea-maker," standing at Ali's side, frowned skeptically. "Well, almost every evening," Ali said, tempering his claim. "I don't do it on Monday or Friday." "I like buying shirts," he wafted dreamily, likely conjuring images in his head of the next extravagant purchase. "But I save a little sometimes, and I have to give to my mother as well." Al-Hajj added meekly that he, too, had tried to earn extra money making bricks but found it exhausting after a full and arduous day at the work site. I suspected that al-Hajj also did not put much effort into his after-hours apprenticeship as a tailor. As it turned out, Ali's hands were also not muddied as regularly as he initially claimed. Some weeks after telling me about his brick-making enterprise, he decided that it was putting too much strain on his body but that he would continue to put in the extra effort when he could muster the energy.

Late one afternoon al-Hajj led me to Ali's secret patch where he moonlighted in the brick trade. I followed the tall, lanky youth along a twisting path through Djoboro's dense urban maze. We squeezed along a narrow passage between dilapidated houses, emerging at the edge of a steep earth embankment overlooking the floodplain to the west. The perimeter of Djenné was used as a dump site, and the shallow water encompassing the town at this late date in the dry season was stagnant and filthy. The many people without running water in their homes, and without the resources to pay for a clean supply at their neighborhood taps, used this source of festering rivulets for bathing and for washing their clothes and cooking utensils. Al-Hajj and I plodded onward along the top of the embankment, trash tumbling beneath our unstable footing, until we arrived at the legendary spot in Kanafa marked by the tomb of the sacrificial virgin, Tempama Djennepo. A land bridge emerged from the subsiding waters, and we crossed to the other side, out of town, heading toward where Ali set up shop. I was relieved to encounter less refuse as we moved away from the edge of town, and hoped, for Ali's sake, that the mud he was handling was cleaner, with fewer discarded objects and razor-sharp scraps of metal and broken glass.

On his brick-making evenings, Ali's mother prepared an early meal after which he headed straight to his secluded spot to work until sunset. Any individual industrious enough to make bricks could claim an empty site along the water's edge and start his own production. Using a hoe, Ali clawed earth from the banks and formed a large, neat pile with a slight conical indent at the center. Hay and water were mashed and trampled into the dense soil with his bare forearms and calves until an even, mucky consistency was achieved. Water was fetched by the bucketfuls from the convenient, nearby source, but obtaining hay involved greater effort. Brick makers who do not want to pay for hay have to journey several kilometers from town to gather long, dry grass from untended fields. Naturally Ali tried to carry back as much as possible each time, and kept his supply under a tarpaulin at his work station. He formed the individual bricks using a standard wooden mold that could be slipped up and off with ease. Ali estimated that he could make about one hundred bricks per session, and, when dry, he sold them to the cart drivers for 13 CFA a pair. In turn, the cart drivers added their own small profit margin to the price they charged the masons. Potentially Ali could earn 650 CFA for an evening's work, nearly doubling his daily wage from the building site.[7] I was delighted to witness his already impressive stacks of several hundred bricks, dried and waiting to be sold.

Al-Hajj and I stayed for a long while, sitting on a dry bank of earth just above Ali, chatting with him while he scooped mud from between his straddled legs and slapped it down with a plop in the mold. Rhythmically he lifted the mold, reset it, scooped mud, slapped and smoothed, again and again. He admitted to enjoying the solitude out here away from town, where he could focus his thoughts on restful matters. A sun the color of ripe papaya was dipping behind us, and al-Hajj rose, gesturing that it was time to depart. As we set off, he pointed proudly to a small pile of dried bricks nearby that he had made himself. They were not for sale; instead, his family would use them to make repairs to their own home after the *Tabaski* celebrations.[8] "It's perfectly safe to leave them here," he confirmed as we walked back. "Nobody would think of stealing them." I asked if he planned to make more. "Maybe," he responded nonchalantly, "but I can't work constantly like Ali. I would age too quickly, and the money's too little." In the distance, across the flat plain to the west, was a low and broad rectangular mud structure that appeared almost fortress-like. Al-Hajj explained that it was a corral, paid for and built by his fellow residents of Djoboro. Many households own a few zebu cattle, and individual quarters of the town communally hire young Fulani herders at a cost of 250 CFA monthly per head. The Fulani bring the animals to pasture on *bourgou*[9] and other grasses during the daytime and return them to the safety of the corral each night. The historic division of labor along caste and ethnic lines remains remarkably consistent with European reports and descriptions from the early twentieth century, and even the notion that Ali, as a Bamana, might be better suited to toiling with mud than his Djennénké friend reflected age-old occupational expectations.

When we arrived back in his neighborhood, al-Hajj invited me for tea. He took me to the room where he boarded with six other young men, and set about lighting charcoal in the portable metal stove and cleaning the tiny enameled teapot and glass. The ground-storey room had a single corrugated-metal door providing direct access from the street, but with no access to the family living quarters of the house to which it was adjoined. As an act of charity, the household head allowed groups of local adolescent males to live there rent-free. This popular arrangement gave al-Hajj a certain degree of autonomy from his nearby kin, though he continued to take meals at home and occasionally slept there. The other laborers and apprentices from the building team likewise had rooms outside their parents' homes. Ali shared one with a fellow age-mate from his quarter, as did Omar in Yobukayna. Yappi had been sharing a room with Abdullahi for the past two years, and the eldest of the Bouaré brothers, Suleiman, rented a space by himself at a modest monthly rate of 1000 CFA.[10]

Al-Hajj's dark, windowless room measured no more than three square meters. The Spartan furnishings consisted of a bare double-bed mattress against one wall, a single mattress painfully bowing on a rickety frame on the opposite side of the room, and a wafer-thin matt neatly rolled and stashed in a corner. When there was a full house of lodgers, some of the boys slept cramped on the earth floor beneath the beds. In most respects, these rooming arrangements serve as adolescent clubhouses. Scrawled in bold red paint on the mud-plaster outside were the letters "JRD." The *Jeunes Révolutionnaires de Djoboro* was the "gang" name adopted by al-Hajj and his comrades. The JRD earned a little money each year by organizing a *soirée* that coincided with the annual plastering of Djenné's mosque, and they tapped profitably into the festive spirit of the town. They sold tickets for 1000 CFA each, and hosted a street party with blaring music from a portable cassette player, soft drinks, and snacks. Rap music was especially popular among the *révolutionnaires* and the name Puff Daddy—a contemporary African American music celebrity— was also painted graffiti-style on their exterior wall.

We sat in the doorway, legs stretched into the dusty street, sipping sweet tea. I raised the topic of women, aiming to strike up a discussion about premarital relations in Djenné. Al-Hajj blushed. "I don't go out with girls," he said bashfully. "It's too difficult and parents object. Well, not all of them, but some. And, you need money!" Evidently money was a prime obstacle to the dating venture, as I equally heard from other teenage men. "After buying the stuff I need . . . tea, cigarettes and other little things, there isn't much left. And girls demand that you have money!" "What about extra tailoring work?" I inquired. "My master doesn't pay me," he said, "And I'm still an apprentice. But my master does give me 500 CFA, and sometimes 1000, at *Tabaski*. That doesn't get me far, though." His gaze dropped silently to his lap. His experiences in love had not yet begun and clearly he had no interest in talking about relationships, so I switched the talk to music. Sadly, however, this topic only further dramatized the generation gap between us, since I was familiar with little more than the names of his favorite American rap performers. Silences between words were growing, and my list of possible subjects was running dry. Al-Hajj was a very pleasant young man, but his somewhat withdrawn nature sometimes made idle chat hard work. Fortuitously darkness was setting in and the time had come to pedal home.

Sarafar Miters

The awaited day arrived. We would start building *sarafar* miters that, literally, would be the crowning glory of our project. Having reached town ahead of my usual morning schedule, I piloted my bike through Kanafa and made a stop at Konamadou Djennepo's house to greet his family, and they graciously invited me to share their breakfast of rice and fish sauce. Konamadou's wife, Ainya, was feeling terribly nauseated, and Konamadou asked me to take a look at her right hand. The young woman's entire hand and fingers were swollen like a balloon, the skin so taught that I feared it would burst. An infection, festering for nearly two weeks, had evidently reached a critical stage. Locally prepared herbs prescribed for Ainya had made no difference, and I implored Konamadou to take

Display of various baked-clay tiles for cladding floors and wall surfaces

her to the town's hospital and to accept a small gift of money to pay for a prescription. They both agreed it was time to try this alternative and see a medical doctor. Their initial hesitation to visit the hospital and purchase antibiotics had been a question of the cost. Like most people in Djenné, they did not particularly prefer "traditional" medicines; their choice was often determined by economics.

Down the road from our project at Marabout Haydarah's, another group of builders were resurfacing the front facade of a house with kiln-baked terracotta tiles. These thin rectangular tiles manufactured by the local potters are occasionally used on floors and stair treads, but masons began applying them to vertical wall surfaces sometime during the past two decades. Entrepreneurial artisans also manufacture a variety of molded shapes, including lozenges, diamonds, hexagons, and hearts. The cost of clay tiles, and of the labor involved in setting them, is relatively high, so tiles have come to signify prestige and clients who can afford them are likely to have their mason use them. Not only are they popular for residential buildings, but some mosques in the region have also been dressed from the base to the tips of their miters with terracotta—often adversely affecting the structural integrity of the building.[11] A broad consensus exists among masons and clients that they provide immediate protection against erosion and alleviate the need for annual re-plastering. Although the clay tiles remain popular, many masons, like al-Hajji, recognize their limitations and the potential problems they cause.

The concrete mortar and the clay tiles it holds in place are materially incompatible with mud walls. The hard impervious shell prevents the building from "breathing," thus trapping moisture in the walls and making the interior damp and moldy. The clay content in the mud lends the material its cohesion, but at the same time clay expands and contracts at a rapid rate. Changes in outside humidity bring about a significant increase or decrease in the actual volume of the walls and ceilings, causing cracks and fissures in the rigid cement mortar. Subsequently rainwater may enter behind the casing and slowly wash away the structural mud wall. Such erosion, concealed by the tile facing, can go dangerously undetected and cause a structure to collapse suddenly. This dilemma also applies to cement renderings on mud walls. Through trial and error, some masons have been made aware that the best rendering for a mud structure is more mud. Even though it must be laboriously reapplied each year or so, mud plasters breathe and expand in harmony with the core of the mud-brick walls below. Despite knowledge of this hazard, many clients continue to be seduced by the aesthetics and consumer status associated with clay tiles and cement renderings, and they commission their masons to apply them. In the short term, these surfaces eliminate the need to renew mud surfaces annually and thereby deprive masons of an important source of work and income.[12] Masons nevertheless realize that, with tiles, they will be eventually called back to fill cracks and restore weakened or collapsed structures.

At Marabout Haydarah's house, like the Brunet-Jailly house in Djoboro, all the construction and plaster rendering would be in mud. For today's *sarafar*-building exercise, the masons erected a simple scaffold to provide easier access to the top of the parapet wall. Yappi stood in the center on the long, raised timber plank with al-Hajji and Bamoy on each side. To start, the three men set out the rectangular bases of the seven *sarafar idye*. Each base measured 40 centimeters wide by 58 centimeters deep and was made with three full bricks. The bases were spaced 16 centimeters apart to evenly fill the 3.80-meter section of parapet wall between the two *sarafar woy* pilasters. The *sarafar idye* miters would reach

244 · *Portraits of Life and Work in Djenné*

Masons and apprentice (*center*) constructing *sarafar idye* decorations

a total height of eight-brick courses, and as the two builders proceeded in perfect tandem, they tapered the width and depth of each successive brick course, achieving a slight convexity in the profile of all four sides. A small stick of palm wood was inserted horizontally in each *sarafar idye* between the third and fourth brick course, projecting slightly from the front face of the gently curving surfaces. These would later be covered with mud and sculpted to create round disc-like projections called *sarafar jutun* (the *sarafar's* "navel"). The tops of the *sarafar idye* were terminated in fine points coined *sarafar déné* (the *sarafar's* "tongue"). This eighth and final course comprised only a tiny, pyramidal piece of brick that was carefully carved with the edge of a *kuuru-bibi* trowel.

Throughout the procedure, a tautly drawn horizontal cord was raised from course level to course level to ensure that the masons and apprentice were producing the same diminishing dimensions on the front and back faces of the pointed projections. The tapering of the inside faces was judged for symmetry by the masons' eyes, and corrections were made regularly to ensure that all the *sarafar idye* matched perfectly. The *sarafar idye* were thickly covered with *laabu-kuntur-kow* (a thick, smooth plaster produced by squeez-

Al-Hajji Kouroumansé positioning sticks of palm for the *sarafar jutun*

ing the mud through the fingers and removing all lumps and stones),[13] and their identical finished forms were sculpted and smoothed with the more delicate French trowels. When the work was completed, all the rooftop decorations would be given a final coat of special mud plaster that is mixed with flour of the baobab fruit for extra durability and *karité* butter (oil of the shea butter nut) for water resistance.[14] The apprentice worked meticulously on the central miter, and the masons built up the three on each side. Yappi was performing well, and al-Hajji paused to exclaim loudly to the laborers passing bricks and mortar nearby, "See! Yappi is a mason today!" This praise encouraged the young man and fostered a sense of confidence. It also publicly affirmed the apprentice's rising status and authority in relation to the other team members.

My chance to sculpt miters never arose, but I worked nearby handing all three men their tools and materials. Al-Hajji made a display of each stage in the process for my benefit, and stressed that a high degree of expertise and considerable experience were required for producing symmetrical and well-proportioned forms. As he worked, Bamoy remarked that in the past *sarafar* were reserved for the houses of influential *marabouts,* established traders, and important government officials, and thus denoted the abodes of the town's elite. The origin of the spiky forms, he claimed, lay with "Moroccans who settled in Djenné long ago"—possibly referring to the Moroccan traders who arrived during the Songhay rule of Sonni Ali in the fifteenth century.[15] "But now," he added, "masons build *sarafar* for any patron who can afford them." The use of vertical extensions to demarcate corners and accentuate height, however, are not restricted to Djenné but are found throughout the Sahel: on houses and mosques along the Niger River, stretching south from Timbuktu to the one-time Bamana Kingdom at Segou; on the grand old mosque of Bobo Dioulasso and the historic mosques of the Kong region in present-day Ivory Coast; and on exuberantly adorned *zaures*[16] in Hausaland where the mud spikes are commonly referred to as *zanko* (sing.).[17] The sculptural protrusions play a practical role of protecting against erosion and structural collapse. Ideally winds and rains will first diminish the mud extensions before reaching the building's vulnerable corners, where adjacent walls, floors, and ceiling constructions join and brace the structure. The pinnacle-like extensions of the *style-Soudanais* thereby guard buildings by providing a period of reprieve during which necessary and periodic repairs can be made. A poorly maintained mud building, especially one with failing corners, can collapse suddenly, transforming a home into a weighty tomb for those trapped inside.

Apprentice Konamadou Konsinantao (aka, "Yappi")

Yappi's Confession

Yappi stepped down from the wooden plank, peered into the courtyard, and hollered to the laborers to dust the reed baskets properly with dry soil or rice husks before filling them with mortar. This made it easier for the masons to re-move the moist contents, like a well-floured cake pan. Relishing the power of his position, he continued instructing his junior team members to add more water to the mud, put greater or lesser quantities of mortar in the baskets, fetch wood, and send bricks. In truth, however, the laborers did not have a great deal to do. As the masons' work moved away from erecting walls and ceilings to the more meticulous tasks of sculpting decorative details, the quantities of materi-als required diminished. Widening lapses between demands for their menial services meant that the laborers were becoming bored. Suleiman Bouaré took more frequent naps in the shade with his woolly hat pulled down over his eyes, and several of the young men carved their names into the mud plaster of the interior rooms. Ali, too, was getting into mischief.

When comparing Yappi to Ali, Yappi was clearly more mature and more focused than his fellow apprentice, a disparity owing partly to the seven-year age gap between the two but also a reflection of the palpable difference in their desires to succeed and perhaps move on in life. As the first Djenné-born son, Ali loyally abided by his mother's plan to secure a proper urban trade for her son. His two older brothers were born in the village and would always be recognized by the townsfolk as farmers, thus the onus was on Ali to secure a Djennénké status for the family. He accepted this destiny unquestioningly and seemed to harbor no desire to leave the town. When Ali was granted opportunities to act as the main apprentice in Yappi's absence, he usually displayed a serious and attentive disposition, distancing himself to some degree from his brothers and the other laborers, and focusing on the task at hand. When Yappi was reconsigned to the top rung and Ali was forced to resume his position among the laboring ranks, his adolescence became more apparent and he engaged in small rebellious acts of defiance. Between half-hearted stints of relaying materials, he shared cigarettes with al-Hajj "the tea-maker," joked and gamboled about, antagonized his workmates (namely Omar), feigned fatigue, and cat-napped at his station. These minor transgressions were largely ignored by al-Hajji and Bamoy but almost never by Yappi. Yappi remained strategically close to the masons and was especially obliging to his master, al-Hajji. Despite his yearnings to quit manual labor and leave Djenné, Yappi conscientiously rose to the challenges and high standards set by his apprenticeship training. Indeed, he recognized the need to maximize all options available to him, and he would undoubtedly try his hand at any other promising opportunity that presented itself. Yappi cleverly played each card in the game for a new life and better circumstances.

As Yappi and I were passing materials to al-Hajji, Yappi paused to adjust the bandage on his right thumb. He had sliced his thumb open on a shard of glass the day before while plastering at the *marabout*'s house across the road. He pulled off the torn rubber dish-washing glove meant to protect his finger from infection and awkwardly retied the filthy blood-stained rag using his left hand and teeth. As he did so, he inquired in a deliberate, calculated tone whether I would join him to pray at the mosque this Friday afternoon. I sensed a ploy and, furrowing my brow dismissively, responded flatly that I could not. "Why," he chimed with false naivety, knowing full well what my answer would be. My anger bubbled at the thought of being badgered to convert. After working together and establishing a rapport of mutual respect, I thoroughly resented the idea of religious difference suddenly becoming a wedge between the builders and me. I answered slowly and pointedly, "Because, Yappi, you know that I am a Christian." His reply knocked the wind out of me, like an unexpected brick to the waistline. "So am I!" he proclaimed, looking me straight in the eyes. "I'm also a Christian" he said, this time reinforcing his admission loud enough for all nearby to hear. If his objective was to astonish, he succeeded. "You're not a Christian, Yappi! Don't tell lies," I protested. Bamoy let his trowel drop, staring on incredulously at the apprentice. Al-Hajji stole a sideways glance and then continued laying bricks. Yappi insisted, confessing that he kept Bibles in his home, all the while directing his gaze on me. I was feeling terribly uneasy with this performance. The existence of a Bozo Christian in Djenné was seemingly riddled with contradiction as well as potential risk, and I could not predict where he was going with this.[18]

Bamoy, with increasing clarity about what he was hearing, exploded: "Liar! Yappi!" The young man initially dismissed the outburst. "How can you be a Christian if you pray at the mosque?" Bamoy demanded angrily. "I only go sometimes, and that's because I must in Djenné," he answered defiantly. Al-Hajji interjected, calmly defending Yappi's decision and reprimanding his mason-colleague for inflicting narrow views: "Even though you went to school Bamoy, you still know nothing!" This sparked the most heated exchange that had yet occurred between any of the builders. With his master having declared his support, Yappi also turned on Bamoy, fervently defending his choice to be Christian. Bamoy frothed with rage, snapping back at his two challengers. Meanwhile, news of the event was speedily conveyed along the chain of laborers, and they shoved and passed one another on the stairs to take up roof-top positions for the event. Their faces expressed amused shades of shock, and several launched remarks from the sidelines supporting Bamoy and mildly taunting and interrogating Yappi. Ali simply burst out laughing and made his way back down the staircase. This time the game point was his. Al-Hajj "the tea-maker" gaped with hanging jaw, and Abdullahi stared fixedly in bewildered disbelief. Overall, the reaction was not as horrifically dramatic as I might have predicted, and eventually al-Hajji's persistently even tone of voice quenched the blaze. The laborers were ordered back to their stations, and work resumed. Bamoy's temper smoldered, and he said little else for the remainder of the morning. In a subdued voice I suggested to Yappi that he might not want to discuss his religious convictions openly, but he persisted that the choice was his and others must learn to respect it. When the midday call to prayer crackled over the loud speakers, he invited me with earnest to his mother's home to see his Bibles.

On our somewhat uncomfortable walk to Djoboro, Yappi explained that he had been raised in a Muslim household and that his father had died four years ago unaware of his son's conversion. "He would not have tolerated it," Yappi said, "but my older brother and some of my friends know." This did not quite tabulate in my mind, since Yappi's roommate, Abdullahi Bouaré, clearly had no previous knowledge of this. Perhaps the friends he referred to were other members of his newly found faith. "I'm not the only Christian in Djenné, you know. There are more in Kanafa and other quarters of the city. And they are starting to make themselves heard!" Many of the Christians are Bobos who have settled since the 1970s draught period in the new areas around the hospital.[19] The overwhelming sentiment in Djenné is that it is a Muslim town and Christian residents are not welcome. Some Bobos seeking acceptance conceal their Christian identities and claim to be Marka. As Yappi spoke, the ugliness of interfaith conflicts and unrest that I knew from Northern Nigeria flashed through my mind, and I wished that it would never be repeated here. From grade 7 to 9 Yappi had been sent away to the village of Togo in Fangaso,[20] where the majority of the Bobo and Dogon population were Christians, and where there was a Catholic school. He made numerous Christian friends and was inspired by their ideas and teachings. "The Christians in Togo condemn alcohol, just like in the Qurʿan," he told me. He was given a French translation of the Gideon Bible,[21] and he confided that what he learned from it was more beneficial than the Qurʿanic lessons he had sat through as a boy. "Can a mason in Djenné be Christian?" I wondered aloud. "Al-Hajji's one of the few who knows," Yappi told me. "I've talked to him about it and he supports me. Al-Hajji is open-minded. He's traveled outside Djenné, and he accepts others for what they are, regardless of creed."

Yappi's older brother was resting on a mat in the small courtyard of their house when we arrived. I greeted him while Yappi slid behind a hanging striped cloth that covered a doorway and soon emerged with his pocket-sized New Testament. He proudly handed it to me for inspection. It made me think of those hundreds of thousands of Bibles left optimistically by Gideon Christians in the drawers of hotel rooms. In this case, the black cover was actually well worn and the pages fingered. "Take it and read it," he beamed. I politely declined, reminding him about his earlier sermon on personal choice. More important, I did not want to be seen as taking sides in any religious rows that might arise on the building site. Yappi moaned about the prevailing intolerance in Djenné, despite current talk of democracy in the country. "No one really has choice here," he said. "Listen to me! If the big man of the house (*chef de la maison*) supports a political party, then all the family members must support the same. If not, it's an insult . . . a challenge to him."

I sympathized with his desire for the freedom to make choices in life and to explore the world beyond the confines of this patriarchal community, but I was dubious about Yappi's motives for embracing Christianity. Since the first day we met, Yappi repeatedly complained about his stifling circumstances and expressed hope to leave behind both Djenné and the building profession. His life's aspirations were ambitious, if not altogether unrealistic. I was therefore left to puzzle the extent to which his disclosure on-site that morning was calculated to achieve an effect greater than merely opening a space of religious tolerance among his peers. It was indeed conceivable that Yappi had counted on the resultant social fission to bring about more substantial transformations in his life. Recognizing the limitations of his own economic and political resources to effect that change, Yappi, by proclaiming his religious conversion, was unleashing social forces beyond his control. If these forces were auspicious, they might expel him from an imprisoning and impoverishing world and move him to a place offering greater opportunities. In other words, Yappi's statement potentially contained the power to activate consequences that would, so to speak, deliver him from the toil of masonry and banish him from town simply because this kind of confession could incite the degree of hostility that it did. Perhaps he hoped that these hostile reactions would crystallize in popular consensus and that subsequent interventions by the community would coerce Yappi into another livelihood. This was a decision that Yappi could not justifiably make as an autonomous individual; rather, it necessitated an alteration to his wider social circumstances and the inclusion of other social players. My hypothesis was entirely logical in the given context: words were being used to bring about change, just as *marabouts* and masons claimed they could.

I escaped Yappi's company without the burden of new reading material, and on my way home I ran into Bamoy. He was already washed and dressed in a fine *boubou* of shiny grey cotton. He paused to greet me politely and then rejoined the colourful current of men winding its way through the brown dusty streets to the mosque for prayer.

View over the mosque's roofscape of skylights/vents and towering pinnacles

10 · Finishing Off

The following morning no mention was made of Yappi's conversion to Christianity, as though yesterday's episode had never occurred. Yappi made no further provocations, and his fellow team members posed no challenges. Their silent collusion suspended the conflict for now, perhaps demonstrating a collective willingness for reconciliation and, more pragmatically, the need to get on with work. Later that day when Yappi boldly requested the shoes on my feet for the hundredth time, I asked, rhetorically, whether it might be un-Christian of me to give my only pair to him and nothing to the others, upon which he withdrew his demands. I had brought baseball caps to Mali for all my colleagues, and with the mounting temperatures it was time to start wearing them.[1] The *harmattan* winds were blowing hot and steady, and the air was choked with dust. From the rooftop of Marabout Haydarah's house we could see no farther than the perimeter of the town, and all colors were saturated in soft shades of brown.

Sarafar Har and *Sarafar Woy*

The two *sarafar har* at opposite ends of the main facade were the focus of today's attention. The *sarafar har* are the "male" pilasters, and their miter-like projections that extend above the rooflines of both Moroccan and Tukolor-style houses are made higher than the centrally positioned mud spikes by dressing them with a pointed *fula,* or "hat." To my mind, these tall projections with bulbous tips appear somewhat phallic, and this imagery is reinforced by the gendered name they have been given. When I asked whether the *sarafar har* were indeed phallic representations as suggested by other European authors,[2] embarrassed murmurs rippled through the circle of men assembled on the roof, and some blushed. "No, no!" replied Bamoy waving his finger, "They're male because they wear a *fula* (hat) like men do in Djenné." "The *sarafar woy*," al-Hajji continued, pointing to the seven we had just completed over the entrance to the house,[3] "do not wear a hat because they are female." I later received the very same explanation from other masons. "The old *sarafar har* had only one *fula*," said al-Hajji, "but some masons now give them two, one on top of the other." The reconstruction of the *marabout*'s house was part of the Dutch-sponsored conservation project for the town, so its *sarafar har* would terminate with one hat only, as did those on the original house. Also, in contrast to some newer structures where the superimposed double *fula* were plastered with cement to preserve their sculpted contours throughout the rainy season, every element of this house would be rendered in a finishing coat of mud.

A *sarafar har* is constructed in the same manner as the *sarafar idye* miters. It is built to a height of eight brick courses, and all four sides of the vertical projection taper evenly inward toward an apex. Unlike the *sarafar idye*, it does not terminate in a point (*sarafar déné*), but has a small flat top that can support the protuberant *fula*. Extending from two of its faces are sleek buttresses angled at ninety degrees to each other, firmly anchoring the tall projection to the corner of the parapet wall on which it is erected. The buttresses also increase the mass of the *sarafar har* and give it a bolder, more "masculine" appearance than the *sarafar idye*. The two masons built both *sarafar har* in tandem, al-Hajji raising the one at the right and Bamoy the one at the left-hand corner of the facade. Today's delivery of bricks contained an enormous quantity of chopped straw which made them crumbly and difficult to carve, but the masons insisted that they were good quality. Al-Hajji completed his structure first, and after applying a coat of *laabu-kuntur-kow* plaster in his characteristically artistic manner, he went down to street level to guide Bamoy's final stages.

Three days later al-Hajji purchased two round clay pots from a *jam-woy* (the potter-wife of a blacksmith) and brought them to the site wrapped in protective layers of old wax-print cloth. These *kusu* (clay pots) would serve as the armature for the *sarafar har fula*. The builders switched, in fact, between calling the "hat" by its proper name, *fula,* and *bumo*, which translates not so distantly to "head." Bamoy first used a *daasi kayna* (literally, "small axe") to carefully smooth away small protrusions and imperfections in the contours of the *sarafar har*. One of the clay pots was filled with a thick mixture of *laabu-*

RIGHT Bamoy Sao, with his son, sculpting the *fula* (hat) of a *sarafar* miter

tyirey and placed upside down on top of a *sarafar har*. Bamoy gave the pot a twist to fit it snugly in place and adjusted it to rest evenly on the pinnacle. Next the mason applied a generous layer of *laabu-tyirey* by hand to the outer surface of the pot, working small shards of brick and additional dollops of the heavy red mud into the composition, slowly building up the onion-dome-like form of the *fula*. While Bamoy was putting the finishing touches to the pointed *fula* with his bare palm and French trowel, Abdullahi Bouaré stood beside him passing on materials. At one point, when Bamoy was fully absorbed in his task, the laborer caught my attention with a devilish grin. Pointing to the nearly completed *sarafar har* with one free hand, Abdullahi performed an exaggerated simulation of masturbation with the other. He was evidently amused by his own charade, and the other laborers on the roof joined in the giddy laughter. I cannot say whether the sculptural detail appeared obviously phallic to him or not prior to posing my question the other day, but he and the others certainly made the connection now!

All the while, al-Hajji preoccupied himself with installing the terracotta *handoro* (downspout) and deliberately ignored Abdullahi's shenanigans. Using his *sasiré* (crowbar), he pierced a hole at the base of the parapet wall and carefully gyrated the iron rod until the opening matched the circumference of the *handoro*. The long downspout was inserted, reaching out as far as possible over the street to evacuate rain water away from the building's facade. His two young sons had accompanied al-Hajji to work today, and they stood by their father to watch the procedure. "This is how a mason's education begins," he said, obviously proud that his sons were showing interest. The youngest, Lasine, would soon start school, and his brother, Abdullahi, who was deaf, would likely apprentice with a tailor. Al-Hajji refused to commit the boys to his own back-breaking profession. It wasn't long before the two children began fidgeting. One stepped on the other's foot, a squabble erupted, and they were marched off elsewhere to play. By contrast, their cousin Komar made more concerted efforts to assist when he accompanied his uncle to the building site. Komar was the son of al-Hajji's senior brother, Baba, and though only slightly older than Lasine and Abdullahi, he did not attend school. Growing numbers of Bozo children were indeed being enrolled in school, unlike in the past when Bozo parents resisted, fearing their children would be corrupted by bad manners. Baba contended that these were not his worries, as he planned for his sons to become masons, and they were exceptionally well disciplined when working.

The *Nyégé*

The last element of the house to be constructed before applying a final coat of plaster to all surfaces was the *nyégé* (toilet). A square tower had already been erected in the courtyard, adjacent to the kitchen, so it remained for the small enclosed toilet chamber to be built above. Dry waste would collect in the tower, and urine would be routed directly out of the toilet chamber to a channel that ran down the outside wall of the house. Because of the intense heat in Djenné, urine normally evaporates before reaching street level. Historically, a part of the masons' duties was to periodically empty the night soil from the dry shafts of clients' homes. This job is now also performed by other entrepreneurs who compete with the masons for the little profit to be had. The work is always done at night, certainly never during the daytime. First, a pit measuring approximately 1.50 meters in depth is dug in the road adjacent to the tower, and then an opening is made at the base of the shaft with a crowbar. The night soil is emptied into the pit, and the hole is covered over with the excavated earth. The tower is then resealed and can be used again until the next removal, which normally occurs every ten to fifteen years.

One special task that remains under the sole jurisdiction of masons is the digging of graves.[4] Narrow rectangular graves, body-length and one meter in depth, are excavated in the cemetery on the outskirts of town.[5] At the bottom of the excavated pit and along one side, a second cavity is dug out. The deceased are interred inside the cavity according to Islamic custom (i.e., on their side facing Mecca), and a mud-brick wall is constructed to separate this subterranean space from the main pit and protect the body from becoming enveloped in soil. The rectangular pit can then be back-filled without disturbing the body. The master mason Beré Yonou claimed that burials were not always executed in this way and that, at some unspecified time in the past, the deceased were buried directly in the earth.[6]

We spent nearly a full day constructing the tiny square toilet chamber above the tower. The masons had once told me that making the *nyégé* (referring to both the night-soil shaft and the chamber) was among the most difficult tasks in house building (*barey térey*). "The reason it requires expertise," Bamoy explained, "is not because a *nyégé* demands special technical skills, but because we must work in such a small, cramped space." The space was indeed constricting. Toilets in Djenné are typically located on the first storey or on a roof terrace, and they are very often free standing structures with their own separate entrance from outside. Inside, the chamber is normally too low to allow one to stand upright. The walls of Marabout Haydarah's toilet were only thirteen brick courses high, allowing a ceiling height of 1.50 meters, and the space was to be roofed with thick branches.

Because the contours of the *marabout*'s property were irregularly shaped, the toilet walls, like other rooms in the house, did not meet at right angles. Where two of its walls intersected at an obtuse angle, one brick in each course of the corner junction had to be modified by lopping an angle off one side to produce a trapezoid-like configuration. Bricks modified in this way are imaginatively referred to as *kaarey niiné* ("crocodile's snout"), and Ali and Abdullahi Bouaré were charged with carving these for the masons. While laying bricks, al-Hajji spotted one of his former apprentices passing in the street below and barked a gruff, friendly greeting. The man waved both arms in an enthusiastic response, steered his horse and cart to the front of the house, and entered the courtyard with a radiant smile. Al-Hajji had begun training this colossal Horso several years ago, but he quit the trade prematurely to work as a municipal garbage collector and to earn a steadier civil-servant's income to support his family. He also operated a grinding mill (*dur-marsiin*) from his home that provided a lucrative service for his neighbors. The Horso immediately launched into a series of jovial attacks, ribbing his former mentor for having erected so mediocre a house and for having such a lazy team of weaklings. He then put on an entertaining spectacle by picking up bricks from the courtyard floor and hurling them one by one in quick succession to al-Hajji, who stood on the storey above. Each of the twenty bricks was rocketed effortlessly upward to a height level with the mason's eyes, and al-Hajji caught them as they dropped, piling them neatly at his feet. The Horso was a Herculean powerhouse, and several of the laborers tried feebly to emulate his show of strength, prompting a good deal of laughter.

Wood branches that are used to construct ceilings but that are not palm wood (*sebe*) are called *bundu*.[7] The same wood branches that are placed horizontally in mud-brick walls to provide lateral support or bracing are referred to as *domba*. A closely spaced layer of *bundu* was arranged over the toilet chamber, spanning the tops of the two side walls. Above these, a second layer of smaller branches was positioned to fill in gaps before finishing the flat roof with a weighty covering of mud.

In the mid-afternoon, several deliveries of fetid grey-colored mud arrived by donkey and cart. This specially prepared mud, called *laabu-batakara*, is made by combining rice husks (*modu*) with grey sedimentary mud taken from the bottom of the marshes and rivulets during the dry season when water levels are

Preparing mud plaster at street level

low. The rice husks serve as a binder, and the mud itself is composed of a rich mix of organic materials deposited by annual flooding during the rainy season. Unlike *laabu-fumbo*, which is made from laterite and fermented in a pit for several weeks with rice husks, the coarser *laabu-batakara* does not need to be fermented for such extensive periods, as it is taken directly from the riverbeds and the mixture smells marginally less putrid than the former. The laborers spent the remaining hours of the day tidying the site and removing caked mud from the floors and stair treads throughout the house to prepare for the monumental plastering job that would commence the following morning. The masons calculated that it would take three days to surface all interior walls and ceilings, and the front facade would only be started once the Moroccan-style wooden door and shuttered windows were installed.

Handu Koray

With the principal construction work now complete, al-Hajji was scheduled to spend the next week or so working on an independent commission at Marabout Djennepo's house in the Konofia quarter. Ridding himself of the *marabout*'s "gangster" intermediary was the prime motive for getting this job over and done with. Following Friday's midday prayers, al-Hajji cast decorative concrete breeze-blocks with a mold and made several long slabs of reinforced concrete on the building site. His task was to erect screen walls in the large openings around the ground-floor veranda of the courtyard. These three-quarter-high walls would be assembled with the perforated breeze-blocks and capped by a coping made from the concrete slabs. I was to assist him in this task, and the following Tuesday morning we climbed the courtyard staircase to retrieve cured blocks from the roof, only to be startled by what we saw at the top of the stairs: a full-grown, yellow-headed *m'baaka* lizard skewered upside down and lengthwise on a stick planted in the parapet wall. The little creature's four legs grasped menacingly at the air. As a mason, al-Hajji was uneasy about working alongside this gruesome display of his trade's totem, but he could do little about the situation. The lizard had been left by Marabout Djennepo to desiccate in the sun and would be used in preparing medicines. The heads of *m'baaka* lizards, for instance, were ground into powder and used in cough remedies. Al-Hajji confirmed that masons could take this medicine without committing an offence, but they must never inflict harm upon the *m'baaka* and unleash its life energies themselves.

The following day I returned to the building site in Yobukayna where plastering of the second-storey rooms had already begun under Bamoy's direction. It was a relief to be working indoors, out of the sun, though interior conditions were far from ideal. The room dimensions were tight, and with both masons working in the same space at the same time the environment quickly became hot and uncomfortable. The wet, grey plaster darkened the rooms, making the air dank and humid, and we were trapped with the stench of the *laabu-batakara* plaster. The men complained that the plastering mud we were using was especially unclean and that it stained the palms of their hands purple. Even after scrubbing several times with laundry soap that evening, my hands were still tinged violet.

In each room Bamoy and Yappi started at corners diagonally opposite each other and progressed in the same direction until all walls were covered. The laborers transported basket after basket of the *laabu-batakara* mud to the two men who scooped generous quantities with both hands and slapped it onto the walls. With their right palms, they first spread the mud in even vertical sweeps to cover a section of wall top to bottom and approximately 1.50 meters wide. Once a section was evenly covered in this manner, they then smoothed the plaster horizontally, beginning at the top of the wall and moving downward with machine-like movements of their right arms, back and forth, in perfectly straight bands. The vertical seams between adjacent sections were smoothed in similar manner to make them blend into one another, and in some rooms a 50-centimeter-high panel at the base of the walls remained plastered in the vertical direction with deeply fingered grooves that gave it texture and distinguished it from the smoother wall surface above. A second layer of finer *laabu-fumbo* is sometimes applied after the *laabu-batakara* dries, but this fermented plaster is costly and is only used where budgets permit.

Ceilings (*hu béné*) present builders with much greater trials than walls. In order to get close enough to the palm-wood surfaces, Yappi and the mason stood balanced on a plank of timber supported by the tops of two battered oil drums. Neck and back muscles were strained from peering straight up at their task and working with arms raised above their heads. Mud dropped into their eyes, and the wooden ceiling beams pricked their hands with painful splinters. The geometric configurations of beams produced a number of different ceiling levels, increasing in height from the corners of the room to its center, thereby demanding greater planned coordination between the two builders. The *fata-taki* arrangement of palm wood, for instance, had three different heights, and the *fata-hinka* ceilings had two. The mud had to be applied thickly and evenly to all surfaces and also well-worked into the crevices between wood members so that it would not detach and come crashing down. The final covering of velvety *laabu-batakara* softened the protruding contours of sticks and beams beneath, like taught skin stretched over the ribs of some prehistoric beast.

For the most part, plastering is a monotonous chore affording few opportunities for creative indulgence. Sculpting decorative compositions onto walls, however, is a welcome respite from the tedium, but ornamentation is normally included in special interiors only. In the second-storey parlor in Marabout Haydarah's house, Bamoy embellished the wall spaces above the main door and above the opposite window with *handu koray* motifs.[8] Standing on top of an oil barrel, the mason spread a second, thin, even coat of plaster over the now dried layer of plaster above the door. With the point of his trowel, he then etched two identical elongated crescent-like shapes into the mud, one above the other, and proceeded to remove any wet plaster lying outside the edges of the defined figures. Using thick handfuls of *laabu-batakara,* Bamoy began to sculpt the forms, raising their contours from the wall surface and slowly building up their mass in bold relief. The horizontal lines of both the upper and lower crescent shapes were extended in either direction and married into the geometries of the *fata-taki* ceiling. He followed the same procedure for sculpting the decoration over the window, across the room.

Bamoy made it clear that the *handu koray* was not a talisman, nor did it have any special symbolic meaning beyond the association of the crescent moon with Islam. Its purpose in the room was primarily aesthetic. "Does it not give you pleasure when you see it?" he asked rhetorically.

One delivery of *laabu-batakara* that afternoon was somewhat reddish in color rather than the typical dark grey and, to my relief, lacked the putrid smell I had come to associate it with. Bamoy immediately rejected the load, complaining that the mud was of inferior quality. Upon sending it back with the cart driver, Bamoy strictly instructed the boy to deliver only the grey. Exercising his command, the mason then sent Ali on an errand to buy sacks of rice husks to mix into the mud plaster. During al-Hajji's absence Bamoy was fully in charge, and Ali's status on-site was normally reduced to carrying out menial tasks with the laborers. Being sent on small quests like this one thus boosted his wounded ego.

The mechanical drudgery of plastering in enclosed spaces was conducive to group conversation. Final results of the African football championships were hotly debated after Cameroon defended its title against Senegal, beating Mali's neighbor three goals to two in a hair-raising round of penalty shots. The men spoke regularly about music and women, and about how they would relax during the upcoming *Tabaski* holidays. Bamoy was a fan of rock music, remarking that he especially enjoyed listening to his favorite band, Dire Straits. "Music isn't just for young people," the forty-two year old asserted, defending his musical tastes against those of the young laborers on the opposite side of the generation gap. "Listening to rock music gives you a sense of spirit," he continued, "and I play my cassettes every evening to unwind." Ali and al-Hajj "the tea-maker" recited lyrics by Peter Tosh and Bob Marley in garbled English, and Abdullahi Bouaré was keenly interested in learning the meanings of choice words. All the laborers were eager to learn some English, but Abdullahi showed the greatest persistence. He habitually carried a leaf of lined paper and ballpoint pen in his shirt pocket and asked me to slowly pronounce words which he then transcribed phonetically in Arabic script. He had received no formal education, but his father, who had been a Qurʿanic teacher, taught all three sons to read and write. Abdullahi and Ali were proud to tell me that even Sulayman, their eldest brother, could read, but perhaps not as well as they since he was a little slow. Sulayman rarely participated in discussions, instead focusing quietly on the piles of mud he was forever churning and trampling, and napping between sessions.

The first English words Abdullahi wrote down were the numbers one to ten. With muddy hands, he slowly and meticulously wrote the Arabic numerals and transcribed the words phonetically. He recited numbers aloud throughout the day, enthusiastically exchanging his own corrections of my Djenné-Chiini for my corrections of his English pronunciation. Pronouncing the letters "r" and "th" posed the greatest challenge for him, making "three" a major stumbling block in his otherwise impressive recitation. He quickly moved onto other words, including greetings and parts of the anatomy such as "hand," "arm," and "head." Every morning Abdullahi recited to me what he had written the day before to verify that he had done so correctly. He continued to record new vocabulary between hauling basketfuls of mud. Some of the later words he requested revealed the kinds of personal interactions he regularly had with physically and mentally impaired people in Djenné. Abdullahi asked for both the English and French terms for "deaf" and "blind," and also for "insane." The *harmattan* carries a significant risk of meningitis (*koo-wirtje*), which causes hearing loss among other complications, and the waterways throughout the Inland Niger Delta are breeding grounds for *Onchocerca volvulus,* the parasitic worm that causes river blindness (*mara*).

Although he dreamed of venturing to America, among other places, Yappi demonstrated little interest in learning English. His preferred topic of discussion was women, and Bamoy never hesitated to join in those fanciful chats. The two held court over their supposedly less experienced colleagues, each one upping the ante with tales of bravado. "Young men and women meet in the streets at night," began Yappi's narration of premarital encounters. "If a boy sees a girl that he likes, he tries to talk to her. And if she agrees, they meet together at a secret place far from her house and her parents. They can continue talking more freely there, and the girl might come back to the boy's room. If other boys are in the room, then they all chat together. After some time, if the desire of both parties is sensed to be serious, then the others leave the couple to the privacy of the room." Like most places in the world, the age that men in Djenné start engaging in sexual relations varies depending on the individual, but Yappi and Bamoy agreed that most boys start in their late teens and early twenties. Bamoy added that it was preferable for men to find younger women, and that girls might become active as early as fourteen years old. This, of course, was difficult to verify since no woman openly spoke about these issues. Given that most parents monitor their daughters' reputations closely, and that people keep a vigilant eye on the goings-on in their neighborhoods, it seems unlikely that midnight encounters were common.[9]

Yappi declared smugly to his fellow workers that he had been in a relationship with a girl from his neighborhood for the past two years. "It's time to find a second . . . perhaps in Tolober," he mused coolly. When I asked what his girlfriend might think of him having a second girlfriend, he shrugged his shoulders and replied blankly that she had no choice in the matter. Abdullahi rolled his eyes, and Ali and al-Hajj "the tea-maker" snickered together. None had girlfriends, and the two youngest did not see the point. "Two girls, two times the money," said al-Hajj dryly. "Girls always ask for money" chimed Ali, "and if you don't have any, they'll call you a liar! I'm not marrying until I have lots of money." Al-Hajj slapped him "five," and the two turned on Youssef, ridiculing the temporary Dogon laborer for having three wives and being left without a single CFA to his name. From their somewhat juvenile perspectives, romance was calculated purely in financial costs. "Not every girl asks for money," Yappi retorted, "My girlfriend doesn't!" But Ali and al-Hajj remained unconvinced, and Abdullahi voiced no opinion whatsoever.

A few days later, standing on the plank of timber to plaster the final ceiling, Yappi made a bid to exalt himself to new heights in the eyes of his workmates. The performance opened with overt displays of contentedness, dressed in broad smiles and cheerful whistling. "Did you notice how happy I am this morning?" he asked loudly enough to address everyone present. "I met my new girlfriend last night," Yappi continued, answering his own question, then added, half-jokingly, "And she's pretty, like me!" This cleared the way for making his ultimate boast: "I've made love to many women in Djenné, and—" Bamoy suddenly arrested Yappi's swagger with a razor-sharp reprimand, "Uh! Cut your tongue!" This sort of bragging transgressed the acceptable limits. Though past talk of women and romance had raised the topic of sex, the men's discussions had remained abstract. Yappi's talk had become too detailed and personal, and Bamoy needed to publicly shame him to stop the situation from further deteriorating.[10]

Once the plastering of all the interior rooms was completed, attention moved to the exterior surfaces in the courtyard (*batuma*). By this point, our membership had been depleted by a couple of laborers. Omar had gashed his foot on a rusty shard of metal in the mud he was trampling, and al-Hajj "the tea-maker" succumbed to a nasty bout of malaria. Following a tetanus booster and bandaging, Omar convalesced for a few days, and al-Hajj spent the better part of a week in bed indulged by his mother and older sister. Al-Hajji Kouroumansé was still working on his project in Konofia, leaving Bamoy and Yappi with the remaining cleanup work. Yappi was assigned to plaster the courtyard walls, and Bamoy to install a wooden nosing on each stair to protect the fragile edges of the mud treads. To do so, Bamoy first bored holes in the staircase walls on either side of each tread, cut the wood sticks to a length slightly longer than the tread itself, and then secured them in place by twisting them into the holes. Although

Marabout Sekou Haydarah's Moroccan-style house completed (*left*)

palm wood is the most durable material for the job, it also punctures the bare soles of climbing feet with splinters. Palm-wood sticks were thus used for the stairs leading from the second storey to the roof only, and smoother *bundu* branches cut from deciduous trees were used to make the nosing of each stair that ascended from the courtyard to the second storey where the traffic would be more frequent. Once the staircase was finished, it was rendered in a thick coat of *laabu-bibi* (black mud). By now Bamoy's hands were riddled with splinters; after washing in the drum of water, he pulled out a sewing needle to remove the prickly devils. Abdullahi lightly rebuked him for not sterilizing the needle before operating, so into the pot of tea it went where it boiled for several minutes before it was fished out with a spoon.

Al-Hajji checked in periodically to ensure that Marabout Haydarah's project stayed on track, but he spent the remaining days leading up to *Tabaski* working independently on other commissions. After finishing the breeze-block

Three designs for recesses in the interior walls of a house. These *al-qūba* niches are sculpted in mud. The third is called *al-qūba saney* after its starburst pattern.

screens for Marabout Djennepo, he transferred his white sack of tools back to the Brunet-Jailly house in Djoboro to execute some truly fine decorative work on the interior walls. In the front and rear vestibules (sing., *siifa*), al-Hajji sculpted elaborate recessed niches in the mud, which he referred to by the Arabic term *al-qūba*.[11] *Al-qūba* niches were built historically to hold copies of the Qurᶜan or oil lamps. Typically arrangements of bold geometric lines and symbols incised in the mud surrounded a series of deeply recessed concentric arches, and the entire composition was framed within an incised line. When I paid him a visit, al-Hajji proudly showed me three that he had completed and explained the symbols involved. He named an upward-pointing arrow a *sasiré*, like the word for the mason's flared-end crowbar. Paisley-like shapes placed symmetrically near the bottom of the frames were called *jōto* which is a ladle for eating *bita*, the staple millet-based porridge. Not surprisingly, al-Hajji referred to the multiple crescent shapes by the Arabic term *hilāl*, like the crescent moons in Islam, and claimed that a peculiar little stickman-like figure was a *fitila bumo*, which, in Djenné-Chiini, means "wick of the oil lamp." The composition that best demonstrated al-Hajji's talent was called *al-qūba saaney* after the four concentric "star"-like patterns that encompassed its simple rectangular alcove.

Winding Down

The last Monday market before the *Tabaski* celebrations was somewhat busier than past weeks, but harvests of rice, grains, and produce had been badly affected by the meager rains, and, compared to previous seasons, fish for sale was scarce. In an economy where most people are directly engaged in fishing or agriculture for their subsistence and livelihoods, this meant far less spending money in circulation. I assisted Konamadou with setting up his stall, neatly laying out the hundreds of flip-flops in color-coordinated patterns along the low wooden table. The flip-flop repairman was installed in his usual spot next door, gradually accumulating a small pile of tortured rubber soles for suturing, and the *donso* vendor of medicines sat cross-legged on the ground before us, theatrically pitching his newest wares. Omar was installed at a short distance from us along the eastern edge of the market, pedaling his sewing machine in the endless column of tailors who fiercely competed for commissions. A cacophony of pulsating bobbins, accelerating and decelerating incongruously with one another, contributed a diffusive hum to the symphony of market commotion.

Yappi came meandering from the direction of the tailors and joined us for a little chit-chat. He was on his way to meet al-Hajji and invited me along. I followed him through the tangle of congested market pathways, narrowly bordered on both sides by hawkers and wares, and we eventually emerged from the crowds at the southeast corner of the mosque. The mosque loomed sentinel-like over the vast and dusty market square. Al-Hajji was sitting close by with a gathering of companions outside one of the dozen or so indistinguishable shops that sold a limited and identical variety of items. He was scrubbed clean and wore a handsome royal-purple *boubou* with golden embroidery around the neckline and down the front of the chest. The three of us strolled casually to his small rented home in Djoboro, where his youngest wife and baby daughter lived. Their two tidy rooms were painted in the ever popular shade of pale green, and the floors were covered in a patchwork of linoleum off-cuts. The modest sitting room was sparsely furnished with a foam mattress and a brand new stereo-cassette player. The stereo, with its multitude of shiny chrome knobs and menacingly large speakers, was conspicuously propped on top of its cardboard packing crate. Al-Hajji had paid 115,000 CFA for the machine, a princely sum equivalent to forty-six days' wages for a mason.

Diabaté Yonou (the apprentice from my very first building site) also came around for a visit, as did Abdullahi Bouaré. Many of the masons and laborers with whom I had been acquainted over the past two years lived nearby in Djoboro, and they frequently socialized together. Al-Hajji offered tea, then disappeared into the adjoining room and returned with a thick envelope of photographs. The pictures were mostly shots of him building the monumental Brunet-Jailly house. He asked me to select one to take home as a souvenir to London. I had taken scores of photos, but al-Hajji had not yet seen the processed results and he wanted to be certain that I had an appropriate image for my memories as well as for my publications. While choosing with enthusiastic, yet unsolicited, help from all those present, al-Hajji's wife came in from the courtyard to join our amusing review of photos. Her daughter was swaddled comfortably to her back, and a blue plastic baby doll was tied in imitation to the little girl's back with a piece of wax-print fabric. The mason's wife assisted with the final choice, heartily commending it to me as a flattering portrait of her husband.

On our return to the market, we paid a visit to al-Hajji's mother and his youngest brother, Hasey, who remained critically ill. The wives of al-Hajji's two other brothers were at the house working in the cramped vestibule and courtyard. In dense urban settlements like Djenné, where available housing space is often too small to accommodate the extended family, forcing married sons to set up independent households, young wives spend considerable time at the home of their mother-in-law, helping with daily chores and preparing meals. We threaded our way cautiously through an obstacle course of playful toddlers and pots bubbling on fires, finally making it to Hasey's room. Al-Hajji greeted his weary mother and sister seated on low stools beside the door. The curtain was drawn tightly to keep out the daylight that so curiously tormented the sick man. We entered quietly so as not to startle him. Hasey, now bedridden, could barely muster the energy to acknowledge our presence. Al-Hajji confided sorrowfully that he did not think his brother could endure this mysterious illness much longer. Our stay was brief and, before departing, I squeezed another small gift into his mother's frail hand to help with the burdensome cost of medicines.

Revisiting Sanuna

Work at our construction sites in Yobukayna and Djoboro had officially ceased until after the holidays. *Tabaski* was only four days away, and I would soon be concluding my second and final season of work with the masons. I decided to visit the project at Sanuna by the river's edge and catch up with my colleagues from the previous year. It was early morning when I set off from Tolober, and as I piloted my bike up the low earth embankment and onto the tarmac road, I spotted Konamadou walking toward Djenné. He carried a bulky parcel of fodder under one arm and, trailing close behind, was an enormous ram affectionately nuzzling his backside. I pedaled over to greet him. Konamadou told me that his family had decided not to sacrifice this valuable ram for the feast and instead had purchased a sheep in the market for 20,000 CFA. Livestock prices were skyrocketing as *Tabaski* approached, and even scrawny sheep were being sold for as much as 25,000 CFA. During the holiday every married male was expected to slaughter his own animal to commemorate Abraham's sacrifice. But, in reality, high costs often meant that family heads would perform the ritual on behalf of their wedded sons. *Tabaski* was also a festive season, when children normally receive a set of new clothing to parade on the feast day, and this posed another significant expense for households. As we spoke, a passing herd of sheep aroused the attention of Konamadou's ram, and it tried to bolt in pursuit of pleasure. Konamadou swiftly restrained the animal, explaining bashfully that he had forbidden his ram to liberally sire lambs for strangers, adding that he would soon provide his own ewes to partner the randy beast.

Hamidou Guindo, the Dogon laborer, spryly passed us on his long trek to Sanuna. I offered him a lift on the back of my bicycle, and we set off for the river together. As I pedaled along the marshy creek that fingered its way to the Bani, Hamidou told me that he hoped to leave Djenné in two months, once he had saved enough money to begin his journey. He planned to slowly make his way home, back to his tiny village near Teli along the Bandiagara Escarpment. He would stop in towns along the way to continue his Qur'anic studies with local *marabouts* and to earn a little money if possible. Although the trip is only a half-day's journey by car, Hamidou estimated that it would take him almost a year to complete the voyage home, but finally uniting with his family would make every hardship bearable.

When we arrived at the nearly completed house, Baba and Bamoy Kouroumansé were already there, squatting at the edge of the roof and busily calculating the spacing between protruding *toron* wood members. Several laborers had also arrived early. Anasse put down his hoe and stepped forward to greet me. He and several others were wearing the straw hats I had given them last year. The brims were a little frayed but still kept the sun off their faces and the backs of their necks. Anasse's shiny skin accentuated the bold, sculptural features of his face. He and Hamidou were among the few remaining laborers I had worked with the year before, and I was happy to see him here. Some of the Qur'anic students had returned to their villages, others found new work in Djenné, and an unfortunate few had fallen ill. "Salam is no longer working," Anasse said flatly. He explained that his friend had contracted a strain of necrotizing faschitis last year while visiting family in Burkina Faso, and the flesh in his fingers was decomposing around the bones. Anasse told me that he, too, had suffered bouts of malaria this season but was doing well otherwise, *alhamdulileh* ("Praise be to God!" الحمد لله). The masons valued his diligence and increasingly delegated him responsibilities for coordinating the preparation of building materials and monitoring the behavior of the other laborers. Anasse knew there was potential for him to remain permanently in the trade as a chief laborer, but because he was neither Bozo nor a native Djennéboro, the prospects of his ever becoming a mason were few. So he had resolved, sensibly, to make this his final season of both work and study in this town.

I spent much of the day under a scorching sun relaying tools and materials to the masons, who positioned the neatly bundled sticks of palm wood high above the entrance to the house. Its grand Tukolor-style facade gazed gracefully upon the waters of the Bani during the rains, but now the river gave way to a bed of grassy mounds dotted with grazing cattle. A relentless breeze leached any moisture from the air, and the afternoon temperature climbed steadily into the high thirties (eighties, Fahrenheit). Hamidou toiled in a long-sleeve sweat shirt because he had no savings to buy a second-hand T-shirt from the market. "I have to give money to my *marabout*," he meekly explained, but Bamoy rebuked him for handing everything to his teacher. "Your master should spare you money for at least two T-shirts and other essentials. It's not right!" the mason protested. I knew now, however, that Hamidou was secretly squirreling away wages for his journey home. Although Bamoy was a full-fledged mason, Baba continued to mentor his younger brother and now patiently demonstrated how to integrate the *toron* into the structure of the wall. Without a site apprentice this season, Baba was able to dedicate more attention to Bamoy, who was honing his existing skills and learning new construction assemblies. The hooded vestibule over the front door was Bamoy's first *gum hu,* and over the next few days he would have his debut at constructing decorative cats' heads and miters.

I was joined on the roof by another veteran laborer, Sedou, the young Dogon "snake-killer." He had grown taller and become considerably more confident since I had last seen him. Sedou came from Djialassougou and spoke a different dialect than his fellow Dogon workers. He could now communicate almost fluently in Bamanankan,[12] but the masons normally shouted their commands in Djenné-Chiini or in an eclectic mix of the two languages with a smattering of French words and Arabic expressions. Sedou had learned to count in the masons' tongue and had memorized the words for the various building materials. This enabled him to get away from his solitary, mind-numbing station next to the well drawing water and to engage more directly in the action. Like Anasse and Hamidou, Sedou was a diligent worker and much appreciated by the masons.

Baba and Bamoy had secured five rectangular bundles of *toron,* and by mid-afternoon they began erecting the parapet wall above the projecting wooden members. The long two-storey facade of this house was divided horizontally into five equal sections and was symmetrically arranged around the hooded *gum hu* vestibule. When finished, the classic roofline decoration above the entranceway would comprise a series of three short pilasters (*gaaga*) alternating with two cat's heads (*musi bumo*), and two cat's eyes (*musi moo toondi*) peeping out from above. This assembly would be crowned with five plump *sarafar idye* miters, each accentuated by a tiny round navel (*jutun*). Five was the standard number of miters above the door to a Tukolor-style home, whereas Moroccan-style houses might have more than twice that number. The length of parapet wall on each side of the central decoration would be punctured by evenly spaced rectangular apertures (*fūney*), and the ends of the building would terminate in majestic *sarafar har* projections capped with *fula* hats. It was an ambitious project and skillfully executed, but unfortunately this house would be in constant combat against the winds that gusted across the wide course of the Bani. Its picturesque position was exposed to the full brunt of elements, and even with generous layers of the sturdiest mud plaster, the walls and decorative features would require regular maintenance.

Anasse and I spent that early evening relaxing together over a glass of sugary tea. He confided that he was strategizing the next stages in his Qurᶜanic education. Anasse was deeply concerned by the tendency of Djenné *marabouts* to horde their *grands secrets* and share them exclusively with members of their own families. He needed to attain deeper knowledge in order to one day return to his village in Burkina Faso and practice as a religious scholar, but by staying here his vocational progress was stagnating. Anasse was one of nine children, and his aging parents would soon grow dependent on him and his brothers. "The *marabouts* in *la brousse* [the bush]," he assured me in a hushed voice, "are more generous with their secrets and knowledge." He paused momentarily to be sure no one was listening: "I plan to follow my older brother's route. He started off in Djenné and now he's a *marabout* in Bobo Dioulasso. I'll leave this place to study in a small village outside Djenné." He would not divulge the name of the place. "After I've learned many secrets, I'll go next to Segou," he continued. "In Segou I'll study with a *marabout* in proper Bamanankan language. The Djenné-Chiini that people speak here is too mixed, and my villagers won't understand." So as not to arouse jealousies and prevent his *marabout* from foiling the plan, Anasse was determined to keep his scheme to himself until arrangements were finalized and he was ready to depart.

Shortly before I left Djenné, Anasse came to my door with a jubilant announcement. His *marabout* had benevolently decided to release him with a blessing, and so he would depart in two days for Gomitogo, the village he had secretly described weeks before. "It's a Bozo village," he said, "and the people there speak Bozo not Djenné-Chiini, but I'll get by in Bamanankan." Hope and the thrill of adventure flickered in his eyes. "I won't have to work as a laborer, and the *marabout* in Gomitogo won't ask me for money. I'll work in his rice fields to earn my lessons." He explained that most village *marabouts* are landowners and their troupes of Qurᶜanic students assist with the sowing and harvesting of crops. "When there's no work in the fields, there'll be plenty of time for studies," he proclaimed earnestly. I sincerely hoped that such better and promising circumstances awaited this honorable young man.

He spoke confidently about learning powerful secrets and about how people would someday seek out his special knowledge and send him their children for Qurᶜanic studies. Again he asked me to keep these thoughts between us. He had not yet shared the plan with his fellow *garibous,* for if he did, his *marabout* might suspect him of trying to influence others and instigate trouble. There was a distinct possibility that his *marabout* might still punish him for leaving and undermine his plan. Step by measured step he was moving toward his goal, shaping his life, and forging his adult identity. Anasse's scheme would surely involve many additional years of study and travel, and also incur significant hardship and a great deal of work. Nevertheless, anticipation for what lay ahead and ultimately for his future career as an accomplished *marabout* overshadowed any apprehension he had about his long, solitary, and arduous journey.

Tabaski Celebrations

On the Friday afternoon before *Tabaski,* Konamadou taught me to perform proper ablutions (*walaa*) and prostrations in his courtyard, insisting that I join the ceremonious congregational prayers the next morning. Initially I wasn't comfortable with this idea and asked whether my being an *annasaara* (white person) and Christian might pose a problem. He assured me that Djenné's community welcomed others to join in the prayers and that he would be especially pleased if I participated with his family in this event.

I arrived at the Djennepo household just before eight o'clock in the morning, and it had been announced by the Imam of the Mosque that prayers would commence at 9:30 AM. This gave me a little extra time to practice my prayer prostrations. Konamadou's wife and sister-in-law prepared a special breakfast of rice and tasty fish sauce that was taken by all the men and boys seated together in a circle on a woven mat (*ténfél*). After washing sticky hands and faces, the young boys changed into their matching new clothes while Konamadou and I made ablutions. He was strict about the procedures and made certain that I followed each step accordingly. We set off together hand in hand with the chil-

Author seated with Konamadou Djennepo (*to his right*) at the *Tabaski* prayers

dren in the direction of the congregational prayer ground. The large open space was located on the west side of town, in Kanafa quarter. The call to prayer had set everyone in motion, and the crowds moved with purpose to their common destination. *Tabaski* prayers were an exclusively male affair with the exception of a few elderly women who prayed at the rear of the assembly. All other women were expected to pray in the privacy of their homes.

Continuous streams of people flowed into the prayer ground from the web of narrow streets that converged from all directions. The normally dusty expanse was soon transformed into a canvas of vibrant colors. Everyone donned their finest, freshly laundered *boubou*, and many wore handsome embroidered flat-topped caps while others carried parasols. The enormous gathering of several thousand fluidly organized itself into a series of straight, long rows facing the *qibla* direction toward Mecca, and we sat waiting for the ceremony to begin. The Imam soon arrived at the front to lead the prayers, flanked on each side by prominent *marabouts*, high-ranking officials, and city dignitaries. The brief prayers were followed by the Imam's sermon and blessings from eminent members of Djenné's religious community. The congregation then waited patiently for the first ram to be slaughtered. The frightened animal suddenly wised-up to its fate and made a final fleeting dash from the prayer ground, but it was quickly apprehended and dragged back bleating to the knife. As patriarch of Djenné's religious community, the Imam performed the first *Tabaski* sacrifice so that all others would be meritorious in the eyes of God.

The return journey set a leisurely pace for the remainder of the day, and everyone mingled in the streets to exchange greetings and holiday blessings: "Yerkoy ma yakubaar ga!"[13] When we arrived at the Djennepo home, Konamadou's father, Baba, whetted his best knife and prepared to slaughter the sheep they had purchased for the occasion. Konamadou and his younger brother, Bamoy, assisted with the task, pinning the animal to the ground and offering up its throat in the sacred direction. One of Baba's older brothers was later summoned to skin and butcher the animal, and the men carved the carcass into small pieces with a host of sharp instruments including an axe and a hoe. The fresh meat was divided into a dozen equal piles, and the younger children were sent out to distribute these among neighboring households in the Semani quarter. Exchanges of this sort occurred throughout the town, and by noon all of Djenné was permeated with the aroma of roasting meat. The Djennepo women used the offal to prepare a thick stew which they served with heaps of steaming rice. The liver was grilled separately, and, in accordance with tradition, Baba, as the patriarch, cut it into small pieces and divided it among the family. In the late afternoon Konamadou and I once more performed prayers together before I returned to Tolober.

On the road back, my head swam with memories of the dazzling colors that filled the prayer ground, the sheep, the butchering, and the communal meal. I reflected contentedly upon the warmth, generosity, and friendship I had experienced throughout my long stay in Djenné, and it made leaving that much harder. In just a few days I would fly home.

Ainya, the wife of Konamadou Djennepo, and their first child, Niabère

Epilogue · Continuity and Change

After my fieldwork in 2002 I visited Mali every year during the dry *harmattan* season, each time clarifying data and, more important, following the changing circumstances and major events in my mason colleagues' lives. In February 2005 I returned to co-produce a documentary film on Djenné's masons.[1] This epilogue, based on episodes and life stories recorded during that visit, underscores the breadth and complexity of building-craft knowledge in Djenné. Throughout this book I have maintained that becoming a master mason in Djenné requires more than merely technical competence. The masons I knew demonstrated a keen ability to innovatively configure building plans and details; communicate their ideas and knowledge with words and actions; negotiate their positions and status; and perform secret knowledge that not only provided guarantees of safety but persuaded the public of their professional expertise and grounded patronage in trust. These ways of acting and knowing were seamlessly woven into coherent performances of "being a mason." Djenné's masons have also adapted their practices to ever changing circumstances by strategically integrating new tools, technologies, and attitudes with existing ones. The vignettes I present here are brief, but my intention is that they, like the accounts of masons' lives and practices in the previous chapters, will stimulate thinking about the dynamic interaction between cultural continuity and change.

The President's Tour and the Talo Dam

The two vehicles carrying our film crew and equipment were stopped at a road block at N'Golosso, a tiny village on the approach to San. Young military personnel directed us off the shoulder of the road into the dry scrubby grass and sternly instructed us to wait there in the long line of idling cars, trucks, and buses. Rumor spread that the president, Amadou Toumani Touré,[2] would be passing this way on his return to Bamako but no one had the slightest idea when that might be. We simply had to wait. At midday under a blazing sun, all traffic along the southern stretch of the country's narrow dual carriageway was halted until further notice. The N'golosso villagers were lined up on the opposite side of the road, patiently waiting there since early morning. Children were dressed in their best clothing and made to stand in place, one beside the other. Any excessive fidgeting was tamed by a self-appointed and overzealous disciplinarian wielding a switch. A large group of women in fine wax-print wraps and T-shirts anxiously prepared to sing the praises of "ATT," and the men anxiously scouted for signs of his approaching car. The main event, however, was still a long way off.

After more than two hours, a convoy of gleaming black vehicles appeared on the distant flat horizon speeding toward N'golosso. Excitement peaked, and a handful of children frolicked daringly out of their designated places. Villagers, standing proudly, preened themselves, and the horde of delayed and weary travelers took up positions along the tarmac. The black cars approached in a flash, and before the women could even finish the first bar of their welcoming song, all heads swiveled 180 degrees following the flicker of shiny chrome and rear license plates as the cars sped off in the distance. The gathering was dumbfounded, though, luckily, their roadside reception had not been mowed down by the high-speed train of VIPs. Not a single pair of eyes had glimpsed Mr. President through the dark-tinted windows. Shoulders drooped and heads hung low in disbelief. Only a few young children continued to cheer, not realizing that the party had passed N'golosso by. Minutes later, however, spirits were resurrected when a second cavalcade was spotted. The earnest villagers took up positions, and the more reluctant travelers trudged back to the roadside. This time the approaching black vehicles reduced their speed, and the president's enormous four-wheel-drive truck came to a halt. The smiling, waving leader emerged onto the dusty shoulder of the road and spent several generous minutes with his countrymen, receiving their praises and shaking elders' enthusiastic hands. Their cheers and celebrations lingered long after his vehicle disappeared from sight.

President Touré had spent that morning near Djenné officially inaugurating the construction of the long awaited Talo Dam. This massive project for the Bani River, located at the village of Talo nearly 150 kilometres upstream from Djenné, was highly controversial.[3] Championed by a government determined to improve farming irrigation in the Inland Niger Delta region and boost Mali's cotton production for international export,[4] the scheme was hotly contested by local and environmental interest groups who claimed that the dam would have disastrous effects on people's livelihoods and on the Bani's fragile ecosystem of waterways and marshes.[5] Those opposed to the project argued that not only would the Talo Dam dramatically alter fishing and agricultural practices,[6] the local economy, the climate, and the natural environment of the inland delta, but it would also deplete precious alluvial deposits from which mud bricks for houses and mosques are made.[7] The soils deposited by the annual floods are rich in fish bones, cow manure, and other organic matter, producing an ideal clay mixture for sun-dried bricks. Apparently the onward march of technology to the beat of global economics, in the form of a dam, was destined to wreak havoc on local livelihoods and stamp out an ancient and distinctive building tradition. The erasure of Djenné's world-renowned architecture would occur not because of the onslaught of more fashionable concrete blocks and corrugated tin roofs, long feared by conservationists, but because of a top-driven economic initiative that could result in no other choice but to replace mud with cement.[8]

Djenné Plugged In

We arrived at Djenné's Cultural Mission in Tolober by early evening and would transfer to accommodations in the old town the next day. The sleepy quarter of Tolober where I had stayed during my fieldwork was changing rapidly. Poles and power lines now delivered electricity, and broad new streets of rectangular one-storey, mud-brick houses fingered their way into the barren landscape. The newly built gas station along the main road was the adopted social hub. Local residents had ceased gathering in the courtyard of the Cultural Mission, and now watched evening television under the bright fluorescent lights of the service station with a backdrop of shiny chrome petrol pumps.

Temperatures were pleasingly cool but exceedingly dry. The expanse of floodplain stretching between Tolober and the boggy eastern perimeter of Djenné's old town was parched, and racing devils lifted swirling columns of fine red dust into the air. A year ago water had been abundant, but the past rainy season was ungenerous and drought-like conditions across the Sahel were further exacerbated by voracious legions of locusts that decimated crops.[9] The lack of water afflicted all sectors of the agricultural economy.[10] Low river levels in the delta brought fewer fish,[11] and vanishing waterways meant that farmers could not paddle to their remote rice paddies in the surrounding countryside. A withering demand for new pirogues and for repairs to existing ones harmed the boat builders, and the resultant drop in demand for their iron tools and implements affected the blacksmiths. For masons, the measly harvests meant that money for building and maintenance was scarce, and there were too few commissions to keep everyone employed. The previous year's bountiful crops and surplus economy provoked the *barey ton* to raise a mason's standard daily wage from 2500 to 3000 CFA, and that of a laborer from 750 to 1000 CFA,[12] but the current economic slump suggested an urgent need to review those increases.

In spite of these bleak circumstances, Djenné had undergone several significant developments since my fieldwork. The combined Malian-Dutch effort to restore one hundred historic monumental houses was complete, and funding was secured for their ongoing maintenance and annual plastering.[13] An equally important achievement for both architectural preservation and the general amelioration of sanitary conditions was the implementation of a wastewater management project.[14] The construction of a pumping tower in 1982 and the subsequent widespread installation of piped water resulted in dramatic increases in water consumption. This earlier initiative, however, failed to establish a sewage system for the evacuation and filtration of water-borne waste,[15] and by the 1990s open gutters and stagnant pools posed a serious health menace and undermined the fragile foundations of Djenné's mud structures. A straightforward and reasonably cost-effective solution was devised by civil engineers to channel waste water from the taps, kitchens, and bathrooms of individual homes directly into the ground, passing first into submerged concrete decantation boxes, and from there into simple filtration beds of sand and coarse gravel that protect groundwater from contamination. Fifty homes were selected for the pilot, and its success led to a more extensive implementation of the scheme by local authorities.[16] Although the system was not yet installed in all quarters, the results were impressive. Swampy, impassable alleys were transformed into dry routes, providing safer environments for living, playing, and traveling.[17]

Before starting to film the documentary, our tiny crew paid a customary visit to Djenné's traditional chief (*Djenné wéré*), Ba Hasey Maïga, at his expertly restored Tukolor home in Sankoré quarter.[18] Official permits had already been arranged through the National Museum and the Cultural Mission, but etiquette requires that the chief's blessing is obtained in carrying out any project in Djenné. He affably consented, and we set off from the tidy public square in front of his home in search of building works and film locations.

On our ambles that first morning, my ears were struck by the ubiquitous sound of mobile phones. In previous years only a small handful of landline telephones serviced the entire town, but satellite technology had evidently beamed Djenné into the global network of telecommunications.[19] It quickly became clear that mobile phones were having an impact on time-honored social conventions. Mobile users interrupted traditional lengthy greetings to answer a host of irksome ring tones, and I witnessed people suspend devotional prostrations to take calls. Even more astonishing was the presence of a cyber café in Kanafa quarter and plans for a second to be opened next to the marketplace. Hourly Internet charges at the air-conditioned facilities were an exorbitant 1500 CFA—equivalent to half the daily wage earned by masons. Screens at the café were nonetheless occupied by a steady clientele with superior financial resources. Though few masons own mobile phones, and many are alienated from the Internet because of costs or illiteracy, the trend toward accelerated communications and electronic access to a global sea of information is surely influencing building practices. As patrons engage more frequently with a vast consumer market, alternative life-style choices multiply and tastes diversify. As always, masons will respond to these social and economic transformations by transforming their practices, planning, technologies, and materials. Unlike in the past, however, the changes are destined to come fast and simultaneously from numerous sources. The study of this impact remains to be done.

Konamadou Djennepo: A Beacon of Hope

Over the past few years Konamadou Djennepo had been subjected to a string of setbacks. Few building projects came his way and, somewhat predictably, his venture in the flip-flop trade had proved disastrous.[20] His father could find no work as a pirogue builder, and all of Konamadou's modest profits from his market stall were thus spent on basic necessities for the family. In addition to his own parents and siblings, the extended family he supported included his stepmother's children, his father's adopted son, and his sister-in-law and her five children whom Konamadou's older brother had abandoned when he quit Djenné for Ivory Coast. The brother took an Ivorian wife and failed to send any remittances, giving no signs of ever returning.

Deprived of cash to reinvest in new stock, Konamadou was eventually forced to give up his stall in the Monday market and sell his remaining wares from home.

His dismal little shop opened onto a quiet and narrow street, attracting few potential customers. To exacerbate an already grave situation, thieves broke in and cleaned out the store. General economic hardship arising from the drought and crop devastation was rumored to be fueling an escalation in local crime. Konamadou then made an innovative attempt at sculpting miniature replicas of Djenné's *style-Soudanais* houses and gates. The well-executed but weighty models were formed with dark grey *laabu-fumbo* mud, and included *sarafar* miters and tiny projecting *toron* made with twigs. He hoped to sell these to touring foreigners, but lacking a proper venue for displaying his artwork, and given that the beaten tourist trail then ran through the center of town, Konamadou found no buyers.

At least one shining star brightened Konamadou's misfortunes. After years of waiting, his wife had given birth to their first child, a healthy little girl they named Niabère in memory of Ainya's eldest sister. Her soft skin glistened with *karité* oil, and kohl-painted eyes and tiny *gris-gris* dangling around her neck and wrists protected the helpless infant from evil *djinn* and other dark forces lurking in the world. "She will go to school," Konamadou vowed, rocking her gently in his arms. "I want my daughter to have a proper education."[21] Although he and his brother, Bamoy, never went to school, the family's younger generation, including the girls, were now attending the local primary school.

Bozo attitudes had changed. Most Bozo parents I knew in Djenné, including many masons, now sent their children to school, and some would possibly go on to secondary levels.[22] Formal education would inevitably expose masons' sons to new professional opportunities and choices, and historic family ties to the trade risked being severed. Some masons nevertheless supported these changes, wanting to spare their children this backbreaking work. Others wanted their children to be schooled in a classroom but hoped that at least one son would follow their path. And a few continued to denounce the school system, convinced that the best education for their sons was on the building site, as it presented fewer risks and carried the guarantee of trade qualifications and a future income.

Bayeré Kouroumansé: Reinvention and Survival

I found two of the Kouroumansé brothers plying their trade on-site. The annual re-plastering of the Brunet-Jailly house was being carried out by Bamoy and, to my surprise, his younger brother, Hasey. After spending more than a year on the brink of death, Hasey fully recovered his strength and health, *al-hamdulileh*. By all accounts, his illness subsided as mysteriously as it ap-

peared. Hasey married his young fiancée, who had devotedly waited throughout the ordeal, and she had recently given birth to their first child.

While visiting the two brothers at the Brunet-Jailly house, I stole the occasion to admire its superb craftsmanship. The annex extending along one side of
the courtyard, which I had helped build, was complete, along with its second-
storey veranda of elegant arched openings. The contours of al-Hajji's sculpted
details and wall niches were crisp and perfect, and his use of various shades of
mud plaster was exquisite. The palm-wood members of the ceilings were left
exposed to marvelous effect, accentuating the *fata-hinka* and *fata-taki* geometries of their structure. Al-Hajji was presently far away in the western city of
Kayes, and the eldest Kouroumansé brother, Baba, was in Bamako. Both were
working on commissions arranged by their entrepreneurial cousin, Bayeré.[23]

For a relatively young mason, Bayeré had cleverly maneuvered his way up
through the ranks to achieve national, even international, recognition. He was
a rarity among masons in that he was numerate, fluent in spoken French, and
literate in Arabic. After completing basic Qurᶜanic studies, Bayeré pursued a
more serious *madrassah* education into his teenage years and assisted his father
with masonry when not in school.[24] At eighteen he turned full attention to the
trade, apprenticing under his father and various other masons in order to receive
a rounded training. Bayeré apprenticed under the tutelage of his *grand frère* and
worked with a maternal uncle erecting mosques in Komba (near Sofara) and in
the Dogon village of Djanvilie (near Koulibala and Yarou), as well as with three
other uncles in the villages of Tjemé, Oura, and Tché in the Burkinian region
of Djibasou, near the frontier with Mali. In Segou he had been employed by a
paternal uncle to do his first work with cement.[25]

In the 1980s Bayeré worked closely with several European researchers,[26]
and he became fluidly conversant in Western discourses of heritage and "vernacular" architecture. As a local contact and reliable informant, Bayeré's relations with foreign scholars multiplied over the next decade. He was assigned an
integral role in the Mali-Dutch restoration project, charged with overseeing the
works of fellow masons and acting as a kind of consultant for the selection committee and the government's Cultural Mission.[27] He learned to read architectural drawings proficiently and acquired valuable project management skills.
Bayeré made himself an authority on "authentic" building practices, and regularly chastised his colleagues' supposed errors. He once pointed to a turn-of-
the-century photograph of a Moroccan-style house and pontificated about the
"mistakes" in its roofline decorations, declaring that many of today's senior masons also lack a correct understanding of Djenné's traditional architecture.

Bayeré maneuvered masterfully within the discourse on authenticity, challenging the age-set authority of his trade and establishing an esteemed and secure position. He regularly tallied his diverse training experiences, his work in distant locations, and the associations he fostered with foreign scholars to substantiate his credentials. He assumed the role of chief mason for two grand houses built for Europeans[28] and forged a role as a building contractor, managing the construction of several projects in parallel but seldom engaging in the actual muddy work of masonry. Bayeré frequently asserted that his new responsibilities were more demanding, both mentally and physically, than those of a regular mason whose workday ends at 3:00 PM. He buzzed around town on his scooter meeting clients and suppliers, arranged endless appointments by cell phone, and worked late into the evening calculating budgets and drawing up project schedules. I had tremendous admiration for his ingenuity and capacity to reinvent himself, taking confident control over the ever shifting conditions that characterize Djenné's fragile economy and building industry.

At the invitation of scholarly friends, Bayeré traveled to Europe on several occasions, and in 2003 he was part of a small delegation of Djenné masons flown to Washington, D.C., for the Smithsonian Folklife Festival to erect a monumental mud-brick gate at the National Mall.[29] Two years later Bayeré won a prestigious contract to build a home for the Malian government minister in the distant western city of Kayes. He employed his mason-cousin, al-Hajji Kouroumansé, to take charge of site works, and al-Hajji made the journey accompanied by his assistants Ali and Abdullahi Bouaré. Bayeré simultaneously deployed al-Hajji's older brother, Baba, to oversee a project in Bamako, and he professionally managed the operations at both sites by mobile phone.

In Djenné there is a popular saying: "One person works, and all others eat." Industrious individuals complain that while they toil, underemployed members of their extended family and social acquaintances expect gifts and financial support. Bayeré, however, shrewdly keeps those close to him gainfully employed, and, by doing so, he has uniquely made himself into a *grand patron* without squandering his capital savings in the form of handouts. Most recently he led a delegation of talented masons, including al-Hajji, to South Korea where they constructed a large-scale model of a Djenné-style mosque in mud bricks for the new high-tech Gimhae Clayarch Museum.

During our film project, Minister of Culture Cheikh Oumar Sissoko paid a diplomatic visit to Djenné for the annual plastering of the mosque; to enthusiastic cheers from the crowd, he participated heartily in the mucky event. Bayeré, who formed part of the town's official reception, remained close to the

RIGHT Mason Konmoussa Tennepo

minister throughout the ceremony, publicly signaling his emergent status as a key spokesman for the masons' community, and possibly for the nation's traditional architecture. In crafting his own representation for the television cameras and onlookers, Bayeré did not sport his mason's attire nor did he participate in the claying activity. At the end of the morning, when posing professionally beside the minister for photos, his starched and shiny pink cotton shirt was astoundingly unsoiled.

Konmoussa Tennepo's Benediction

Our documentary would focus on just one mason, and a principal concern was to avoid instigating conflict between those with whom I had already established relations. After some deliberation, we made the film with a mason who had not been part of my field research. Konmoussa Tennepo and his team of laborers were well suited for the role. The mason had excellent camera presence, an effervescent personality, and a unique and confident style.

We first encountered Konmoussa[30] on a construction site in Farmantala quarter. He was straddling a mud-brick wall high above the street and sporting a fluorescent yellow-and-orange Tommy Hilfiger™ cloak and a white bicycle helmet with a red stripe down the center. The helmet was for protection, and underneath he wore a tight woolen cap. Konmoussa was thirty-nine years old and impressively fit. He was compactly built and renowned in the eastern quarters of Djenné as a talented football player. His eyes were bright and playful, and he sported a long, neatly groomed beard. The beard conveyed his membership in the dawat'Islamiyyah ("Convocation of Islam" دعواة اسلامية), a local religious association headed by the master mason Beré Yonou who solemnly believed that, in order to be a good mason, one must have sound knowledge of the Qurʿan and Islamic principles. This expressly apolitical group is an exponent of proper Islamic conduct, and its members convene to discuss moral issues that offer spiritual guidance.[31]

Like many of his Bozo colleagues, Konmoussa once fished the rivers around Djenné in the wetter months between building seasons. Over the years, however, his reputation as a mason had flourished, and he now received an assortment of commissions that kept him employed almost continually. "During the heavy rains I stop for a few weeks to rest, but otherwise I'm building," he declared. The summer and rainy seasons were periods for executing small-scale tasks, including fixing leaky roofs and clay downspouts, realigning doors, and patching plasterwork. He attributed his ample work to a combination of com-

Re-plastering the historic Tukolor-style Nientao house in the Samsey quarter

petence and good fortune. "Others don't have luck. That's why they have little work. But I've been blessed with good luck." Konmoussa went on to explain that becoming a master of the trade is not necessarily associated with age; rather, it has to do with one's knowledge and, most important, the recognition one achieves. He proudly described himself as a *maître maçon*, and then moderated his boast by saying that one is designated a *maître* by one's colleagues and the public, not by oneself. He then asserted that, despite his youth, his knowledge made him *plus grand* than many of his older colleagues, but later reflected that he could not stroll about trumpeting this sort of thing. "My father is a master mason," he continued, "but even he will say that he is just *un petit maçon* because he wouldn't call himself a master in the presence of others."

On the rooftop of his humble one-storey home in the dense Semani quarter, we interviewed Konmoussa Tennepo about training, professional practice, and life as a mason. The topic of trade secrets inevitably arose, and Konmoussa insisted that a mason must have a cache of incantations to protect against the jealousies of others: "Once you've achieved success, whether you're a mason or a *marabout*, you must be able to protect yourself against those who might try to destroy you." Though relations among the *barey ton* masons are principally cordial, rivalries can brew beneath the surface. "My father is still my main master," he said with pride. Konbaba Tennepo, one of Djenné's most venerated craftsmen, was his son's first teacher and played a continuing role in Konmoussa's formation.[32] Konbaba established intimate ties with all his apprentices, whether kin or not. He believed that many young men today enter the profession expressly to make money, but he staunchly upheld the tradition whereby apprentices remain close to their master over a long period and are motivated by the pursuit of knowledge. "My father teaches me secrets little by little," said Konmoussa, gripping his stomach with two hands to indicate where he stored them. "Gradually I'm becoming a powerful mason," he added confidently. "I possess the knowledge that my father teaches me, and other masons have their own." He hoped to pass these secrets onto a son. Though he and his young wife Nana Kayantao vowed that their children would attend a Franco-Arab school, they also hoped that their sons would remain in the trade.

I queried Konmoussa about the benedictions he practiced, merely expecting him to confirm that a mason's secret knowledge was a mixture of *bey-bibi* and *bey-koray*. Instead, he generously offered to perform a benediction and invited the cameraman to record the event. He descended the stairs from his rooftop into the cramped little courtyard of the house, and after several minutes reappeared in his yellow-and-orange cloak with a long, thin instrument concealed within its folds. It was dusk, and in the waning daylight Konmoussa sat poised on the edge of a rusted iron bed frame. He initiated the blessing with full ablutions, using water from a zebra-striped plastic kettle to clean his mouth, nostrils, forehead, and face. He then scrubbed his forearms—right and left—and the top of his head and ears, finishing with his feet. While still seated, he again cupped a handful of water into his mouth, swished it about, spat it into his right hand, and lifted his gaze skyward following the direction of his pointed finger. He twisted his neck briskly and mechanically, facing forward, left, right and behind over his shoulder, and reciting secret incantations to sanctify the empty space around him.

Next, Konmoussa removed the instrument from his cloak. The iron rod (*guuru-bono*) was jet black and nearly half a meter long, with a leather wrist strap attached to one end. While uttering inaudible verses, he slipped the strap around his right wrist and began writing on the dusty surface of the roof terrace with the rod's blunt end. He etched the name "Allah" in giant and rectilinear Arabic script, starting with a tall *alif* (ا) and ending the word with a peculiar forked tail. Additional lines transformed the second *lam* (ل) in God's name into a spacious empty square at the center of the diagram. Konmoussa entered the square from the left-hand side through an unfinished segment of the line, and closed it like a door once inside. Within the protected sanctum, he prostrated in prayer, facing east to Mecca and in alignment with the *qibla* of the town's imposing mosque.[33] Starting on the eastern side of the square and using his baton, he then traced smaller versions of "*Ya! Allah*" (يا الله). He wrote this outside the perimeter of each of the four sides, completing his circle in counter-clockwise rotation.

Konmoussa took a protective amulet belt from inside his cloak and tied it around his waist, and then grasped prayer beads from his pocket. After praying and making benedictions in the sacred direction, the mason fingered the entire string of beads before turning counter-clockwise to efface each small "*Ya! Allah.*" Again he recited benedictions, spat into his hand and purified his head, then rapidly pulled the dust of the surrounding vanished letters into the interior of the square with his palms. The loose earth was gathered together in a little mound, more benedictions were muttered, and then Konmoussa scooped the pile with cupped hands, lifted it to his face to spit, and transferred the power of his invocation to the dust. Once more he made ablutions, but this time miming the cleansing of his body with the blessed earth. When finished, the dust that had fallen about his body was gathered again in a pile, and the benediction was complete. He prayed with crossed arms, issued greetings of peace (*Salam alaykum*) in all directions, and then exited the square through the same passage that he had shut with a line.

Konmoussa explained that his benediction protects against the jealousies and curses of other masons. The blessed earth it yields is also used at the start of new projects, and put into foundations or walls to protect the building and builders from harm. He described the metal rod as being "pure black without any traces of white," even though it was made with both *bey-bibi* and *bey-koray*. When questioned further about its origins, he denied that local smiths had forged this instrument, and would say nothing more about its source or significance. The rod was extremely powerful, and, like many of Konmoussa's secrets, he would never reveal the full contents of his knowledge.

The Annual Plastering of the Mosque

A proliferation of cultural and music festivals throughout Mali prompted the planning of a weeklong Djenné celebration that would attract tourists and showcase the town's ethnic diversity.[34] The dates for the very first Djenné Festival were set for February 2005.[35] There would be a crafts fair in the grain hall with a poster exhibit by the Cultural Mission on local architectural heritage and archaeology; performances would include evening concerts and traditional dances by various troupes from the town and surrounding villages; and the main attraction would be the plastering of the mosque, which was scheduled for the Thursday of festival week.[36]

Normally the annual plastering occurs toward the end of the dry season in March or April. At this late period a few remaining ponds dot the surrounding floodplain, and their stagnant water is used for mixing the mud. The precise date of the event has always been determined by elaborate negotiations between elders of the town quarters and the master masons of the *barey ton*, who are responsible for organizing the materials and the work. Astrology and lunar calculations are employed for identifying an auspicious day, and this is typically determined just a few weeks (sometimes only days) prior to the event.[37] In past years plastering occurred in two stages spaced a week or so apart, and the populations of the northern and southern quarters of the town were responsible for plastering the surfaces on their respective halves of the building.[38] Mounting pressure from organizers to make the new festival a success, however, coerced the elders and masons to agree on the proposed Thursday in February.[39]

Massive, coordinated preparations began Wednesday afternoon. On the outskirts of town, armies of little boys frolicked in shallow ponds of soupy brown water, trampling, scooping, and gathering piles of dark oozing mud. In a cacophony of shouts, chants, and banging metal pots, squadrons of older boys and young men arrived with horse carts and woven baskets to collect the mud, and then rampaged back to town behind fluttering flags and banners. Groups of adolescent girls and unmarried women sang praises and made music with cowry-laden calabashes along the sides of the road, tossing and spinning the instruments and cheering the mud-spattered hordes of men as they sprinted to the mosque and up the wide stairs onto the raised platform that envelops the enormous building. Idle onlookers were aggressively pelted with fistfuls of pasty mud, and globs of the stinking stuff clung tenaciously, like tar, to hair and clothing. Cartloads and baskets were dumped in ever growing piles at the base of the mosque walls and in the market square. This activity continued through the afternoon with raw energy and mounting intensity. The rambunctious squadrons became fully engrossed in their task; as they charged through the streets, some of the individuals gazed unwaveringly ahead with feverish, wild stares. People said these boys drank infusions of *almukaykay*[40] to boost vigor and sharpen their focus. Referred to locally as a "drug," *almukaykay* is a stimulant concocted from the leaves of a plant growing at the water's edge. The question of how widely it is consumed remains uncertain, but *almukaykay* is a performance-enhancing substance typically associated with such rituals as the mosque plastering.

That evening, pre-plastering revelries were organized throughout Djenné. In a neighborhood of Yobukayna, a blue plastic tarpaulin was stretched between rooftops to shade the open space below, and stereo speakers were mounted in windows and doorways. Metal-framed lawn chairs with corded rubber seats and backs were lined up in neat rows facing one another, and a colorful display of plastic flowers was arranged on a low wooden table positioned at the center of the public square. Music soon crackled over the speakers, luring a slow but steady trickle of residents to the street party. As the day's heat subsided, the blare of music grew louder. The mix of popular Malian hits and heavy-metal rock drowned out all possibility for conversation, and guests sat sedately in the long rows of chairs sipping bottles of sugary soda water. The gathering lasted until half past two in the morning, the stragglers strolling home under the bright light of a full moon.

A shrieking whistle pierced the dawn at 6:20 AM, signaling the start of the event. Drums beat madly to a chorus of cries, and what seemed like a thousand bodies rushed forward carrying baskets and pots of every description. Legions of sinewy, muscular arms hoisted colossal wooden ladders against the walls, creating the scene of a fortress under siege. Scores of men scrambled up the front face of the building, climbing the ladders and acrobatically scaling the armature of projecting *toron*. A continual relay was set in motion, delivering basket after

basket of mud from the ground to the highest pinnacles that adorned the towers and parapet wall. In his vibrant account of the event, Bourgeois describes a popular belief that, if a plasterer should fall, "quick as a wink he will change into a lizard and scamper down the wall," regaining human form when he reaches the ground.[41] Companies of women hastily transported colorful plastic pails brimming with water from the marshes, pouring them from the top of their heads in steady streams upon the gigantic piles of mud. Masses of young boys trampled the mucky mess, churning it into plaster and playfully painting one another from toe to head. Other young ones colonized their own small patches of the building, spreading plaster over the podium walls and nearby saints' tombs with tiny sweeps of their palms. Even foreign tourists who dared venture from the relative safety of the sidelines lent a hand in the plastering work. Musicians ferociously pounded drums, and young women spun their calabash instruments, heightening the frenetic tempo of the festivities.

The masons and apprentices were centrally involved, shouting instructions to the squadrons of young men and commandeering the plaster work from the highest rungs of the ladders, straddling *toron* in midair and organizing the waves of deliveries that wound their way up the mosque staircases to the roof. Konmoussa Tennepo and his tall and brawny apprentice, Yusuf Traoré, worked side by side throughout the morning, and Konamadou Djennepo was likewise accompanied by his apprentice, Konbakary. Konamadou hollered over the boisterous clamor to attract my attention. He shimmied up the ladder to the rooftop of the long women's gallery at the rear of the mosque where I stood with my camera, and greeted me with a broad smile and mud-speckled face. He asked me to take his picture, and we were soon joined by other faces barely recognizable beneath their caked strata of mud. All clothing was muted in shades of browns and greys, perfectly harmonized with the tones of the newly dressed mosque.

Yappi Konsinantao spotted our gathering and gleefully joined the grimy portrait session. Since working together three years ago, Yappi had renewed his Muslim faith and humbly acquiesced to the building trade. He prudently reckoned that most people would have derided his flirtations with Christianity, and that the search for work and a secure life elsewhere in the country was saddled with too many risks. Yappi therefore completed his mason's training, and his master, al-Hajji, formally presented him with a *kuuru-bibi* trowel and *sasiré* crowbar to mark his professional qualifications. Yappi also married and now had a child, affirming his readiness to stay. While al-Hajji was away, building in the distant town of Kayes, he entrusted Yappi to monitor his local projects, thereby granting the young man greater responsibility and furthering his learning expe-

LEFT Annual re-plastering of the Djenné Mosque in 2005

rience. Yappi told me that Ali Bouaré, who had traveled west with al-Hajji, had quit his apprenticeship to take up another in metalworking but that Ali continued to work as a building laborer to earn wages and support his widowed mother.

Every able-bodied man and boy, and hundreds of women, participated in this extraordinary feat of coordination, energy, and speed. By 7:30 AM, the eastern facade and towers of the mosque were complete, and the remainder of exterior surfaces, including the courtyard walls and the roof, were finished a few hours later. By late morning the task was over. Unlike in the past—when half the building was plastered and the other half tackled a week or so later—the entire building was covered at once. Because of the enormity of this year's mission, accurately estimating the total quantities of mud required was difficult. As a result, supplies ran dry before all the surfaces could be adequately covered. It was rumored that a second coating would be needed once the first layer dried. This miscalculation ignited debates about the procedures and preparation, and many elders and *marabouts* alleged that the plaster shortage occurred because the tradition of selecting an auspicious date for the ritual had been discarded in favor of the new festival calendar. The mosque's centenary would be celebrated in a year, and popular sentiment was that Djenné must revert to hosting this important event on a specially chosen day.

By noon weary crowds trailed off home, and hundreds journeyed by foot, bicycle, and in the back of trucks to bathe along the banks of the Bani River at Sanuna. Children jumped from the docked ferryboat and splashed about in the gently flowing waters, while mothers laundered soiled clothing. Back in Djenné individual neighborhoods hosted celebrations, and handfuls of candies were distributed among the throngs of anxious children. A group of women cooked a special meal of rice and lamb that later would be shared by the *barey ton* in the courtyard of the mosque. Seventy-odd members of the masons' association gathered on the west side of the mosque to hear the closing words from their chief, Sekou Traoré. They sat closely together on the ground, shaded by the high walls, and, as they listened, casually peeled dried splotches of mud from their clothing, limbs, and faces. Before rising to their feet, the masons graciously raised upturned palms toward the sky and made a communal benediction for the safety of the town and prosperity in the year ahead.

A Future in Flux

Djenné, like every other place and every period of history, confronts changes and challenges that alter its present and reconfigure its imaginings of the past.

The dam project was implemented by Mali's government to boost agricultural production in the Inland Niger Delta, but it could equally jeopardize the region's fragile riverine ecosystem and its historic interweave of economies and livelihoods. Below the dam, lower water levels could adversely affect fishing and agriculture. Controlled flooding, moreover, threatens to diminish the rich alluvial deposits vital to making mud bricks and thus reproducing the region's architectural heritage.

Computers and telecommunications promise new relations and faster links with the world, and although Djenné's unique qualities will become more widely known and appreciated around the globe, new values, alternative life-styles and marketing forces, as well as changing consumer tastes will infiltrate the town at increasing speed. Climate change, drought, and plagues of locusts, as well as shifting attitudes toward state education and employment will draw young men and women into new trades and careers at home and abroad. By en-rolling their children in classrooms rather than apprenticeships, parents, includ-ing masons, are knowingly complicit in the growing defection from the tradi-tional trades. Some masons are purposely diversifying their own "traditional" practices by learning to build with concrete and steel and to decorate with ce-ramic tiles and commercial paints, or by reinventing themselves as lucrative building contractors and thereby challenging and redefining the existing age-set hierarchy and power structure of Djenné's *barey ton* association.

As new configurations of work, life, and urban space emerge in the twenty-first century, the people of Djenné also embrace their rituals, skilled practices, and the material expression of their buildings in a longing for rootedness and con-tinuity. In combination, Djenné's UNESCO World Heritage status, the Malian-Dutch restoration project, and local associations like Djenné Patrimoine have served to promote international and local discourse about architectural conserva-tion and the use of vernacular building materials and methods. The *barey ton* has been revitalized as a result of these efforts, and the masons enjoy prestige and un-precedented wages. Individual masons strategically take up positions of authority within the politics of "authenticity," and a small but growing number claim com-plete autonomy over the reproduction of their *style-Soudanais* architecture. For now, this reproduction continues to wed a technological know-how and concep-tual ability for design with situated Islamic principles, benedictions, and secret incantations. Throughout this book I have demonstrated how these seemingly different ways of knowing unfold together and inform one another in the crafts-man's everyday practices. Together they produce and reproduce the masons' dis-tinct identity, as well as the living, changing character of Djenné.

Glossary

Ar. = Arabic; Bam. = Bamanankan; Boz. = Bozo; Dj.-Ch. = Djenné-Chiini (indigenized form of Songhai); Fr. = French; Fu. = Fulfuldé (Peul); and Hau. = Hausa. A question mark indicates that the linguistic origin or spelling or both are uncertain.

albarka (Dj.-Ch.) blessing or benediction (derived from *baraka* [Ar.] meaning "grace")

albida (Dj.-Ch./Ar.) (heretical or untrustworthy form of) secret knowledge

alfinta (Dj.-Ch.) fried cakes made with rice or millet (*gallettes* [Fr.]; *m'omi* [Bam.])

alharma-alharma (Dj.-Ch.) to labor for free, as a favor to someone

almukaykay (Dj.-Ch.) intoxicant made from the leaves of a marsh plant (*Datura* spp.)

al-qūba (Ar.) "dome," referring to wall niches for oil lamps or books

ʿaql (Ar.) reason or rational thought

aru-kuru (Dj.-Ch.) evil spirits that inflict illness or injury (*kama limba* [Bam.])

baakawal (Dj.-Ch.) protective amulet worn around the waist

bana-hay (Dj.-Ch.) wage

banco (Fr.) mud, referring to mud construction and architecture

baobab (?) very large African tree (*Adansonia digitata*) (*koo-nya* [Dj.-Ch.])

barey (Dj.-Ch.) mason

barey amir (Dj.-Ch./Ar.) master mason

barey bumo (Dj.-Ch.) chief of the *barey ton* (*bumo* = "head")

barey ton (Dj.-Ch./Bam.) masons' association (*ton* [Bam.] = "association")

bari (Dj.-Ch.) horse

batuma (Dj.-Ch.) interior courtyard of a house

bey-bibi (Dj.-Ch.) black-African secret knowledge (*bey* = "knowledge"; *bibi* = "black")

bey-koray (Dj.-Ch.) Islamic-based secret knowledge (*koray* = "white")

bita (Dj.-Ch.) millet-based porridge

bogolanfini (Bam.) mud-dyed cloth

boubou (Fr.) (derived from Malinké, *bubu*) long flowing gown worn by men and women, sometimes embroidered

boubou de tjete "the wall's boubou," referring to a coat of mud plaster over brickwork (*tjete* [Dj.-Ch.] = "wall")

bulanga (Dj.Ch.) shea butter (*karité* butter)

capitaine (Fr.) Nile perch (*Lates niloticus*) (*ham-koray* [Dj.-Ch.])

daarey (Dj.-Ch.) jujube (*Ziziphus mauritiana*), a small tree bearing tiny yellow fruit

daasi (Dj.-Ch.) composite hammer and axe-like tool

daasi kayna (Dj.-Ch.) small axe

djenné-ferey (Dj.-Ch.) handmade cylindrical "Djenné" mud bricks

djennénké (Dj.-Ch.) urban identity of Djenné residents, regardless of ethnicity

djenné wéré (Dj.-Ch.) title of Djenné's traditional chief

djinn (Ar.) spirits, frequently referred to in the Qurᶜan

doni doni (Bam.) little by little

donso (Bam.) hunter

donso ton (Bam.) association of hunters

dyente (Dj.-Ch.) learn a trade or do an apprenticeship

dyente idye (Dj.-Ch.) pupil or apprentice (*idye* = child)

dyiney dyisi do (Dj.-Ch.) storeroom

farka banda (Dj.-Ch.) "donkey's back," referring to the curved profile of the parapet wall

fata-hinka (Dj.-Ch.) "two-winged" ceiling, i.e., two opposite corners are spanned diagonally

fata-taki (Dj.-Ch.) "four-winged" ceiling, i.e., all four corners are spanned diagonally

fatihah (Ar.) opening, referring to the opening *sūra* of the Qurᶜan

fitila bumo (Dj.-Ch.) wick of the (oil)lamp

fūney (Dj.-Ch.) window, and also the rectangular aperture in the parapet wall

furufuru (Bam.) deep-fried millet cakes

futey (Dj.-Ch.) kitchen

gaaga (Dj.-Ch.) pied crow, but in construction referring to the squat pilasters in the decorative ensemble above a house entrance

gaara (Dj.-Ch.) blessing or benediction

gabriyyer (Dj.-Ch.?) construction formwork, i.e., for constructing arches

galia (Dj.-Ch.) parlor room

ganda karfoo (Dj.-Ch.) snake

garboy-honno (Dj.-Ch.) wild date (*Balanites aegyptiaca*), thorny tree bearing a berry-like fruit

gar-bundu (Dj.-Ch.) thick branches (used as beams for constructing ceilings)

garibou (Bam./Ar.) migrant student of a Qurʿanic school (from *gharib* [Ar.] = "stranger")

garsi (Dj.-Ch.) porridge-like mixture made from millet and milk

gris-gris (Fr.) protective amulet

gum hu (Dj.-Ch.) covered portico characteristic of Tukolor-style houses

guuru bari (Dj.-Ch.) literally "iron horse," but meaning "bicycle"

guuru bono (Dj.-Ch.) iron rod

guuru karfoo (Dj.-Ch.) plumb line

hajj (Ar.) Holy pilgrimage to Mecca, one of the "Five Pillars" of Islam

handoro (Dj.-Ch.) long, clay downspout

handu koray (Dj.-Ch.) "white moon," but in building decoration *handu koray* refers to curved decorative lines incised in the mud plaster

harmattan (Ar.) winter period of dry, dusty winds blowing south from the Sahara

har terey hu (Dj.-Ch.) room reserved for the household patriarch, situated above the vestibule

hu (Dj.-Ch.) living quarters or room

hu béné (Dj.-Ch.) ceiling

jaari benté (Dj.-Ch.) auspicious day

jaari futu (Dj.-Ch.) inauspicious day

jam-woy (Dj.-Ch.) potter-wife of a blacksmith

jihad (Ar.) struggle or war, often used to refer to an Islamic Holy War

jiminta (Dj.-Ch.) sweet snack made with peanuts, sugar, and chilli pepper

jōto (Dj.-Ch.) large wooden ladle

kaarey niiné (Dj.-Ch.) "crocodile snouts," referring to a wedge-shaped mud brick

kabi (Dj.-Ch.) totem

kado (Fu.) derogatory term for the Dogon (derived from *kad* [Fu.] = "potash")

kalikali (Dj.-Ch.) staircase

kalikali sunduku (Dj.-Ch./Ar.) small enclosure (*sunduq* [Ar.] = "box") on the roof at the top of the stairs

kamba baakawal (Dj.-Ch.) protective amulets worn around the upper arm

kamba-hiiri (Dj.-Ch.) bracelets, i.e., beaded ones that women make to sell in the market

kani hu (Dj.-Ch.) bedroom; and also the room in a house for unmarried men, normally with a separate entrance

karamogo (Bam.) expertise or mastery

karité (Bam.) shea tree (*Vitellaria paradoxa*) (*bulanga-idye-nya* [Dj.-Ch.]), producing shea butter

kaydiya (Dj.-Ch.) rainy season

kayna kayna (Dj.-Ch.) little by little, or slowly

kola (or *cola*) small tree (genus *cola*) bearing seed containing caffeine

koo (Dj.Ch.) baobab fruit

koyra-boro (Dj.-Ch.) a town person or a Songhay

kumbu (Dj.-Ch.) wooden-handled hoe

kusu (Dj.-Ch.) bulbous clay pot (used for making the *sarafar fula*)

laabu (Dj.-Ch.) mud

laabu-batakara (Dj.-Ch.) plaster prepared with grey mud from marshes, mixed with rice husks

laabu-bibi (Dj.-Ch.) "black" mud

laabu-fumbo (Dj.-Ch.) a resilient plaster prepared with fermented *laabu tyirey* and rice husks

laabu-kuntur (Dj.-Ch.) mud containing small stones or gravel

laabu-tyirey (Dj.-Ch.) "red" mud

lakha (Boz.) Bozo temporary fishing encampment along the riverbanks

lutu (Dj.-Ch.) deaf person

maale-banya (Dj.-Ch.) "slave of the master," referring to an apprentice

madrassah (Ar.) a place of study, usually referring to as an Islamic religious school

marabout (Fr./Ar.) religious scholar or holy man

maraboutage (Fr./Ar.) *marabout* practices of preparing amulets and making benedictions

m'baaka (Dj.-Ch.) species of lizard (*Agama agama*); the *m'baakahar* (male) has a bright yellow head

mihrab (Ar.) niche or tower in a mosque wall indicating the orientation to Mecca

mina bara (Dj.-Ch.) laborer

modu (Dj.-Ch.) rice husks

muezzin (Ar.) person responsible for making the call to prayer

musi bumo (Dj.-Ch.) cat's head (*musi* = "cat"; *bumo* = "head"), but, with regard to construction, refers to the small half-columns with pill-like capitals

musi moo toondi (Dj.-Ch.) full cat's eye (*moo* = eye; *toondi* = full), but, regarding construction, refers to the small aperture made above the "cat's head" (*musi bumo*)

nasi (Dj.-Ch.) medicine prepared by washing away Qurᶜanic scriptures with water

noor-foo (Dj.-Ch.) scorpion

noor koray (Dj.-Ch.) money in the form of cowry shells (*nor* = "money"; *koray* = "white")

numu (Bam.) blacksmith (pl., *numuw*)

nyama (Bam./Mandinka) vital force that animates all things

nyamakalaw (Bam.) a Mandé caste group

nyégé (Dj.-Ch.) toilet, usually referring to the tower-like toilet stack

pelle (Fr.) shovel

pinasse (Fr.) large wooden boats used to transport goods on the Niger

pirogue (Fr.) canoe-like boat

potigé (Dj.-Ch.) decorative facade of a traditional Djenné house

prix de thé (Fr.) "the price for tea," referring to a small gift of money

qibla (Ar.) wall in a mosque containing the *mihrab*

saaney (Dj.-Ch.) star

sahel (Ar.) littoral or coast, referring to the dry scrubby region south of the Sahara

sâho (Boz.) communal house for unmarried Bozo males

salafal (Dj.-Ch.) minaret, but occasionally used to refer to a *sarafar*

santal (Dj.-Ch. ?) arch

saraa (Dj.-Ch.) alms

sarafar (Dj.-Ch.) pilasters terminating in vertical projections

sarafar déné (Dj.-Ch.) "*sarafar*'s tongue," referring to the pointed tip of the *sarafar idye*

sarafar fula (Dj.-Ch./Fu.) "hat" of the *sarafar*, i.e., the bulbous top on the *sarafar har*

sarafar har (Dj.-Ch.) "male" *sarafar*, i.e., the pilasters on the ends of a house facade

sarafar idye (Dj.-Ch.) "offspring" *sarafar*, i.e., the miters positioned between the *sarafar woy*

sarafar jutun (Dj.-Ch.) "*sarafar*'s navel," referring to the circular projections on the *sarafar*

sarafar woy (Dj.-Ch.) "female" *sarafar*, denoting the pilasters on either side of the entrance

sasiré (Dj.-Ch.) flared-end crowbar

sebe (Dj.Ch.) ronier palm (*Borassus aethiopum*), used for ceiling construction

segi (Dj.-Ch.) thickly woven baskets (for transporting mud mortar)

shaytān (Ar.) devil or Satan

siifa (Dj.-Ch.) vestibule

simaan (Dj.-Ch.) cement

sirri (Dj.-Ch.) secret or secret knowledge

soro (Dj.-Ch.) flat terrace roof

sūra (pl., *suar*) (Ar.) chapter of the Qurʿan

taa-koy (Dj.-Ch.) tailor

Tabaski (Wolof) *eid al-kabir* or *eid al-Adha* (Ar.) Islamic feast commemorating the willingness of Prophet Abraham to sacrifice his son

talibé (Bam./Ar.) student of a Qurᶜanic school, (from *talib* [Ar.] = "student")

tarikh (Ar.) history, sometimes used to refer to a land-claim document

tasika (Dj.-Ch.) ante-room frequently used for sleeping

tira (Dj.-Ch.) protective amulet worn around the neck

tjirkaarey (Dj.-Ch.) breakfast

tjirkosé (Dj.-Ch.) lunch

toguere (Fu.) large mound-like landform in a floodplain area

toron (Dj.-Ch.) protruding bundles of palm-wood sticks

toron di djumbu doo (Dj.-Ch.) thick palm-wood stick embedded in the parapet wall and used as a step

truelle française (Fr.) "French" trowel, referring to the mason's smaller, imported trowel

truelle kuuru-bibi (Fr./Dj.-Ch.) "black-skin" trowel, referring to one locally produced by blacksmiths

tubaabu (Bam.) "white" person, or a European

tubaabu ferey (Bam./Dj.-Ch.) rectangular "white-man's bricks" made with a wooden mold

tuguri (Dj.-Ch.) wood or timber

voussoir individual wedge-shaped stones (or masonry units) that compose an arch

walaa (Dj.-Ch.) wooden boards used by students for writing Qurᶜanic verses from the Arabic *alwāh* (sing., *lauh*); also ablutions

waliju (Dj.-Ch./Ar.) saint

wakoloni (Dj.-Ch.) tiny supernatural creatures

yer koy naarey (Dj.-Ch.) "Asking for God's blessing" or "Pray to God"

zakat (Ar.) alms giving, i.e., one of the "Five Pillars" of Islam

zanko (Hau.) vertical, miter-like roof extensions on buildings in Hausaland

zaure (Hau.) entrance vestibule to an extended family compound in Hausaland

Notes

Introduction

1. *Soumbala* is a condiment made from the pounded seeds of the African locust bean tree (*Parkia biglobosa; néré* in Bamanankan) and formed into balls that can keep for several months.

2. Djenné's mosque has been closed to non-Muslims since the 1990s. It is popularly reported that an incident involving a Western photographer and his troop of fashion models raised local concerns when they were found conducting a photo shoot inside the prayer hall. Signs were subsequently posted at the entrances to the building strictly forbidding entrance to non-Muslims.

3. Marchand 1993 (unpublished report to CIDA). *Gidan Hausa*.

4. Marchand 2001.

5. The term *harmattan* derives from a combination of the Arabic words for "hot" (*hār* حار) and "time of" (*matān* متا). The *harmattan* is the name of the hot dry season occurring during the winter months. It is characterised by strong winds blowing south from the Sahara carrying immense quantities of dust and sand over West Africa.

6. Translation: "There is no God but Allah." This is the first line in the Islamic affirmation of faith, or *šahāda* (شهادة).

7. Park 1983 [1799], 209.

8. Ligers 1964, 1:v.

9. On the use of apprentice-style field methods in anthropology, see Coy 1989a.

10. For a more detailed examination of nonverbal communication between craftspeople, see Marchand 2003a; 2007b; 2008; and forthcoming.

11. Marchand, forthcoming.

12. In the past, plumb lines made with clay bobs were produced locally. Because these broke easily when they fell or bounced against wall surfaces, masons now use imported lead plumb bobs. A second, though less popularly used Djenné-Chiini term for plumb line is *kadomamé karfoo*.

13. The French term *mètre* is used, and the numerical measurements made with it

are commonly cited in French, not the local Djenné-Chiini language. The seldom-used term for measuring tape in that language is *nési-haya* ("measure-something").

14. Only the French term *pelle* is used, and there is seemingly no local indigenous term for shovel.

15. At the time of her study in the early 1980s, LaViolette records that the four tools at the core of the masons' kit were the iron bar, trowel, stick of wood, and string or rope. The stick of wood, she writes, "is used to align bricks and measure out door and window openings" (1994b, 91). During my fieldwork, sticks of wood were indeed used for taking measurements, which is illustrated in chapter 4.

16. LaViolette, too, notes that despite the "traditional feel of Jenne," the architectural style has changed over time and "masons and their clients innovate" (1994b, 91).

17. The term *style-Soudanais* translates from the French as Sudanese style, and is sometimes referred to as the Sahelian or Sudanic style. In her erudite account on the *style-Soudanais*, Prussin writes: "The colonial *tata* or citadel of French West Africa at the Marseille Colonial Exposition of 1922, by combining the minaret of the Djinguereé Ber mosque at Tombouctou with the traditional Muslim facade of a house at Djenné, Mali, established an architectural prototype for France's entire West African empire" (1986, 18). She notes, however, that a precise definition of the *style-Soudanais* is elusive (1986, 103). Denyer's somewhat ambiguous definition listed the main features as a courtyard plan, walls constructed of mud bricks and mortar, flat or dome-shaped vaulted roofs supported on palm joists, and parapets pierced with drainage pipes or channels (1978:160–61). Indeed, Maas and Mommersteeg (1992, 77) note that the *style-Soudanais* characteristics defined by various authors (Prussin 1986, 161; Engeström 1955, 122; Denyer 1978, 160–61; Domian 1989, 24; and Trimingham 1970, 69) can be attributed to building types across a wide geographic territory stretching from Tunisia to Ghana, and they regard these as secondary to their focus on the Djenné style. In their exploration of the *style-Soudanais*, Maas and Mommersteeg (1993) concentrate on the prototypical courtyard house of Djenné and its relation to the urban morphology. They list the standard features of Djenné's architecture and the arrangement of domestic spaces. LaViolette, too, focuses on Djenné and writes that "it is appropriate . . . to think of at least the nineteenth and twentieth century sudanic building style about which we know the most as a Jenne school of architecture, which has evolved with different regional characteristics within an extensive and deep tradition in the Western Sudan" (1994b, 89).

18. Prussin 1974b; Maas and Mommersteeg 1992; Blier 2004; Bedaux, Diaby, and Maas 2003a.

19. LaViolette 1995, 171.

20. Jansen 2000, 37. Note that the Mandé term for *griot* is *jeli,* whereby *jeli-ké* refers to a male and *jeli-muso* to a female.

21. Marchand 2003c.

22. Lave and Wenger 1991.

23. Casey 1996b; Heidegger 1993.

24. LaViolette 1987; for an earlier version of my studies of the masons' association, see Marchand 2003d.

25. Monteil 1932, 160–61.

26. Based on archaeological evidence (McIntosh and McIntosh 1981), specialized building activity has existed in Djenné (Djenné-Djeno) since at least the eighth or ninth century, but, as LaViolette points out, material evidence is lacking for the origins of the masons' traditions and their professional organization (1994b, 90–91).

27. Mandé country is located in the southwest of present-day Mali and was the heartland of the Mali Empire which ruled over a vast territory from the thirteenth to the sixteenth century.

28. *Koyra-boro* translates either as "town person" or "a person of Songhay descent," but the term is used regularly by established Djenné residents of various ethnic origins who speak Djenné-Chiini as their mother tongue and who are fully immersed in the town's urban culture.

29. Bourgeois 1987, 60. LaViolette (1994b, 90) also records that members of the Traoré lineage have acted as head of the *barey* since the late nineteenth century.

30. Monteil 1932, 252. My translation from the French: "Le chef de la corporation des baris est choisi par le chef de la ville de Djénné parmi les plus intelligents et les plus capables: c'est une manière d'architecte local généralement fort habile. Il est obéi et écouté des autres bari qui n'entreprennent rien sans ses ordres."

31. More specifically, the drought hit hardest in 1972–74 and 1984–87.

32. Sanankoua (1999, 95) reports cases of young women also leaving Djenné during this period of hardship.

33. Monteil 1932, 253. My translation from the French: "un bon maître bari reçoit une solde journalière de 400 cauris; le bari qui fait le mortier est payé 200 cauris et les goujats reçoivent chacun 100 cauris."

34. In the eighteenth century the Germans were well known for their trade in cowry shells which they exported from the East African coast and shipped around the Cape to West Africa where cowries were popularly used as currency (Gilbert 2004, 34).

35. Insoll 2003, 249–50.

36. At that time the currency in Mali was the Malian franc. The Malian franc was adopted in 1962 to replace the CFA, but the CFA was reintroduced in 1984 (1 CFA = 0.2 U.S. cents; U.S. \$1 = 417 CFA; 1 CFA = 0.15 Euro cents; 1 Euro = 655 CFA [2008 exchange rate]). Older craftsmen informed me that a mason's wage in 1970 was equivalent to approximately 750 CFA.

37. For further discussion of the syntheses of styles incorporated in new one-storey constructions of the expanding quarters, see Maas and Mommersteeg 1992, 200–205.

38. The threat to mud architecture posed by new materials and technologies, as well as by cultural change and foreign influences, was noted by at least the early 1980s (see, for example, Haberland 1981, 44).

39. Bedaux et al. 2000, 205. On the struggle between national and local positions over Djenné's architecture as a form of cultural capital, see also Rowlands 2003. Fontein (2000) provides an in-depth study of the politics and challenges of using the label "world heritage" in Africa, as well as the struggles that emerge over its ownership and control. Fontein notes that "while the heritage idea originated in Europe, it has been 'indigenised'—at least in the sense that it has been thoroughly utilised for the purposes of African nationalist revival" (64).

40. Bedaux et al. 1995. See also Bedaux et al. 2000 and Bedaux, Diaby, and Maas 2003b for further reports on the Dutch-Mali collaboration for the restoration of houses in Djenné.

41. Bedaux et al. 1995, 24.

42. LaViolette (1994b, 89) records that there were approximately one hundred masons in 1983. The significantly smaller number of masons at that time may have been a result of the droughts in the 1970s and 1980s, and the decreased demand for building work.

43. The strictly observed hierarchy and the use of intermediaries are also exemplified in the *kama blo*, the great meeting hut of the Mandé rulers in Kangaba. This ancient institution may have served as an early model of controlled discourse throughout the Mandé cultural region.

44. Maas and Mommersteeg 1992, 186.

45. The Horso are defined more by their low social position as intermediaries in the service of Djenné families than by any specific ethnic identity. Horso act as guardians for

the young sons of their patron families during the fifteen-day period following circumcision; they are also guardians of brides and grooms during wedding ceremonies. Their services and benedictions are rewarded with small gifts of money and kola nuts. See also Brunet-Jailly (2004) on the role of Horso in Djenné's circumcision and excision ceremonies; and Diallo (2004, 176) on the role of caste members as gatekeepers of initiation rites. It is notable that, in recent decades, some Horso have undergone apprenticeships to become masons.

46. Bourgeois 1987, 62.

47. Monteil 1932, 252. My translation from the French: "Les bari se recrutent surtout dans le pondo méridional, ils sont souvent originaires des cantons de Djénnéri et de Pondori. A quelque classe de la société qu'il appartienne, un indigène peut se faire bari; mais c'est une déchéance pour les gens de bonne famille parce que, bien que les bari soient des gens libres non castes, ils participent de la mésestime qui atteint tous les artisans."

48. Prussin 1970, 18. Also noteworthy is that masons, unlike other corporate groups in Mali such as hunters, bards, leatherworkers, blacksmiths, and potters, are not *nyamakala*, a "caste" group with endogamous marriage prescriptions.

49. Prussin 1986, 46.

50. LaViolette 1994b, 90.

51. Marchand 2007a.

52. *Suar* is the plural of *sūra*, a verse in the Holy Qurᶜan.

53. Brenner (1984, 76), in his discussion of Qurᶜanic education, similarly notes that "the relationship between student and teacher went much further than the transmission of commentaries . . . [whereby] the teacher could become the most fundamental and pervasive influence in the student's moral and personal development."

54. Statistics from the United Nations Development Programme (UNDP) Human Development Report (2004, 129).

55. The term *marabout* refers to scholars of Islam and Qurᶜanic schoolteachers. The title is a French corruption of the Arabic term *murābit* (مرابط) meaning 'garrisoned troops," the plural of which is *al-murabitun,* or the Almoravids. The eleventh-century Almoravid conquerors of Morocco established a capital at Marrakech and were responsible for converting the Berber population of North Africa and the Western Sahara to Islam. The term *marabout* was used throughout the French West African colonies to refer to Islamic proselytisers, religious scholars, and teachers. According to Imperato (1977, 51), the French disseminated the term from their North African colonies to West Africa. The Djenné-Chiini term for *marabout* is *alfaa,* but the former is more commonly used in Djenné.

56. Masons are increasingly using measuring tapes in combination with their more traditional means of body-based measurements. Slick, imported tape measures that retract automatically with a "snap" are prestige items.

57. For Mali's cultural heritage, see D. H. Ross, ed., special issue of *African Arts* 28, no. 4 (fall 1995); and on the state of conservation of the old town of Djenné, see the United Nations Educational, Scientific, and Cultural Organization (UNESCO) World Heritage Report (2006, 86).

1. Back to Work

1. The geographic term *Sahel* comes from the Arabic term *sāhil* (ساحل), meaning littoral or coast, and refers to the large band of dry grasslands and shrub that border the Sahara (صحارى), meaning desert.

2. See introduction, note 5.

3. *Djinn* refers to the spirits that populate the world in various forms. Similarly, in English, these rotating winds are often called "dust devils."

4. See S. Keech McIntosh (1995, 374) on the satellite settlements of Djenné-Djeno. Djenné-Djeno was a thriving urban center situated to the southeast of present-day Djenné. Archaeological excavations reveal that the site was continuously occupied from as early as the third century BCE until the fourteenth century CE (see also R. J. McIntosh 2005).

5. Bamoy was a common Songhay (or Djenné-Chiini) name given to boys who were "named after" (*moy*) their "father" (*ba* or *baba*). The boy comes to be called Bamoy by others, and his real name (i.e., the name of his father) will rarely be used. The equivalent appellation for girls is Nyamoy, where *nya* is "mother." Because Djenné-Chiini was the dominant language of Djenné, many Bozo residents were given Songhay names. On the politics of naming and giving children the homonyms of family relatives, see Samoura, Ouane, and Cissé 1999, 61–63.

6. *Hasey* means "uncle," or, more precisely, "mother's brother" in Djenné-Chiini, and this nickname is given to boys named after an uncle. The female equivalent, *Kondé,* is given to girls named after an "aunt."

7. *Tubaabu* is a Bamana word and is more commonly used than the Djenné-Chiini term for white person, *annasaara* (derived from the Arabic word for a Christian, Nasrani نصراني).

8. See Heath 1999 and Nicolaï 1981.

9. Ligers 1964; Tymowski 1974, 12; Maas and Mommersteeg 1990, 24. Monteil (1933, 265) claims that the Bozo are recognized by all inhabitants of the region as the most ancient masters of the earth and water, but their mastery was achieved not by conquest but because they were there first.

10. Conrad and Frank (1995a, 11) legitimately recognize that, "while ethnic categories remain a viable means of recognising difference, the boundaries between them are by no means absolute or immutable." Rather, "ethnicity might more accurately be viewed as one of a number of negotiable aspects of one's identity" (Frank 1995b, 144).

11. According to Mommersteeg, Djenné has approximately thirty-five schools for elementary Qur'anic education and about a dozen secondary-level schools for the study of Arabic grammar, law, and the traditions of the Prophet (*hadith*) (1999, 30). For more detailed studies on Qur'anic education in Djenné, see Mommersteeg 1991a, 1991b, and 1998; and on religious education in Mali more generally, see Brenner 2001. By contrast, the curriculum of the town's more scholarly *madrassahs* includes a proper formation in reading and writing Arabic, as well as mathematics, history, and other subjects. *Madrassah* (مدرسة) is the Arabic term for "a place of study," and these are sometimes referred to locally as *médersa,* a French corruption of the Arabic.

12. Abu Bakr (أبو بكر), a popular Arabic male name, translates directly to "father of a young camel."

13. Cypermethrin is a synthetic chemical similar to the pyrethrins of chrysanthemum flowers. It kills insects by affecting the central nervous system, and is highly toxic to fish and bees. Its typical half-life in soil is thirty days. People working with cypermethrin develop symptoms of dizziness and skin irritations. In America, the chemical has been classified as a possible human carcinogen.

14. Djennénké refers to the native, cosmopolitan, and ethnically mixed population of Djenné (Konaré 1999, 42).

15. Laterite is a red soil with a high clay content, and is rich in iron and aluminium oxides. Laterite often forms the topsoil layer in tropical and subtropical regions. When dry, its hard and durable qualities make it an ideal building material.

16. Lauber 1998, 59.

17. Maas and Mommersteeg 1992, 36.

18. On the ecological properties of mud construction, see Lauber 1998, 58.

19. In relation to the river, also see my discussion in the epilogue about the Talo Dam project on the Bani River upstream from Djenné. The dam may decrease the quantity of alluvial deposits throughout the downstream water system. These annual deposits are rich in fish bones, manure, and other organic materials, and provide excellent soil for making mud bricks. The abundance of cow manure along the river comes from the Fulani herds that graze year-round on the banks and along the grassy bed during the dry season.

20. Following Roberts (1987, 68ff.), La Violette (1995, 172) describes the Somono as mainly fishers and farmers who were originally recruited or captured in the late seventeenth and early eighteenth centuries "to perform fishing and transporting services for the Bamana empire in Segu." She notes that, despite being of Bamana, Marka or Soninke, Bobo and Bozo origins, contemporary Somono identity in Djenné functions like an ethnic category (La Violette 1995,173).

21. A *pirogue* is the French term for a canoe, and it is used locally to refer to the sleek black wooden boats made from wide planks and used by fishermen of the Pondo.

22. The 2:00 PM prayer time is called *aluula* in Djenné-Chiini.

23. *Koyra-boro* means, literally, "town person."

24. Maas and Mommersteeg (1992, 173–175) include several versions of the Tempama legend in their analysis of Djenné's sacred layout. These include versions from Monteil 1932, 34–36; Daget, Konipo, and Sanankoua 1953, 127–28; Tall 1977, 183; and Yaro 1989. For another version of the Tempama (or Tapama) legend, see McIntosh 1998, 104); and for a discussion of Tapama and other Djenné saints, see Diakité 1999, 55–59.

25. The bedrock below Djenné was considerably deep, so stone was quarried from a place east of Djenné, beyond the crossroads with the main motorway to Mopti and in the direction of the Bandiagara escarpment, and transported back to town by truck. Archaeological evidence also suggests that the sandstone used for tools and grinding implements was imported to ancient Djenné-Djeno from outside the immediate region (S. K. McIntosh 1995, 390; McIntosh and McIntosh, 1981, 414).

26. See also Maas 1990, 29. Note that, in Djenné-Chiini, *dyente* means "apprenticeship" or "learn a trade" and *idye* means "child."

27. *Barey* is the Djenné-Chiini word for "mason," and *amir* derives from the Arabic word *āmir* أمر, meaning "lord" or "master."

28. People in Djenné commonly did not know their precise age. Some individuals merely cited the year of their birth when asked their age; others identified their birth date with reference to a coinciding major event. I had particular difficulty ascertaining the ages of my Bozo colleagues compared to members of other ethnic groups on the building site. Aside from age not being an especially salient item of cultural information in this region, the ambiguity also relates to the fact that people operate according to two different calendar systems: the solar-based Gregorian calendar and the lunar-based Islamic one.

29. McIntosh 1998 [1988], 208–9.

30. The word for a workday in Djenné-Chiini is *jaari kakwego* and for a holiday *jaari kakwaysi*.

31. McNaughton 1982, 57.

32. Brett-Smith 1994.

33. For an earlier study on worksite banter in Djenné, see Marchand 2003b.

34. See, for example, Laboret 1929, 244–54; Evans-Pritchard 1933, 369–401; Paulme 1939, 433–44; Pedler 1940, 170–73; Radcliffe-Brown 1940, 195–210; Radcliffe-Brown 1949, 133–40; Griaule 1948, 242–58; Irvine 1974, 167–89; Freedman 1977, 154–65; Stevens 1978, 47–71; Drucker-Brown 1982, 714–27; and Heald 1990, 377–92.

35. See Liger 1964, for a comprehensive description of Bozo fishing practices; and, for a more contemporary account, see Beaudoin 1998, 33–39.

36. Like the geographic and environmental distinctions I describe between the Bozo

and Dogon, Phillips Stevens's (1978, 50, 63) investigation of Bachama joking categories in northeastern Nigeria also considers relations of "privileged familiarity" between ecologically determined groups, including those who reside along the riverbanks (*Ji-zaŋe*) and those who reside inland (*Ji-bawe*).

37. I take note here of Mary Douglas's differentiation between an obscenity and a joke (1968, 371–72). Although I agree that labeling something (a gesture, action, or remark) as "obscene" implies that it is offensive, and that this may be cross-culturally problematic, I nevertheless maintain that the nature of the insults exchanged between Bozo and Dogon are meant to shock and offend, and therefore "obscene" is an apt description. Arguably, this effect continually, and productively, puts their nonviolent alliance to the test, and thereby reproduces and strengthens it.

38. Radcliffe-Brown 1940.

39. Paulme, 1939, 441–44.

40. Griaule 1948.

41. For example, see discussions about *nyama* in Mandé societies in the work of Bird 1971; Brett-Smith 1994; Imperato 1975; McIntosh 1998, 27–28; McNaughton 1988; and Monteil 1971 [1932], 29–30.

42. See van Beek 1991, 148. Also see Jansen 2002, 30 n. 40, who notes that several contemporary scholars working in the Mandé region have critically questioned the importance of *nyama*.

43. Rouch 1960, 24–29.

44. Bird 1971.

45. Paulme 1939. Dieterlen (1941, 89) also refers to this legend in describing the cathartic relation between Dogon and Bozo.

46. Evans-Pritchard's 1933 study of the Zande also demonstrates the coexistence of a blood-brotherhood form of alliance and a joking relationship. Radcliffe-Brown (1940, 208) suggests "four modes of alliance or consociation, (1) through intermarriage, (2) by exchange of goods or services, (3) by blood-brotherhood or exchange of names or sacra, and (4) by the joking relationship," which, he states, "may exist separately or combined in several different ways."

47. Paulme 1939, 441–44. One Bozo colleague explained that "a Bozo cannot marry a Dogon because everyone knows that a marriage easily results in dispute. Our two groups of people want to avoid any potential hostility so that we can maintain our brotherly relationship."

48. The Bamanankan term for inter-ethnic joking relations, or *cousinage à plaisanterie*, is *sinakuya*.

49. Griaule (1948, 246) notes that Fulfulde (the Fulani language) was used as the lingua franca between Dogon and Bozo where he conducted fieldwork, and it remains an important language for inter-ethnic communication throughout the Inland Niger Delta region.

50. Leach 1972, 42.

51. Griaule 1948, 246–47. Also note the similarity in the content of the insults expressed here with those exchanged between the Bachama *Ji-zaŋe* (people of the river banks) and *Ji-bawe* (people of the bush) studied by Phillips Stevens (1978, 63).

52. Legend has it that long ago a group of Fulani came across a group of Dogon. The Dogon could neither make themselves understood nor did they understand Fulfuldé. The Fulani became frustrated with these stubborn people and proclaimed that "Les Dogons sont méchants comme le potasse" ("The Dogon are nasty like potash"). The Fulfulde word for potash is *kad*, which was transformed to *kado* in referring to the Dogon. The reason potash is considered "nasty" is because of its acidity and bitter taste. It is worth noting that the Dogon add potash to their staple dish, *Tõ*, which other ethnic groups view as a notoriously bad-tasting meal.

53. In his study of Mandé blacksmiths in oral lore, McNaughton (1995) similarly notes that smiths are portrayed as both cultural heroes and sorcerers, and that these two capacities are not considered mutually exclusive. Hoffman (2000, 12) writes that accomplished griots master a wide range of ritualized speech (*kilisi*) that can either "benefit or harm the target."

54. Historically Islam and so-called traditional African knowledge have been tightly interwoven but, as in the rest of the country and throughout West Africa more generally, this symbiotic relation has coexisted with a vocal current of religious conservatism and imagined orthodoxy within the religious discourse. Many *marabouts* continue to be prominent suppliers of protective amulets and incantations that blend Islam and animism, while other religious leaders and Muslim spokespersons denounce such practices as pagan.

55. Brennies 1988, 229.

56. Parkin 1980, 57.

57. McIntosh 1998 [1988], 105.

58. Urciuoli 1995.

2. Staking a Claim

1. Also hear the interviews in Ton van der Lee's documentary film, *Heavenly Mud,* produced in 2003.

2. Blake 1976.

3. Rykwert 1981, 14–18.

4. Herrmann, 1962, 49.

5. Ibid., 48.

6. Viollet-le-Duc, *Entretiens sur l'Architecture* (1858–72).

7. Prussin 1994, 102.

8. Ibid., 110.

9. Ruskin 2001 (1836–7).

10. Ruskin 1984, 142.

11. Ibid., 100.

12. Ibid., 101.

13. Ibid., 141.

14. Levi-Strauss 1963.

15. Maas and Mommersteeg 1992, 40. My translation from the French: "Les ruelles et les petites places ressemblent à des veines taillées dans la masse homogène de la ville. De caractère labyrinthique et capricieux, ces veines forment des structures qui apparemment ne semble pas dérivées des méthodes de planification urbaine rationnelles comme nous les connaissons en Occident. On les appelle des structures prérationnelles."

16. Lefebvre 1991, 14, 47.

17. Rykwert 1981, 28.

18. See, for example, Asquith and Vellinga 2005; Denyer 1978; Dmochowski 1990; Fathy 1973; Oliver 1976, 1987, 1997; Prussin 1974, 1976, 1986; Rapoport 1969; Rudofsky 1965; Schoenauer 1981; and Schwerdtfeger 1982.

19. Prussin 1968, 34.

20. Prussin 1986, 21.

21. Oliver 1971, 11.

22. Maas and Mommersteeg, 1994, 93 n. 1. Van Eyck published photos of Djenné in *Forum voor Architectuur en daarmee Verbonden Kunsten* 1961, 15, 3, 85–116.

23. See a description of the sanitation project by the engineers Langevelde and Alderlieste, in Bedaux, Diaby and Maas 2003a.

24. Bedaux and van der Waals 1994.

25. Brunet-Jailly 1999a.

26. Bedaux, Diaby, and Maas 2003b.

27. Bourgeois 1983.

28. Ibid., 70.

29. See, for instance, Asquith and Vellinga 2005; and Oliver 1997.

30. Blier 2004, 185.

31. Le Corbusier 2000 [1948].

32. Bedaux et al. 2000, 205.

33. In Djenné-Chiini, Fulani is *filan*, and Rimaïbe is *filan-kombe*.

34. The term "usufructuary," from the Medieval Latin root *usufructus*, is defined as possessing the right to make use of another's property short of causing damage to it.

35. More than two centuries earlier, Mungo Park (1983, 200) observed during his travels through the Sahel that an individual in need of land "applied to the chief man of the district, who allowed him an extension of territory, on condition of forfeiture if the lands were not brought into cultivation by a given period."

36. The *m'baaka* is *Agama agama*.

37. The female of the species is locally referred to as *m'baakawoy*.

38. Gardi (1974, 57) also notes that construction commences only on auspicious days.

39. Ligers 1964, 42.

40. The Djenné-Chiini term *jaari benté* is translated as "auspicious day," and *jaari futu* as "inauspicious day." The French terms *jour ouvert* and *jour fermé* are also used, respectively.

41. Similarly, Jansen (2002, 18–19) notes in his study of Mandé *griots* (*jeli*) that secrets are not hidden information but rather information that, if used inappropriately or abused, will be dealt with by sanctions and punishment. He constructively suggests that secrecy might be studied as a sociological phenomenon rather than focusing on the informational content of secrets (12). Hoffman (2000, 193) writes that it is a basic principle among *griots* never to reveal everything during a performance, and the more skilled bards strategically include statements "referring to that which will not be revealed."

42. R. van der Velden (1989; in Mommersteeg 2003, 26) recorded that masons blessed stones prior to making foundations by asking Allah not to destroy the house and not to let it fall into ruins. Masons also frequently invoked the Prophet Abraham (Ibrahim) in their benedictions. Mommersteeg quotes an old mason's explanation for this: "In the beginning of the world there was Abraham, son of Adam, who constructed the first building: the Kāba. It still exists. That is how masonry began. You must invoke that force in order to make buildings that endure. That is why it is impossible to demolish the Kāba" (2003, 26; my translation from the French).

43. Stoller 1989, 100.

44. Park 1983 [1799], 32.

45. In his study of Bamana practices and beliefs, Imperato (1977, 51) also notes that "magic and religion are not clearly separated."

46. In Djenné-Chiini, grain is translated as *attaam;* and cottonseed, sorghum, millet, maize, fonio, and rice grains are translated, respectively, as *haabu-idye, bimbiri, hayni, masara-haamaa, finji,* and *moo-kogosi.* In discussing the prevalence of claims in local oral tradition to a common origin for the Bozo, Dogon, and Nono peoples, R. J. McIntosh (1998, 101–2) notes that "ethnicity is expressed as a triumvirate of grains. Each recognizes the mythical quality and equivalence of grains of fonio (the Bozo), millet (the Dogon), and rice (the Nono)."

47. Further consideration of masons' contemporary practices of burying blessed articles at property boundaries may furnish archaeologists with an important clue to their

finds. Describing patterns of artifact distribution in archaeological finds, R. J. McIntosh (1998, 226) notes that "there appears to be a cardinal-point presentation of classes of materials offered in these ash-filled depressions," and asks "to what degree is this cardinal-point orientation to sacrificed objects merely happenchance? Or is it a reflection of an ancient Middle Niger material culture *imago mundi*?" Citing previous work co-authored with R. McIntosh, S. Keech McIntosh (1995, 369) writes that "kneeling statuettes, complete or fragmentary, have been found in wall niches . . . [and] beneath floors" which may have had a protective function.

48. More specifically, this refers to the Almoravid conquerors of the Ghana Empire (see Levtzion, 1973, 45).

49. Ligers 1964, 43. My translation from the French: "En effet, tu as bien travaillé et nous te remercions beaucoup. Chaque fois que quelque partie du sâhô sera endommagé, par exemple une colonne décorative (hôn'an'djuon) écroulée, on t'appellera. Également si l'on veut faire le crépissage (hô sigi), on fera appel à toi."

50. In Djenné-Chiini: *ay dan no ni haya* (I give you "something," i.e., the price for tea); *ay dan no ni goro* (I give you a present for kola nuts); and *ay dan no ni nyerfu* (I give you a present of money).

51. Maas and Mommersteeg 1992, 27; see also Daget, Konipo, and Sanankoua 1953, 8.

52. Rouch 1960, 10–11.

53. Bafaro is a Bamana name for the female spirit of the river, a name equally used by the Bozo. *Ba* is translated as "river" and *faro* as "god." Daget, Konipo and Sanankoua (1953, 7) record that the official master of the waters, the *dyi tuu*, acts as the intermediary between the Bozo peoples and the water spirits (the *yegu* or *dyenye*) that need to be appeased. The Bozo performance of the *kono* (bird) puppet also attracts the favor of the water spirits (Arnoldi 1976).

54. Imperato 1977, 16.

55. de Grunne 1982, 12. Note that *toguere* is a Fulfuldé word meaning an "archaeological mound."

56. McIntosh 1998, 104.

57. Ibid., 97.

58. Prussin 1986, 47.

59. McNaughton (1988, 3) describes *nyamakala* as a group comprising "clusters of clans that own the rights to arcane spiritual and technological practices . . . [and] they are organized by profession—smiths, bards, leather workers." The social role and identity of the *nyamakalaw*, however, are not rigidly defined, but rather research demonstrates that members of these groups continually redefined their identity "in response to changing social, economic and political circumstances" (Conrad and Frank 1995a, 11). See also R. J. McIntosh 1998, 178–79, for a persuasive hypothesis on the evolution of *nyamakalaw*, or corporate castes such as blacksmiths, hunters and *griots* (or *jeli*). In her discussion of the development of caste systems in West Africa, Tamari (1991, 245) explains that the compound word is derived from *nyama* meaning "energy or life force" and *kàla* meaning "receptacle or handle." See also Bird, Kendall, and Tera (1995) for a comprehensive discussion of the various etymologies of this highly ambiguous term.

60. Herbert 1993; Jansen 2000, 5–6; McNaughton 1988, 102–3; Rouch 1960, 277.

61. Laude 1973, 42; McNaughton 1988, 64–66; Erza 1988, 25.

62. Brett-Smith 1994, 38; McNaughton 1988, 20–21.

63. Brett-Smith 1994, 36.

64. Herbert 1993, 21; McIntosh 1998, 178; McNaughton 1988, 22. See Frank 1998, for a comprehensive study of Mandé potters.

65. Brett-Smith 1994. Note, however, that, unlike Mandé blacksmiths, Djenné's masons are not members of a caste group (i.e., they are not *nyamakalaw*).

66. Brett-Smith, 1994, 38.

67. In his Djenné-Chiini dictionary, Heath (1998) defines *nyama* as "to be crazy or wild." In Djenné-Chiini, the word *hunde* translates as "life force" or "spirit," but again it does not share the same significance with the more potent Mandé concept of *nyama*.

68. LaViolette (1995, 170–72) also notes that Djenné lies close to the northeastern periphery of Mandé influence, and is strongly influenced by the Fulani and Songhay social systems. Her study of potters and *nyamakala* in Djenné produced significantly different results from the general scholarship on Mandé society (171).

69. Bird 1971.

70. Bird, with Koita and Soumaouro, 1974; Stoller 1994, 354.

71. Soares (2005, 84) discusses the continuing importance and status of French language in postcolonial Mali, noting that the "bureaucrats, civil servants, technical and administrative experts and personnel involved in the running of the affairs of the so-called modern sectors of the economy and state have been educated for the most part in French language schools the state has promoted."

72. Park 1983, 28.

73. Jansen 2002, 14.

74. Prussin 1976, 18.

75. Hoffman 1990, 136.

76. The Manding term for the "science of the trees" is *jiridon,* and is a specialized form of knowledge typically associated with the hunters, or *donso* (McNaughton 1982, 56).

77. Rouch 1960, 271.

78. Maas and Mommersteeg 1992, 180. My translation from the French: "Les pratiques magico-religieuses diverses telles que la divination et la fabrication des amulettes."

79. See, for example, Mommersteeg 1988, who details the fabrication of love amulets that are used for bringing about sexual attraction between a man and woman. See also Mommersteeg 1990.

80. Brett-Smith also notes that, at the birth of a Bamana blacksmith, the family head announces the event to the anvil and sacrifices a kola nut to appease the forces of *nyama* contained within (1994, 39).

81. Maas and Mommersteeg 1992, 31.

82. My translation from the French: "En principe, il y a deux métiers ici à Djenné: le travail de petit guide, et quand on est agrandi, le maraboutage."

83. The local Djenné-Chiini word *walaa* is derived from the Arabic *lauh* (لوح), plural *alwāh.*

84. The word "Qurᶜan" is derived from the Arabic verb *qara'a* أقرَ, meaning "to recite."

85. Jujube tree, *Ziziphus mauritiana.*

86. *Balanites aegyptiaca.*

87. Marchand, unpublished CIDA Report, 1993.

3. Magic and Mortar

1. In Djenné-Chiini "Tolober" means "large mound," and the name refers to the expansive rise in the floodplain upon which the settlement is built. Tolober is a fairly recent settlement dating to the 1960s.

2. The Djenné-Chiini term *guuru-bari,* referring to a bicycle, translates literally as "iron horse." Bicyles are also called by the more standard word *negeso.*

3. Harts-Broekhuis and Verkoren (1994, 119) likewise note in their study of Djenné's economy that most townspeople engage in numerous activities in order to survive severe economic and environmental fluctuations.

4. See also Maas and Mommersteeg (1992, 80), who recorded the word *al-hayti* for foundations, a term clearly derived from the Arabic.

5. *Borassus aethiopium*, also known in English as the African palmyra palm and the deleb palm.

6. Maas and Mommersteeg 1992, 65, 97. Bourgeois (1987, 62) also suggests that the arch, like that employed in Djenné's mosque, arrived via the French. Several spectacular mud mosques have been erected in nearby villages that display imaginative interiors of slim round columns and superimposed arches.

7. *Tasika*, in fact, translates as "anteroom," but because this space is almost invariably used for sleeping, I refer to it as sleeping room or bedroom.

8. According to Maas and Mommersteeg (1992, 220), the term *terey* means "to communicate the idea of an art or craft" and presumably relates in this context to the space in the home where the man does his work.

9. The word *sunduku* describes the small box-like room built on the rooftop to provide protection for the staircase. The term is derived from the Arabic word for box or cabinet, *sundūq* صندوق.

10. Literally, "covered room."

11. Prussin 1973, 39.

12. At the time of their study, Maas and Mommersteeg (1992, 79) noted that there were few remaining Tukolor-style homes in Djenné, but a handful of new Tukolor-style facades have since been constructed. In addition to the one in Sanuna, a second for another European patron was erected in the Djoboro quarter. Although the latter includes a small interior courtyard and its planning more closely resembles the town's older houses, it is distinguished from traditional houses in that it has two monumental facades: one is Moroccan-style and addresses the street, and the other, at the rear, is Tukolor-style. There is no historic precedent for this combination in Djenné.

13. The Arabic word for devil, *shaytān* شيطان, was frequently used in Djenné.

14. In her study of Mande *griots*, Hoffman (2000) records that healers commonly transfer the curative powers of words by spitting "into a liquid which the patient will either drink or wash with" (169). In Djenné-Chiini, this action of spitting into one's hand while making a benediction is called *sumburku*.

15. The French term *brouette* was mainly used for "wheelbarrow," although the Djenné-Chiini word *otoro* was sometimes employed instead.

16. More than half a century earlier, Daget, Konipo, and Sanankoua (1953, 8) also noted that the Bozo rarely married outside their ethnic group.

17. Imperato (1977, 10) notes the importance of oral secrets in Mandé culture and the historic opposition to openly written forms of language. McNaughton (1988) also discusses the importance of trade secrets (*gundow*) in Mandé society, noting that "every significant activity and profession has its secret expertise" (41).

18. Violent unrest in Ivory Coast erupted on September 19, 2002, as opposing factions of Houphouet-Boigny's successors battled for power.

19. The kola nut is indeed one of the few stimulants sanctioned by Islamic code (Konaré 1999, 28).

20. Konamadou was referring to the Islamic concept of *halāl* حلال, "that which is allowed," in contrast to *harām* حرام, "that which is forbidden."

21. Semani (or Seymani) derives its name from the numerous "blacksmiths" installed in that quarter.

22. The female name *Ainya* translates as "my mother" in Djenné-Chiini, and is given to girls who are named after their mother. According to social convention, the name *Ainya* replaces the child's real given name so as not to invoke the mother's name when the child is reprimanded or shamed.

23. *Pinasse* is a French term referring to the large, black wooden boats that ply the Niger and Bani rivers with cargoes of goods and people.

24. Sanankoua 1999, 83.

25. See Diakité (1999, 49–51) on basic Qur⁽anic schooling and the submission of students to their masters; and Mommersteeg 1991b.

26. Brenner 2001, 276–77.

27. Older Qur⁽anic students at the secondary level of studies are frequently referred to as *talibé* (derived from the Arabic *tālib* طالب, meaning "student").

28. Maas and Mommersteeg (1990, 31) also note that the Bozo's barter in fish and fish oil for rice and millet observes historic trade relations established between a fisherman and a particular family of cultivators or a village.

29. Marchand 2001. *Hājl* هاجل was a local term used by the builders in Yemen's capital, San⁽a.

30. Large branches sold in the market place for fuel are called *tuguri-dubi* (*tuguri* is "tree"), but, when cut for construction, they are referred to as *gar bundu* (*bundu* meaning "wood" or "stick").

31. Termite infestation owes in part to the substitution of palm wood with cheaper and more readily available softwood timbers.

32. *Toron* in everyday parlance refers to a wooden stake driven into the ground to which animals are tethered. In an architectural context, it refers to the sticks of palm wood that are embedded horizontally in the walls of houses and mosques and that protrude on the exterior face, lending the region's building a distinctive appearance. *Toron* serve to distribute the lateral loads within the thick mud walls and provide exterior scaffolding for maintenance and plaster work to the building.

33. Literally, "four-winged" ceiling.

34. Literally, "two-winged" ceiling.

35. The shea-butter tree, in Latin, is *Vitellaria paradoxa*, also called *Butyrospremum parkii* in honor of the Scottish explorer Mungo Park.

4. Conflict and Resolution

1. Though quartered palm trunks were available in lengths of up to 3.8 to 4.0 meters, masons advised maximum spans of no more than 3.5 meters.

2. On *griots*, Jansen (2000, 32) writes that while members of the older generation are alive, younger *griots* will not admit to having the equivalent knowledge of their parents because this would demonstrate a lack of respect.

3. In her study of Mandé *griots*, Hoffman (1995) similarly argues that, because of its ambiguous nature, *griot* speech is relegated to the realm of the occult. Since noble patrons (*horon*) have no access and no power over the occult, they are forced to seek protection through the *griots*.

4. These terms translate, respectively, as "black mud," "red mud," "prepared mud" (usually for making bricks), "mud containing small stones or gravel," and "fermented mud."

5. Lauber 1998, 59.

6. Some masons used the word *sarafar* interchangeably with *salaafal* which literally means "minaret" in Djenné-Chiini, and in this case refers metaphorically to the vertical projection of the pilaster above the roofline. More specifically, *sarafar* are the pilasters that extend the full height of the building and terminate in pinnacles. The *sarafar har* ("male" pilasters) frame the ends of the building facade and the two slender *sarafar woy* ("female" pilasters) frame the entrance to the house. The *sarafar woy* support a series of *sarafar idye* miters that crown the roofline above the doorway. *Idye* means "child," and therefore these

sarafar symbolically connote the offspring of the male and female ones. Family and procreation are recurrent themes, as similarly suggested by the juxtaposition of towering mud pinnacles and white ostrich eggs that crown the roofs of mosques throughout the region.

7. For example, choosing a total number of eight *sarafar idye:* 460—(8 × 40) = 140 cm; 140/(8–1) = 20 cm spacing between each.

8. For example, see Ryle, 1949; Bourdieu, 1977; Lave and Wenger, 1991; Bloch 1998; Farnell 2000; Wacquant 2004. See also Marchand 2001; 2003; 2005; 2007b; 2008.

9. See, for example, Gerdes's (1999) work on ethnomathematics and visual mathematics.

10. Prussin (1986, 82) suggests that the five projecting pinnacles on Djenné houses represent the five pillars of Islam. This explanation, however, was not offered by the masons I worked with, and many houses in town have more than five pinnacles above the doorway.

11. *Gaaga* means "pied crow" (*Corvus albus*), and in this case makes a metaphorical connection between the pied crows that perch on rooftops and the squat pilasters tucked inside the recess of the decorative parapet.

12. In fact, the total number of pilasters and "cat head's" may vary from one house to another, yielding a minimum of five, with a maximum of ten or more *sarafar idye* miters above. Some masons, like Bayeré, are adamant that the correct quantity is always an odd number, but historic houses with an even number exist, and the quantity ultimately depends on the arrangement of all decorative elements below.

13. The intermediary's fluid and strategic adoption of the opposing stances expressed by the rivaling parties is also discussed by Jansen (2000) in his study of *griots* and their skilled ability to frame social interactions.

14. One of the traditional roles of the Mandé bards (*griot* or *jeli*) was as the principal spokespersons for the rulers and chiefs, and they continue to act as mediators to negotiate marriages and settle family disputes (Conrad and Frank 2005, 1; Jansen 2000, 40). Individuals of this *nyamakala* group serve as intercessors between the temporal and spiritual worlds, as mediators between parties involved in rites of passage, as lineage spokespersons, and as intermediaries between conflicting parties (Johnson and Sisòkò 1992, 4). McNaughton (1988, 64) also discusses Mandé emphasis on "mediators, intermediaries, and advisers" who "work as instruments of moderation and reason," and he reports on the participation of blacksmiths in this role.

5. Master and Apprentice

1. This year the wood was being doused with salt water rather than the noxious cypermethrin poison, but the masons believed that this would not be an effective deterrent against the voracious termites.

2. The name "Yobukayna" (or "Yoboucayna") translates to "the little market."

3. According to al-Sadi's seventeenth-century Tarikh as-Sudan, Djenné's King (*koi*) Konboro converted to Islam in AD 1180 (Hunwick 2003, 17–19). From this date on, Djenné-Djeno was gradually abandoned and, by about AD 1400, was completely deserted. Popular legend claims that the newly Islamicized population deserted the old settlement because of its former association with animist practices, and they established a new settlement nearby at present-day Djenné.

4. Brunet-Jailly (1999b, 171) notes that the introduction of piped water and the advent of plastic bags have created a serious sanitation problem in the town.

5. *Sarafar idye* means, literally, "children of the *sarafar*," referring metaphorically to the offspring of the "male" (*sarafar har*) and "female" (*sarafar woy*) pilasters that decorate the facade of a house.

6. Djenné Patrimoine is a locally based, non-political association whose objective is

to promote the preservation of the town's cultural, architectural, and archaeological heritage. The association publishes a regular bulletin that includes news and scholarly reports about Djenné's urban environment.

7. On strategies to avoid appearing nepotistic in the selection and training of apprentices, see also Graves 1989, 55–56.

8. In discussing the training of a Songhay bard (*griot*), Hale (1996, 6) records that the endless process began with seven-year-old children. Each night around the campfire the children learned three more names in the genealogy of the Epic of Askia Muhammad. After several years they went off to learn from other wordsmiths.

9. At the time, Monteil (1932, 252–53) notes that the mason's only tool was his flared-end crowbar used for demolishing old masonry and for tailoring bricks to size. All else was done with the mason's bare hand, and verticality was judged by eye.

10. On children making clay toys, see Mandel and Brenier-Estrine 1977.

11. Members of all three families were still active in Djenné's building trade at the time of this writing. The Nassiré and Yonou lived in Djoboro, and the Salamantao lived in Yobukayna. For an alternative version of the origins of Djenné's masons, see Monteil (1932, 195–96), who recounts how the people of the town were taught to build by a certain Moroccan, Mallam Idriss. Prussin (1986, 47) develops this claim further, stating that Mallam Idriss and his Songhay brother, Mallam Yakouba, came from Timbuktu at the time of the Moroccan invasions in 1591 and built the first mosque at Djenné. Following Prussin, Domian (1989, 56) also recounts the legend of Mallam Idriss as the founder of Djenné's architecture.

12. De Ceuninck and Mayor 1994.

13. LaViolette 1994a. Notably, a number of contemporary blacksmiths in Djenné are Bozo. Imperato (1975, 56) describes how Bozo blacksmiths in the region of Segou and San produce twin fetishes for the predominantly Bamana population; in this region, the Bozo are believed to descend from two female twins made by the creator Faro and are thus closely associated with twins.

14. Coy 1989a; Goody 1989; Singleton 1989, 17. Citing Goody (1982) and Peil (1970), Coy (1989b, 119) notes in his own study of apprenticeship with a Tugen blacksmith in Kenya that father-son, master-apprentice relations are potentially disruptive, and Goody (1989, 245–46) suggests that non-kin relations allow for a more effective division of labor and more efficient work.

15. Smiths were normally specialized either in making jewelry (popularly in silver and gold) or fabricating tools, machine parts, and household wares. One well-respected blacksmith forging tools such as the trowels and *sasiré* crowbars at the time of my study was Alfamoi Sunkuro, who operated a shop in Semani, the traditional blacksmiths' quarter in Djenné.

6. The Michelangelo of Djenné

1. "Fulani" designates the Fulfuldé-speaking ethnic group, and "Peul" is a term other ethnic groups use to refer to the Fulani. Perou was Rimaïbé, a group that was former slaves of the Fulani, and the men teasingly called him "Peul" because he regularly behaved "above his station."

2. *Alfinta* are small, fried cakes made from rice or millet flour and water, and sometimes sweetened with sugar. They are also referred to by the French name *galettes* or by the Bamana word *m'omi*. Another popular breakfast snack is *furufuru* (Djenné-Chiini), which are similar to small, plain, deep-fried donuts.

3. Historically arches were not part of Djenné's architectural repertoire until the arrival of the French. Prussin (1986, 150) notes that arches built in the twentieth century of sun-dried bricks are "a result of and in part inspired by the French military construction ef-

forts." Aradeon (1989) also contends that the technology for arch and dome construction in the Western Sudan was not indigenous but was imported from outside the region. See also Domian 1989, 20, 25, 29.

4. The spring line is the vertical point on a wall, pillar, or column from which the curve of an arch begins.

5. Note that many Bozo patronymics are derived from Bamanankan (the Bamana language), and in Djenné an "o" is regularly added to the end of the name. For example, Djennepo translates to "the girl is dead"; Tennepo to "your totem is dead"; Salamantao to "the man who catches eels"; Tomotao to "here it stops"; and Kontao to "here you are again." In the case of the last two, a legend explains the origin of these patronymics and how the two families named each other. The Kontao people were hunters, and the Tomotao habitually stole meat from them. One day the Kontao decided to attach a punctured bag of ashes to a piece of meat, and when the Tomotao stole it the Kontao followed the trail of ashes. At the place where the trail stopped, they found the Tomotao and declared, "Here it ends." The surprised Tomotao exclaimed, "Here you are again!" (Hady Ballo, personal communication, January 2006).

6. Maas and Mommersteeg (1992, 208–9) note that masons work within a set of enduring constraints but that possibilities for individual expression lie in the creative arrangements of spatial elements and decoration.

7. Mason Mama Kourani died in 2002 during my second fieldwork season.

8. Although the tea contained no alcohol, the boys referred to it as "African whisky" because the combination of caffeine and sugar gave them an energetic boost.

9. Omar's maternal grandfather, Badara Salamantao, was a master mason who erected all the Sounfountera houses in Yobukayna, including the renowned *maison du capitaine* built for a prominent family member who was a decorated officer of the French Army in World War II. At the time of this writing, the Sounfountera's family mason was still a related member of the Salamantao family.

10. See Samoura, Ouane, and Cissé (1999, 74) on the stigma attached to being educated in the French school system and the resistance on the part of parents to send their children. Stoller (1989, 149–50), too, notes that among the Songhay of Niger "there was large-scale indirect resistance to French education" based on the belief that foreign Christians would corrupt the minds of their children.

11. In fact, Tolober may now be regarded as a quarter of Djenné, since the once open land between the perimeters of the village and town is being filled in by houses and other structures.

12. *Gris-gris* were not restricted to being worn on the body but might also be manufactured to protect buildings such as homes and granaries or other vulnerable objects such as motor vehicles. *Marabouts* of the Inland Niger Delta also produced amulets for protecting boats. Blessed bicycle chains were sold for around 20,000 CFA, and these were nailed to the front of pirogues and wrapped around their wooden prows like chokers. One Bozo fisherman explained that this was the most effective place to put the *gris-gris*, because it faced the direction of the moving vessel and also because the prow was the most vulnerable part of their boats.

13. Other sorts of protective amulets worn on the body include *baka* held in the hand, *jinde tira* worn around the neck, *jéré tira* worn on the side of the body, and *jiiba tira* kept in the pockets of clothing

7. Vulnerable Craftsmen

1. *Bogolanfini* is a Bamana word meaning "mud-dyed cloth." *Bogolan* cloth was traditionally worn by hunters but is now used more popularly in contemporary fashion and

produced for tourists. Similarly, *basilanfini* (leaf-dyed cloth) and *galanfini* (blue-dyed cloth) are produced for these purposes.

2. Maas and Mommersteeg 1992, 31. According to Mommersteeg, the figures are from a report published in 1988, based on a survey conducted two years earlier (personal communication, March 2008).

3. Saad 1979, 14.

4. Tilapia and eels were also a good catch, fetching a handsome price at the market.

5. This practice is similarly described by Imperato (1975, 52) in his study of Bamana and Maninka twin figures.

6. *Donso* is a Bamana/Mandé term designating a hunter, and translates more precisely to "house (*so*) of knowledge (*don*)." Hunters are thought to possess wide and varied forms of knowledge related to the bush, animals, and the spirit world.

7. This corrupted term is likely derived from the Arabic word *safūf* (سفوف), meaning "medicinal powder."

8. *Nasi* can also be prepared by wiping away Qurʿanic *suar* from *alwāh* (*walaa*) boards with a swab of cotton. The cotton is then stored in a sealed bottle and, when needed, the holy contents absorbed by the cotton can be diluted in water and used in the manner described above. An especially powerful verse in the preparation of protective amulets and *nasi* was the *ayat al-kursi* in *surat al-baqara* ("The Throne" verse in the *sūra* of "The Cow," 2:255). This verse was thought to be extremely powerful when recited backward by a *marabout*. On the subject of *nasi*, see also Mommersteeg 1994, 69. LaViolette (1994a, 150) reports that the water blacksmiths keep in a receptacle and use to temper the iron is also sought by people as a form of medicine. As elsewhere in West Africa, blacksmiths are believed to have secret powers.

9. *Kani hu*, literally, means a "sleeping room."

10. In addition to the *sâhos* at Kouakourou and Kolenzé, another remarkable example survives in the village of Kotaga along the banks of the Niger. Kotaga is a mixed village of Bozo and Jénéma. A knowledgeable *marabout* of the village explained that the Jénéma were originally a Marka population who settled here and gradually adopted the local Bozo language, which they now refer to as *Jénéma sé*. Although the Jénéma believe that they are culturally superior to their Bozo neighbors, young men (age fifteen until married) from both ethnic groups reportedly share the *sâho* situated close to the village mosque. It is notable that the rather grand *style-Soudanais* mosque sheathed in kiln-baked clay tiles was built in 1992 by two Jénéma brothers, Tiema and Tié-Tié Kébé. An especially beautiful mosque, with an interior of daring arcades of mud arches supported on columns, is located in the nearby village of Segou-Bongo and was built by another family relation, Mama Kébé.

11. There were no *sâhos* per se in the temporary encampments along the river since the ephemeral huts were erected with simple wood frames and grass. *Sâhos*, in contrast, were usually elaborate constructions. Also, the age-set organizations in the village settlement reportedly broke down when the community was migrating along the river. This was because all able-bodied young men were too busy fishing to engage in the sort of leisurely age-set socializing that occurs in the *sâho*.

12. See Ligers 1964, 3:38–141, for a comprehensive ethnographic discussion of the *sâho* and associated social relations in the 1950s; see also Blier 2004, 198–200, on the architecture, social function, and demise of the *sâho* (*sakho*).

13. Samoura, Ouane, and Cissé (1999, 64–65) recount the stories told to children and adolescents about devils that inhabit certain alleyways and the square in front of the mosque. The stories caution them about the dangers of being out at night. Maas and Mommersteeg (1992, 42) also mention the existence of forbidden alleys (*rues interdites*) in Djenné, thought to be inhabited by spirits. Houses typically border these alleys with blind facades, and they constitute "dirty" spaces where waste water and garbage collect.

14. *Waliju* is derived from the Arabic word *walīy* (ولي), meaning saint or holy man.

15. *Kurukuru* is the typical Djenné-Chiini term to describe this sort of snack, and it regularly includes peanuts. Peanuts (*maatigan*) are harvested throughout Mali, and production is especially concentrated west of Bamako in the region around Kita.

8. Cat Heads and Mud Miters

1. Other non-Bozo residents also differentiated the Bozo from the general Djennenké population. One Marka gentleman explained to me that "the Djennenké are not a particular race. All Djenné's people are a mixture of ethnicities, except the Bozo." The Bozo comprise less than 20% of the town's population.

2. Grimes (1988, 257) estimated that there were between 30,000 and 87,000 Bozo speakers in Mali, whereas Blecke (1996, 9) suggests that there were almost 120,000 above the age of six. Population growth accounts for some of the discrepancy. According to Dwyer's classification, Bozo is a Niger-Congo language, and it constitutes a sub-branch of the West-Mandé languages along with Soninké (1989, 47–66; cited in Smeltzer, Smeltzer, and Sabe 1995, 57). In fact, Delafosse (1972 [1912]) proposed that the Bozo were related to the Soninké who traveled eastward to this region sometime after the fall of the Ghana Empire in the eleventh century. In their study of Bozo speakers, Smeltzer, Smeltzer, and Sabe (1995, 58) divided bozophones into four distinct linguistic groups occupying different regions of the Inland Niger Delta, including the Sorogo who speak the so-called Sorogama dialect and occupy the Pondo region around Djenné and Mopti.

3. Blecke 1996, 9.

4. In Bamanankan, *bo* means "bamboo" and *so* means "house." The term designating the fisher folk may be written as either *Boso* or *Bozo*. I have chosen the latter, more conventional spelling throughout.

5. Smeltzer, Smeltzer, and Sabe 1995, 58. During the rise of the Segou-Bamana Empire in the eighteenth century, the Bozo made a pact with the *faama* (king) Biton Coulibaly that in return for being left in peace to fish the rivers they would recognize the *faama*'s sovereignty over the Niger (*Joliba*). The Bozo's *kona* pelican puppet was performed annually in a masquerade renewing this agreement between the two peoples (Arnoldi 1976).

6. Note that *koyra-boro* means, literally, "town person," but also refers to a "Songhay" person.

7. In his study of the Bozo language, Monteil (1933, 261) also notes that Bozo of the Djenné region refer to themselves as *sorogo*, which the author questionably equates with the term *sorko*. Smeltzer, Smeltzer, and Sabe (1995, 58), however, recognize the Sorogo (i.e., speakers of sorogama) to be one of four Bozo language groups.

8. Nicolaï (1981, 20) suggests that, presumably during the period of the Songhay Empire (1464–1591), Songhay would have been the language of commerce from Djenné in the West to Agadez in the East, and it remains so in Djenné today.

9. R. McIntosh (1998, 126) similarly notes that the Bozo and Sorko are frequently confused in the literature.

10. Monteil (1933, 264) also records that, according to legend, the Bozo emerged from the earth at Dia-Kolo and Wotaka on the Niger. Like Daget and colleagues, R. McIntosh (1998, 104) similarly questions whether such legends of autochthony have been fabricated to bolster claims to power over the land and water.

11. Daget, Konipo, and Sanankoua 1953, 6; my translation from the French.

12. Note that languages commonly borrow numerical vocabulary or words expressing time and other measurements from languages that either possessed these concepts earlier or were politically dominant. Turkish, for instance, has borrowed the term *sifr*

(zero) from Arabic, as well as the words *zamaan* (time), *dakika* (minute), and *saat* (hour). Similarly, the words for "time" in Djenné-Chiini are *alwakati* and less commonly *waati*, both derived from the Arabic word *waqt* وقت, meaning "time."

13. On buildings where *toron* protrude from planar wall surfaces, such as the towers of the Djenné Mosque, the horizontal wooden reinforcements set into the wall also distribute the lateral load of the bulky mass, as well as the stresses that arise because of expansion and contraction in the mud.

14. Brenner 1993, 77.

15. Ibid., 61–62.

16. At the time of his stay in Djenné, Monteil (1932, 195–96) records the masons' claims that the house of Babèr Tawati was built by Mallam Idriss, the legendary founder of the town's architectural style who supposedly constructed the palace and mosque of Koi Konboro in the thirteenth century.

17. Rooms of the deceased were sometimes bolted shut, and surviving relatives believed that their spirits haunted these places. Belongings were usually left undisturbed, and visitors were forbidden to enter those rooms. In the case of *marabouts*, these possessions might include copies of the Qurᶜan and other manuscripts, including historical works. Some of these are thought to be of significant cultural value, but conservators and historians are denied access to them by house owners. Those in academic circles worry that these potentially important sources of information are being devoured by insects and spoiled by damp. Other rooms from which visitors are typically barred are those containing fetishes or rooms where *marabouts* store their paraphernalia for making *gris-gris* and amulets. Van Gijn (1994, 99) notes that the room of an influential head of household may be closed and abandoned by his family for as long as forty years.

18. More fully, *musi moo toondi* translates approximately as "full cat's eye," but I have chosen to use "cat's eye."

19. To work for free, as a favor to someone, is termed *alharma-alharma* in Djenné-Chiini.

9. Yappi's Confession

1. Mommersteeg (1994, 72) notes the importance of the *marabouts'* benedictions (*gaara* in Songhay) in Djenné's daily life and rituals.

2. The official organization of civil servants who manage and operate the public standing water taps is referred to as the *robinet-ton*.

3. Langeveld and Alderlieste 2003.

4. Bamoy Kouroumansé was the younger brother (*petit frère*) of al-Hajji's father, Lasine.

5. Literally, "How is your work?" and "Good health to you."

6. Marchand 2001.

7. Ali was earning a daily wage of 750 CFA on both the Brunet-Jailly and Marabout Haydarah's houses. Normally an apprentice worked for his own master for free, but since these sites were being administered by Bayeré, and not Ali's master, al-Hajji, he was paid the same salary as his fellow laborers.

8. *Tabaski* is a Wolof term for "sacrifice" and refers in this context to the Islamic Feast of the Immolation (Arab.: *Eid al-Adha*, عيد الاضحى), or Greater Bairam, commemorating Abraham's sacrifice. The Djenné-Chiini term is *jingar-bér* ("big feast"). The Wolof term spread with French colonization, and is now used throughout West Africa. The feast takes place on the tenth of *zu'lhijja,* and the date is determined each year according to the lunar calendar. It is also popularly known throughout the Islamic world as *Eid al-Kabir* (عيد الكبير).

9. *Echinochloa stagnina.*

10. Van Gijn (1994, 99) notes that after boys are circumcised at around the age of twelve, they are no longer permitted to sleep in their mother's "house" or quarters, and spend the night with age-mates in an available room of the family house or in the vestibule (*siifa*). By the time boys reach eighteen, they will have normally moved into a room with other young men connected to either the family house or another house in the neighborhood with independent access to the street. Van Gijn claims that the ethnic mix of boys in the latter rooming arrangements contributes to the social solidarity of the town's diverse population.

11. For instance, the exterior surfaces of the mosque in the riverside village of Kotaga, south of Kona on the Niger, were covered in clay tiles. Within a few years they began falling off in sheets, demanding constant repair.

12. LaViolette (1994b, 94) notes that commissions for re-plastering account for a large proportion of a mason's annual work.

13. *Laabu-kuntur* describes mud that contains stones and lumps, and it becomes *laabu-kuntur-kow* by removing (*kow*) all small objects.

14. Mud plasters made with these ingredients endure longer than regular mud plasters, but their high costs and lengthy preparation time means that they are reserved for the building elements most vulnerable to sun, wind, and rain erosion. In fact, few home owners can afford to include these plasters in their construction and maintenance budgets, and some with adequate resources prefer to spend it on cement.

15. Sonni Ali's troops took Timbuktu in AD 1468 and Djenné in 1473, significantly expanding the realms of the Songhay Empire. The reign of Askia Muhammad Touré (1493–1528) ushered in a great period of stability and prosperity throughout the region, and trade and Islamic studies flourished. During this period a large number of Songhay from the region of Gao moved south, settling in Djenné.

16. A *zaure* is the entrance building to an extended family compound in Hausaland.

17. When I conducted fieldwork in Zaria, Northern Nigeria, in 1992–93, the so-called big men who lived in the walled city of *birnin* Zaria commissioned their masons to decorate the facades of their family compounds with *zanko* extensions and geometric designs of sculpted mud. Contemporary relief decoration was often rendered with cement plaster and then brightly painted with commercial paints. It was considered inappropriate, however, for a person of meager economic and political status to emulate this ostentatious display on their own homes; were they to do so, they would be publicly ridiculed for their social blunder and misguided aspirations (Marchand 1993; Schwerdtfeger 1982; Schwerdtfeger 2007).

18. An estimated 90 percent of Muslims comprise Mali's population, 4 percent are Christian, and the remaining 6 percent adhere exclusively to local religious practices. One man in Bamako, in describing the population, emphasized the pervasiveness of local forms of spiritual belief: "In Mali we have 90 percent Muslims, 5 percent Christians, 5 percent other, and 100 percent animists!" In Djenné, however, the proportion of Christians is almost negligible, and the town vehemently purports itself as exclusively Islamic.

19. Regular expansion of the town began after World War II. Maas and Mommersteeg (1994, 90) note that Djenné's open spaces were gradually filled in with houses, and a new orthogonally planned quarter spread westward.

20. Fangaso is a rural community in the Tominian *cercle* (an administrative district within one of Mali's eight official regions), located south of Djenné in the direction of San.

21. The Gideon's Association was founded in 1899 in Wisconsin, and the name comes from that of a man described in the Old Testament Book of Judges who was willing to do whatever God asked of him. The association's key purpose is to evangelize through the distribution of Bibles and New Testaments, and it claims members in 181 countries (http://www.gideons.org.uk/Gideons/index.asp [accessed July 2008]).

10. Finishing Off

1. Only al-Hajji and Bamoy would wear their baseball caps to work. The other men refused, wanting to keep them clean and tidy for important occasions. At least one laborer sported his to the communal prayers during the *Tabaski* celebrations.

2. For example, in his illustration and description of a Djenné house facade, C. Monteil (1932, 191–92) labels the *sarafar har* as *lōburu*, which he defines as having phallic connotations. Following Engeström (1955), Prussin relates the origins of the decorative pinnacles to the protruding forms of ancestral shrines, and in describing the roofscape of Djenné's mosque, she contrasts the "masculine" verticality of the pinnacles with the "feminine [and] . . . softly rounded miniature domes" of the clay skylights (1986, 189; see Plate 50). Konaré (1999, 44) declares that the "clearly phallic forms" on house facades are the remnants of Bozo pagan culture in which sexuality was more openly displayed, and, as of yet, Islamic efforts to suppress paganism have not eliminated this aspect of Djenné's cultural heritage. Maas and Mommersteeg (1992, 182–83) speculate on the phallic imagery of Mandé architectonics, including the pilasters and pinnacles of Djenné's Tukolor and Moroccan-style facades. In an interview with Beré Yonou, Maas and Mommersteeg (1992, 200), however, note the mason's rejection of this European interpretation as well as his insistence that the *musi bumo* was built for its aesthetic qualities and signified the economic status of the inhabitants.

3. The masons used the terms *sarafar woy* ("female" *sarafar*) and *sarafar idye* (*sarafar* that are "progeny" or "sons") interchangeably to refer to the set of seven miters that were built on top of the decorative assembly above the house entrance. *Sarafar woy,* however, was used consistently to describe the two pilasters on either side of the main doorway.

4. Monteil (1932, 253) also notes that masons were the official grave diggers.

5. Djenne's cemeteries were historically located within the city quarters. Use of these cemeteries ceased in the twentieth century during the period of French colonial rule. Today they remain as walled enclosures surrounded on all sides by streets and houses. The ground elevations inside are raised above street level and overgrown with shrubs and grasses. There are especially good examples in Yobukayna and on the border between the Konofia and Samsey quarters. Other burial sites within the city include those of saints, typically located at crossroads and built against the sides or corners of houses. Some of these are marked by low mud enclosure walls.

6. Prussin (1986, 47) notes that according to Islamic prescriptions for burials, a part of the excavation must be sealed off by a wall of bricks.

7. *Hu di gum bundu* means, literally, "wood covering a room," *hu* meaning a "room" and *gum* meaning "to cover."

8. *Handu* is translated as "moon" or "month," and *koray* as "white," but in the context of the plaster decorations it refers to "crescent moon shapes in bas-relief."

9. Flirtations between men and women occurred regularly, and, from my observations, women initiated the playful teasing as frequently as the men. The vast majority of interactions remained innocent. It was generally understood that unmarried women must comport themselves with modesty and were expected to remain virgins until they are married (see Diallo 2004, 174, 181). On the morning after a wedding, the bride and groom's bed sheets were customarily inspected for blood by one of the older women to satisfy the question of the girl's chastity and the boy's sexual performance. Divorced women, on the other hand, tended to be more direct in their flirtations, and, according to one middle-aged divorcee, they could do as they pleased without worrying about the consequences their unmarried sisters faced.

10. Diallo (2004, 173) notes that, in Mali, "open discussions about sexual issues are taboo and often perceived as a lack of virtue."

11. *Qūba* (قُبَة) is the name of the first mosque that was built outside Medina during the time of the Prophet. *Qūba* also means "dome" and is derived from the verb *qabba* (قَبّ), meaning "to rise or ascend."

12. Although most ethnic groups continue to speak distinctive languages and dialects, Bamanankan is spoken or understood by approximately 80 percent of the Malian population. Bamanankan and French are Mali's official languages, and Bamanankan is widely used in the country's marketplaces where diverse ethnic groups come together to trade.

13. Literally, "May God grant it!"

Epilogue

1. Co-producers of the fifty-six-minute documentary *Future of Mud: A Tale of Houses and Lives in Djenné* were Susan Vogel (director), professor of African art and architecture at Columbia University, and Samuel Sidibé, the director of Mali's National Museum. The film is distributed by First Run/Icarus Films, New York.

2. Retired general Amadou Toumani Touré (aka, "ATT") was head of state during Mali's transition (1991–92) after the overthrow of the Traoré government. He was elected president in the general democratic elections in June and July of 2002, replacing the outgoing president Alpha Oumar Konaré.

3. The primary beneficiaries of the Talo Dam project will be the towns of San and Bla. Despite strong resistance from Djenné's residents, including representatives of Djenné Patrimoine and *marabouts* who cast powerful spells against those who dared lay the first stone, the project was approved in 1998. After a long delay construction finally commenced in 2005. The French introduced plans for dams at both Talo and Djenné, but the projects were aborted with the advent of the Second World War. Talo was later deemed the superior site because of its more accessible layer of bedrock, necessary for anchoring the dam (Childs 2004).

4. Mali, one of Africa's largest cotton producers, achieved record production levels in 2003– 2004 because of abundant rains, and this was a source of tremendous national pride. Civil war and the closure of Abidjan's ports in neighboring Ivory Coast, however, forced Mali to export its cotton through other West African countries, creating significant increases in transport costs. Mali's state-owned cotton company, CMDT [Malian Company for the Development of Textiles], was forced to slash profit forecasts by 67 percent. Cotton harvests were predicted to fall back to normal levels in 2004–2005.

5. According to a report from the International Development Office at Clark University, Massachusetts, the Talo Dam will have a highly questionable impact on the region. The report, commissioned by Cultural Survival and submitted to the Malian Government and African Development Bank in 2001, predicts losses of grazing land in the project's target area, and losses of agriculture, grazing, and fishing in the downstream region where Djenné is situated. The report estimates that up to 20 percent of the Bani's water will be diverted from the downstream flow while the reservoir fills during the rainy season, dramatically altering the riparian ecosystem of the region—and the livelihoods of those who depend on it (for the full report, see www.cs.org). In response to the Clark Report, a construction moratorium was imposed to further assess the situation and consider the validity of dissenting views. Although a majority of Djenné residents were opposed to the dam, most were poorly informed about the surrounding issues (Fink and Meierotto 2002). By 2004 new designs included sluice gates to increase flexibility in water management (Childs 2004). Physical design changes to the dam, new impact studies, and increased participation by downstream residents in the negotiations led Cultural Survival to offer its endorsement to the project that year (Petrillo and Childs 2004).

6. Fish stocks were expected to decline dramatically, gravely affecting the livelihoods of the local fishermen. The dam was also expected to have a detrimental impact on rice production located downstream. Rice cultivation is an ancient practice in the Inland Niger Delta, and historically it has represented a vital source of subsistence and trade. Clearly future water management schemes must ensure a continued and adequate supply downstream of the dam. Future schemes must also strive to keep the river and its system of rivulets and marshes around the city clean in order to supply a sanitary source of water and a hygienic source of mud for bricks and plaster. Garbage and toxic waste in the mud are hazardous to brick makers and builders, as well as to gardeners, bathers, fisher folk, and wildlife.

7. See also Gallier 2002.

8. Ian McIntosh, the director of Cultural Survival, predicted that the town of Djenné may one day be deserted as a result of the dam's ecologic and economic impacts (see "New dam in Mali will cause starvation and destroy ancient city," July 20, 2001, at www.edie.net [accessed July 2008]). See also Mitchell's (2002) account of the Aswan Dam's effects on the Nile Valley. Not only have diminished annual deposits of alluvial silt negatively impacted agriculture but local building traditions have also suffered. Depletion of good soils for making bricks, Mitchell argues, made a mockery of Hassan Fathy's heroic attempts to introduce so-called traditional architecture at New Gourna (ibid.).

9. In 2005 a steady stream of reports warned of devastating drought and starvation in the neighboring republic of Niger that had been unfolding since August 2004. Desperate pleas for assistance from the international community were issued ("Timeline: how Niger's food crisis unfolded," at www.alertnet.org [accessed March 2006; no longer available]). An estimated 3.6 million people, nearly one-third of Niger's population, were in need of food aid in 2005. Mali, Burkina Faso, and Mauritania were also threatened by food crises because of drought and locust plagues in 2004. It was expected that at least 1.1 million people in Mali would require food aid in 2005, and an estimated five thousand children in the north of the country were suffering acute malnutrition (see "Niger neighbours also face hunger," http://newsvote.bbc.co.uk [accessed July 2008]). Although Mali's head of food security stated that Mali was at no risk of famine, the UN World Food Programme reported on July 21, 2005, that 20 percent of the country's population were likely to suffer food insecurity or famine. The hardest-hit regions were those in the remote north, but the region of Mopti was also listed as an area of "hardship." The UN estimated declines in agricultural production of 42 percent within the year, and 25 percent lower than the previous five-year average (see "Mali: No risk of famine says government, but aid workers disagree," at www.alertnet.org [accessed March 2006; no longer available]).

10. An estimated 70 percent of Mali's labor force is engaged in agricultural activities including livestock and fishing, providing 36 percent of the country's measured GDP in 2003, according to U.S. government sources.

11. Mali's fishing industry has declined steadily since 1980, largely because of insufficient water levels in the rivers. Though there have been better-than-average rainfalls since 1993 (with the exception of 2002 and 2004), levels in the Niger and Bani rivers have been low primarily because water has been diverted for agriculture.

12. Young *garibou* laborers (i.e., those under twelve years of age) were now earning 400 CFA per day on building sites. Mali's per capita annual income in 2003 was approximately 155,000 CFA.

13. For an illustrated report on the restoration project of Djenné houses, see Bedaux, Diaby, and Maas (2003b, 62–66).

14. This project was piloted with technical and financial support from the Dutch.

15. The water tower was financed and built by the Canadian government.

16. See Langeveld and Alderlieste 2003, 67–69. More specifically, the filtration

mechanism consists of an excavated pit of coarse gravel approximately 25 millimeters in diameter, to a depth of 2 meters below grade, and this is covered with a bed of sand and backfilled. Recycled rice sacks made of woven plastic are used at the interface between the gravel and sand to keep the layers separated.

17. In his early-nineteenth-century description of Djenné, Landor (1907, 459) writes: "The streets were winding and beautifully clean. The whole place was entrancingly interesting and picturesque." This remained a reasonably accurate depiction of the town's streetscape until the 1990s.

18. The restoration of the chief's home played a pivotal role in the Mali-Dutch project to convince apprehensive home owners that if their houses were selected for inclusion in the restoration program, they would not be displaced. Written contracts were used initially, but residents were wary about signing, believing that the paper documents might contain hidden clauses transferring ownership to the government. Verbal agreements were therefore made between the Cultural Mission and individuals that families would refrain from making changes to their houses once restoration was complete (Rogier Bedaux, personal communication, January 27, 2001).

19. Brunet-Jailly (1999b, 171) reports that in 1999 there was one telephone line in Djenné, and mail arrived weekly.

20. Konamadou Djennépo had assisted Baba Kouroumansé on at least one recent commission for a house. This new Moroccan-style house in Bamana quarter belonged to a wealthy trader living in Bamako, and was occupied by his older brother, Marabout Traoré. Though constructed of *tubaabu-ferey* mud bricks, the surface finishes included such imported materials as cement, ceramic tiles, and a concrete Italianate balustrade.

21. Four types of schooling are available to children in Djenné: Qurʿanic schools, where children learn to recite the Holy Book; *madrassahs*, which emphasize Qurʿanic education but also include basic reading, writing, and arithmetic in their curricula; Franco-Arab schools, which again emphasize religious education but offer a formal curriculum taught in French and Arabic; and the state public schools, which follow a European-style curriculum. Many children who attend the state schools or Franco-Arab schools also attend Qurʿanic schools in their local neighborhoods for supplementary religious training.

22. In response to the growing number of students a new primary school was built near the water tower in Kanafa quarter, and its classrooms are brimmed to capacity. A Franco-Arab school had also been built in the expanding suburb of Tolober. UNICEF raised the proportion of female students through a successful campaign that paid families monthly stipends for each daughter sent. The small stipend was calculated to compensate families for the extra assistance in household chores for which they would have to pay in the absence of their daughters. Although figures for both boys and girls had improved, Djenné was still reputed as having one of the poorest attendance rates in the country. According to the U.S. government's 2003 country profile on Mali, nationwide attendance at primary school was 64.3 percent and the national literacy rate was 31 percent (www.state.gov).

23. The father of the four brothers was the *petit frère* of Bayeré's father. Both men were born of the same father but different mothers.

24. Boubacar (aka, "Bayeré") Kouroumansé was born in 1961. His older brothers left Djenné in search of work during the late 1970s and early 1980s at a time when the local economy was devastated by drought, and Bayeré quit school to work full-time with his father.

25. Bayeré's maternal side of the family was named Tementao, and his mother came from the village of Sirimou. His paternal Kouroumansé extended family members were dispersed along the Niger, from Mopti to Timbuktu.

26. The researchers with whom Bayeré worked included the architect Pierre Maas and

the anthropologist Geert Mommersteeg, authors of *Djenné: chef d'œuvre architectural* (1992).

27. Bayeré was also centrally involved in local authority efforts to install the aforementioned waste-water drainage system throughout the town.

28. These were Ton van der Lee's house in Sanuna, by the banks of the Bani, and Joseph Brunet-Jailly's house in Djoboro.

29. The delegation included Boubacar Kouroumansé, Bakayna Tennepo, and the master mason Beré Yonou with his son Omar and his apprentice Mahmoud Kontao. Washington 2003 Smithsonian Folklife Festival emphasised the cultural heritage of Timbuktu and Mali in general, and the summer event hosted music, songs, dances, arts and crafts, and other performances.

30. The prefix *kon* added to male names is a Bozo term meaning "father," and it is given to sons who are named after their father in the same way as the Songhay name Bamoy translates to "namesake of father." *Ainya* is the female equivalent name in Songhay, meaning "my mother."

31. Some residents of Djenné confused the dawat'Islamiyyah with a larger Bamako-based organization called ansār dīn ("Followers of the Faith"). Ansār dīn was led by Marabout Sharif Ousman Madani Haydarah and is a reform movement that, like dawat'Islamiyyah, calls for comportment based on the teachings of the Qurʿan and Hadīth. According to Schultz (2003), ansār dīn combines traditional elements of religious authority with "new credentials" including radio broadcasting to attract listeners' aesthetic sensibilities. Schultz claims that the popularity of Marabout Haydarah's teachings signifies the importance of religious debate in contemporary Malian state politics (ibid.). Soares (2005) also discusses how certain Muslim leaders and activists make use of new media technologies to articulate political and spiritual messages, but he claims that, with the exception of Sharif Haydarah, "most members of the new Bamako-based Muslim elite lack religious authority and consequently do not have many followers" (86).

32. Konmoussa's paternal grandfather was a pirogue builder—a typical Bozo trade—but his father, Konbaba Tennepo, had always been a mason.

33. The *qibla* is the wall of a mosque containing a prayer niche and orienting the building toward Mecca.

34. These included, most famously, the annual music "Festival in the Desert" that was started in the sand dunes outside Timbuktu in 2001. Other festivals included the more recent "Festival on the Niger" hosted in Segou.

35. "Festival du Djenneri," February 19–25, 2005. The politics and organization of this festival were studied by the anthropologist Charlotte Joy (2008).

36. Sekou Amadou, founder of the Fulani Empire at Macina (1818–1843), preached a conservative Islam and was responsible for the closure of all neighborhood mosques, "fearing they would prove rallying points for anti-Peul resistance" (Bourgeois 1987, 55). Like the Great Mosque, their roof gutters were blocked and they collapsed as a result of water infiltration. The neighborhood mosques were not rebuilt, and to this day Djenné has only the one mosque.

37. Interview with Sekou Traoré, chief of the *barey ton*.

38. Bourgeois 1987, 62. See, too, Bourgeois' 1987 article, "The History of the Great Mosque of Djenné," for an erudite history challenging prevalent notions that Djenné's mosque is a French creation and asserting the oft-neglected importance of local authorship. On the idea that the French created the mosque, see Landor 1907, 461; Dubois 1911, 185–89; Marty 1920–21, 2:235; Bâ and Daget 1984, 156; and Prussin 1974, 21; 1977, 73–75; 1986, 184–86), See also Blier 2004, 197–98, for a summary of the scholarship on French involvement in the 1906 reconstruction.

39. Geert Mommersteeg reports that, during the 1980s, the re-plastering of the

330 · *Notes to pages 291–93*

mosque sometimes took place in late February and early March (personal communication, March 2008). These early dates were possibly the result of the drought conditions afflicting the Sahel at the time.

40. A species of *Datura*.

41. Bourgeois 1987, 62. Note that the reference to a lizard refers to the masons' totem, the yellow-headed *m'baaka*.

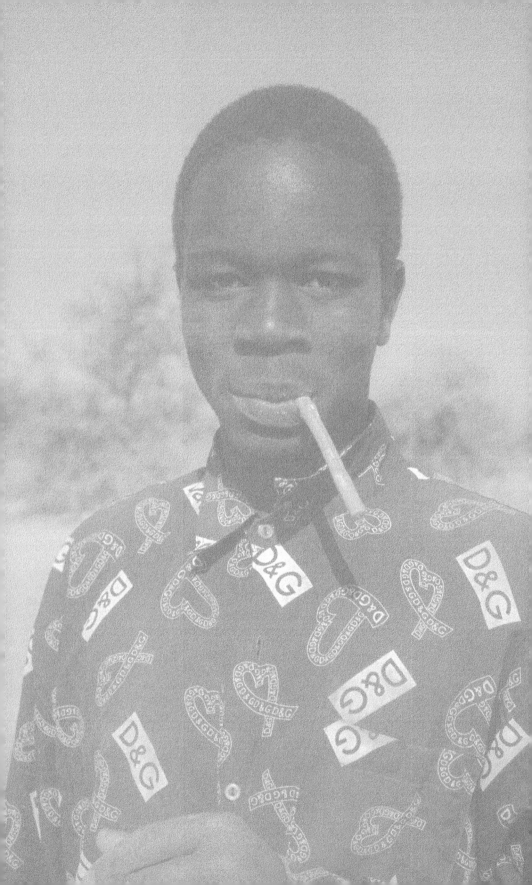

Bibliography

Aradeon, S. B. 1989. "Al-Sahili: The Historian's Myth of Architectural Technology Transfer from North Africa." *Journal des Africanistes* 59:99–131.

Arnoldi, M. J. 1976. *Bamana and Bozo Puppetry of the Segou Region Youth Societies: From the Collection of Joan and Charles Bird.* Department of Creative Arts at Purdue University.

Asquith, L., and M. Vellinga, eds. 2005. *Vernacular Architecture in the Twenty-first Century: Theory, Education, and Practice.* London: Routledge.

Bâ, A. H., and J. Daget. 1984. *L'Empire Peul du Macina: 1818–1853.* Abidjan: Nouvelles Éditions Africaines.

Beaudoin, G. 1998. *Soudan Occidental: histoire et architecture.* Paris: BDT Éditions.

Bedaux, R., B. Diaby, M. K. Keita, P. Maas, and S. Sidibe. 1995. *Plan de Projet Réhabilitation et Conservation de l'Architecture de Djenné (Mali).* Bamako and Leiden. Republished in 1996 by *ICOMOS Scientific Journal* 7:45–76.

Bedaux, R., B. Diaby, P. Maas, and S. Sidibe. 2000. "The Restoration of Jenne, Mali: African Aesthetics and Western Paradigms." In *Proceedings Terra 2000: The 8th International Conference on the Study and Conservation of Earthen Architecture,* 201–7. London: James and James.

Bedaux, R., B. Diaby, and P. Maas, eds. 2003a. *L'Architecture de Djenné: la pérennité d'un Patrimoine Mondial.* Leiden and Gand: Rijksmuseum voor Volkenkunde and Éditions Snoeck.

Bedaux, R., B. Diaby, and P. Maas. 2003b. "Resultats." In idem, eds., *L'Architecture de Djenné: la pérennité d'un Patrimoine Mondial,* 62–66. Leiden and Gand: Rijksmuseum voor Volkenkunde and Éditions Snoeck.

Bedaux, R., and J. D. van der Waals, eds. 1994. *Djenné: une ville millénaire au Mali.* Leiden and Gand: Rijksmuseum voor Volkenkunde and Martial.

Bird, C. 1971. "Oral Art in the Mande." In *Papers on the Manding,* ed. C. T. Hodge, 15–26. Bloomington: Indiana University Press.

Bird, C., with M. Koita and B. Soumaouro. 1974. *The Songs of Seydou Camara,* vol. 1, *Kambili.* Occasional Papers on Visual Communication, African Studies Center, Bloomington: Indiana University Press.

Bird, C., M. Kendall, and K. Tera. 1995. "Etymologies of Nyamakala." In *Status and Identity* in West Africa: Nyamakalaw of Mande, ed. D. C. Conrad and B. F. Frank, 27–35. Bloomington: Indiana University Press.

Blake, P. 1976. The Master Builders: le Corbusier, Mies van der Rohe, Frank Lloyd Wright. New York: W.W. Norton.

Blecke, T. 1996. Lexikalishe Kategrien und Grammatische Strukturen im Tigemaxo (Bozo, Mande). Köln: Rüdiger Köppe Verlag.

Blier, S. P. 2004. "Butabu: Adobe Architecture of West Africa." In Butabu: Adobe Architecture of West Africa, ed. J. Morris and S. P. Blier, 185–216. New York: Princeton Architectural Press.

Bloch, M. 1998. "The Resurrection of the House amongst the Zafimaniry of Madagascar." In How We Think They Think, ed. M. Bloch, 85–99. London: Westview.

Bourdieu, P. 1977. Outline of a Theory of Practice. Cambridge: Cambridge University Press.

Bourgeois, D., and C. Pelos. 1983. Spectacular Vernacular: A New Appreciation of Traditional Desert Architecture. Salt Lake City: Peregrine Smith Books.

Bourgeois, J. L. 1987. "The History of the Great Mosque of Djenné." African Arts 20 (3): 54–62.

Brenner, L. 1984. West African Sufi: The Religious Heritage and Spiritual Search of Cerno Bokar Saalif Taal. Berkeley: University of California Press.

———. 1993. "Constructing Muslim Identities in Mali." In Muslim Identity and Social Change in Sub-Saharan Africa, ed. Brenner, 59–78. London: Hurst.

———. 2001. Controlling Knowledge: Religion, Power and Schooling in a West African Muslim Society. Bloomington: Indiana University Press.

Brennies, D. 1988. "Language and Disputing." Annual Review of Anthropology 17:221–37.

Brett-Smith, S. C. 1994. The Making of Bamana Sculpture: Creativity and Gender. Cambridge: Cambridge University Press.

Brunet-Jailly, J., ed. 1999a. Djenné: d'hier à demain. Bamako: Éditions Donniya.

Brunet-Jailly, J. 1999b. "Demain: Djenné!" In Djenné: d'hier à demain, ed. J. Brunet-Jailly, 171–89. Bamako: Éditions Donniya.

———. 2004. "Une Saison de Circoncision et d'Excision." Djenné Patrimoine Informations 17:5–8.

Casey, E. 1996. "How to Get from Space to Place in a Fairly Short Stretch of Time." In Senses of Place, ed. S. Feld and K. Basso, 13–52. Santa Fe, N.M.: School of American Research Press.

Childs, L. 2004. "Talo Dam Construction Delays Holds: African Development Bank and Malian Government Implement Cultural Survival Recommendations." Cultural Survival Quarterly 28 (1).

Conrad, D. C., and B. F. Frank. 1995a. Introduction to Status and Identity in West Africa: nyamakalaw of Mande, ed. D. C. Conrad and B. F. Frank, 1–25. Bloomington: Indiana University Press.

———, eds. 1995b. Status and Identity in West Africa: Nyamakalaw of Mande. Bloomington: Indiana University Press.

Coy, M., ed. 1989a. Apprenticeship: From Theory to Method and Back Again. Albany: State University of New York Press.

———. 1989b. "Being What We Pretend to Be: The Usefulness of Apprenticeship as a Field Method." In Apprenticeship: From Theory to Method and Back Again, ed. M. Coy, 115–36. Albany: State University of New York Press.

Daget, J., M. Konipo, and M. Sanankoua. 1953. La Langue Bozo. Institut Francais d'Afrique Noire: Gouvernement de Soudan: Centre Ifan.

de Ceuninck, G., and A. Mayor. 1994. "La Poterie Traditionelle: de sa production à sa consommation." In Djenné: une ville millénaire au Mali, ed. R. Bedaux and J. D. van der Waals, 131–38. Leiden and Gand: Rijksmuseum voor Volkenkunde and Martial.

de Grunne, B. 1982. *Ancient Treasures of Terracotta in Mali and Ghana.* New York: African-American Institute.

Delafosse, M. 1972 [1912]. *Haut-Sénégal, Niger.* 3 vols. Paris: Maisonneuve et Larose.

Denyer, S. 1978. *African Traditional Architecture: An Historical and Geographical Perspective.* London: Heinnemann.

Diakité, D. 1999. "L'Islam à Djenné." In *Djenné: d'hier à demain,* ed. Brunet-Jailly, 45–60. Bamako: Éditions Donniya.

Diallo, A. 2004. "Paradoxes of Female Sexuality in Mali." In *Re-thinking Sexualities in Africa,* ed. S. Arnfred, 173–89. Sweden: Almquist and Wiksell Tryckeri.

Dieterlen, G. 1941. *Les Âmes des Dogons.* Paris: Institut d'Ethnologie.

Dmochowski, Z. R. 1990. *An Introduction to Nigerian Architecture.* 3 vols. Jos, Nigeria: Ethnographica and the National Commission for Museums.

Domian, S. 1989. *Architecture Soudanaise: vitalité d'une tradition urbaine et monumentale.* Paris: Éditions l'Harmattan.

Douglas, M. 1968. "The Social Control of Cognition: Some Factors in Joke Perception." *Man* (n.s.) 3:361–79.

Drucker-Brown, S. 1982. "Joking at Death: The Mamprusi Grandparent-Grandchild Joking Relationship." *Man* 17 (4): 714–27.

Dubois, F. 1911. *Notre Beau Niger.* Paris : Flammarion.

Engeström, T. 1955. "Contribution aux Connaissances des Styles de Construction au Soudan Français." *Ethnos* 2–3:122–26.

Evans-Pritchard, E. E. 1933. "Zande Blood-brotherhood." *Africa* 6: 369–401.

Ezra, K. 1988. *Art of the Dogon: Selections from the Lester Wunderman Collection.* New York: Metropolitan Museum of Art.

Farnell, B. 2000. "Getting Out of the Habitus: An Alternative Model of Dynamically Embodied Social Action." *Journal of the Royal Anthropological Institute* 6 (3): 397–418.

Fathy, H. 1973. *Architecture for the Poor.* Chicago: University of Chicago Press.

Feld, S., and K. Basso, eds. 1996. *Senses of Place.* Santa Fe, N.M.: School of American Research Press.

Fink, R., and L. Meierotto. 2002. "Moratorium on Talo Dam Construction Still Holding." *Cultural Survival Quarterly* 26 (4).

Fontein, J. 2000. *UNESCO, Heritage, and Africa: An Anthropological Critique of World Heritage.* Edinburgh: Centre of African Studies, University of Edinburgh.

Frank, B. 1995. "Soninke garankéw and Bamana-Malinke jeliw: Mande Leatherworkers, Identity, and the Diaspora." In *Status and Identity in West Africa: nyamakalaw of Mande,* ed. D. C. Conrad and B. F. Frank, 133–52. Bloomington: Indiana University Press.

———. 1998. *Mande Potters and Leather Workers: Art and Heritage in West Africa.* Washington, D.C.: Smithsonian Institution Press.

Freedman, J. 1977. "Joking, Affinity, and the Exchange of Ritual Services among the Kiga of Northern Rwanda: An Essay on Joking Relationship Theory." *Man* 12 (1): 154–65.

Gallier, F. 2002. "Analyse du Projet de Barrage de Talo et de ses conséquences prévisibles sur les systèmes de production ruraux du Djenneri." *Djenné Patrimoine* 13:15–27.

Gardi, R. 1974. *Indigenous African Architecture.* New York: Van Nostrand Reinhold.

Gerdes, P. 1999. *Geometry from Africa: Mathematical and Educational Exploration.* Washington, D.C.: Mathematical Association of America.

Gilbert, E. 2004. *Dhows and the Colonial Economy of Zanzibar, 1860–1970.* Oxford: James Curry; Zanzibar: Gallery Publications; Athens: Ohio University Press.

Goody, E. 1982. *Parenthood and Social Reproduction: Fostering and Occupational Roles in West Africa.* Cambridge Studies in Anthropology series 35. Cambridge: Cambridge University Press.

———. 1989. "Learning, Apprenticeship, and the Division of Labour." In *Apprenticeship: From Theory to Method and Back Again,* ed. M. Coy, 233–56. Albany: State University of New York Press.

Graves, B. 1989. "Informal Aspects of Apprenticeship in Selected American Occupations." In *Apprenticeship: From Theory to Method and Back Again,* ed. M. Coy, 51–64. Albany: State University of New York Press.

Griaule, M. 1948. "L'Alliance Cathartique." *Africa* 18: 242–58.

Grimes, B., ed. 1988. *Ethnologue: Languages of the World.* Dallas: Summer Institute of Linguistics.

Haberland, E. 1981. "West African Mud Architecture: Research of the Frobenius Institute." *African Arts* 15 (1): 44–45.

Hale, T., and N. Malio. 1996. *The Epic of Askia Mohammed.* Bloomington: Indiana University Press.

Harts-Broekhuis, E., and O. Verkoren 1994. "Populations et Activités." In *Djenné: une ville millénaire au Mali,* ed. R. Bedaux and J. D. van der Waals, 115–21. Leiden and Gand: Rijksmuseum voor Volkenkunde and Martial.

Heald, S. 1990. "Joking and Avoidance, Hostility and Incest: An Essay on Gisu Moral Categories." *Man* (n.s.) 25 (3): 377–92.

Heath, J. 1998. *Dictionnaire Songhay-Anglais-Français, tome II—Djenné Chiini.* Paris: L'Harmattan.

———. 1999. *A Grammar of Koyra Chiini: The Songhay of Timbuktu.* Berlin: Mouton de Gruyter.

Heidegger, M. 1993 [1977]. "Building Dwelling Thinking." In *Basic Writings,* ed. D. F. Krell, 343–64. 2nd rev. ed. San Francisco: HarperCollins.

Herbert, E. W. 1993. *Iron, Gender, and Power: Rituals of Transformation in African Societies.* Bloomington: Indiana University Press.

Herrmann, W. 1962. *Laugier and Eighteenth Century French Theory.* London: A. Zwemmer.

Hoffman, B. 1990. *The Power of Speech: Language and Social Status among Mande Griots and Nobles.* Ph.D. diss., UMI Dissertation Service, Ann Arbor, Michigan.

———. 1995. "Power, Structure, and Mande *jeliw.*" In *Status and Identity in West Africa: Nyamakalaw of Mande,* ed. D. C. Conrad and B. F. Frank, 36–45. Bloomington: Indiana University Press.

———. 2000. *Griots at War: Conflict, Conciliation, and Caste in Mande.* Bloomington: Indiana University Press.

Hunwick, J. 2003. *Timbuktu and the Songhay Empire: al-Sa'dīs Ta'rīkh al-sūdān Down to 1613 and Other Contemporary Documents.* Leiden: Brill.

Imperato, P. J. 1975. "Bamana and Maninka Twin Figures." *Africa Arts* 8 (4): 52–60.

———. 1977. *African Folk Medicine: Practices and Beliefs of the Bambara and Other Peoples.* Baltimore, Md.: York Press.

Irvine, J. 1974. "Strategies of Status Manipulation in the Wolof Greeting." In *Explorations in the Ethnography of Speaking,* ed. R. Bauman and J. Sherzer, 167–89. Cambridge: Cambridge University Press.

Jansen, J. 2000. *The Griot's Craft: An Essay on Oral Tradition and Diplomacy.* Munich: LIT Verlag.

———. 2002. *Les Secrets du Manding: les récits du sanctuaire kamabolon de Kangaba (Mali).* Leiden: CNWS University of Leiden.

Johnson, J., and F-D. Sisòkò. 1992. *The Epic of Son-Jara: A West African Tradition.* Bloomington: Indiana University Press.

Joy, C. 2008. "Enchanting Town of Mud: The Politics of Heritage in Djenné, a UNESCO World Heritage Site in Mali." Ph.D. diss., University College London.

Konaré, A. 1999. "Djenné des origins à la penetration coloniale: un apercu historiques." In *Djenné: d'hier à demain*, ed. J. Brunet-Jailly, 27–44. Bamako: Éditions Donniya.

Labouret, H. 1929. "La Parenté à Plaisanteries en Afrique Occidentale." *Africa* 2 (3): 244–54.

Landor, H. Savage. 1907. *Across Widest Africa*. London: Hurst and Blackett.

Langevelde, J., and M. Alderlieste. 2003. "Approvisionnement en Eau et Assainissement." In *L'Architecture de Djenné: la pérennité d'un Patrimoine Mondial*, ed. R. Bedaux, B. Diaby, and P. Maas, 67–69. Leiden and Gand: Rijksmuseum voor Volkenkunde and Éditions Snoeck.

Lauber, W. 1998. "L'Architecture de Terre Traditionelle des Dogon." In *L'Architecture Dogon: constructions en terre au Mali*, ed. W. Lauber, 56–61. Paris: Adam Biro.

Laude, J. 1973. *African Art of the Dogon: the Myths of the Cliff Dwellers*. New York: Brooklyn Museum in association with Viking Press.

Laugier, M. A. 1985 [1753]. *Essai sur Architecture*. Santa Monica: Hennessey and Ingalls.

Lave, J., and E. Wenger. 1991. *Situated Learning: Legitimate Peripheral Participation*. Cambridge: Cambridge University Press.

LaViolette, A. 1987. "An Archaeological Ethnography of Blacksmiths, Potters, and Masons in Jenne, Mali (West Africa)." Ph.D. diss., Washington University, St. Louis.

———. 1994a. "Forgerons, Menuisiers, Orfèvres et Piroguiers-Charpentiers." In *Djenné: une ville millénaire au Mali*, ed. R. Bedaux and J. D. van der Waals, 149–58. Leiden and Gand: Rijksmuseum voor Volkenkunde and Martial.

———. 1994b. "Masons of Mali: A Millennium of Design and Technology in Earthen Materials." In *Society, Culture and Technology in Africa*, ed. S. Terry Childs, 87–97. Philadelphia: University of Pennsylvania Museum of Archaeology and Anthropology.

———. 1995. "Women Craft Specialists in Jenne." In *Status and Identity in West Africa: nyamakalaw of Mande*, ed. D. C. Conrad and B. F. Frank, 170–181. Bloomington: Indiana University Press.

Le Corbusier (Charles Edouard Jeanneret). 2000 [1948]. *The Modulor*. Birkhäuser: Basel.

Leach, E. 1972. "Anthropological Aspects of Language: Animal Categories and Verbal Abuse." In *Mythology: Selected Readings*, ed. P. Maranda, 39–67. Harmondsworth: Penguin.

Lefebvre, H. 1991. *The Production of Space*. Oxford: Blackwell.

Leiris, M. 1988 [1934]. *L'Afrique Fantôme*. Paris: Gallimard.

Lévi-Strauss, C. 1963. *Structural Anthropology*. Translated from the French by C. Jacobson and B. Grundfest Schoepf. New York: Basic Books.

Levtzion, N. 1973. *Ancient Ghana and Mali*. London: Methuen.

Ligers, Z. 1964. *Les Sorko (Bozo): Maîtres du Niger*. 4 vols. Paris: Librarie des Cinq Continents.

Maas, P. 1990. "Djenné: Living Tradition." *Saudi Aramco World* 41 (6): 18–29.

Maas, P., and G. Mommersteeg. 1990. "Fishing in the Pondo." *Saudi Aramco World* 41 (4): 22–31.

———. 1992. *Djenné: chef-d'œuvre architectural*. Bamako, Eindhoven, Amsterdam: Institut des Sciences Humaines, Université de Technologie, Institut Royal des Tropiques.

———. 1993. "L'architecture dite Soudanaise: le modèle de Djenné." In *Vallées du Niger*, ed. J. Devise, 478–92. Paris: Musée National des Arts d'Afrique et d'Océanie.

———. 1994. "Une Architecture Fascinante." In *Djenné: une ville millénaire au Mali*, ed. R. Bedaux and J. D. van der Waals, 78–94. Leiden and Gand: Rijksmuseum voor Volkenkunde and Martial.

Mandel, J.-J., and A. Brenier-Estrine. 1977. "Clay Toys of Mopti." *African Arts* 10 (2): 8–13.

Marchand, T. H. J. 1993. "Gidan Hausa." Report for the Canadian International Development Agency, Ottawa, unpublished.

———. 2001. *Minaret Building and Apprenticeship in Yemen*. London: Curzon.

———. 2003a. "A Possible Explanation for the Lack of Explanation; or, 'Why the Master Builder Can't Explain What He Knows.' Introducing Informational Atomism against a 'Definitional' Definition of Concepts." In *Negotiating Local Knowledge*, ed. J. Pottier, A. Bicker, and P. Sillitoe, 30–50. London: Pluto.

———. 2003b. "Bozo-Dogon Bantering: Policing Access to Djenné's Building Trade with Jests and Spells." *Traditional Dwellings and Settlements Review, Journal of IASTE* 14 (2): 47–63.

———. 2003c. "Process over Product: Inverting the Emphasis in Sustainable Conservation." In *Managing Change: Sustainable Approaches to the Conservation of the Built Environment*, ed. J-M. Teutonico and F. Matero, 137–59. Los Angeles: Getty Conservation Institute.

———. 2003d. "Rang Professionel Laborieusement Acquis: devenir maître maçon à Djenné." In *L'Architecture de Djenné: la pérennité d'un Patrimoine Mondial*, ed. R. Bedaux, B. Diaby, and P. Maas, 29–43. Leiden and Gand: Rijksmuseum voor Volkenkunde and Éditions Snoeck.

———. 2005. "Endorsing Indigenous Knowledge: The Role of Masons and Apprenticeship in Sustaining Vernacular Architecture." In *Vernacular Architecture in the 21st Century: Essays in Honour of Paul Oliver*, ed. L. Asquith and M. Vellinga, 46–62. London: Taylor and Francis.

———. 2007a. "Fortifying Futures on Blessed Foundations: Masons, Secrets, and Guarantees in Djenné." In *Mande Studies 7: Divination in the Mande World*, guest editors: J. Jansen and A. Schmidt, 89–98.

———. 2007b. "Crafting Knowledge: The Role of Parsing and Production in the Communication of Skill-Based Knowledge among Masons." In *Ways of Knowing*, ed. M. Harris, 181–202. Oxford: Berghahn.

———. 2008. "Muscles, Morals, and Mind: Craft Apprenticeship and the Formation of Person." *British Journal of Educational Studies* 56 (3).

———. Forthcoming. "Embodied Cognition, Communication, and the Making of Place and Identity: Reflections on Fieldwork with Masons." In *Reclaiming the Human: Reflections upon a Complex Singularity*, ed. N. Rapport. Oxford: Berghahn.

Marty, P. 1920. *Etudes sur l'Islam et les tribus du Soudan*. Vol. 2. Publisher unknown.

McIntosh, R. J. 1998. *The Peoples of the Middle Niger: The Island of Gold*. 2nd ed. Oxford: Blackwell.

———. 2005. *Ancient Middle Niger: Urbanism and Self-Organising Landscape*. Cambridge: Cambridge University Press.

McIntosh, R. J., and S. K. McIntosh. 1981. "The Inland Niger Delta before the Empire of Mali: Evidence from Jenne-jeno." *Journal of African History* 22 (1): 1–22.

McIntosh, S. K., ed. 1995. *Excavations at Jenné-Jeno, Hambarketolo, and Kaniana (Inland Niger Delta, Mali), the 1981 Season*. Berkeley: University of California Press.

McNaughton, P. R. 1982. "The Shirts That Mande Hunters Wear." *African Arts* 3:54–58.

———. 1988. *The Mande Blacksmiths: Knowledge, Power, and Art in West Africa*. Bloomington: Indiana University Press.

———. 1995. "The Semantics of Jugu: Blacksmiths, Lore, and 'Who's Bad' in Mande." In *Status and Identity in West Africa: Nyamakalaw of Mande*, ed. D. C. Conrad and B. E. Frank, 46–59. Bloomington: Indiana University Press.

Mitchell, T. 2002. *Rule of Experts: Egypt, Techno-politics, Modernity*. Berkeley: University of California Press.

Mommersteeg, G. 1988. "He Has Smitten Her with Love: The Fabrication of an Islamic Love-Amulet in West Africa." *Anthropos* 83:501–10.

———. 1990. "Allah's Words as Amulet." *Etnofoor* 3 (1): 63–76.

———. 1991a. "Learning the Word of God." *Saudi Aramaco World* 42 (5): 3–10.

———. 1991b. "L'Education Coranique au Mali: le pouvoir des mots sacré's." In *L'Enseignement Islamique au Mali*, ed. B. Sanankoua and L. Brenner, 45–61. Bamako: Jamana; London: SOAS.

———. 1994. "Marabouts à Djenné: enseignement coranique, invocations et amulettes." In *Djenné: une ville millénaire au Mali*, ed. R. Bedaux and J. D. van der Waals, 65–75. Leiden and Gand: Rijksmuseum voor Volkenkunde and Martial.

———. 1998. *In de Stad van de Marabouts*. Amsterdam: Prometheus.

———. 1999. "Qur'anic Teachers and Magico-Religious Specialists in Djenne." *International Institute for the Study of Islam in the Modern World (ISIM) Newsletter* 3:30.

———. 2003. "Au-dèla du Banco: quelques remarques sure les secrets des maçons de Djenné." In *L'Architecture de Djenné: la pérennité d'un Patrimoine Mondial*, ed. R. Bedaux, B. Diaby, and P. Maas, 24–27. Leiden and Gand: Rijksmuseum voor Volkenkunde and Éditions Snoeck.

Monteil, C. 1972 [1932]. *Une Cité Soudanaise: Djénné: métropole du Delta Central du Niger*. Paris: Éditions Anthropos.

———. 1933. *La Langue de Bozo: population de pêcheurs du Niger*. Paris: Librarie Larose.

Nicolaï, R. 1981. *Les Dialectes du Songhay*. Paris: CNRS.

Oliver, P., ed. 1971. *Shelter in Africa*. London: Barrie and Jenkins.

———, ed. 1976. *Shelter and Society*. London: Barrie and Jenkins.

———. 1987. *Dwellings: The House across the World*. Oxford: Phaidon.

———. 1997. *Encyclopaedia of Vernacular Architecture of the World*. Cambridge: Cambridge University Press.

Park, M. 1983 [1799]. *Travels into the Interior of Africa*. London: Eland.

Parkin, D. 1980. "The Creativity of Abuse." *Man* (n.s.) 15 (1): 45–64.

Paulme, D. 1939. "Parenté à Plaisanteries et Alliance par le Sang en Afrique Occidentale." *Africa* 12 (4): 433–44.

Pedler, F. J. 1940. "Joking Relationship in East Africa." *Africa* 13 (2): 170–73.

Peil, M. 1970. "The Apprenticeship System in Accra." *Africa* 40:137–50.

Petrillo, J., and L. Childs. 2004. "Cultural Survival Endorses Revised Plan for Talo Dam Construction." *Weekly Indigenous News*, June 11, 2004.

Prussin, L. 1968. "The Architecture of Islam in West Africa." *African Arts* 1 (2): 32–35, 70–74.

———. 1970. "Sudanese Architecture and the Manding." *African Arts* 4 (4): 13–19, 64–67.

———. 1974a. "An Introduction to Indigenous African Architecture." *Journal of the Society of Architectural Historians* 33 (3): 182–205.

———. 1974b. "Architecture of Jenne." Ph.D. diss., Department of History of Art, Yale University.

———. 1976. "Fulani-Hausa Architecture." *African Arts* 10 (1): 8–19, 97.

———. 1977. "Pillars, Projections, and Paradigms." *Architectura* 7 (1): 65–81.

———. 1986. *Hatumere: Islamic Design in West Africa*. Berkeley: University of California Press.

———. 1994. "Vérité et Imaginaire de l'Architecture." In *Djenné: une ville millénaire au Mali*, ed. R. Bedaux and J. D. van der Waals, 102–11. Leiden and Gand: Rijksmuseum voor Volkenkunde and Martial.

Radcliffe-Brown, A. R. 1940. "On Joking Relationships." *Africa* 12 (3): 195–210.

———. 1949. "A Further Note on Joking Relationships." *Africa* 19 (2): 133–40.

Rapoport, A. 1969. *House Form and Culture* (Foundations of Cultural Geography series). Upper Saddle River, N.J.: Prentice Hall.

Roberts, R. 1987. *Warriors, Merchants, and Slaves: The State and the Economy in the Middle Niger Valley, 1700–1914*. Stanford: Stanford University Press.

Ross, D. H., ed. 1995. "Disturbing History: Protecting Mali's Cultural Heritage." Special issue of *African Arts* 28, no. 4 (fall 1995).

Rouch, J. 1960. *La Religion et la Magie Songhay*. Paris: Presses Universitaires de France.

Rousseau, J. J. 1973 [1762]. *The Social Contract and Discourses*. Translation and introduction by G. D. H. Cole. London: Dent.

Rowlands, M. 2003. "Patrimoine et Modernité à Djenné: identités nationale et locale." In *L'Architecture de Djenné: la pérennité d'un Patrimoine Mondial*, ed. R. Bedaux, B. Diaby, and P. Maas, 79–81. Leiden and Gand: Rijksmuseum voor Volkenkunde and Éditions Snoeck.

Rudofsky, B. 1965. *Architecture without Architects: A Short Introduction to Non-pedigreed Architecture*. Santa Fe: Museum of New Mexico Press.

Ruskin, J. 1984 [1849]. *The Seven Lamps of Architecture*. Toronto: Harper Collins Canada.

———. 1859. "The Work of Iron in Nature, Art, and Policy." In *The Two Paths*. Republished in *On Art and Life*. London: Penguin, 2004.

———. 2001. *The Poetry of Architecture*. IndyPublish. Published initially as a series of articles in *Architectural Magazine*, 1836–37.

Rykwert, J. 1981. *On Adam's House in Paradise: The Idea of the Primitive Hut in Architectural History*. Boston: MIT Press.

Ryle, G. 1949. *The Concept of Mind*. London: Hutchinson.

Saad, E. N. 1979. "Social History of Timbuktu, 1400–1900: the role of Muslim scholars and notables." Ph.D. diss., Northwestern University.

Samoura, K., I. Ouane, and H. Cissé 1999. "Enfances à Djenné." In *Djenné: d'hier à demain*, ed. J. Brunet-Jailly, 61–80. Bamako: Éditions Donniya.

Sanankoua, O. 1999. "Femmes de Djenné." In *Djenné: d'hier à demain*, ed. J. Brunet-Jailly, 81–96. Bamako: Éditions Donniya.

Schoenauer, N. 2000 [1981]. *6000 Years of Housing*. New York: W.W. Norton.

Schultz, D. 2003. "Charisma and Brotherhood Revisited: Mass-Mediated Forms of Spirituality in Urban Mali." *Journal of Religion in Africa* 33 (2): 146–71.

Schwerdtfeger, F. 1982. *Traditional Housing in African Cities: A Comparative Study of Houses in Zaria, Ibadan, and Marrakesh*. Chichester, U.K.: Wiley.

———. 2007. *Hausa Urban Art and Its Social Background: External House Decorations in a Northern Nigerian City*. London: International African Institute; Berlin: LIT Verlag.

Scott, J. 1992. *Domination and the Arts of Resistance: Hidden Transcripts*. New Haven, Conn.: Yale University Press.

Singleton, J. 1989. "Japanese Folkcraft Pottery Apprenticeship: Cultural Patterns of an Educational Institution." In *Apprenticeship: From Theory to Method and Back Again*, ed. M. Coy, 13–30. Albany: State University of New York Press.

Smeltzer, S., B. Smeltzer, and M. Sabe. 1995. "Compte-rendu des enquêtes cartographique lexicostatistique et sociolinguistique des parlers Bozo." *Mandekan* 30:55–101.

Soares, B. 2005. "Islam in Mali in the Neoliberal Era." *African Affairs* 105 (418): 77–95.

Stevens, P. 1978. "Bachama Joking Categories: Toward New Perspectives in the Study of Joking Relationships." *Journal of Anthropological Research* 34:47–71.

Stoller, P. 1989a. *Fusion of the Worlds: An Ethnography of Possession among the Songhay of Niger*. Chicago: University of Chicago Press.

———. 1989b. *The Taste of Ethnographic Things: The Senses in Anthropology*. Philadelphia: University of Pennsylvania Press.

———. 1994. "Ethnographies as texts/Ethnographers as Griots." *American Ethnologist* 21 (2): 353–66.

Tall, M. Ly. 1977. *Contributions à l'histoire de l'Empire du Mali, XIIIe au XVIe siècles: limites, principales provinces, institutions politiques*. Dakar, Abidjan: Les Nouvelles Éditions Africaines.

Tamari, T. 1991. "The Development of Caste Systems in West Africa." *Journal of African History* 32 (2): 221–50.

Trimingham, J. S. 1970. *A History of Islam in West Africa*. London: Oxford University Press.

Tymowski, M. 1974. *Le Développement et la Régression chez les Peuples de la Boucle du Niger à l'Époque Précoloniale*. Warsaw: Éditions de l'Université de Varsovie.

United Nations Development Programme (UNDP). 2004. *Human Development Report 2004: Cultural Liberty in Today's Diverse World*. New York: UNDP.

United Nations Educational, Scientific, and Cultural Organization (UNESCO). 2006. World Heritage Report: "Convention Concerning the Protection of the World Cultural and Natural Heritage," 13th Session, July 2006. Paris: UNESCO.

Urciuoli, B. 1995. "Language and Borders." *Annual Review of Anthropology* 24:525–46.

Van Beek, W. 1991. "Dogon Restudied: A Field Evaluation of the Work of Marcel Griaule." *Current Anthropology* 32(2):139–167.

Van der Lee, T. 2003. *Heavenly Mud*. Documentary film, 52 minutes. Produced by Jokestar Film and AVRO television.

Van der Velden, R. 1989. "Moskeeën en Metselaars in de Regio van Djenné." Master's thesis (architecture), University of Technology, Eindhoven.

Van Eyck, A. 1961. Photos of Djenné. *Forum voor Architectuur en daarmee Verbonden Kunsten* 15 (3): 85–116.

Van Gijn, A. 1994. "La Maison: structure et organisation d'espace." In *Djenné: une ville millénaire au Mali*, ed. R. Bedaux and J. D. van der Waals, 95–101. Leiden and Gand: Rijksmuseum voor Volkenkunde and Martial.

Viollet-le-Duc, E. E. 1858–72. *Entretiens sur l'Architecture*. Paris: A. Morel.

Vogel, S. (director), co-produced with T. H. J. Marchand (consulting anthropologist and writer) and S. Sidibé. 2007. *Future of Mud: A Tale of Houses and Lives in Djenné*. Documentary film, 56 minutes. Prince Street Pictures, distributed by First Run/Icarus Films, New York.

Wacquant, L. 2004. *Body and Soul: Notebooks of an Apprentice Boxer*. Oxford: Oxford University Press.

Yaro, A. B. ibn al-Hâdî Ko. 1989. *Hadiyyatu al-bashar fi al-qarni al-khamis cashar* (*Le don à l'humanité au XVe siècle [année hegire]*), manuscript, Djenné.

Index

Page numbers in italics refer to figures.

Dmochowski, Z. R., 312n18
documentary film, 277, 286, 312n1, 326n1
Dogon, 49–57, 91, 229, 264, 270, 283, 310n36,
    311nn37,47,49,52, 313n46
Dogon country, 1, 6, 25, 269
Dogon laborer. See laborer
Domian, S., 306n17, 319n11, 320n3
Douglas, M., 311n37
dowry, 195
drawing (architectural), 10, 19, 85, 88, 96, 97,
    125, 126, 170, 283
drought, 3, 16, 23, 86, 120, 154, 193, 230, 250, 279,
    282, 295, 307nn31,32,42, 327n9, 328n24,
    330n39
Drucker-Brown, S., 310n34
Dubois, F., 329n38

economy, 3, 16, 18, 19, 23, 27, 46, 74, 84, 86, 120,
    156, 165, 192–193, 212, 220, 242, 250, 264,
    266, 279, 280–281, 282, 284, 295, 315n71,
    327n8, 328n24
ecosystem. See riverine ecosystem
education, 11, 22, 49, 77, 86, 118, 148–149, 154,
    156, 165, 184, 237, 256, 263, 282, 283, 295,
    320n10, 328nn21,22
Egypt, 79
Eid al-kabir. See Tabaski
Eindhoven University of Technology, 62
endogamy, 156, 212, 308n48
Engeström, T., 306n17, 325n2
English (language), 262–263
environmental conditions, 46, 92–93, 212, 279
Epic of Askia Muhammad, 319n8
erosion, 42, 134, 137, 214, 243, 246, 271, 324n14
ethnicity, 46, 47, 49, 50, 56, 64, 102, 153, 154,
    210–212, 240, 290, 309n10, 310n20,
    313n46, 322n1, 324n10, 326n12
Europe, 284
Evans-Pritchard, E. E., 310n34, 311n46
excision, 308n45
exogamy, 51
expertise, 6, 13, 19, 22–23, 68, 81, 85, 96, 97, 118,
    146, 157, 160, 207, 215, 219, 246, 277, 316n17
Ezra, K., 314n61

Fangaso, 324n20
Farnell, B., 318n8
Faro, 319n13
Fathy, H., 312n18, 327n8
festival, 290, 294, 329nn34,35
Fink, R., 326n5

fish stocks, 327nn6,11
flirtation, 325n9
Fontein, J., 307n39
food, 18, 51, 53, 69, 102, 137, 207, 210, 216, 274,
    311n52
food crisis, 327n9
formwork, 18, 45, 91, 144, 169, 173
Frank, B., 309n10, 314nn59,64, 318n14
Freedman, J., 310n34
French (language), 51, 74, 97, 108, 118, 153, 167,
    184, 205, 211, 213, 283, 305n13, 315n71, 326n12
French Sudan, 60, 306n17
Fulani, 64, 80, 138, 167, 180, 183, 184, 191, 198,
    205, 230, 232, 240, 310n19, 311n52, 313n33,
    315n68, 319n1
Fulani Empire of Macina, 329n36
Fulfuldé, 311n49, 319n1
furufuru, 319n2

Gallier, F., 327n7
Gao, 16, 34, 193, 212, 324n15
Gardi, R., 313n38
garibou. See Qur'anic student
Gaudi, Antonio, 60
gender, 8, 75, 196, 254, 273, 291, 293, 325n2,
    328n22
general building contractor, 47, 86, 146,
    283–284, 295
Gerdes, P., 318n9
Ghana Empire, 314n48, 322n2
Gideon's Association, 324n21
gift, 48, 66, 67, 73, 81, 106, 128, 157, 163, 202, 205,
    217, 229, 284, 308n45, 314n50
Gilbert, E., 307n34
Gimhae Clayarch Museum, 284
Gomitogo, 271–272
Goody, E., 319n14
Gothic, 61
grain, 68, 69, 85, 89, 90, 91, 168, 193, 194, 198,
    266, 313n46
grave, 257, 325nn4–6
Graves, B., 319n7
Griaule, M., 49, 50, 51, 53, 56, 59, 310n34,
    311nn40,49,51
Grimes, B., 322n2
griot. See jeli
gris-gris. See amulet
gross domestic product (of Mali), 327n10

Haberland, E., 307n38
hadīth, 329n31

Author with his reliable "iron-horse" bicycle in Djenné

Trevor H. J. Marchand is Senior Lecturer in Social Anthropology at the School of Oriental and African Studies, University of London.

Printed and bound by CPI Group (UK) Ltd, Croydon, CR0 4YY

09/06/2025

14685951-0001